防御船舶撞击桥梁的柔性防撞装置论文集

Proceedings of Flexible Anti-collision Device Used for Defending Ship-Bridge Collision

CHEN Guoyu WANG Lili YANG Liming CHEN Mingdong NI Buyou etc.

陈国虞　王礼立　杨黎明　陈明栋　倪步友等

上海科学技术文献出版社
Shanghai Scientific and Technological Literature Press

图书在版编目（CIP）数据

防御船舶撞击桥梁的柔性防撞装置论文集 / 陈国虞等著 . —上海：上海科学技术文献出版社，2015.11

ISBN 978-7-5439-6793-9

Ⅰ. ① 防… Ⅱ. ①陈… Ⅲ. ①桥梁工程—防撞—文集 Ⅳ. ① U443.8-53

中国版本图书馆 CIP 数据核字（2015）第 187709 号

责任编辑：祝静怡　王茗斐
封面设计：许　菲

防御船舶撞击桥梁的柔性防撞装置论文集
陈国虞　王礼立　杨黎明　陈明栋　倪步友等　著
出版发行：上海科学技术文献出版社
地　　址：上海市长乐路 746 号
邮政编码：200040
经　　销：全国新华书店
印　　刷：上海市印刷七厂有限公司
开　　本：787×1092　1/16
印　　张：20.25
字　　数：467 000
版　　次：2015 年 11 月第 1 版　2015 年 11 月第 1 次印刷
书　　号：ISBN 978-7-5439-6793-9
定　　价：78.00 元
http://www.sstlp.com

目　录

第五部分 桥梁防船撞遇到的几个具体问题

第六部分 对国内外一些桥梁防船撞规范的评析

CONTENTS

Part 1 The demand for defends collision of ship with bridge

Part 2 The impact force between ship and bridge

Part 3 How does the flexible anti-collision device implement

Part 4 The experimental basis and test validation of flexible anti-collision technology

Part 5 Some detail problems of bridge anti-collision technology

Part 6 Analysis on some guides for defends collision of ship with bridge

序 言 1

我国桥梁防船撞装置的实践，确切地说应该是在建设黄石长江公路大桥时才开始的。由于该桥桥型采用了主跨 245 m 的五跨预应力混凝土连续刚构，设有双薄壁墩及群桩基础，桥位又处在 $R=30\,000$ m 的弯河道上，通行 5 000 t 的船只及驳船队，而当时规范采用的船撞力明显偏少，因此开展了防撞装置的研究，最终采用了以钢刚架为主，加护舷的浮式弹塑性耗能的防撞装置。

十几年后，在 21 世纪初建设湛江海湾大桥，要通行 50 000 t 船只。由于桥位处 10 m 等深线宽约 800 m，只有解决 50 000 t 船只的防撞问题，才有可能选用主跨小于此宽度的较经济桥型方案。在设计投标方案比选中，由于采用了黏滞性防撞圈为主的柔性防撞装置方案，完善地解决了突出的防撞问题，使主跨 480 m 的双塔混合梁斜拉桥方案中标并建成。

这种柔性防撞装置经专家会议鉴定是世界首创。与过去的装置相比，标志着防撞装置已进入了新的一代：

从理念上，已由过去的单纯防止桥梁破坏，发展到“三不坏”的理念，即桥梁不坏，船只不坏，防撞装置不坏；

从措施上，采取了拨转船头，带走大部分动能，以及用耗能效果良好的多层黏滞性钢丝绳胶圈，大大减小了船舶撞击力；

从计算理论和方法上，依托宁波大学，采用冲击动力学、黏弹性的本构模型以及相应的有限元方法，引入了应力波和波阻抗的概念，并应用实测的钢丝绳胶圈参数，使计算更符合实际。为了证明计算理论和这种装置的有效性，还在宁波象山港大桥，由宁波高指、宁波大学和上海海洋钢结构研究所一起作了实船实桥的撞击试验，即用实船撞击装有柔性防撞装置的桥墩，取得了满意的结果。

在上述工作的基础上，上海海洋钢结构研究所还制定了《桥墩的船撞力计算及柔性防撞装置设计指南》的企业标准。

在柔性防撞装置的研究和建造中，陈国虞教授在桥梁防撞这一学科中，作出了重要的、开拓性的贡献。与有关大学与产业部门共同协作，不断探索、不断实践，为一系列桥梁设计和建造了柔性防撞装置，并总结提高，共同编写了《船撞桥及其防御》及《桥梁防撞理论和防撞装置设计》两本专著，并在杂志和国际国内专业会议上发表了大量有关论文。现在又把这些论文经过优选精编，出版这本《防御船舶撞击桥梁的柔性防撞装置论文集》，内容丰富、翔实、全面。对于从事桥梁防撞的广大工程技术人员，这是一个大好消息，可以提供他们阅读、应用和钻研，也有利于桥梁防撞学科的进一步发展提高。

交通运输部公路科学研究院　研究员

2015 年 4 月 18 日

Preface 1

To be precise, the practice of the Chinese bridge anti-collision device began at when Huangshi Yangtze river highway bridge constructed. Since this bridge adopted the bridge-type of five spans prestressed concrete continuous rigid frame with 245 m mainspan, and the substructure adopted double-walled pier and group piles foundation, and also the bridge was at $R=30\ 000$ m curved river. At that time, the builder required 5 000 t ship and barge train to go through, nerveless the ship crash force of the design specification was obviously lower. For this reason, the investigation of anti-collision device was carried out. Finally the floating elastic-plastic energy dissipation anti-collision device which was composed of steel frame and fender was used.

After ten years, construction of Zhanjiang bay bridge in the early 21st century, 50 000 t ship needed go through. If they wanted to choose the economic bridge scheme with mainspan of less than 800 m, they must solve the anti-collision problem of 50 000 t ship, because the bridge location in 10 m isobath was about 800 m wide. In the selection of the design bidding scheme, as the scheme of the flexible anti-collision device that was using viscosity steel wire rings would perfectly solve this problem, and finally this device helped the twin towers hybrid girder cable-stayed bridge with 480 m mainspan win the biding and construction.

The flexible anti-collision device via expert meeting appraisal was word's first. Compared with the past device, it marked the anti-collision device has entered a new generation:

In concept, it has developed the anti-collision concept from purely preventing bridge damage in the past to ' three-uninjured ', that is bridge uninjured, ship uninjured and anti-collision device uninjured.

In measurement, it employs v-shape to change the bow's direction and brings lots of kinetic energy. It also uses the high energy absorption element of layers viscosity steel wire rings to greatly reduce the impact force of the ship.

In computation theory and method, relying on the Ningbo University, it adopts impact dynamics, visco-elastic constitutive model and the corresponding finite element method, and introduces the concept of stress wave and the wave impedance, and uses the test parameters of steel wire ring to agree the results.

In order to validate the calculation theory and the effectiveness of the device, they, Ningbo highway headquarters, Ningbo University and Shanghai Marine Steel & Structure Research

Institute (SMSSRI), did a real impact test between ship and bridge at Ningbo Xiangshan bay bridge, that is a ship crash with bridge added flexible anti-collision device. The test is with satisfactory results being attained.

On the basis of the above work, SMSSRI also set an enterprise standard of Impact force calculation for bridge and flexible anti-collision device design guide. In the research and construction of the flexible anti-collision device, Professor CHEN Guoyu has made an important and pioneering contribution in the area of anti-collision discipline for bridge. He Works together with the university and industry departments, continues to explore and practice. Flexible anti-collision device were designed and constructed for a series of bridge. He summarized and wrote two monographs of ship-bridge collision and its defense and Theory and design of crashworthy device against ship-bridge collision, and also published a large number of relevant papers in the magazine and the international/domestic professional meeting. Now he puts these papers through optimizing choreography and publishes this book Proceedings of Anti-collision device used for defending ship-bridge collision, this book is rich in content, detailed and comprehensive. This is big good news for general engineers who engage in bridge anti-collision areas. This book should be useful, therefore, as a textbook to read, apply and investigate. And it is also beneficial to the further development to improve bridge anti-collision discipline.

Researcher of Research Institute of Highway Ministry of Transport

2015 年 4 月 18 日

序 言 2

铁路的新建直接影响到国民经济的顺利发展，尤其是高速铁路建设已是当今国家的战略重点，铁路桥梁是铁路的重要组成部分。研究探讨我国铁路桥梁的发展历史及其经验教训，为从事铁路桥梁建设和养护工作者提供有益借鉴。原铁道部领导吕正操、刘建章、李颉伯等同志曾多次倡议编写中国铁路桥梁史。1980 年 4 月，铁道部和铁道兵联合组成了中国铁路桥梁史编辑委员会及其办公室。中国第一座长江大桥——武汉长江大桥的总设计师、第一届中国工程设计大师王序森先生和大桥局第一任局长彭敏同志为首席顾问等 66 位领导和专家组成的编辑委员会，于 1980 年 4 月—1987 年 10 月，历时 7 年多编辑出版的《中国铁路桥梁史》。其中的第五章："中华人民共和国成立以来铁路桥梁重大灾害"第三节第四部分专论"船舶碰撞桥梁事故"。不仅详细介绍了我国通航河流上的铁路桥梁被船舶或漂流物碰撞造成灾害的事故情况和原因，并且特别提出了最早的："漂浮式或固定式的缓冲装置，除具有吸收撞击的动能外，还有调整改变船舶的偏航方向和撞击速度的作用……"。向后人提示了既保护桥也能保护船的"双保护"的先进设计思想。然而我们一些铁路大桥建养部门，迄今自以为铁路桥梁桥墩的设计的安全系数较大，长江上的几座公铁两用大桥虽经多次碰撞，仍安然无恙，所以对船撞桥及其防御的问题不够重视。但"人无远虑，必有近忧"，事物必然会发展变化的规律是千万不能忽视的。我国在防灾、减灾、免灾的国策中，保护人的生命总是摆在第一位的，绝不能按西方用工程投资大小与人的生命价值的比值公式来考虑问题。而应从以人为本科学发展的观点来处理当今船撞桥及其防御的难题。就以笔者亲历参与修建的四座长江大桥，从 1959 年至 1984 年统计：共发生碰撞桥梁事故 62 次，其中武汉大桥 45 次，南京大桥 12 次，枝城大桥 3 次，九江大桥 2 次。62 次事故中，碰撞桥墩的占 60 次，碰撞钢梁的占 2 次。有的严重事故造成船沉、人亡、物损的惨状，令人目不忍睹。1986 年有代表向全国人大提出议案，要求解决船舶碰撞桥梁采取有效的措施问题。但始终未得到解决。从 1994 年起，以陈国虞先生等多位老专家，他们先后花了 8 年时间从调查研究和收集国内外的有关船撞桥及其防御措施的资料，进行了分析，坚持走中国自己的路，通过多学科的理论研究和力学论证并通过模型试验制造出黏滞性防撞圈。2001 年得到宁波大学王礼立副校长等多位教授负责仿真数值分析；2011 年由宁波高指牵头，杨黎明教授等在象山港进行了实船撞墩实验。使得理论分析、实验验证和数值计算等三种方法结合起来，共同创造了国际领先的柔性、吸能、缓冲的“三不坏”防撞装置。这种装置设计思想的机理是非常先进的，利用黏弹性防撞元件抓住了刚柔相结合的技术关键，将发生的船舶冲击集中动能转化为分散的环带受力圈，因而使桥墩受到的水平力至少降低50 %以上，换言之，也就是使桥墩防撞的安全系数提高了一倍。无疑这种安全、实用、经济、耐久的先进装置已完成了桥梁界先辈们的期望，而且进一步将两保护（保护桥梁同时保护船的安全）飞跃发展成了三保护（防撞装置不坏）。现在荟萃了历年来多种期刊的精辟文章，汇编成这部《防御船舶撞击桥梁的柔性防撞装置论文集》，是一本难得的新书，无疑会对今后这方面工作的进一步创新和发展起到推波助澜、画龙点睛的作用。

原中铁大桥局资深高级工程师（教授级）、工程测量专家

Preface 2

New railway construction directly affects the smooth development of the national economy, especially the high-speed railway construction is today's national strategic focus, railway bridge is an important part of railway. Research on the development history of railway bridges in China and its experience and lessons, it is beneficial reference for railway bridge construction and maintenance workers. The former leaders of MOR, Mr Lu Zhengcao, Mr Liu Jianzhang and Mr LI Jiebo etc. had repeatedly initiative to write Chinese railway bridge history. In April 1980, the MOR and railway corps merged to form the editorial board and office of China railway bridge history. The editorial board was composed of Mr Wang Xusen, China's first Yangtze river bridge — Wuhan Yangtze river bridge's chief designer, the first Chinese engineering design masters, and Mr PENG Min, the first director of Major Bridge Bureau, and other 66 leaders and experts. Mr WANG Xusen and Mr Peng Min were the principal consultant. From April 1980 to October 1980, China railway bridge history was edited and published which was lasted more than seven years. There is a monograph "Ship-bridge collision accident" in the fourth part of the 3rd quarter of chapter 5 of this book. The monograph not only introduced the accident caused by the collision between ship/waif and railway bridge pier on navigable rivers in China in detail and its reason, but also specially put forward the earliest demand: "Floating or fixed buffer device, besides absorb the impact kinetic energy, and also adjusts to change the yaw's direction and the impact speed ...". This prompted posterity to adopt the "dual protection" advanced design thought which is both protecting bridge and protecting ship. But the bridge construction and maintenance department always ignored the problem of ship-bridge collision, they thought that the railway bridge had bigger safety factor, and that was an example such as some highway-railway bridge on the Yangtze river. There is a Chinese proverb "Those who do not plan for the future will find trouble at their doorstep", The rule of things change is never ignored. In the national policy of disaster prevention and mitigation, protecting life comes first always. Using a ratio between project investment and value of human life to consider problems is not advisable. We should be in human science development view to deal with the problems of ship-bridge collision its defense. Take the four Yangtze river bridges of author personally participate in building as examples, the statistics data was from 1959 to 1984: there were 62 times accidents, such as 45 times at Wuhan bridge, 12 times at Nanjing bridge, 3 times at Zhicheng bridge, 2 times at Jiujiang bridge. In the 62 times accidents, 60 times collision with pier, 2 times collision with steel grider. There were miserable situations of ship sank, died and thing damage. In 1986, a representative brought a bill that ask to solve the problem of ship-bridge collision to NPC, but this still hasn't been solved.

Since 1994, Mr. Chen Guoyu and many aged experts took 8 years to investigate and collect material about ship-bridge collision from domestically and internationally. And they insisted on Chinese method, enentually fabricated the visoelastic anti-collision element by multi-disciplinary theory and mechanics knowlege. In 2001, Mr. Wang Lili, Ningbo university vice President, and other professors were responsible for the numerical simulation analysis; In 2011, led by ningbo highway headquarters, Pro. Yang Liming did a full-scale impact experiment at Xiangshan bay. They put theoretical analysis, experiments and numerical calculation together to create an internationally advanced flexible, energy absorption, buffer "three-uninjured" anti-collision device. The mechanism of the device design idea is very advanced, visoelastic anti-collision element was the key technology of rigid and soft. This technology can reduce 50% of impact force by steel ring outside the bridge pier. In other words, that makes the safety factor of the bridge pier anticollision doubled. The device, integrated with safety, practical, economic and durable, has finished the expectation of predecessors engaged in bridge engineering. And further they devolop two protection (protect bridges and ship together) into three protection (anti-collision device doesn't damage). Now the insightful articles of variety journals were gathered together to assembly the book *Proceedings of Anti-collision device used for defending ship-bridge collision*. This is a rare new book, and will be sure to help the further innovation and development.

ZHU Haitao

Former experienced senior engineer and engineering survey specialist of

China Railway Major Bridge Bureau

前　　言

“船撞桥及其防御”是一个新兴的、交叉性综合性的、工程力学应用小学科。1983年在北欧由国际桥梁和结构工程协会(IABSE)指定了该学科的分委员会,该分委会参考美国联邦公路局的公路规范和有关指南、丹麦海峡大桥和日本本州-四国联络桥等具体工程实例,提出了该分委会的“综述与指南”,1991年于列宁格勒召开的年会上定稿。中国的上海海洋钢结构研究所也组织出版了:《船撞桥及其防御》(中国铁道出版社,2006)和《桥梁防撞理论和防撞装置设计》(北京:人民交通出版社,2013)等两本专著。可以说,中、外都同期到了这个小学科蓬勃发展的时期。

现在,按照向航运界和桥梁界发送“三不坏”桥墩防撞装置的研究和工程进展资料的愿望,上海海洋钢结构研究所将其发表于各杂志的论文,依照论文性质分类汇印成册,在汇印时将图标和表头注上英文,便于更多的读者使用。原来发表的期刊和媒体,包括连续出版物:中国造船、中国水运、航海技术、航海科技动态、船舶工程、上海造船、广东造船、铁道标准设计、重庆交通大学学报、城市道路与防洪、桥梁、中国海洋产业海洋工程(国联资源直投媒体)、桥梁工程与技术(国联资源直投媒体)和海洋工程装备等;学会年会连续论文集包括:中国公路学会桥梁和结构工程分会全国桥梁学术会议论文集、中国土木工程学会桥梁及结构工程分会全国桥梁学术会议论文集、国际冲击工程学会论文集(ISIE Book of Proceedings)和国际自动化和工程控制会议论文集等;公开发行的单本论文集或专著有:科学中国人十年优秀论文选、应用力学进展(论文集)、桥梁船撞研究与工程应用(论文集)、船撞桥及其防御、桥梁防撞理论和防撞装置设计和国际船桥相撞及其防护学术研讨会论文集等;工程技术网站有:道客巴巴网www. doc88. com;豆丁网www. docin. com;中国桥梁网www. chinabridge. org. cn;桥梁工程与技术网www. bridge. ibicn. com;中国海洋产业海洋工程网www. coi. com. cn;共29家媒体。发表在不同的媒体是为了方便不同的读者群体,汇印在一起是为了使用者全面地了解这项技术的情况。

这本论文集从桥梁防船撞的要求、船对桥的撞击力、柔性防撞装置的设计等三方面展开论证,说明柔性防撞装置的必要性及可行性。通过冲击动力学理论、缓冲吸能元件实验和实船撞击实验等方法讨论该装置的科学性。同时采用数值分析的方法进一步验证防撞装置的设计方法及可行性。最后对设计中常见的具体问题进行解答,并对历史上、国内外一些防撞装置进行评价。使读者全面地了解该领域国内外的研究进展,深入系统地掌握

柔性防撞技术。

同时论文集体现了我国在桥梁防撞领域的若干进展，具体包括：

第一，着眼各类水域防撞问题，突破某些国家偏重于研究内河航运的局限性。我国现在于国、内外承建的桥梁，从上中游发展到下游、由内河走向港湾、由大陆通向离岸的岛屿、并且跨过海峡连接陆块、甚至承建洲际大桥。跨越航线的桥梁愈来愈多，桥下通过的船舶愈来愈大。所以我国防御船撞桥，一开始研究就不局限于内河。并指出从内河航运得来的结论，对我们有局限性，不适用。例如，驳船的情况，河渠化的航道，河道宽度在船长3倍以内的航速横向分布规律以及内河船与海船撞桥力估算的差别等。针对以上问题，我们都根据调查测定，作了具体分析，取代了曾经借用的外国假定。

第二，采用"应保尽保"及"三不坏"的先进设计理念。检阅了历年桥梁防撞研究的纪录，认为船撞桥的样本搜集比较少(与相邻的学科相比较，以及使用中由于样本少产生的误差等方面而言)，因此使用"年撞塌概率"作为建与不建防撞装置的决定性指标，就不合适。提出了新的方法："万一撞上也能保护桥梁、船舶和环境的安全"的原则。

第三、总结中外16种船撞力半经验公式。经过研究，指出他们都是同源的。由于在有了桥墩等设计图纸之后，可以用较精确的计算方法，所以半经验公式仅用在开始设计时对船撞力进行估算，在这个阶段对跨航线的桥梁决定桥型、桥跨和桥墩分布等都会有用。

第四、仿真分析与实船撞击试验。依托宁波大学引入通用有限元软件LS-DYNA辅助船撞桥问题研究及防撞装置的设计，并且使用材料动态受力变形时的性能指标(材料破坏临界值等)，作为衡量构件失效的标准。我们专门设计实船撞墩试验，特别研制传感器系统，以测定力、变形、转角等的时程数值，检验软件程序的计算结果。

第五、充分利用桥梁自身抗力，节约资源。现行设计有一种倾向是不愿利用桥墩和桥梁其他构件的水平抗力，而要"御敌于国门之外"。换言之，只要间接式防撞装置，不愿设计直接式防撞装置。我们通过严谨的理论推导和实验验证，证明合理利用桥墩自身抗力进行防护装置设计是可行的，并且具有尺寸小，性价比高的特点。

第六、防御船撞桥的设计指南是给谁用的？现实往往和人们想的不一样，粗略一看防御船撞桥应该是桥梁设计的一部分，但是从上世纪80年代开始传入的文献看，研究防御船撞桥的人除了桥梁设计者之外，还有一部分力学家。而文献内容中大量引用船的资料。我国最先引进防御船撞桥文章的是桥梁专家，但1994年交通部科技司(委)将一项防撞装置任务下达给部属船舶运输研究所和交通院校。不久在桥梁界出现了一个意见："研究船撞桥的人以船舶和水运工作者比较合适"，于是在上海、重庆、黑龙江和武汉出现了一批船舶和水运专业的研究者；在宁波和重庆出现了研究力学和材料的研究者参加进来。现在形成的认识是：研究防御船撞桥必须结合船舶和桥梁两个方面的专业知识，研究的方法是工程力学的三种方法(理论分析、数值计算和实验验证)。因此设计指南应该是提供给设计桥梁的人使用的。而桥梁设计和防御装置、设施设计的人，不可能从事很多船撞桥方面的理论研究和进行现场实验等工作，因此指南需要简单明了、可供桥梁设计者使用。

在本书中，以上几点是新论，是骨架，专业人士只要阅读这些内容就可以了。但是为了更多的人认识“防御船撞桥”，文章中就写进很多科普性的介绍和系统性的内容。对于青年学生和非本专业读者，是一本比较全面而有用的参考书。

执笔　陈国虞　英文翻译　赵振宇

2015 年 5 月 10 日

Foreword

"Ship-bridge collision and its defense" is a new, overlapping, comprehensive and small discipline of engineering mechanics. The subcommittee of this discipline was assigned by the international association of bridge and structural engineering (IABSE) at Northern Europe in 1983. The subcommittee raised "Review and Guide" referencing the guide of FHWA and anti-collision engineering of Denmark Strait bridge and Japan Honshu-Shikokurode contact bridge. And that book was finalized at the meeting of Leningrad in 1991. Shanghai Marine Steel and Structure Research Institute (SMSSRI), China, also published, *ship-bridge collision and its defense*, (China railway publishing house, Beijing, 2006), and *Theory and design of crashworthy device against ship-bridge collision*, (People's traffic press, Beijing, 2013). That is to say, we enter the booming period of the small subject at the same time.

Now, According to wish of sending research progress of "three-uninjured" anti-collision device to shipping interests and bridge interests. SMSSRI published the paper that was published at various magazines by paper properties classification. In order to facilitate more readers to use, figures and table title were translated to English. The 14 journals and media, including continued publication, are, China Shipbuilding, China Water Transport, Marine Technical, Marine Technical News & Trends, Shipping Engineer, Shanghai Shipbuilding, Guangdong Shipbuilding, Railway Standard Design, Journal of Chongqing Jiaotong University, Urban Roads Bridges & Flood Control, Bridge, China's Marine Industry and Marine engineering (direct investment media resources), Bridge engineering and technology (direct investment media resources), Marine engineering equipment and so on. Conference proceedings including continuously, Proceedings of Bridge Conference of Bridge and Structure subcommittee of China Highway and Transportation Society, Proceedings of Bridge Conference of Bridge and Structure subcommittee of China Civil Engineering Society, ISIE Book of Proceedings and Proceedings of Conference of International automation and engineering control. Single proceedings and books of public offering, the excellent paper anthology of *Scientific Chinese* in the past ten years, Advances in Applied Mechanics, research on ship-bridge collision and its engineering application, ship-bridge collision and its defense, Theory and design of crashworthy device against ship-bridge collision, Proceedings of International Symposium on Ship-Bridge Collision and Its Protection. 5 engineering websites, www. doc88. com, www. docin. com, www. chinabridge. org. cn, www. bridge. ibicn. com, www. coi. com. cn. There are 29 media agencies in all. Publishing in different media is for the convenience of different reader groups, printing together is for users to fully understand the situation of this technology.

The demand of ship-bridge collision, the impact force between ship and bridge and the design of anti-collision device were discussed in this book, and that indicates the necessity and feasibility of flexible anti-collision device. Scientificity of this device was proved by the theory of impact dynamics, experiments of buffer energy-absorption element and full-scale test. The design method and feasibility were further verified by numerical analysis. At last, we answered some question about ship-bridge collision technology, appraised some other devices at home and abroad in history. Give readers a comprehensive understanding of the field research progress both at home and abroad, systematically master flexible anti-collision technology deeply.

While this book embodies some progress in the field of bridge anti-collision in our country, specific include:

First, collision problem with all kinds of waters, the breakthrough in some countries those focus on research limitations of inland waterway transport. Now in our country the bridges construction of domestic and international are from the upper and middle reaches to downstream, from inland to harbor, from mainland to the offshore islands and across the strait connecting landmass, even intercontinental bridge construction. The more bridges across lane, the bigger ships which go under bridge. So the study on defending collision in our country is not limited with inland waterway. And points out that the conclusion from the inland waterway transport, we have limitations, do not apply. For example, the condition of the barge, the speed transverse distribution in watercourse which has 3 times length of ship width and the difference impact force between inland vessel and seagoing vessel. To solve above problems, we are all according to the survey, made a concrete analysis, replaced the foreign assumption that we used ago.

Second, the advanced design concept of "must be where should be" and "three-uninjured". We surveyed the record of bridge anti-collision research for many years, and we deemed that the sample was less than that in other disciplines. So the probability of collapse per year is not suitable to do the qualitative index of choosing anti-collision device. We put forward a new concept that is, "the safety of ship, bridge and environment should be protected in the collision."

Third, 16 empirical formulas of impact force were summarized. We pointed out they are isogeny after we studied. As the exact calculating method is used after design, so empirical formula is used to estimate the impact force before design. In the period, impact force is useful for choosing bridge type, bridge spans and the distribution of bridge pier.

Forth, simulation analysis and full-scale experiment. The finite element software LS – DYNA was firstly used to assist ship-bridge collision research and design of anti-collision device

supporting by Ningbo University. And we used the performance parameters (such as damage threshold) of material's dynamic deformation to measure component failure. Full-scale experiment was being designed, in specialty; sensor system was being developed to measure the history data of force, deformation and angle of rotation. Result by software was validated by experiment.

Fifth, make full use of the bridge itself resistance, save resources. There is a trend of device design that doesn't use the resistance of bridge itself. In other words, they only choose the indirect type device, don't choose direct type. We demonstrated that making full use of the bridge itself resistance to design device was feasibility by rigorous theoretical derivation and experimental verification, and the device had the characteristics of small-size and high cost performance.

Sixth, who will use this guide? Reality often is not the same as people think, at first glance, defending ship-bridge collision is part of bridge design, nevertheless, Judging from the literature of beginning in the 1980s, there were also mechanical who researched on it. And a lot of ship information reference was in literature content. In our country, who introduced firstly the article of defending collision was bridge expert, but a mission of anti-collision device was being given to shipping research institute and traffic colleges. In the near future, an opinion was appeared in bridge interests, "people who research on ship-bridge collision are better with ship and water transport workers". So there are some researchers major in shipping and water transport in Shanghai, Chongqing, Heilongjiang and Wuhan. There are some researchers major in mechanics and material in Ningbo and Chongqing. Now the formation understanding is that people who research on ship-bridge collision must have ship and bridge professional knowledge at the same time, and use the study method of theoretical analysis, numerical calculation and experimental verification. So the design guide should be provided to people who design bridges. But these people have little knowledge of ship-bridge collision and full-scale experiment, so the guide should be simple to bridge designer.

In the book, above is new and skeleton, professionals just read the content. But in order to let more people to know ship-bridge collision, the science popularization introduction and the content of systemic are been written. It is a more comprehensive and useful reference book for young students and non-professional reader.

When the proceedings were collected, PhD student ZHAO Zhenyu of XJTU was in charge of sorting and supplements translation, and Pro. CHEN Guoyu revised.

Actual writing: CHEN Guoyu; English Translation: ZHAO Zhenyu

2015 - 05 - 10

第一部分

桥梁防船撞的要求

The demand for defends collision of ship with bridge

长江中游桥墩防撞——防撞要求的分析

Anti-collision of bridge pier in middle reaches of Yangtze River — Analysis on the characteristic which they need

陈国虞

(交通部上海船舶运输科学研究所 200135)

CHEN Guoyu

(Shanghai Ship and Shipping Research Institute,
Ministry of Communications, 200135, China)

摘　要　回顾近年长江中游船撞桥的事故之后,首先对长江中游的桥墩防撞提出了8点要求:兼顾水运、桥梁和航道维护等几方面的需要;在桥墩、码头等的周围不应占很多地方,以致碍航;适应水位变化的要求;吸掉动能的能力要大;被撞后应能恢复,方便维修;安装、运输方便;不妨碍捕捞养殖,少影响冲刷沉积和防撞装置的造价便宜等。接着对长江中游700 t以上的船舶的动能进行统计。最后用统计结果加以判断、归纳,绘制直方图,利用直方图正态分布99.75%保证率的动能的船舶,作为防撞装置撞击动能的设计工况。

关键词　船撞桥　长江中游　动能正态分布　保证率　设计工况

Abstract: After review the accidence of ship collision with bridge in the recent years happening in middle reaches of Yangtze River, this paper at first analysis on the characteristic which the bridge pier need, and raise 8 points of them: Take care the request of carriage, bridge and maintenance of sea water way; near the dock and bridge does not occupy so much places; adapt the request of the water level variety; dissipating the energy as much as possible; after collision should recover and facility to repair; itself convenience transportation, install and maintain; don't hinder to fishing and breed; fewness scour and sediment and builds price cheapness.

Second, this paper make a statistics on kinetic energy of ships above 700 t in the middle reaches of Yangtze River. Use the result of statistics to take in judge, we draw the square diagram. And use the ship at normal distribution of the square diagram with the 99.75% assurance rates as the design work condition to design the anti-collision equipment.

Keyword: ship collision with bridge, middle reaches of Yangtze River, normal distribution of kinetic energy, assurance rates, and design work condition

从葛洲坝往下到江西湖口为止的江段,通称长江中游,通航里程为 902.5 km。现有的、在建的和规划中的跨江桥共有:枝城、洪湖、金长、银长、武汉长江大桥、武汉长江公路桥(二桥)、兴长、宝长、埠长、黄石、九江等十余座长江大桥,它们大多建有水中墩柱。(上游跨江桥易于作成岸边墩塔,一跨过江,便能取消水中墩柱)因此,都有桥墩防撞的问题,至于下游,由于通过的船较大,桥较少,防撞设施工程费用亦较大,故另行讨论。

1 长江中游船碰事故分析

长江上最大的水运公司——长江轮船总公司,下属重庆、武汉、芜湖、南京、上海 5 家分公司,共有 1 227 艘船驳,其他 14 家地方公司共有 66 艘船驳,合计1 293 艘(700 t 以上船驳)。现以 1985—1990 年 6 年为统计期,从重庆到上海通航内发生的事故中,碰撞、触礁和搁浅三项统计如表 1 所示。

表 1 **长江轮船总公司 1985—1990 年重庆到上海通航内事故统计表**

Table 1 **The navigation accident statistics of the Yangtze river shipping corporation from Chongqing to Shanghai during 1985 to 1990**

次/%

年 份	碰 撞	触 礁	搁 浅	合 计
1985	69/66	9/9	26/25	104/100
1986	44/66	11/16	12/18	67/100
1987	42/63	17/25	8/12	67/100
1988	52/65	10/125	18/225	80/100
1989	47/71	13/20	6/9	66/100
1990	5/56	0/0	4/44	9/100
6 年总计	259/66	60/15	74/19	393/100

注:表 1 由林树人同志提供。

由表 1 中可以看出碰撞是三种事故中最多的一种,但若仔细分析,首先将下中游事故分开因上游触礁较多,中游搁浅和碰撞较多;再将碰撞中船碰船(碰撞)和触损(船碰固定物,包括船碰趸、船碰墩等)分开。如表 2 只分析长江中游的事故。

表 2　长江轮船总公司 1985—1990 年重庆到上海通航内事故统计表(分类细化)(次)

Table 2　The classification-refined navigation accident statistics of the Yangtze river shipping corporation from Chongqing to Shanghai during 1985 to 1990 (times)

年 份	碰 撞	触 损	搁 浅	触 礁	其 他	合 计
1985	10	6	8	0	8	32
1986	6	1	1	0	3	11
1987	5	3	2	1	6	17
1988	14	4	7	1	11	37
1989	7	0	4	0	4	15
1990	0	0	1	0	0	1
合 计	42	14	23	2	32	113
占比/%	37	12	21	2	28	100

注：表 2 据林树人同志提供资料整理，触损 14 次中多为船撞趸，而船撞墩仅有 1 次。

分开统计之后可知，触损所占比例是小的，仅为事故总数之 12%，而船碰墩则不到 1%。

属于本文分析范围内的长江中游船碰墩实例在统计期内只有一次，将其他几次上下游的、未成事故的苗子和船碰梁等事件一并举例如下：

1987 年 7 月 11 日下午 04:38，长江 220××号船对九江长江大桥 7 号墩“擦道”，当时该船顶推节甲 210××号等驳船下水航行，行经九江大桥时，擦伤 7 号墩的混凝土表面保护层，相接触的节 210××号甲板驳轻损；

1985 年 12 月 30 日下午 06:00，长江 08××号船对重庆长江大桥前面造成触损事故，当时长江 08××号船上水行驶，船撞灯船，触损灯一盏，三脚架一个，浮标船裂口；

1989 年 9 月 29 日早上 05:40，长江 48××号拖 5 艘重载驳船撞南京长江大桥第 5 墩，造成甲 410××驳船轻伤，并撞致 2#红浮、1#红浮移位；

1990 年 7 月 28 下午 16:37。大庆 4××号触损南京长江大桥第 5 墩，致桥墩表面混凝土脱落，大庆 4××号船之 100 ~ 115 肋间凹入 150 mm；

1978 年 8 月 13 日，挂巴拿马旗载有近万吨货物的“大鹰海”号船准备借用宝钢原料码头卸货，这时适逢长江退潮，该外籍船在落潮冲泻下，十几根缆绳在几分钟之内全部断裂，船尾向宝钢主副原料码头中间的一段栈桥撞去，混凝土栈桥将船尾反弹 20 m，使船头向栈桥撞去，将四跨 16 m 栈桥桥面翻坠江中，豁开的大口子把肇事巨轮死死咬住，为此栈桥上皮带运输机停止运转 83 天；

1994 年武汉长江大桥上游几百米的武昌船厂码头上的打桩船失缆，该船离开系泊码头顺流移动，漂向江心撞上大桥，撞坏桥面使钢梁和桥面受影响；

×年×月×日，某船队下水航行至武汉长江大桥上游不远处，离岸较近，欲操满舵向江心调头改为上行，但船头回转到指向对岸时船队不再回转，横于江中向下游漂去，幸而向岸边发出求救信号，几艘拖轮驶来协助调头，方将船队调为向上游，化险为夷。

以上 7 个例子可以看出，虽然船撞墩在各类事故中只占 1%，但当船标不明显或新设水中墩柱、趸船而未被驾驶人员熟知时则易被撞，例如：

1993 年 4 月 16 日至 1993 年 9 月 11 日的 5 个月内船碰撞黄石长江公路桥施工设施有 15 起；

1993 年 5 月 22 日至 1993 年 9 月 13 日的 5 个月内船碰撞武汉长江公路桥施工设施有 16 起；

基于上述分析，船撞墩的事故确实存在，防撞设施应该建设，但亦不可将事故说得过于危险，致防撞设施过大、太贵。

2　吸能防撞设施的综合要求

现将桥墩吸能防撞设施的要求逐一叙述如下：

（1）兼顾水运、桥梁和航道等几方面的利益。只有兼顾才能被几方面同时接受。一般来说桥墩能经受的力比船大，通常船撞墩是船受损，墩的混凝土表面保护层裂开或剥落，表面钢筋外露，影响桥墩使用寿命。驾驶人员通常认为墩是在原有航道中后建的人工岛礁，本身就是个碍航物，是人为的事故隐患；桥方认为已设有标志的墩则船不应撞上去，在桥墩已建成之后船撞上去则船方为肇事者，航道管理方则希望防撞设施不应碍航，不应增加航道维护负担。所以防撞设施应该既保护桥，又保护船，同时不增加航道维护负担，这样便会受到三方的欢迎。

（2）通航要求。水中桩柱墩的周围是要通航船只的，因此在桥墩、码头、渡口、桩柱的周围不应因防撞设施而占去很多地方，以致碍航。

（3）适应水位变化的要求。沿海设施应适应潮水要求，长江中游应适应洪水、枯水的水位要求，有的设施在汛期失效（如桥柱边上的阶梯护台汛期便失效），因此防撞设施多作成浮式。

（4）吸能能力要大。对撞上的船所具有的动能要能吸掉相当一部分，而这时船应不破坏，其余部分传递到墩上时应该不破坏，防撞装置同时应使受撞时墩的混凝土表面层不被破坏。

（5）撞后恢复。防撞设施应能多次使用，小撞应不需维修，大撞应能方便地维修。

（6）安装、运输方便。不应要求过多的施工条件，以使架设方便，这也会使设施的总成本下降。

（7）不应因防撞设施而产生新的问题。如增加水下构筑物，妨碍捕捞养殖，回流沉积等等。

（8）价格便宜。

3　桥墩吸能防撞能量要求的统计分析

防撞工作可分为一对矛盾的两个方面；需要防多大的撞击；设置多大的防撞设施。这儿

存在一个保证率和风险的问题，如果将防撞设施按最大的船、最高的航速，取其最大的冲量、能量，则设计出的防撞设施硕大无比，难以承受，而这样大的能量撞到墩上则是多年不遇的，其概率非常小。这问题的性质有点类似于水利工程中按百年一遇洪峰还是五十年一遇洪峰来计算拦洪坝相类似，要视统计结果和财力，运筹决定。

船撞水中构筑物的力和能量要视相撞时的角度而定，日本同行和我国港工规范中对船撞墩的角度均有分析，分析中将行进中的船撞墩的角度分为三种类型。如图 1 所示。

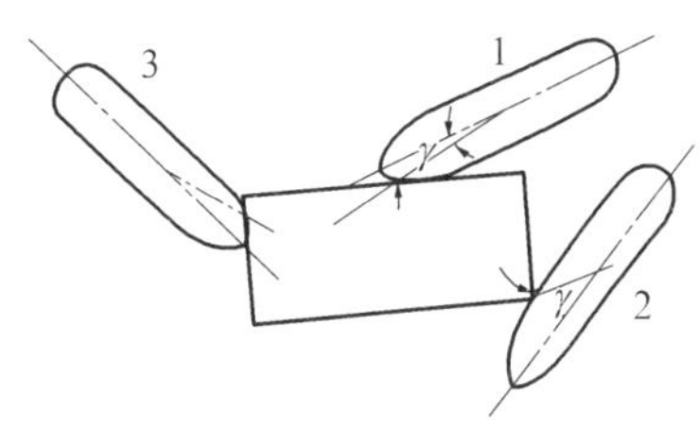

图 1　船墩碰撞时的三种位置关系

Fig. 1　Three collision relations between ship and pier

对漂流船舶和靠趸船，着力点和重心的连线与船的纵轴间的夹角 γ 接近 90°，$\sin\gamma$ 接近于 1，因其速度很低，我国港工规范给出其靠船力如表 3 所示。

表 3　**我国港工规范靠船力表**

Table 3　**the list of berthing impact in China's Port engineering specification**

船舶载重量/t	撞击力/kN
200	100
700	200
1 000 ~ 2 000	250
3 000 ~ 6 000	300

对行进中的船，其接触力与侧向分速度有关，现将其通常出现的情况分为三类，第一类 γ 小于 6°，分速度 $v\sin\gamma$ 小于 $0.1v$；第二类 γ 小于 12°，$v\sin\gamma$ 小于 $0.2v$；第三类 γ 小于 30°，$v\sin\gamma$ 小于 $0.5v$。实际上船在快撞上墩时或者停车，或者打倒车，如用船的最高速计算，是偏安全的。

附连水质量是指船在波浪中运动时，刚性船体带动液体的作用看作相当于船体质量的增加，在无速度时对纵摇、横摇和垂荡都有影响，有航速时通常以一定的系数计入船的质量中，影响这个系数有很多因素。

我国港工规范附录中规定计算有效冲击时附连水系数取 1.1 ~ 1.5。

日本横跨本洲四国的大桥桥墩防撞设计说明书中对前进中的船舶取为 1.1；对没有速度（横漂）的船取为 1.4。

本文计算取较大的航速，故取前进中船舶的附连水质量系数。

船速以新船速乘以 0.08 ~ 0.9 再加上水流速；船队的速度以拖船自由航速乘以 0.58 再加上流速；快船不加流速。

船舶数量分国营、地方国营等归口统计，只算加上附连水质量后超过 700 t 的船只，最大船队的数目以大推轮数目计算，其他船队以驳船及其编队数计算。

船队碰撞时只损坏单只驳船，可知其“碰撞能”不能以整队计算，除碰撞角随船队加大而减小外，还能乘以一个驳船相互碰撞消耗能量的系数（因较难估算，本次未计入）。

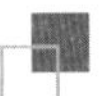

表 4　**船舶能量计算表**

Table 4　**The calculation table of ship kinetic energy**

序	船　型	主要参数 m				满载排水量 t	连附水总质量 t	数 量 艘/队	船速 Km/h /m/s	动能 (mv^2) 10^5 J	角度系数 $\sin\gamma$	计及角度的动能 10^5
		L	B	H	T							
1	江申 1 型	113.0	16.4	4.7	2.6	3 240	3 572	22	20/5.5	54.0	0.2	10.4
2	江申 103 型	62.5	10.4	3.2	2.2	686	755	1	22/6.1	14.0	0.2	2.8
3	江申 107 型	82.5	13.3	3.8	2.75	1 163	1 609	8	22/6.1	29.9	0.2	6.0
4	江申 115 型	90.3	14.2	4.0	2.9	1 791	1 970	1	22/6.1	36.7	0.2	7.4
5	江汉 11 型	84.5	13.0	3.4	2.35	1 333	1 708	1	22/6.1	31.8	0.2	6.4
6	江汉 51 型	84.5	14.0	3.5	2.6	1 174	1 622	7	22/6.1	30.1	0.2	6.0
7	江汉 55 型	77.0	13.0	—	2.63	1 233	1 412	3	22/6.1	26.3	0.2	5.2
8	江汉 119 型	68.5	12.0	3.5	2.7	1 053	1 158	7	24/6.7	26.0	0.2	5.2
9	800 客沪渝班船及平头涡尾	76.0	14	—	2.1	1 300	1 430	2	31/8.4	48.5	0.2	9.7
10	800 t 自卸驳	62.3	10.5	3.6	2.7	1 091	1 310	4	20/5.5	19.8	0.5	9.9
11	集装箱船	62.3	10.5	3.6	2.1	1 058	1 164	4	20/5.5	17.6	0.5	8.8
12	5 500 t 油船	127.0	22.0	3.8	4.25	5 399	6 250	1	21/5.8	101.8	0.1	10.2
13	5 000 t 油船	126.0	16.0	—	5.0	5 000	5 500	8	25/6.9	139.9	0.1	13.0
14	2 400 t 油船	100.4	13.8	4.8	3.6	2 100	2 610	8	24.5/6.0	47.5	0.1	4.8
15	5 000 t 油驳	—	—	—	—	5 000	5 500	6	14/3.9	41.8	0.2	8.4
16	3 000 t 油驳	86.5	15.6	4.0	3.3	3 000	3 300	113	14/3.9	25.1	0.2	5.0
17	1 500 t 油驳	—	—	—	—	1 500	1 650	6	14/3.9	12.5	0.2	2.5
18	1 000 t 油驳	62.0	11.0	3.5	2.76	1 000	1 100	82/41	14/3.9	8.4	0.2	1.7/3.4
19	1 000 t 自航驳	62.0	11.0	3.5	2.6	1 000	1 100	2	14/3.9	8.4	0.2	1.7
20	1 500 t 货驳	72.0	13.0	3.5	2.3/2.7	1 710	1 892	22	14/3.9	14.4	0.2	2.9
21	1 000 t 货驳	62.0	11.0	3.5	2.4	1 107	1 280	48/24	14/3.9	9.3	0.2	1.9/3.8
22	800 t 货驳	56.2	10.0	2.8	2.3	869	956	30	14/3.9	7.3	0.2	1.5
23	1 500 t 甲板驳	75.0	13.0	3.5	2.6	1 727	1 900	138/220	14/3.9	14.4	0.2	2.9/5.8
24	1 000/1 200 t 甲板驳	72.0	13.0	2.5	2.0	1 274	1 401	26	14/3.9	10.7	0.2	2.2
25	2 000 t 甲板驳	—	—	—	—	2 300	2 530	32	14/3.9	19.2	0.2	3.8
26	5 000 t 分节驳	81.0	20.0	5.0	4.1	5 300	5 843	62	14/3.9	41.4	0.2	8.9
27	3 000 t 分节驳	—	—	—	—	3 200	3 500	—	14/3.9	23.6	0.2	5.3
28	2 000 t 分节驳	60.8	10.67	4.21	3.8	2 150	2 355	120	14/3.9	18.0	0.2	3.6
29	1 000 t 分节驳	53.0	10.6	3.5	2.6	1 220	1 342	147/37	14/3.9	10.2	0.2	2.0/8.0
30	1 100 t 矿驳	—	—	—	—	1 320	1 442	21	14/3.9	11.0	0.2	2.2
31	上水最大船队	351	54	—	—	15 000	16 500	2	7/1.9	20.7	0.2	6.0

续表

序	船　型	主要参数 m				满载排水量 t	连附水总质量 t	数量艘/队	船速 Km/h /m/s	动能 (mv^2) 10^5 J	角度系数 $\sin\gamma$	计及角度的动能 10^5
		L	B	H	T							
32	下水最大船队	290	54	—	—	12 000	13 200	2	10/2.8	51.7	0.2	10.2
33	地方 14 公司船	—	—	—	—	6 030	6 600	13	20/5.5	99.8	0.1	10.9
34	地方 14 公司船	—	—	—	—	3 500	3 850	9	20/5.5	58.2	0.1	5.8
35	地方 14 公司船	—	—	—	—	1 500	1 650	2	20/5.5	23.0	0.1	2.3
36	地方 14 公司驳船队	—	—	—	—	3 000	3 300	2	14/3.9	23.1	0.2	3.0
	统计样本总数	1 293/889										

注：本表得到林树人、严似松和毛渭清等同志提供资料，特此鸣谢！

考虑到上述5、6个因素之后可综合得到船撞墩能量直方图。图中每栏由表4所列项目组成，直方图及高斯分布曲线见图2所示。

由图2的直方图可以看出当 $\bar{x}=50.97$，$\sigma_{n-1}=22.09$ 时，取 2σ 区间（连同小于 2σ 以外部分）保证率为97.5%时，应取船或船队的碰撞能量为 9.52×10^6 J；取 3σ 区间（连同小于 3σ 以外部分）保证率为99.75%时应取船或船队的碰撞能量为 1.17×10^7 J。

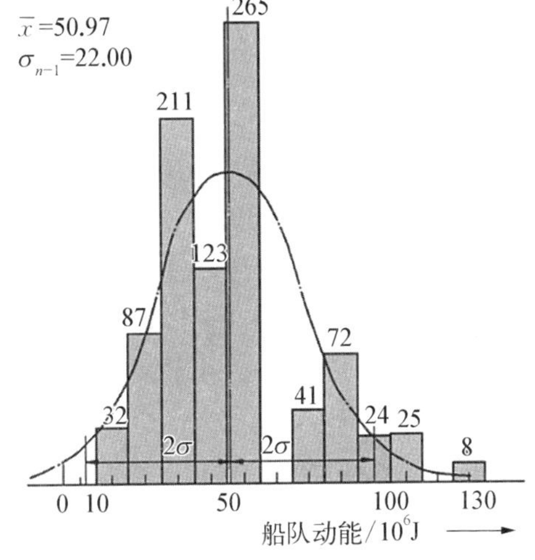

图2　船舶能量直方图及高斯分布曲线

Fig. 2　Histogram and gaussian distribution curve of ship kinetic energy

4　总结

防撞要求的分析告诉我们：根据长江中游桥梁、航道和水运三方面的情况，设置的防护设施应综合地满足8点要求，并在各方能接受的条件下具有上述的足够的吸能能力，以保证船和桥的安全运行。

本文之后将续文讨论吸能防撞设施的种类和特点以及长江中游对吸能防撞设施的选择；符合上述8项要求的吸能防撞设施及其吸能能力的试验标定等。

发表于：航海科技动态，1995(3).

Published at: Marine Technical News & Trends, 1995(3).

长江中游桥墩防撞(续一)——防撞设施的种类及其特点

Anti-collision of bridge pier in middle reaches of Yangtze River (continue 1) — Kind of anti-collision equipment and its characteristic

陈国虞　林树人

(交通部上海船舶运输科学研究所 200135)

CHEN Guoyu, LIN Shuren

(Shanghai Ship and Shipping Research Institute, Ministry of Communications, 200135, China)

摘　要　在前文对长江中游的桥墩防撞提出了8点要求之后,回顾了历史上有过的:势能法、绳拦法、束流推船法、石阶法、墩外护桩法、钢格子结构浮围、复合材型防撞围子等7种方法,然后根据他们的不足,顺理成章地发展出第8种柔性吸能防撞设施。继续阐述了几种材料的吸能特性,讨论了防撞设施的吸能刚性,从而研究设计出一种新的柔性防撞设施——钢丝绳吸能防撞器。

关键词　船撞桥　防撞设施　材料的吸能特性　防撞设施的吸能刚性　钢丝绳吸能防撞器

Abstract: After the afore paper has been raise 8 points characteristics of the anti-collision equipments, this paper reviews 7 kinds of equipment had been used by the people in history: potential energy method, obstruct by rope, control the flow and push the ship, stone stairs method, column outside the pier, steel grid structure pontoon cell around the piers, composite material surround etc.. After that, according to those defect, follow a rational line we got the 8th kind of anti-collision equipments. This paper compares some characteristics of several materials, and discusses the rigidity of absorbing energy process. So, we established new soft energy-dissipating anti-collision equipments: steel rope composite soft energy-dissipating anti-collision equipments.

Keyword: ship collision with bridge, soft energy-dissipating anti-collision,

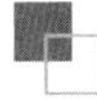

characteristic of anti-collision equipment, defect of anti-collision equipment, steel rope composite soft energy-dissipating anti-collision equipments.

前文《长江中游桥墩防撞——防撞要求的分析》提出防撞设施要能被桥梁、航道和水运三方所接受,桥梁方指铁路或公路(或二者联合)的建设者、桥梁使用和维护单位(有时不止一个);航道方应包括航政管理部门、航道工程部门和日常维护保养部门;水运指的是航运轮船公司和港务系统等,三方面各有各的要求,出发点也不全一样[1]。

前文提出综合各方对防撞设施的要求为 8 条,有点读者认为全部符合 8 条要求比较难,下面讨论以完全符合 8 条为追求目标和筛选原则。

1　防撞设施的种类

文献[6]将桥墩防撞设施分为直接和间接两大类,每大类分为弹性变形型、压坏变形型和变位型故共六类。本文按桥方能接受的、桥航两方能接受的和桥航船三方均能接受的顺序简述如下。

① 势能法　日本称为变位型,即用重物的上升吸收势能(同时伴有运动阻力吸能、加速度吸能),以消耗船舶运动的动能,这种方式如图 1 示意。它的优点是设施不大却能建造出吸收 10^6 J 能量的设施,而且多次反复使用不会坏;其缺点是占据航道,价钱也不便宜;且设施吸收的能量正比于缆绳与桥墩的距离,要增大能量就得多占航道,这是一种古老的方法,最近不多见使用的实例。

② 绳拦法　以大抓力锚或水中桩柱系粗钢绳作为横纲,横向拦阻船只,竖向为细钢绳,用浮子或桩柱使横纲处于水线附近,文献[6]认为此种方式对小船有用,但因碍航,在三年前曾在我国进行讨论,后未被采用,如图 2 示意。

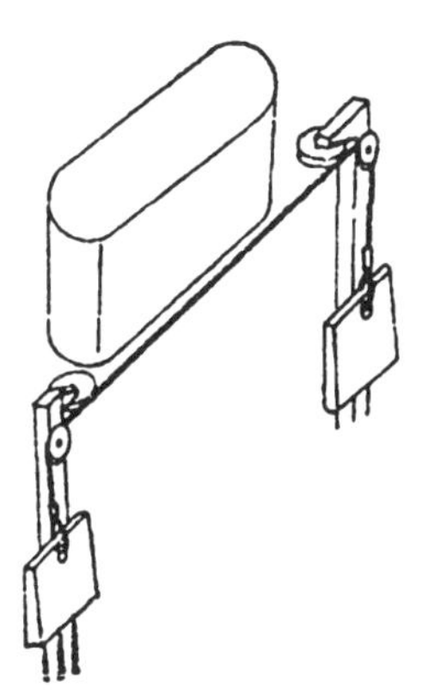

图 1　势能法防撞装置示意图

Fig. 1　The schematic of anti-collision device designed by potential energy method

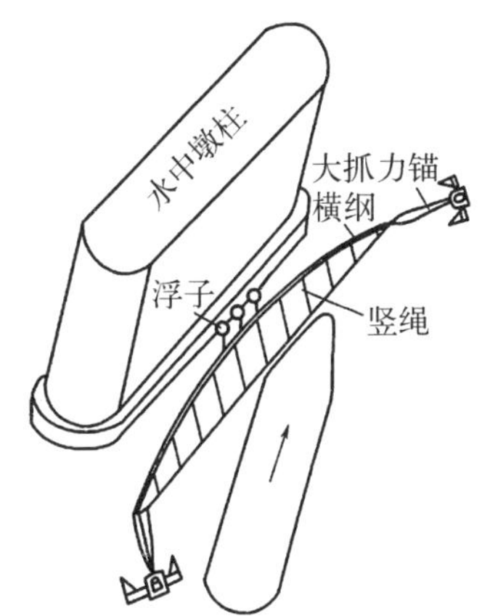

图 2　绳拦式防撞装置设施示意图

Fig. 2　The schematic of anti-collision device designed by blocking wires

③ 束流推船法　在桥墩的上游方向修筑永久性束水导航堤堰，产生将船推离墩的水流和推力，如图 3 示意。其缺点有二：一为增加人工建造的水中永久性碍航物；二为定向水流推船后在船边高速流过使船体两侧流速不一，根据柏努利原理负压产生吸力将船吸向桥墩。

④ 石阶法　用石或混凝土将桥墩周围修出人工岛礁，使船未到墩前先被人工岛礁搁浅触礁。这种方法等于扩大了桥墩，本来桥墩就是占了航道，此法更多占航道，激化矛盾，但水位变化不大的地方使用较多，洪峰来时水位超过石阶即失效，见图 4 示意。

⑤ 墩外护柱法　在桥墩外另建护柱。其缺点与上法相同，且占航道更多，但当洪峰未淹没柱顶前仍然有效，也见图 4。

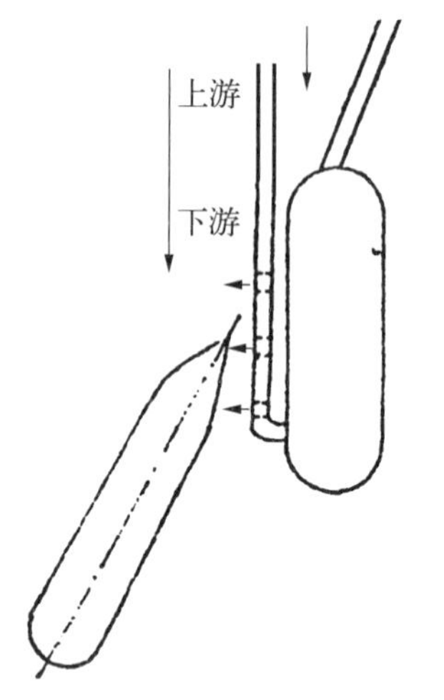

图 3　束流推船法

Fig. 3　The beam on ship method

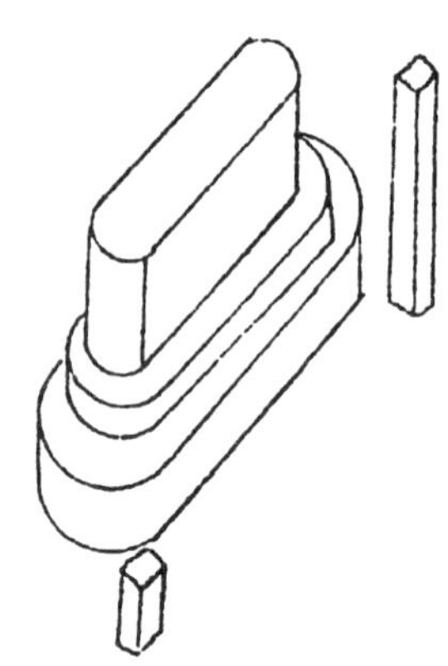

图 4　人工岛式和桩式防撞设施

Fig. 4　Artificial islands and pile type anti-collision facilities

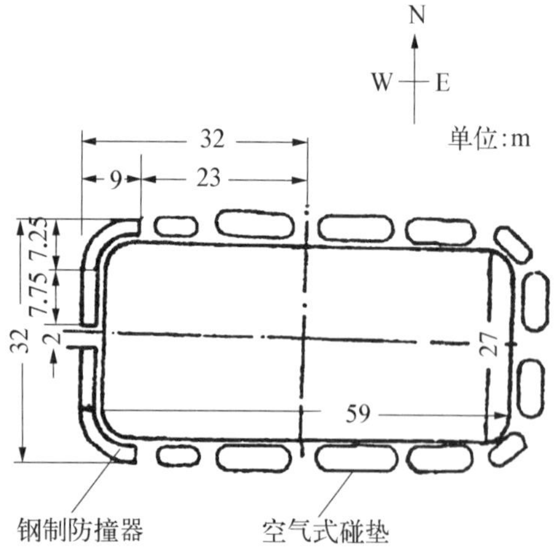

图 5　濑户大桥 5P 桥墩防撞设施

Fig. 5　The anti-collision device of 5P pier at Seto Great Bridge

⑥ 钢格子结构浮围　日本称蜂窝格子型[2]就是在墩柱的周围用钢格子结构作成浮围。其机理是在相撞时压坏船和围子，保护桥墩。这种方式按大船相撞时吸能要求制作，小船撞坏少、大船撞坏多，逐步撞坏逐步吸能。由于此围子在吸能相当大时大致与一艘船的尺寸相当，故两败俱伤，撞后需要修理。通常在钢结构外面还包以橡皮，以改善小能量撞击时的损坏，参看图 5 濑户大桥左侧的实例。

⑦ 复合材型防撞围子　这是一种组合的形式，在格子钢结构内填塞弹塑性物质，如泡沫塑料等。能改变吸能曲线形状，并增加吸能，但未能改变每次撞后要修理的特点。

⑧ 柔性吸能防撞设施　柔性吸能防撞器通常有三种可能的类型,一种为橡皮膜内填充泡沫塑料,但泡沫塑料吸能正比于其容重,容重大了虽然吸能多了,但性质较脆[5],易于在内部压碎成粉末;另一种是内充气体的橡皮碰垫,参看图 5 的右面[3],最大作到 400 t · m(4×10^6 J),是国际上可用的商品,但较贵,其保养工作量大;第三种是钢丝绳作成的吸能防撞器,我国最新专利 93 224 217.0,组合成吸能防撞装置(1×10^7 J 左右),它能保护船,能反复多次使用,其浮筏用低容重的闭口泡沫填塞,不易碎裂。这就满足了 8 条综合要求,见图 7 示意。

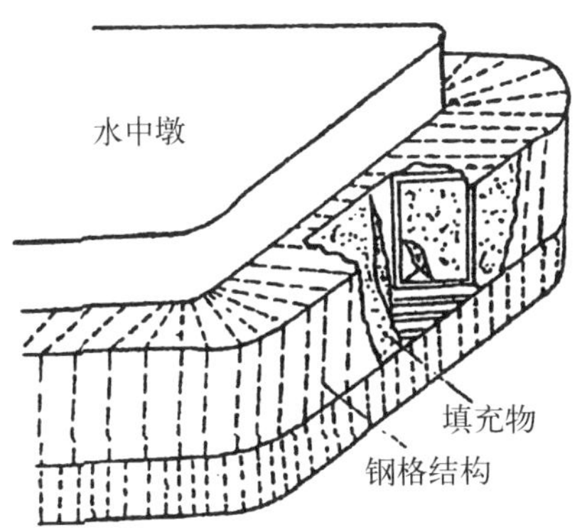

图 6　复合材型防撞设施

Fig. 6　The composite material anti-collision device

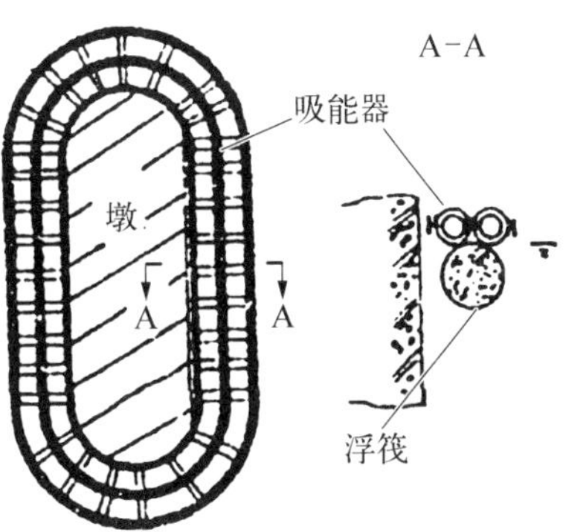

图 7　钢绳柔性吸能防撞设施图

Fig. 7　The schematic of steel-wire flexible energy-absorption anti-collision device

2　几种防撞器结构材料吸能特性

要分析桥、航、船三者的主要矛盾和矛盾的主要方面,必须先分析桥墩、防撞器和船体三者相撞时的材料变形、吸能和断裂特性,才能进一步分析吸能防撞装置整体刚度。

由图 8 看出,钢的弹性模量(杨氏模量)最大,刚性最强,$E = 2\times10^5$ MPa (2×10^6 kgf/cm^2);混凝土小 10 倍 $E = 2\times10^4$ MPa (2×10^5 kgf/cm^2);柔性物质诸如橡胶、泡塑和钢绳圈等其他材料或制成品的刚性要小几十倍。在图上前两者曲线是凸的(二次导数为负值),后者为凹的(二次导数为正值)。

利用这种特性,应能设计制造出这样的柔性防撞器,当其达到与钢格围子同样吸能时,其力小于钢格围子,这样就可以做到桥墩不受过大的力而船也不损坏,图 9 就是这个原理图。

船与墩相撞时,撞击的能量大小取决于船的质量 m,和速度 v,能量为$\frac{1}{2}mv^2$;冲量的大小也决定于质量和速度,为 mv;撞击力与冲量有关,表达式为 $mv = Ft$, mv 可以用冲撞前后的两个状态之冲量差来表示,Ft 可用冲撞过程的力函数在时间坐标轴上积分值(面积)表达,如果是恒力可以直接相乘。这就是说碰撞力的大小与碰撞过程的时间有关,柔性防撞设施使碰撞过程时间延长,因而力就小。

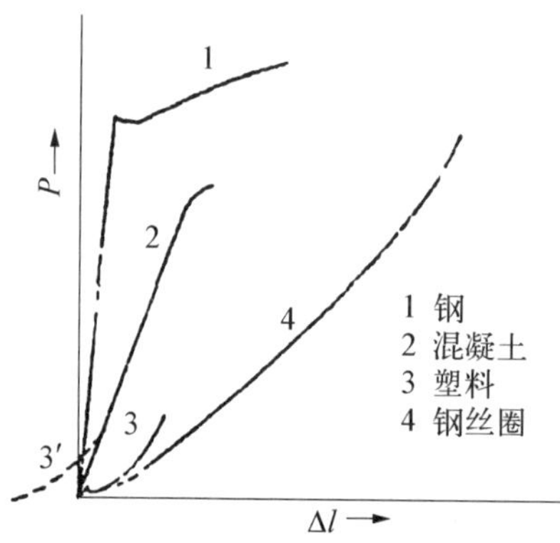

图 8 防撞设施、墩和船的材料压力特性

Fig. 8 The material pressure characteristic of anti-collision device, pier and ship

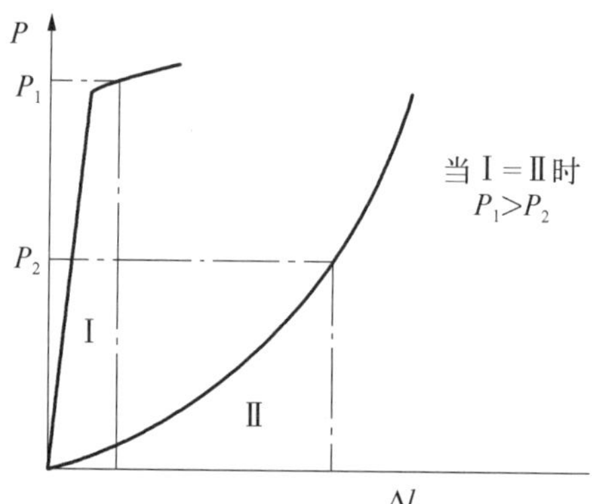

图 9 刚性和柔性材料的力和功

Fig. 9 The force and work of stiffness or flexible materials

船直接撞到水泥墩上力就大,撞在另一艘船上力就小些;船以同样速度撞在钢板桩码头上力就大,撞在防撞器上力就小些[8]。

长江中游及支流除个别的桥用石墩外,绝大多数桥墩由混凝土建成。混凝土的抗压强度极限 σ_c 为 5 ~ 60 MPa(50 ~ 600 kgf/cm^2),取其中等强度的混凝土来举例:σ_c = 45 MPa (450 kgf/cm^2),剪切极限强度 τ_b = 15 MPa (150 kgf/cm^2),长江中游桥墩大致尺寸为 12 m×4 m,其抗剪强度达几万吨力;跨海大桥的桥墩更大,濑户大桥截面积约为其 10 倍,岩黑岛桥约为 8 倍,剪断抗力均为几十万吨,而撞坏一艘船的力仅以几千吨计,相差几十倍之多。据此,桥墩防撞的问题可以归结为两点:船不要撞坏(人命和货损等问题);桥墩表面层不要被撞坏(钢筋暴露,影响寿命)。

3 防撞设施的吸能刚性

各种材料的特性如上所述,但构成防撞设施之后,设施的刚性和吸能特点又有所不同。

混凝土的弹性系数虽然小于钢,但因其构件(构筑物)的整体性和脆性,变形小,不能吸能,船与混凝土桩柱或台基相撞时损坏的首先是船。

钢的弹性系数 E 很大,但是作为钢蜂窝格子的目的是要一小块一小块地屈曲和撕裂[4],所以它的构件刚度与钢块试验刚度不同,桥墩用的防撞钢围子其尺寸与一艘船相当,所以借用钢船碰坏的情况,引入一个整体刚度(最大力/位移)的概念。[8]中给出的几个实例,其整体刚度为 900 t/2.3 m, 900 t/1.4 m, 1 600 t/0.75 m, 1 600 t/4.65 m, 1 200 t/2.4 m,范围从 344 t/m ~ 2 133 t/m,钢围子的破坏是逐渐的,破坏深度加大时抗力增大、能量增加,接触面积也加大。

气动力式的柔性碰垫[3],单个吸能从 2.6 t/m 到 401 t/m,当 2.6 t/m 时直径为 1.0 m;401 t/m 时直径为 4.5 m;以其可压缩直径 80% 估计,其整体刚度是 2.6 t/0.8 m 至 222 t/3.6 m,即 3 t/m ~ 62 t/m。

钢绳吸能防撞器是一种新式柔性防撞器[9],为解决现有防撞器之不足而研制的,它用了几项新技术:选用内摩擦大的钢丝绳;采用钢绳堆垒紧密排列成圈技术,使在最小的体积内得到最大的吸能能力;采用铝合金套压接技术,使吸能防撞器在多次冲击使用过程中不会松散。

钢绳吸能防撞器组成吸能防撞设施时可以串联和并联,不论串联和并联其吸能总量不变;串联时其加到桥墩上的力不增加,位移增加;并联时位移不增加而作用于桥墩上的力增加。

钢绳吸能防撞器现有系列的单个吸能功为 350 ~ 12 000 J;相应的宏观平均刚度4.5 ~ 36 t/m,如图 7 的形式共 800 个吸能防撞器采用 2 串 400 并的方式,位移为单个的两倍,力为单个的 400 倍,这个整体刚度约为 2 000 t/m。

4 总结

讨论了 8 种桥墩防撞设施之后,得到钢绳柔性吸能防撞装置,它能被桥梁、航道和水运三方所接受,满足三方所要求的 8 点综合要求。

参 考 文 献

[1] 日・本州四国连络桥公团:复合材型缓冲工的设计要领(案)[R],1981 - 03.

[2] 日・本州四国连络桥公团:蜂窝钢格子型缓冲工的设计要领(案)[R],1981 - 03.

[3] YOKOHAMA Catalog. Floating-Type Pneumatic Rubber Fenders[M]. CN - 03035 - 01E,日本.

[4] 王绍祖.船体钢室冲击断裂时的启裂与失稳[J].船舶工程,1985(2).

[5] 吴用舒.硬聚氨酯泡沫塑料动态压缩特性的一次试验测量[J].振动与冲击,1986(1).

[6] 岩井・聪.关于船舶对桥梁的安全措施[J].中国航海,1986(2).

[7] 陈国虞.长江中游桥墩防撞——防撞要求的分析[J].航海科技动态,1995(3).

[8] 杨家祥,梁文娟.桥墩碰撞力的计算[J].交通部上海船舶运输科学研究所学报,1994(2).

[9] 陈国虞,倪步友.吸能防撞器[P]中华人民共和国专利 93224317.0.中国专利授权公告.1994 - 11.

发表于:航海科技动态,1995(4).

Published at: Marine Technical News & Trends, 1995(4).

桥墩防撞设施的选择

How to choose the anti-collision equipment of bridge

陈国虞

（交通部上海船舶运输科学研究所 200135）

CHEN Guoyu

（Shanghai Ship and Shipping Research Institute,
Ministry of Communications, 200135, China）

摘　要　要正确选择防撞设施，必须了解人们曾经用过那些防撞设施。20世纪80年代，日本岩井・聪将防撞设施分为直接构造和间接构造两大类，每类均分为3种类型4种方式，是从变形种类（弹性变形、塑性变形）和吸能原理（位能、变形能）来区分的。1991年欧洲的学者将他列举的8种方式中选其常用的5项，即：防护板，墩外桩，拦船缆，人工岛和浮动筏。因为重力变位式只适应冲击能量较小的船舶他就不提了。根据工程力学的发展指出：弹性变形复位很好但耗掉能量太少；塑性变形耗能较多但恢复不易。理想的防撞装置应该将船头拨开，能量保留在船上，交换少损坏就少，交换的动能应尽量消耗掉，船和防撞装置损坏就少。于是发明了高耗能的黏滞性防撞元件，加上外钢围的弹性恢复作用，使三不坏的防撞装置可能实现。保护桥和船的同时也保护了环境。

关键词　防撞设施　弹性变形　塑性变形　黏滞性　外钢围

Abstract: For the choosing of anti-collision equipment of bridge, people must be to know there are how many kinds of collision equipment which the man had been used. In 1980's of last century, a Japanese scholar named Satoshi Iwai has been classify the anti-collision equipment to 8 kinds include direct and indirect construction two types. He was classified from the theory of deformation and the way of energy-dissipating (elastic deformation or plastic deformation; more dissipating or very few dissipating). In 1991 the scholars of Europe only let the anti-collision equipment divide to 5 kinds: the protection plank; pole outside the pier; stop the ship by towrope; human island and float pontoon around the pier. Might be due to potential energy for the big ship is too small they haven't mentioned the method of potential changing.

This paper notice out, the engineering mechanics indicates that: equipment after elastic deformation can be easy to replace, but it dissipate energy very little; plastic deformation can dissipate much energy but it can not replace; viscosity deformation can dissipate very much energy. If we can combine use the viscosity dissipation by the soft anti-collision element and use the elastic replace by the outer steel surrounding, and at the same equipment we turn out the bow of the ship. Let the energy transformation in this impact system is very small. So, we can establish a new anti-collision equipment, it can protect the pier, protect the ship at the same time, it also protected the environment.

Keyword: anti-collision equipment, elastic deformation, plastic deformation, viscosity dissipation, outer steel surrounding

近年来,国内外出现桥墩被撞的情况较多。国际上对桥下船舶通行需要多大的水平宽度和垂直净空,上下游要求多长的平直段均有所约定。今后新建桥梁就得按此约定选择好位置和尺寸,以减少桥墩被撞的危险。这些约定促进了大跨度、高桥身或一跨过江新桥的建设。

桥墩被撞设施的选择应从两个方面考虑:一方面是综合衡量以往措施,那些是切实有效的。在吸收前人经验的同时,应采用最新科技成果。另一方面就是认定选择原则,所选择的设施种类应能被各有关方面接受,最新科技成果往往就是在为满足各方要求、解决各种矛盾中产生和发展的。

1 防撞设施的种类

20 世纪 80 年代,日本岩井·聪提出:桥墩防护措施按设置地点可分为直接构造和间接构造两大类;每大类内再按吸收船舶碰撞能量方式分为弹性变形型、压坏变形型和变位型三型。在两类六型中列举了 8 种方式,如表 1 所示。

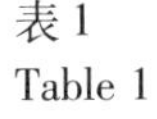
表 1 防撞装置分类

Table 1 The classification of anti-collision devices

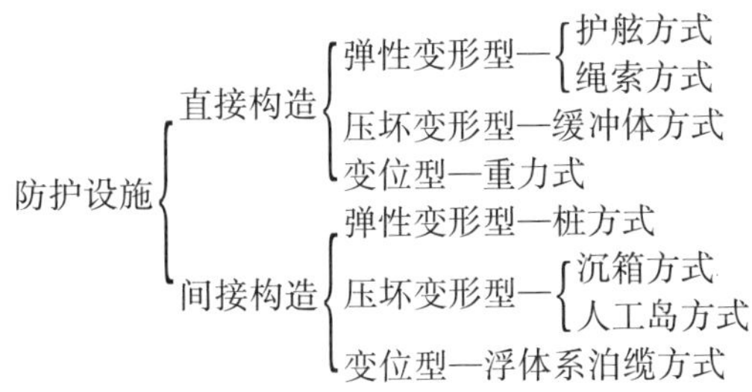

1991年国际桥梁和结构工程协会(IABSE)将通常使用的桥墩保护结构分为5类:

(1) 防护板系统;

(2) 支撑桩系统;

(3) 系缆桩保护;

(4) 人工岛或暗礁保护;

(5) 漂动保护系统。

2 选择的原则

在长江天堑第一桥建成后38年来,发生了几十起船撞桥事故。有关各方因利益不同而有不同的想法和要求。

桥方认为:桥上运量往往超过桥下水运量若干倍,尤其是铁路桥,不但有很大的经济效益,还有其战略意义,所以船受损失是次要的,确保桥面畅通是第一位的。

船方则认为:未建桥前,航道是完整的,桥墩是人工碍航物,是人工岛礁,分割了航道,使航道变窄。应不建或少建,尤其是一些桥墩选位不当,建在航道转弯处,不符合国际上的约定,以致产生船撞桥事故,其责任首先是桥方,不应对船方罚款而应由桥方赔偿。

港航监督方面的要求是保护设施不应多占航道,也不应造成维护困难。例如在墩前设导柱,不占航道和采用某些浮式护圈,占航道较少,都是可以接受的。至于设置灯船、船标,桥上下游设导航站,制定过桥规则,甚至采用先进的设施,都要投资,都将会增加港航方的维护负担。

所以桥墩防护设施必须符合三方要求,兼顾三方利益,能被三方欣然接受,以此归纳出桥墩防撞设施的8点综合要求。

3 桥墩防撞设施的综合要求

(1) 当船与桥撞上时,防撞措施要既保护桥又保护船。

(2) 桥墩防撞设施本身要小,尽量少占航天道宽度,与护堤、护坝和海洋平台保护等有所不同。

(3) 适应水位变化。为了适应潮差及洪枯等水位的变化,防撞设施最好做成浮式。

(4) 吸能能力要大,撞击研究结果表明:撞击产生正半波之后的负半波极易损坏结构物。吸能率高的防撞器,在正半波内消耗掉大量的能,可减少对结构的破坏。

(5) 撞后恢复。防撞设施在大能量撞击下能多次使用,小能量撞击后不需修理。

(6) 安装运输方便。设施不应要求过高的施工条件,以使总成本不致过高。

(7) 不因防撞设施而产生新问题。诸如出现环境保护、捕捞养殖、回流沉积等方面的问题。

（8）价格便宜。

4 防撞设施新成果的应用

最近几年建成的大能量桥墩防撞设施，如日本的濑户大桥、岩黑岛桥等，使用了钢格子缓冲体、橡胶——空气碰垫、钢丝方式等防撞设施。

为了少占航道，桥墩防撞基本上不采用间接构造；由于直接构造中的重力式（变位型或称势能型）其附加机构比较大，采用得也较少，而压坏变形型则只能保护桥不能保护船，且每次撞后要修理，修理时工程较大，不符合上述综合要求。因而只剩下护舷方式和绳索方式两种可供选择了。

岩黑岛桥所用的是绳索方式，在墩身上设置离墩侧表面约 2 m 的支撑，将直径 20 mm 的钢绳拉住支撑（共拉 17 根），利用钢绳受力变形吸能防撞。

护舷方式大多为浮式，有多种防撞元件，如实心橡胶、Ω 型橡胶、气囊式橡胶元件等。最新的一种是 1994 年年底才获中国专利的钢绳圈吸能防撞器。

钢绳圈吸能防撞器能在浮筏上以串联、并联方式组成防撞装置，其吸能量叠加，但反力可因设计而异。它的优点在于既保护桥又能保护船；多次大能量撞击后吸能量下降甚少；位移恢复达 80% 左右；反复使用也不须维修；使用海洋平台不干性水舱涂料保护，在使用期内钢绳能保持银亮表面；所占位置也不大；实测吸能率为 70% ~86%，高出橡胶 2 倍。这足以说明推广最新科技成果可以实现三方兼顾的综合要求。

5 桥墩防撞工作程序

（1）立法。颁布桥梁工程规范，规定桥墩防撞设施与桥梁同时设计、同时施工、同时投入使用。设计时三方会签通过，这样就免除了三方的争议。由于防撞设施仅占大桥工程投资的 5% 左右，要求“三同时”是有可能做到的。

（2）外载的确定。要根据桥、船和港监三方的要求研究确定防撞设施的大小，有关资料已给出一些计算的原则；也有具体计算的方法和步骤；最好能进一步形成规范。

（3）工程图设计、施工设计（包括安装设计）。

（4）典型部件试验和防撞能力验证。因为若对整个防撞设施验证则所需试验规模较大，可采用实际撞击速度来验证其元件的能力。

（5）施工制造和安装。

如能按以上程序设计施工，就可使桥墩防撞设施的建造建立在科学、准确、可靠的基础上。

发表于：中国水运，1995(9).

Published at: China Water Transport, 1995(9).

关于“船撞桥”问题的几点浅见

Some views about ship collision with the bridge

陈国虞
（交通部上海船舶运输科学研究所 200135）
CHEN Guoyu
(Shanghai Ship and Shipping Research Institute, Ministry of Communications, 200135, CHINA)

摘　要　船撞桥问题近20年来被人们所重视。1991年国际桥梁和结构协会(IABSE)在总结153篇报告的基础上公布了船桥相互关系的《综述与指南》，为桥方和航运方取得共识作出了贡献。介绍了该指南的要点，并对若干问题作了补充分析。提出了既要保护桥、又要保护船、防撞器本身也不坏的柔性防撞器，经过分析提出船撞桥的4种情况。

关键词　船撞桥　桥梁保护　航船撞损

Abstract: The problem about the ship collision with the pier is value by people in the recent 20 years. On the foundation of summarize 153 reports, in 1991 the International Association of Bridge and Structure Engineers (IABSE) publicize <The Interaction between Vessel Traffic and Bridge Structures>, give out the contribute for obtain the common view of the bridge side and the traffic side. This paper introduced the important points of that guidebook, and made the complement analysis to some problems. Putting forward a soft anti-collision equipment, it can protect the pier, protect the ship at the same time itself does not damage. Though the complement analysis this paper raise 4 diagram of all situation when the ship collision with the bridge.

Keyword: ship collision with the bridge, protection of the bridge, Vessel Traffic damage

近20年来，跨江桥梁不断增加，船撞桥的问题愈来愈为人们所重视。尤其是大陆和岛屿、岛屿和岛屿之间的桥梁，需通过较大吨位的船只，一旦船撞桥，能量交换很大，造成损失可观。

1983 年，国际桥梁和结构工程协会就“船与桥的撞击”问题编制了一本《综述与指南》，内容包括：

对新桥和航道的规划与建设的建议；

对老桥和航道改进的建议；

对碰撞预防和桥梁保护的建议；

对人员和环境的安全进行评估。

经 8 年实践，在总结 153 篇工作报告的基础上，于 1991 年 9 月正式公布了此《综述与指南》。公布后获得桥梁界和航运界的高度重视。笔者认为，它有很多问题提得很对，可为桥方、航运方、港航管理方所接受，有些问题可进一步探讨。但因《指南》公布时间尚短，有些桥梁早已建成，有些建桥者还未采用，故在本文中，笔者对认为《指南》提得很对的几个问题，从体会和推广的角度说明拥护的理由，有两个问题作者认为可作进一步探讨，并提出一些浅见。现分述如下：

(1) 在繁忙航道上，最好建设一跨过江（或过海峡）的桥，取消航道中的墩柱。如美国旧金山的金门大桥、我国珠江口的虎门大桥、长江下游的江阴长江公路桥、长江三峡的西陵桥、黄浦江上的南浦大桥和杨浦大桥等及香港沿海的青马大桥。因为对原有航道来说，桥墩无疑是新增的碍航人工桩柱，当然愈少愈好，一旦建有桥墩需设置灯标，要求航行船舶避让。有的桥方规定对撞桥的船处以罚款，所以对航行船舶来说最好是航道上不建或少建水中墩柱，对港航管理方来说，也是这样。

《指南》根据通航船舶所需的垂直空间和水平空间（即净高和净宽），提供了一系列图表供桥梁设计者遵循，这就是尊重了通航船舶的权利，并且提醒桥梁工程师在不能分别满足《指南》中根据通航船舶的大小而要求的净高、净宽尺寸时，则应少设或不设水中墩柱，而选择大跨距，甚至一跨过江的桥梁形式。

(2) 桥要建在航道平直段。《指南》规定，“从桥中心线到航道线转弯处的最短距离至少要有桥下通航最大吨位船舶 8 倍船长，最好是 20 倍。否则影响船舶通过桥梁”[1]。黄石公路桥正好建在航道弯段开始处，船撞桥事故时有发生，故防撞任务非常迫切和艰巨。

(3) 碰撞概率的统计计算。《指南》说明“船只碰撞桥梁结构的事故是相当少的，因此碰撞概率的估计不能仅建立在船舶和桥梁已发生的碰撞的统计基础上”[1]，应以桥下通过的船只数量、速度、碰撞质量、碰撞角度、企望保证率等综合因素进行统计分析，以决定外载。文献[2]就是用了这种方法。

(4) 附连水质量系数的选取。船的吨位乘上附连水系数便可算出船的碰撞质量。《指南》中说：“流水动力质量——船只周围与之一起运动的水的动态质量，一般可取为船只轴线方向质量的 10%”[1]，即附连水质量系数选取为 1.1。日本横跨本州、四国两岛的大桥，防撞设计中，对附连水质量系数亦取为 1.1[1]。因为附连水质量系数对左右摆动和往复振动的船来说,其作用显著,系数选取应较大,对具有一定前进速度的船,其附带水质量可取较小,故《指南》中所选取的1.1系数值是较适合的。

(5)新桥应有防护船撞墩设施。文献[1]列出了1964年到1990年中19个典型的船桥相撞例子。其中桥梁落水者14例,桥梁表面损伤者1例;缆车入水者1例。撞损船墩者3例,其中桥墩移位者1例,排桩损坏者1例,桥墩毁坏者1例。可见船撞桥事故中多为船撞桥致桥梁落水而桥面损坏的严重事故。船撞桥墩擦伤桥墩表面,撞破桥墩表面水泥保护层(武汉长江大桥最严重的一次撞破表面保护层深度达55 mm)虽然算不上严重事故,但这类事故多了(武汉长江大桥37年中桥墩被撞65次之多)亦会导致桥墩偏歪或位移,影响桥梁应力[7],从而导致小事故酿成桥梁塌下的严重事故,所以对新建的或在建的桥梁应有桥墩防护设施[9]。

(6)碰撞动能计算。《指南》认为:"船只行驶速度可分解为计算纵向动能平行于船轴线的分量和计算横向动能垂直于船轴线的分量。""如果船只完全停止,其碰撞总动能将耗尽;如果船只仅仅转向,碰撞能量可以碰撞前后船只动能的矢量分析来确定"[1]。这一点,共识者较多,但具体分析时可能有些差别[8],要是防撞装置按"动能耗尽"来设计,设计出来的防撞设施将硕大无比,且造价大,影响了防撞设施的普遍采用。这一点在后面将作补充分析。

(7)桥墩防撞设施的分类。按保护形式分,有防护板式、群桩式、系缆桩式、人工岛或暗礁式以及浮动式5类保护[1];按防护结构分,有直接构造和间接构造两大类[9]。笔者理解间接构造即不将力直接传给桥墩,而是在墩外设置结构物承受撞击的能和力,如墩外的柱、板、索、锚等等。笔者认为应按桥方、船方和港航管理方能接受的程度分类[3],这符合文献[1]所论述防护设施的目的:"保护系统的设计不仅要保护桥梁结构,而且要保护船和环境。"历史上用过的保护桥墩设施约有10种,现按能被桥、船和港航三方共同接受的程序为序分三类叙述如下:

第一类包括人工岛礁、阻船群桩、门式桩柱。这几种防护桥墩的设施有两个特点,一是占航道宽,二是船撞上去时非毁即伤,港航管理和船方均难接受。

第二类如台阶墩脚式、桩板式、浮动格子钢圈式、缆桩式等保护设施,其特点是占航道少,航道维护管理方认为问题不大,但船撞上去仍是硬碰硬,两败俱伤,船方不易接受,桥方在每次碰撞后均要修理。

第三类是既要保护桥,又要保护船,每次撞后不需修理的柔性防撞器[2],能被桥、船、港三方所接受。现有橡胶(或塑料)柔性防撞器(包括内有气体的形式)和钢丝绳柔性吸能防撞器等,它们的特点是在设计能量范围内,船撞桥时,船不坏,桥墩不坏,防撞器本身也不坏。防撞器可维修后使用。

柔性防撞器中由于耗能机理不同,吸能率相差很大,用钢丝绳制作的防撞器因其变形时借助于几百根钢丝之间内摩擦发热耗能,故其吸能率为橡胶的3倍[4],[11]。

(8)采用横向分速度计算能量的方法时如何对待奇点极值。第一种情况:直航前进的船大都是船头部位碰撞桥墩,其分速度夹角为γ。γ决定于船的宽长比(B→船宽,L→

船长)B/L,通常速度较高的船设计成 $B/L \leqslant 1/7$,这时夹角为 8.1°;速度较慢的船、货驳等,设计成 $B/L \approx 1/5$,这时夹角为 11.3°;拖船、渡船设计成 $B/L \approx 1/4$,这时夹角为 14°,横向分速度分别为原向航速的 0.14/0.2 和 0.75 倍,其能量 $1/2mv^2$ 分别为原能量的 0.02/0.04 和 0.06 倍,相撞情况如图 1 所示、图中剖面线是桥墩,它的周围两头尖的部分是笔者设计的防撞设施。

第 2 种情况:船除前进速度外,尚有横漂和转弯,所以碰到了平行中段,有点像船靠码头的情况,水流和舵起作用。此时船不能维持轴向前进。由于船横漂的横向速度比前进速度小很多,算出的能比直航速度所代表的能小得多。相撞情况如图 2 所示。

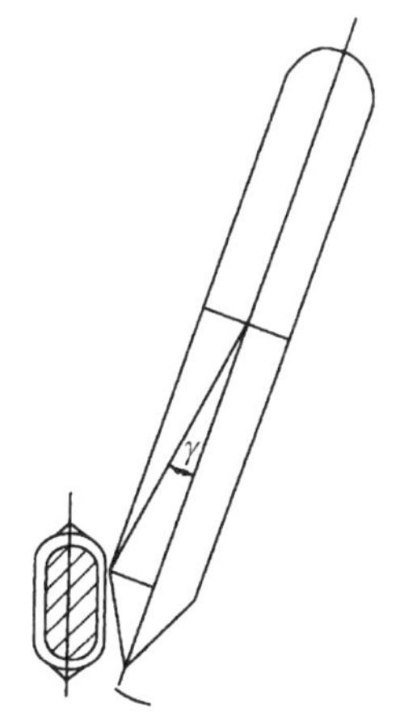

图 1　前进中船首部撞墩

Fig. 1　The bow of a going ship collision with the bridge pier

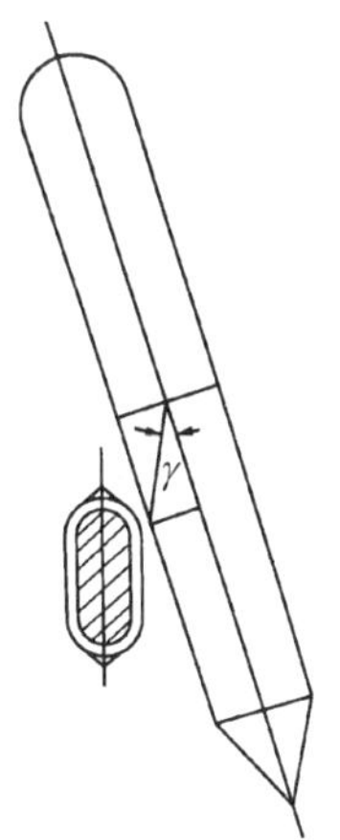

图 2　横漂船船侧碰墩

Fig. 2　The driven ship and ship side collision with the pier

第 3 种情况是一种极端情况,即船正对桥墩开过来,如图 3 示。如果相撞后顶住不动,则船与墩交换全部动能(船舶具有的最大动能值)。但因设计的防撞设施外箍板作成尖型,两相遇瞬间即滑开变成第 1 种情况。由此可以理解为:以横向分速度计算能量时,对正撞住不动的情况时“能量-角度”曲线上的一个奇点,此时横向速度分量为 0 而能量交换最大。笔者建议用保证率的办法处理此奇点,即认为此种状态的概率非常小,置于保证率之外。

第 4 种情况也是一种极端情况,横漂的船正好顶在船的重心上(如果不是顶在重心,则船的惯性力会使船转动,变为第 2 种情况),这时的碰撞能是以全部横漂速度 v_H 计算的 $(1/2mv_H)$,瞬间之后,由于水流合力与船的重心不重合,船头即慢慢旋转,实现“船到桥头自然直”,变为顺流而下,见图 4。

所有船与桥相撞均离不开上列 4 种情况。

(9) 防撞器的尺度和试验速度。如欲对整个桥墩防撞设施进行 1∶1试验,则规模太大。笔者根据国内现有试验机情况,建议对防撞设施的构成元件——防撞器进行 1∶1实体试验,当组成防撞设施时只要保证各元件之间力和能量的传递即可(我们选用最经典的

螺栓连接方法)。

在中国船舶结构测试中心(无锡)分别以船撞桥的实际速度(5 m/s 或 6 m/s)对橡胶柔性防撞器和钢绳柔性防撞器的元件进行了冲击总功、吸能率、位移和恢复等项目的试验测定,并绘图分析。测定结果对设计建造整个防撞装置提供了可靠的依据,也验证了计算的结果。

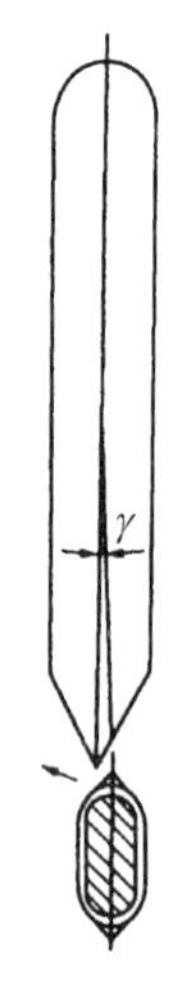

图 3 船对正撞墩后滑开

Fig. 3 Ship slide out after frontispiece collision with the pier

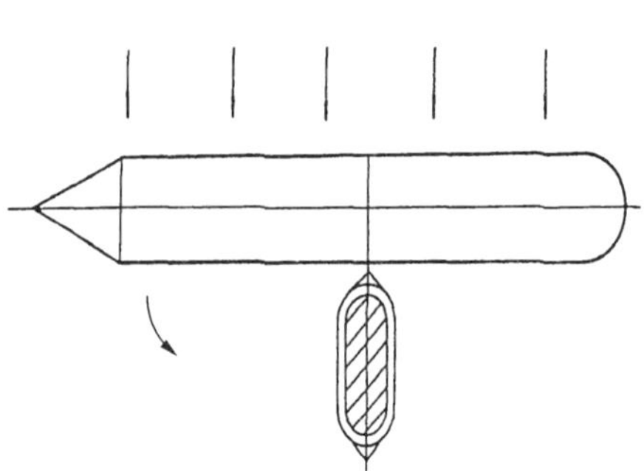

图 4 横漂船重心正好撞在墩上的极端情况

Fig. 4 The center gravity of transverse driven ship collision with the pier

参考文献

[1] 国际桥梁和结构工程协会(IABSE)(丹麦). 交通船只与桥梁结构的相互影响《综述与指南》. 1991-09.

[2] 陈国虞. 长江中游桥墩防撞——防撞要求分析[J]. 航海科技动态,1995(3).

[3] 陈国虞,林树人. 长江中游桥墩防撞(续一)——防撞设施的种类及其特点[J]. 航海科技动态,1995(4).

[4] 陈国虞,倪步友,贾关林等. 长江中游桥墩防撞(续二)——钢绳柔性系能防撞器试验研究[J]. 航海科技动态,1995(5).

[5] 本州四国连络桥公团. 复合材型缓冲工四的设计要领(案)[R],1981(3).

[6] 吴湘韩. 武汉长江大桥创伤累累[N]. 中国青年报,1994-10-27.

[7] 徐世立,王平辉. 长江大桥 37 年被撞 65 次[N]. 武汉晚报,1995-4-8.

[8] 黄石大桥主墩柔性防撞设施试验成功[N]. 长江日报,1995-1-25.

[9] 岩井·聪. 关于船舶对桥梁的安全措施[J]. 中国航海,1986(12).

[10] 李建军. 撞桥事故分析及对策[J]. 中国水运,1995(3).

[11] 李国华,冯子钧. 冲击法则测量橡胶隔振器的动态特性[R]. 第八届全国振动技术交流会.

发表于:上海造船,1995(3).

Published at: Shanghai Shipbuilding, 1995(3).

桥墩防撞设施的历史及其功能——“三不坏”桥墩防撞装置的诞生

The history of pier protection equipment and it's functions — The “three-uninjured” collision protection equipment is born

陈国虞

(上海海洋钢结构研究所 201204)

CHEN Guoyu

(Shanghai Marine Steel and Structre Recarch Institute)

摘　要　江河是船的航道,桥是跨航道的重要通道,桥墩是航道中的障碍物,由于自然和人为条件的多变,出现船撞桥墩的事故。历史上有大承台、人工岛等行之有效的防撞设施,长期地保护了桥;后来出现木栅、钢链和浮舟等设施,希望除了保护桥之外也保护船;但这些设施比较易坏。人们进一步要求桥、船和防撞设施三者都不坏(简称三不坏),这样就出现了会后退的外刚内柔的三不坏防撞装置,从分析防撞要求入手,得出理想的防撞“力-位移”曲线的型式,制造出这种形式的元件,这种元件构成的防撞装置关键在于初撞时会后退,从而改变船的方向,使船的动能保留在碰撞后的船上。交换的能少了,三不坏防撞设施就易于实现了。给出三不坏防撞设施及其设计程序,供业内人士参考使用。

关键词　船撞桥　桥墩防撞　三不坏　冲击

Abstract: River is the waterway of the ship. Bridge is the important way crossed the river. Bridge pier is the obstacles in the waterway. In order to polytrope of nature and the manual condition, the collision of ship to pier happened. In history, there are big foundation, manual island ..., as the effective equipment to protect the collision for bridges. Later people used the timber, steel cable and the pontoon. They hope, at the same time, to protect the bridge and the ship. As a result of these equipment are breakables and needs always repair. So, we found the “three-uninjured” collision protection equipment. At the same time, it protects the bridge and the ship, and the protection equipment is non-destructive. When the collision happened, this equipment would step back. This equipment is outwardly strong but inwardly soft. We found out the best load-deformation curve is hollow curve, that means it's y'' is positive. When the ship is collision with the bridge protection equipment, it steps back. Then the direction of the collision point is changed the most movement energy of the ship would retain on the ship. It does not join to change. When the part of movement energy which join to change is decreased, the three-uninjured protect equipment is easy to build up. In this paper give out the general outline of the three-uninjured protect equipment and it's design procedure for the specialists.

Keyword: ship collision bridge, pier collision protection, three-uninjured, impact

1 前言

江河的存在早于人类的历史,前者以若干万年计,后者不足一万年。人类将江河作交通之用,始有独木舟,后来发展成各种各样的船,人们要横跨江河所以出现用船过江的渡口,一般情况下,由于渡口输送的能力不够,出现桥梁。从有桥梁那天开始就有了船和桥的矛盾。

建桥者考虑到船要通过桥下,把桥孔建得足够宽(净宽)和足够高(净高)。梁是架在桥墩上的,架得足够高船就不撞梁了。但是由于自然条件和人为条件的多变性,船有时还会撞桥墩。建桥时船通过的密度总是较后来稀少,随着人类社会发展,人越来越多,船也越来越多,越来越大,且愈来愈快。这样原有的桥也出现建桥时想不到的船撞桥问题。中国的大运河建成于隋朝,运河上有一道著名的桥叫通济桥(在浙江塘栖镇)有一千多年的历史[1]。桥七孔,现当中三孔通航,与1996年在桥墩外加修8个岛桩就反映了这种情况(图1)。

图1 大运河塘栖镇通济桥于建桥1 000年后加修8个墩外岛桩防撞设施

Fig. 1 8 anti-collision piers was set up after the Tangxi tongji bridge of Great cannel was constructed 1 000 years

长江形成千万年，一直是靠船摆渡的，直到1958年才建成第一桥，武汉长江大桥（后称武汉长江一桥）。该桥自建成后到1999年12月18日共被撞70次（图2）。

图2　武汉长江一桥被撞第70次，图示捞起的分节驳1001号
Fig. 2　The 70th crashed of Wuhan Yangtze 1th Bridge, section 1001 barge was fished up in the picture

长期从事江河航运和航道管理的人们，基于船撞桥后事故的惨重损失，也基于防灾减灾认识的提高，提出了撞桥事故分析和对策[2]，指出，在桥未建之前江河是船的航道，建桥后，桥墩是航道中或航道边上的障碍物，构成人为的隐患，应该多建一跨过江的桥。桥建成后，设有标志，船舶不应撞上去。船撞桥墩除各种因素外，往往有人为因素，对每一艘桥下通过的船而言，桥的通过量是大的，但桥塌下来阻碍江河时，对交通，水利各方面的影响则更大，所以解决船和桥的矛盾，必须兼顾各方。

桥多是建在已有航道上的，因此建桥的时候就必须也有可能充分地考虑到船的需求，但船的需求在发展（越来越大、越来越快、越来越多），桥建成后要使用成百上千年，这样原来考虑解决矛盾的办法会变成不适合，产生新的矛盾。随着人类活动的发展，人们将桥建到从大陆到沿海的岛屿上，这时桥所跨越的航道通航的是海船，尤其是进出港口的远洋船，船和货的总值达若干亿元，这样就迫切地要求防灾和减灾的装置既要保护桥也要保护船。

2　防撞设施应达到的要求

20世纪人类文明明确提出防灾减灾的要求，在联合国已组成相应机构，国内的研究结果明确提出桥墩防撞装置应满足下列要求[2-3]：

（1）防撞装置能被桥梁、船舶运输和港航管理三方面共同接受；

（2）防撞装置要少占地方，不碍航；

（3）防撞装置应适应水位变化的要求：枯水、洪水、涨潮、退潮；

（4）防撞装置的吸能能力要大，但更重要的是将船的动能仍保留在船上，最新的办法是防撞装置将船头拨歪，使船离开墩而不被镶住，即不咬住船头；

(5) 撞后应自行恢复,不需维修;

(6) 该装置应安装、施工方便,成本低,便于桥梁方在建桥时同时建设,现在一般可做到只占桥梁建设费用的5%左右;

(7) 不因设置防装置装置而增加新的问题,如回流沉积、妨碍捕捞养殖等。

3 历史上使用过的防撞设施[4],[6]

20世纪80年代,日本岩井·聪,提出桥墩防护设置地点(力的承受点)可分为直接构造和间接构造两大类,直接构造指其直接设置于桥墩上而言。每大类内在按吸收船舶碰撞能量的方式分为弹性变形型、压坏(弹塑性)变形型和变位(重力和阻力)型,其中有两种可分为二型,故共8种形式。

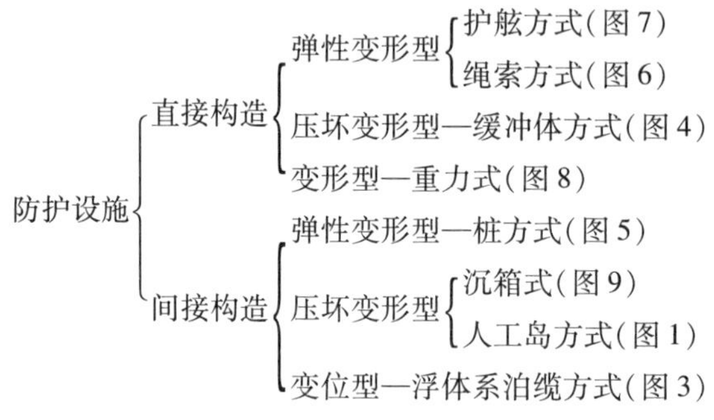

1 大抓力锚
2 横钢
3 竖绳
4 浮子
5 水中墩柱

图3 1990年为武汉长江一桥设计之绳缆式防撞装置示意图

Fig. 3 The wire anti-collision equipment was designed for Wuhan Yangtze 1th Bridge in 1990

1991年国际桥梁和结构工程协会(LABSE)将通常使用的桥墩保护结构分为5类:

· 防护板系统(图7)

· 支撑桩系统(图5)

· 系缆桩系统(图3)

· 人工岛或暗礁保护(图1)

· 浮动保护系统(图4)

如文献[7],按照桥、船和防撞设施三者损坏与大损坏来区分(1995年发表,可将发展设施分为三类):

· 保护桥墩,防撞设施也不会撞坏。例如加大的承台、抛石人工岛等,它们的刚性很大,不变形,因而也不吸收能量,撞上去的船必须吸收全部的碰撞动能,这样对船损坏最大。

· 保护桥墩的同时防撞设施会损坏。例如欧洲内陆河流使用较多的木板围栏、木桩围栏、压坏沉箱、浮动吸能结构等。压坏变形就是吸能过程,防撞设施吸收了一部分船的动能,船的压坏变形便相应小一些。

· 保护桥墩、保护船的同时防撞设施也不坏。例如1995年提出的三不坏吸能防撞装

置(以前有雏形)。

该文认为,历史上还用过一些弹性护舷、桩索拦阻、锚链拦阻、重力变位等办法,对较小的船曾起过作用。

图1,3,5,6,7,8都是防撞设施的举例。

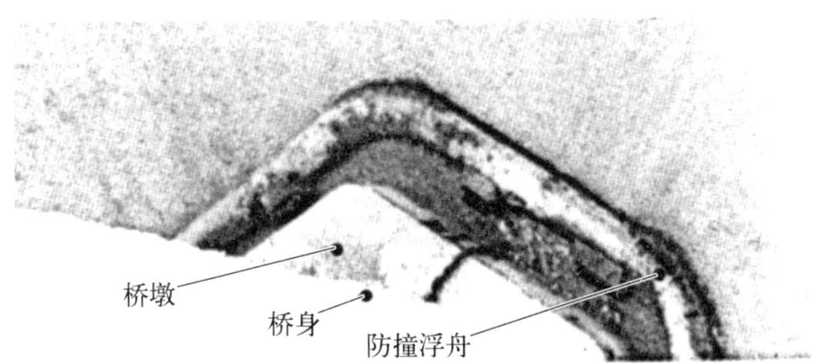

图4　上海奉浦大桥压坏变形型缓冲体防撞装置

Fig. 4　The crushing damage deformation type anti-collision equipment of Fengpu Bridge at Shanghai

图5　广东解放桥桥墩护桩围

Fig. 5　The pile-supported protection system at Guangzhou Liberate bridge

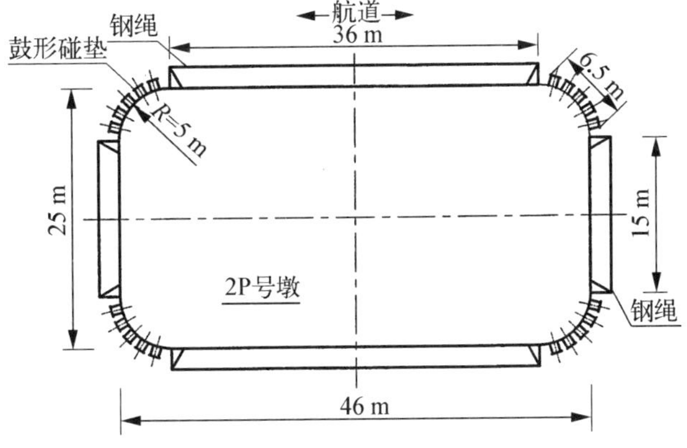

图6　岩黑岛桥2P号墩的鼓形碰垫

Fig. 6　The drum fender for No. 2 pier at Iwakuro-Jima island bridge at Japan

图 7　固定在桥墩上的典型板排护舷

Fig. 7　The timber fender was fixed on the pier

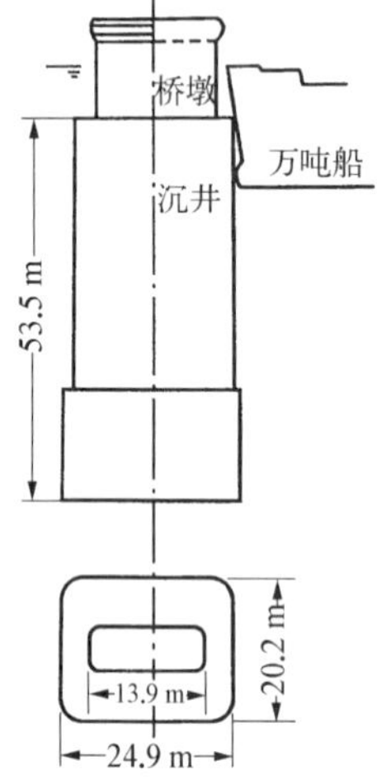

图 8　南京长江大桥 1 号桥墩与沉井

Fig. 8　The No. 1 pier and open caisson of Yangtze River Bridge

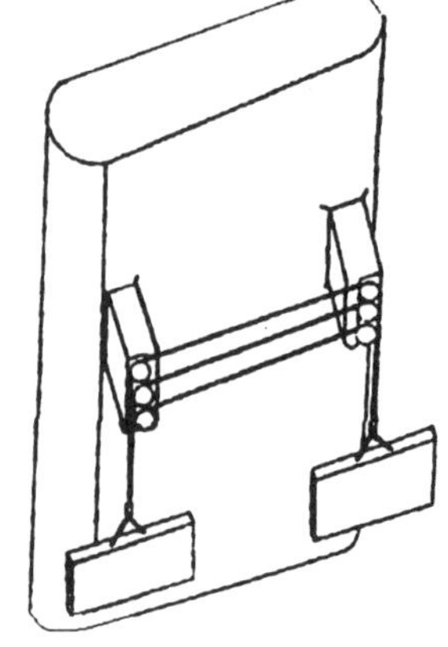

图 9　变位型防撞装置

Fig. 9　The dislocation type anti-collision equipment

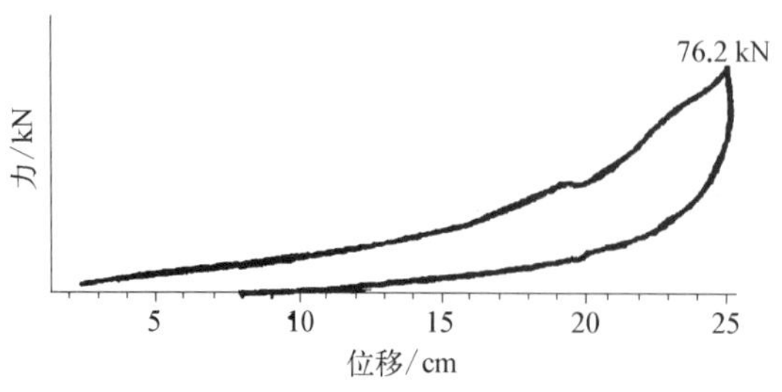

图 10　吸能防撞器准静态标定曲线

Fig. 10　The quasi static calibration curve of energy absorption bumper

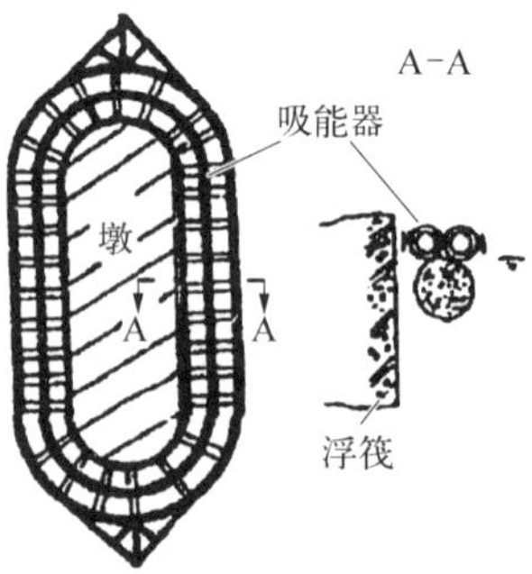

图 11　钢绳柔性吸能防撞设施图

Fig. 11　The steel wire, flexible, energy absorption anti-collision facility sketch

4 从二不坏到三不坏的飞跃

最古老的桥墩防撞人工岛,可以保护桥不坏,而且人工岛也是撞不坏的,自古以来就是两不坏。但船坏了总不是个事,北欧很早就用原木保护桥墩,由于木材易变形,以求保护桥的同时保护船,这就是三不坏的思想,那时船较小(直到现在欧洲内河仍有使用,见[10]),木板、木桩也需频繁修、换。

岩井・聪[6]说的压坏变形型,现在用得较多,如图5,它在船侧撞墩时起较好的作用。如果防撞装置和船体都变形,变形能由防撞装置分担了一部分,船的损坏轻了。但若船头较小、较尖撞入时镶入钢结构格子内,全部的动能都由压坏变形吸收。若船较大,防撞装置的比例小,则由船体变形吸收大量的动能,船的破坏就大了。

三不坏的原理就是分析了撞来船的能量很大,但只要能将船头拨开(不镶住)能量仍保留在船上而参加交换的能量就很小。要能拨开船头必须防撞装置后退,这样就要求防撞系统的“力-变形”曲线是凹形的,即曲线的二次导数 y'',如图10所示。这就是船撞上来时反力很小变形很大,防撞外圈往后退,后退的同时反力逐渐增加,船的接触点有滑动。这样就拨动了船头的方向。如图11所示。

笔者对长江武汉一桥、上海乌镇路桥、浙江大榭岛(黄峙江)桥、广东汕头港湾副航道桥、广东广州鸭鬙沙大桥等桥梁作过三不坏防撞装置设计,体会了设计程序,并总结出该类防撞装置造价大约占全桥成本5%。设计原理和步骤将另文述之。

5 桥梁防撞设计程序

要做到防灾减灾,任重而道远,必须有建桥、航道和船舶三方面努力,但建桥方作用最大。

(1) 制定桥梁防撞系统设计规范,规范中应规定桥墩防撞设施与桥梁同时设计、同时施工、同时投入使用。

(2) 桥位选定与防撞的关系,规定那种情况必须设置防撞系统,那种桥位可以不设置,并进行经济对比论证。

(3) 外载的确定,要根据桥、船和港航管理三方面的要求,进行航道通过的船只大小、种类、航速等分析,确定防撞设施的大小。

(4) 防撞设施设计,防撞效果计算,工程图设计,安装设计。

(5) 典型部件试验以验证防撞能力。

6 总结

桥墩防撞问题的学科多样性,涉及水力学、岩土力学、地质学、桥梁工程、船舶驾驶、

(航海)、铁道公路运输、船舶结构力学(外力和响应)、碰撞力学(冲击动力学)、船舶导航、通讯、仪表以及船舶材料力学等,从历史上,从世界上出现过防撞体系介绍。可看出目前在承继和发展"船撞桥"科技方面是一个很迫切的任务。

船撞桥问题的全面性,多科性宣告了"船撞桥"作为一门分支科学的存在和发展,这一点也可供我国桥、船工作者参考。

参 考 文 献

[1] 浙江省测绘局. 浙江省地图[M]. 地图出版社,1981.

[2] 李建君. 撞桥事故分析及对策[J]. 中国水运,1995(3). 32 - 33.

[3] 陈国虞. 长江中游桥墩防撞: 防撞要求的分析[J]. 航海科技动态,1995(3). 16 - 19.

[4] 陈国虞,林树人. 长江中游桥墩防撞(续一): 防撞设施的种类及其特点[J]. 航海科技动态,1995(4). 14 - 17.

[5] 陈国虞,倪步友,贾关林,邹劲松. 长江中游桥墩防撞(续二): 钢绳柔性吸能防撞器试验研究[J]. 航海科技动态,1995(5): 15 - 17.

[6] [日] 岩井・聪等. 关于船舶对桥梁的安全措施. 中国航海,1986 - 12.

[7] 陈国虞. 桥墩防撞设施的选择. 中国水运,1995(9): 27 - 28.

[8] 陈国虞,倪步友. 水中桩柱用钢绳柔性冲击吸能器试验研究[N]. 交通部上海船舶运输科学研究所学报,1995(2).

[9] 陈国虞. 关于"船撞桥"问题的几点浅见[J]. 上海造船,1995(3).

[10] 国际桥梁和结构工程协会(IABSE)交通船只与桥梁结构的相互影响(综述与指南)[R]1991 - 09. 同济大学顾翔、交通部公路规划设计院鲍卫刚译. 同济大学张乃华校,1993 - 03.

[11] [丹] H. 格罗弗,D. 奥耳逊. 船撞桥分析的当今惯例[C]. 鹿特丹: 船桥相撞国际会议文集,1998 - 5 - 10.

发表于: 科学中国人十年优秀论文选,北京 2002.

Published at: The excellent paper anthology of Scientific Chinese in the past ten years, Beijing 2002.

评议桥梁防撞设计的依据

How to evaluate the design on anti-collision equipment of the piers in the water way

陈国虞
(上海海洋钢结构研究所 201204)
CHEN Guoyu
(Shanghai Marine Steel and Structre Recarch Institute)

摘 要 水运是货物运输5种方式中最大量的方式。很多船撞桥墩的实例表明,船舶被撞损、沉没和桥梁被撞坏、塌落造成很大的危害。从我国公路和铁路两个桥梁设计规范已经规定的条文,说明桥梁设计者按照规范进行桥梁防撞设计是必要的,如果没有按规范中的多处规定进行防御船撞桥的设计,这项桥梁设计是不合规范的。例如有的桥墩处于航道中,却没有考虑船撞桥的力这一偶然载荷。除了对已有规范引经据典之外,本文还指出,水运在发展中,桥梁设计规范也是在发展中的。社会和谐要求达到既保护桥梁又保护船舶和环境才是充分的,才是科学的发展观。因此,试论充分的防撞设计的概念和方法,也是规范需要发展和补充的地方。

关键词 桥梁防撞 必要性和充分性 充要条件

Abstract: Water transport is the most great quantity kind in the 5 kinds in goods to transport. A lot of examples of the ships damage and the bridge falls from ship collision with pier indicate it is a very big bane. This paper focus both to the rule of Chinese highway and the rule of Chinese railway to mentions the Necessary and Sufficient Condition of the bridge design on ship collision with piers. If some designer without consider the accidental force due to the ship collision with pier, this design is disagreement the rule — the Necessary Condition. Point out immediately after, the sea mail is in the fast development, the rule of bridge design also is in the development. So, the sufficient condition is according to the development view of science, attain the protection bridge, protection the ships and environmental just is full. This paper also mention the concept and the method to carry out the fully protections equipment for ship collision with pier.

Keyword: The ship collision with bridge pier, Necessary condition, Sufficient condition, Necessary and sufficient condition

1 桥梁防船撞的客观任务
——和谐与共赢要求既保护桥,又保护船和环境

水域是船舶千年来航行的地方,经过实践选择出最适合航行的水中线域,一般就是航道,桥梁跨越航道如果在水域中设置桥墩便增加了水中碍航物,产生了船与桥的矛盾。世界上近百年来桥梁建设骤增,我国近几十年建设跨过长江、珠江、黄河和沿海航线的桥梁增多,航道通过的船舶越来越大、越来越多、越来越快,所以船与桥的矛盾越来越突出。

"桥梁上通过的车多,运送的货多、人多"这种观点对客运是正确的,对货运就不符合我国长期来的实际。实际上 50 年的统计数据指出[1]:我国的铁路、公路、水运、空运和管道运输 5 种运输方式中,国际贸易货运的 90% 由水运承担;国内货运周转量(t - km)中,建国以来水运量不但绝对量上升,与其他 4 种运输方式相比的相对百分数也在上升,成为百分比最大的运输方式(53%),超过其他 4 种运输方式(铁路、公路、空运和管道运输)货运量的总和(见图 1)。

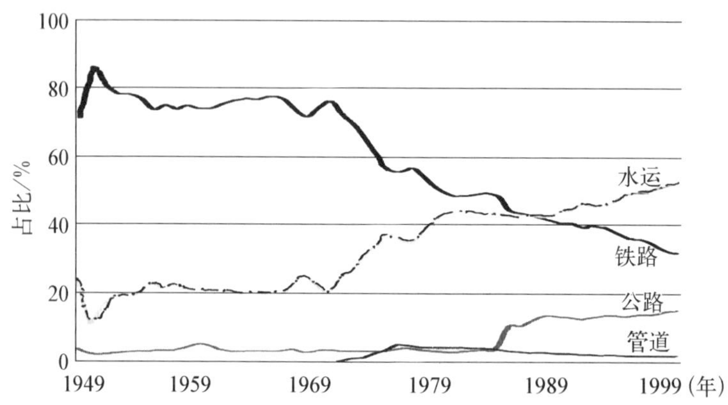

图 1　5 种运输货物周转量 50 年来百分比的变化(因航空货运只占 0.1%,曲线贴着横坐标)
Fig. 1　The movement (in%) of turnover amount of 5 type cargo transportations at 50 years (Cargos transportation by air about 0.1%, the line near the abscissa)

因此,这种观点影响了船和桥两种运输方式的共赢发展与和谐共处。最近,交通运输部在审议长江某铁路桥时要求增加通航孔。并指出:"应该将水域尽量多地留给原来的航道"(大意)。这样才会有利于水陆两种运输方式共赢发展与和谐共处。

跨越航道的桥梁,在进行可行性研究和初步设计时,都进行通航论证研究,召开评议会,那么,应该根据什么原则进行评议呢? 首先应该引经据典地考核其是否达到了规范规

定的要求,这是必要性方面。然后看其是否符合了可持续发展的科学发展观,是不是考虑了水路运输和陆路运输的和谐共处与共赢发展。

2 应按我国现行桥梁设计规范设计桥梁防撞装置(必要性)

我国两个现行桥梁设计规范[2,3]中涉及桥梁水平抗力的规定各有多处。

2.1 我国现行《铁路桥涵设计基本规范》TB10002.1—2005[2]

此规范4.4节共规定6种"其他载荷"(风载荷、流水压力、冰载荷、混凝土浇筑收缩的影响、墩台受船只或排筏的撞击力和汽车撞击等),其中指出:墩台承受船只或排筏的撞击力 F 可按下式计算:

$$F = \gamma \cdot v \cdot \sin\alpha \sqrt{\frac{W}{C_1 + C_2}} \tag{1}$$

式中:γ 为动能折减系数;v 为船只撞击墩台时的速度;α 为船只与墩台撞击点处切线所成的夹角;W 为船只重;C_1, C_2 为船只的弹性变形系数和墩台的弹性变形系数。

据此,可以认为:凡有船舶撞击可能性,而所设计墩台水平抗力不能满足按此公式计算的船撞力时,都应认为是不符合该规范的桥墩。

能不能在设计桥型时就对桥墩的水平抗力加以深入一步的考虑呢?以下面的立面图为例(图2下中有墩11个,从左到右为0#到10#):船从航道往边上偏航,由于角度关系,按上式算出撞向桥墩的水平力愈往边上愈小,(6#→0#,递减),能不能设计桥型时照顾到此项要求将6#墩到0#墩的水平抗力设计为:最强,次强,强,弱,次弱,更弱,最弱呢?(现在从6#到0#水平抗力为最强,最弱,弱,强,弱,强,弱。)

图2 某桥从主航道到边上桥墩抗水平力波动(6#到0#为:最强,最弱,弱,强,弱,强,弱)

Fig. 2 The undulate on lever force resistance from route to the side of a bridge

船撞水平力是从航道往边上递减的,如果桥墩抗御水平力的能力忽高忽低,就算设计防撞装置的人花了九牛二虎之力去降低桥墩受力,仍然可能达不到那个弱桥墩的要求。

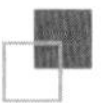

一般的桥梁设计人，首先照顾垂向载荷（结构重力等永久作用），然后照顾桥向载荷（车辆载荷及制动力等可变作用），第三，不要忘记了水平方向（横桥向）的载荷（船舶和漂流物的撞击等偶然作用）。这样才能符合规范的要求。

使用铁路规范 4.4 节的这一个公式，需要长期积累数据，广泛收集数据和正确选用数据。这方面国内在 4 年前已有公开资料出版[6]。

同期建设的另一座桥梁，由于反复考虑桥型：增加通航孔的数目，增加通航孔的宽度，将水域尽量多地留给原来的航道。它设计选用从中间到边上跨度递减，既有利于大中小各种船舶分道行驶，又得到了桥墩的水平抗力从中间到边上递减的合理结果，如图 3 所示。

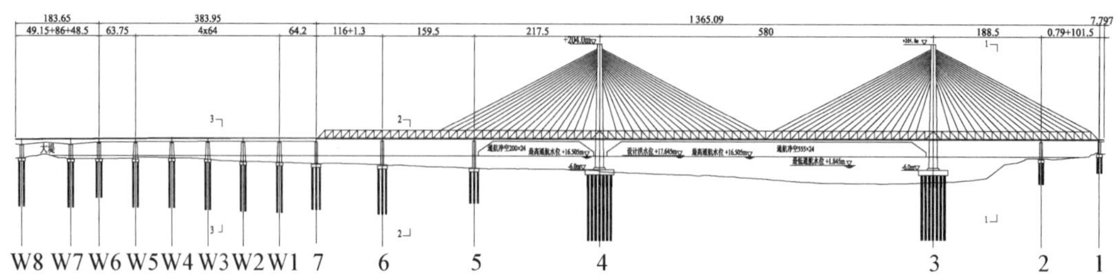

图 3　某长江大桥桥型立面图（包括水中全部桥墩）

Fig. 3　The panorama of a big bridge at Yangtse river (include all the piers in water)

2.2　我国现行《公路桥涵设计通用规范》JTG D60—2004[3]

此规范有关水平力及水平撞击有多处规定，计有：3.1.3 节“桥梁纵轴宜与主流流向正交，墩台轴线应与最高通航水位时的主流方向一致，必须斜交时其偏角不应超过 5°”的规定；3.1.5 节“通航海轮桥梁的桥孔布置和净空应满足相应通航标准（JTJ311）规定，内河通航桥梁的桥孔布置和净空应满足《内河通航标准》（GB50139）的规定”；4.1.6 节之 2，“偶然组合。永久作用标准值效应与可变作用某种代表值效应、一种偶然作用标准值效应相结合”的规定；4.3.8 节“作用于桥墩上的流水压力的规定”；4.3.9 节桥墩冰压力的规定和“强烈流冰”作用的规定；4.4.2 节“位于通航河流或有漂流物的河流中的桥梁墩台，设计时应考虑船舶或漂流物的撞击作用”和漂流物横桥向撞击力的规定；以及 4.4.2 之 3 可能遭受大型船舶撞击作用的桥墩，应根据桥墩自身抗撞击能力、桥墩的位置和外形、水流流速、水位变化、通航船舶类型和碰撞速度等因素作桥墩防撞设施的设计等 6 项。以下分述之。

2.2.1　桥梁纵轴宜与主流流向正交

可以认为，凡是桥梁纵轴与流水角度超上述标准的，都应该调整（见图 4）；增加桥梁通航净宽。举例说明之：

湖北黄石长江大桥桥位定在河流的弯道上，桥梁纵轴与主流流向明显地超过规定，宜增加通航孔净宽，此桥在江中立了 4 个主墩，因为净宽不够，发生船撞事故。

例如 1998 年 9 月 2 日洪水消退恢复通航当晚，长 22033 号推船，顶推 7 艘 1 000 ~ 1 500 t 空驳船，顺水而下，撞 3#主墩。3 艘驳船损坏严重，多根钢丝绳绷断，船队撞散。

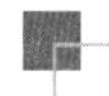

解决的方法也比较简单，要坚持在河流的弯道建桥梁，江中不设桥墩就可以了。2008年，已经在黄石长江大桥上游一公里处，建成了鄂东长江大桥，原来与黄石长江大桥连接的公路已经与鄂东长江大桥连接好了。距离黄石长江大桥建成通车(1995 年)只有 13 年(两桥均见图 4)。

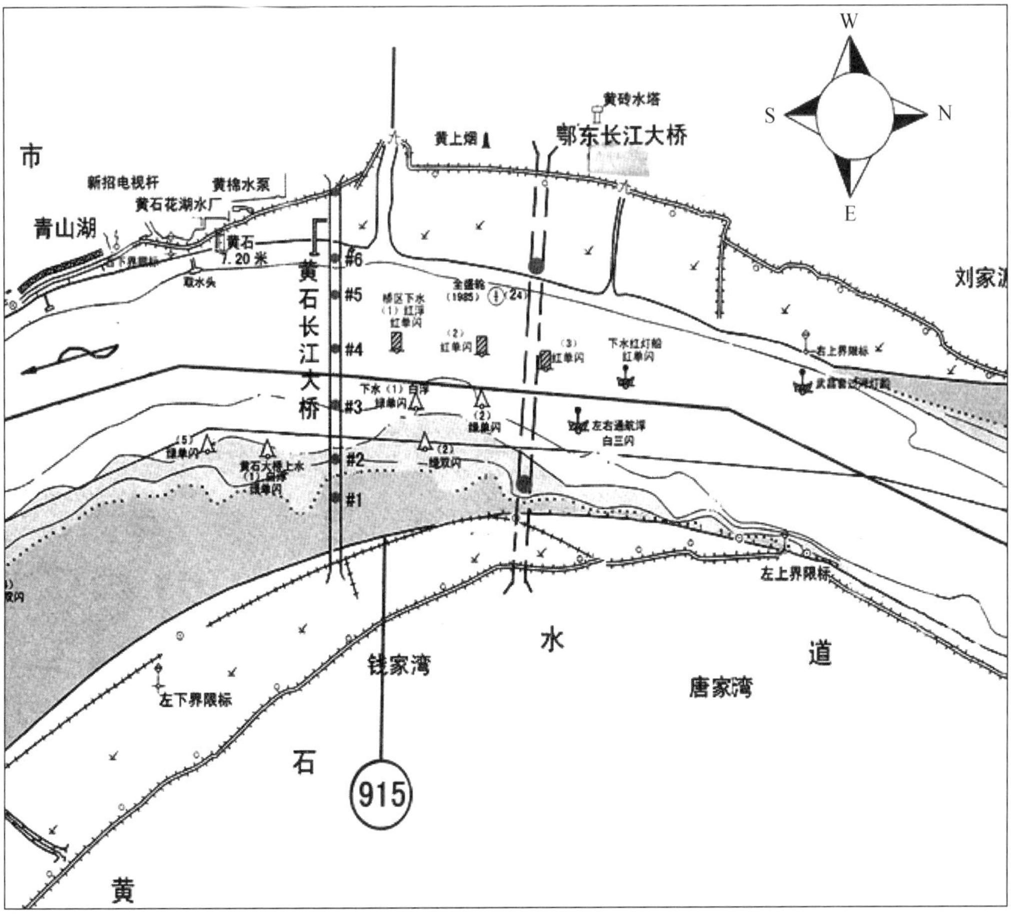

图 4　黄石长江公路桥桥址选在弯道上斜交偏角超过 5°

Fig. 4　The Huangshi highway bridge over Yangtse River, its bridge site design on the curve of the river (drift angle over then 5°)

2.2.2　关于偶然组合的规定

4.1.6 节之 2，有："偶然组合。永久作用标准值效应与可变作用某种代表值效应、一种偶然作用标准值效应相结合"的规定。

4.1.6 节之 2，还规定："偶然作用的效应分项系数取 1.0，与偶然作用同时出现的可变作用，可根据观测资料和工程经验取用适当的代表值。"例如在桥墩防船撞设计中经常会碰到船撞力与流水压力相结合。

某海湾桥 7#墩，旁边通航 3 000 t 江海联运货船，建设方委托桥梁防撞的研究设计单位为该墩设计防撞装置(见图 5)，设计结果被桥墩设计人拒绝。原因是该桥墩用水流力作为控制，根本没有考虑船撞力这一偶然作用的组合。建设方只好花费很多倍的投资另行建设不接触式的墩外防撞装置（见图6）。

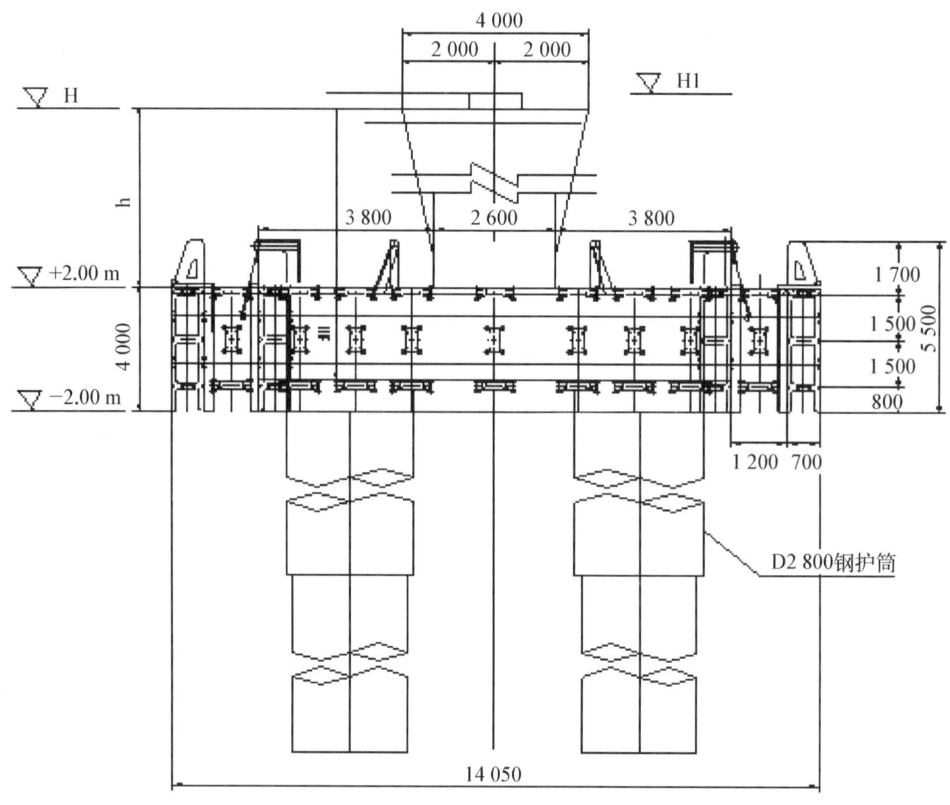

图5　7#墩投资较省的直接式防撞装置

Fig. 5　Saving active anti-collision equipment for 7# pier

图6　该桥墩因未考虑应有的水平抗力改用墩外拦船装置，造价很高

Fig. 6　Due to this pier haven't consider the lever resistance force, then adopt the obstruct equipment out side the pier, it is expensive

2.2.3　流线型桥墩

在4.3.8节规定了流水压力标准值公式：$F = KA(\gamma V^2/2g)$

式中，K为桥墩形状系数，规定如下：方形桥墩为1.5；矩形桥墩（长边与水流平行）为1.3；

圆形桥墩为0.8;尖端形桥墩为0.7;圆端形桥墩为0.6。

在4.3.9节规定:受冰作用的部位宜采用实体结构,具有“强烈流冰的河流的桥墩柱,其迎冰面宜做成圆弧形、多边形或尖角”。

船撞的水平力较冰作用为大,应采用类似的更为有效的措施;航道中的船撞力较流冰冲击力更大,桥墩桥塔墩柱应按此原理设计成流线型或斜面。没有对桥墩水平抗力做出符合规范设计的桥梁,都应认为不符合规范要求(见图7a,b,c.)。

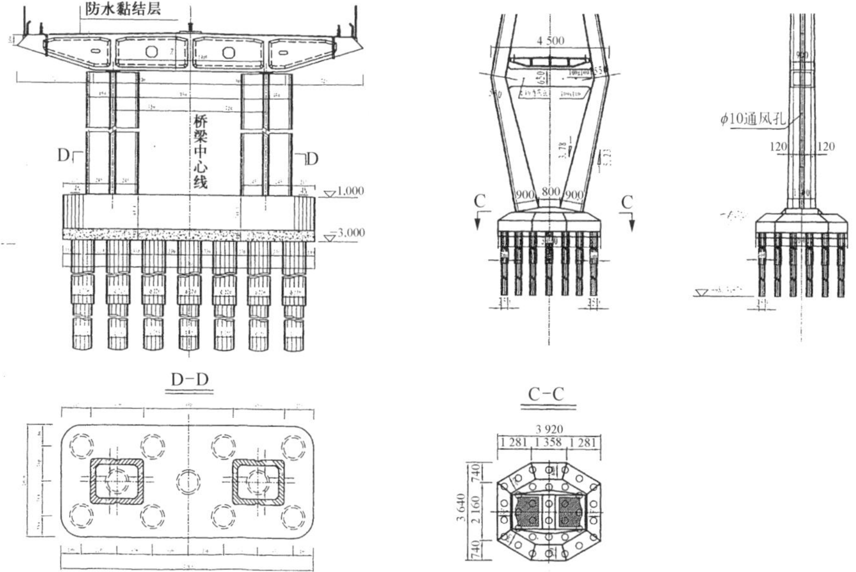

a 通航孔桥墩不应设计成方形
a The pier near the route do not ought to squareness

b 该斜拉桥主通航孔进出两方向均不应设计成平面
b The pier between two main route do not ought to plane

c 日本岩黑岛大桥通航孔两侧的方桥墩
c Japan bridge across the Iwakuro-Jima island with squareness pier between two route

图7 主辅通航孔均应设计成流线型
Fig. 7 The pier near the main route and the supplementary route must be design to streamline form

2.2.4　船舶或漂流物的撞击力

4.4.2 节一开始就有“位于通航河流或有漂流物的河流中的桥梁墩台，设计时应考虑船舶或漂流物的撞击作用”和漂流物横桥向撞击力的规定；

4.4.2 节之3，可能遭受大型船舶撞击作用的桥墩，应根据桥墩自身抗撞击能力、桥墩的位置和外形、水流流速、水位变化、通航船舶类型和碰撞速度等因素作桥墩防撞设施的设计；

4.4.2 节之4 给出了漂流物撞击力的计算公式，该公式是有理论根据的，但是所选数值必须仔细厘定。漂流船是一种漂流物，可按漂流物横桥向撞击力标准值公式计算。

在正常情况下之位于通航河流的桥梁墩台设计时应考虑船舶的撞击作用；该节中 1 和 2，船舶撞击作用的标准值分为内河船舶和海轮两表，已有发表多年的专文讨论[4]，认为此 2 表不适用。并建议两个规范使用同一个公式，这样就解决了公铁两用大桥的问题。

可以认为，在正常情况下，可能遭受大型船舶撞击作用的桥墩，均应作桥墩防撞设施的设计。调查发现大量桥梁达不到这项必要性的要求，在建设桥梁时究其原因：(1) 建造时的设计未能符合现在的规范；(2) 通过桥下的船舶越来越大、越来越多、越来越快。因此校核老桥、补建防撞装置的任务相当迫切。

3　按桥梁防撞任务充分考虑防撞设计(充分性)

现在根据持续发展与和谐共赢的精神，桥梁防撞任务应该考虑既保护桥又保护船同时充分考虑保护环境。这样的防撞设计才是充分的。

3.1　规范需要发展

情况在不断变化，国民经济在发展。航道中通航的船舶越来越多，越来越大，越来越快。因此规范也应不断地修订和发展，举例说明：

对于船舶撞击作用在公路规范分为内河船舶和海轮两表，实际上长江、珠江等河流的下游大量通行江海直达型船舶，近 30 年来设计的这类船舶可从日本、韩国、东南亚各国港口直达我国的南京、武汉、广州等港口，将河船与海船对墩的水平作用力规定为大小各异，没有理论依据也不符合 4.4 节第 4 条的公式，急需改变[4]。一艘江海直达型载重量 3 000 t(3 000*DWT*)的船，撞击力在两表中分别查出为 1 400 kN 和 19 600 kN 相差十多倍，此船从海入江不过仅仅跨越海图上的一条线，船重、船速都不会改变，船撞力也不会改变。这两表让桥梁设计者无所适从[4]。

3.2　设计人的能动性

因此规范必须相应发展才能符合现在桥梁防撞的要求，桥梁设计人必须在考虑永久作用的同时也考虑可变作用和偶然作用，必须在计算桥墩垂向力的同时也考虑足够的水平抗力。船舶受各种因素影响会偏航，在丰水期会驶到距离岸边较近的水域，万一还会撞上航道两侧离航道中心较远的桥墩。因而要求设计人增大桥梁跨距，减少桥墩数量，将水域尽量多地留给原来的航道。减少桥墩数量，必然会加强桥墩，从而提高每个桥墩的水平抗力。在方案设计阶段，估算出船撞力，让该船撞力传到桥墩时应小于桥墩能够抵受的水平力，否则

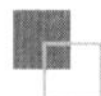

应该加大桥墩或更改桥型，让桥墩能够抵受的水平力大于该船撞力传到桥墩时的值。

很明显，要增大桥梁跨距，减少桥墩数量；要尽量多地将原来的水面留给航道，就必须从桥型开始考虑。因此，桥梁防船撞问题应该在桥梁设计的方案阶段加以论证和设计。

3.3 两个实例

下面是两个外国桥梁跨过较宽水域和河谷的实例，见图 8、图 9。按此原则加大跨距，减少桥墩，从而提高了每个水中墩的水平抗力。

在我国也有实例，见图 10。该桥在 2 680 m 的水面设有 6 个较大的水中墩，5 个 428 m 的跨度，如能在水中墩设置柔性防撞装置，保护撞上去的船，便可实现既保护桥又保护船的目标。

图 8　将水域尽可能多地留给航道——希腊 里约-安特里翁(Rieu-Antirion)大桥

Fig. 8　Be stay the surface of water to the full for the route — Greece Rieu-Antirion bridge

图 9　加大跨距，桥墩少而强——法国 米劳(Millau)大桥，七塔八跨

Fig. 9　Be bigger the span, the pier will few and strong — France Millau Bridge, 7 towers and 8 spans

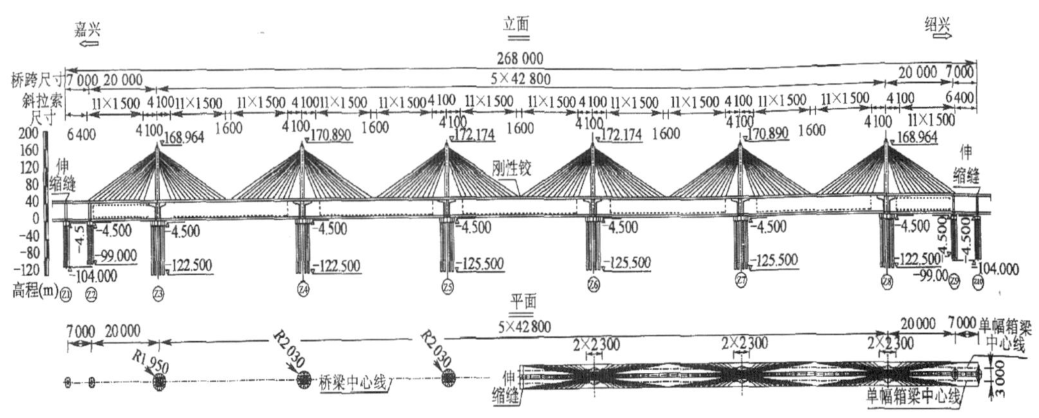

图 10 主跨为 5 × 428 m 的浙江嘉绍大桥

Fig. 10 The Zhejiang Jiashao Bridge, its main span is 5 × 428 m

4 解决桥梁防船撞任务的原理和方法

4.1 解决桥梁防船撞任务的原理

为了防止船舶撞上桥墩而损坏船舶甚至撞塌桥梁,历史上产生了很多种桥墩防撞装置。一般地说如果水较浅,可以建设:墩外围堰、人工岛、墩外桩群等防撞设施,它们扎根于河床中,建筑在桥墩之外,撞上它们时桥墩并不受力,因此称作间接式防撞装置。一位专家称为“御敌于国门之外”。若桥墩处水较深,上述这些防撞设施很费钱,因为它需要挡住桥墩挡不住的船,它就需要抵御比该桥墩能抵御更大的水平力,因此它工程量大,可能比桥墩贵。对环境的影响也更大,还会对河流、港口造成永久性的堵塞,影响回流等等。

更重要的是这类防撞装置通常刚性较大,船撞上去时反力较大,因此船受损很大,船舶若损坏,货舱内的液货(油类或化学品)外泄,或撞上机舱、燃油舱引起的油料外泄,都足以造成水体污染和环境污染。

直接式防撞装置的防撞原理更巧妙一些,首先它是利用桥墩本身的抵抗水平撞击的能力,加大桥跨使桥墩本身设计得大而强;经常我们同时能降低传到桥墩上的水平力,使其达到低于桥墩能承受的程度,就保护了桥梁。另一方面,降低水平力同时也降低了对船的反作用力,船舶受损坏的程度就会降低,从而可使船舱的油料和化学品不外泄,保护水体和环境。

4.2 解决桥梁防船撞任务的方法

怎样完成降低船对墩的力又降低墩对船的力这两个任务呢?研究出了柔性防撞圈和防撞钢围,后者是一个在强度和刚性都设计得适当的闭口钢结构围子,由于他在相撞时与船舶首先接触,称为外钢围。多数是个浮体,就像一个不要船底的开底泥驳,套在桥墩周围,随水位上下浮沉。防撞外钢围与桥墩之间,并联、串联地分布着几层柔性耗能复合防撞圈,外钢围的外形顺着流向做成尖头,有一个迎撞角(见图 11),以便能在船墩相撞时产生分力。法向分力使防撞圈变形,外钢围后退;切向分力使船舶沿着外钢围的外面滑动,这样船的动能大部分保留在船上。法向分力将正面的防撞圈压扁(钢围背面会将防撞圈拉长),这时防撞圈发挥它的黏滞性功能,在较长的时间(10°秒级)不发生反向位移,以便船头贴着外钢围滑动,达到拨开船头使船继续前进,实现“四两拨千斤”的作用[5]。

外钢围位移通常可使各防撞圈内,中空的内径处,变形至相贴(内径为0),由于防撞圈有橡胶复合,橡胶还有弹性变形,做实验时内径处可压至相互接触,位移可以大于内径。实验可以测出额定的冲击载荷下的耗能值,外钢围使各防撞圈同期作用,这些防撞圈耗能总和设计为相当于来撞船舶动能的20%左右。

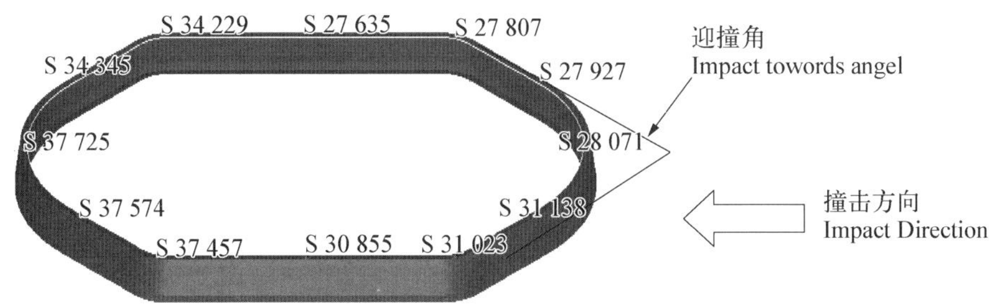

图 11　柔性耗能防撞设施外钢围的迎撞角

Fig. 11　The impact towards angel in the outer steel gate of flexible consume-energy anti-collision equipment

延长冲击时间,消耗一部分动能,产生向前分力使船舶向前滑动、减小船对桥墩的力和减小对船舶的反力等5项结果,体现了船撞桥墩过程的柔性防撞。

上述的复合耗能柔性防撞圈和长圈形防撞钢围的专利号分别是ZL200520042237.2和ZL200520042238.7,已经一起在广东湛江海湾大桥实现。

如果防撞装置只能保护桥而不能保护船,不管船舶液货的泄漏而造成的人、财损失和环境污染的长期破坏,防撞装置只照顾到一半要求,是不符合科学发展观的。于是就需要在刚性的防撞装置外面,再增加一些柔性装置,有人在围堰外加橡胶轮胎就是这种方法,只是他设置的柔性装置还不大够。

5　总结

从上面讨论可以得出结论,最好的方法是一跨过江,江中无墩(如图4,鄂东大桥)。如果必须在水中设置桥墩则应考虑将水域尽量多地留给航道。按照现行的铁路和公路桥梁设计规范,船撞桥的作用力是作为偶然作用,广东九江大桥的撞塌说明设计当年对此偶然作用的考虑与20年后的实际相比较显得不足。通过桥下的船越来越多、越来越快、越来越大。设计桥梁防撞的必要条件是:遵守规范中对于船撞桥这一偶然作用中有关的规定;充分条件是:除规范外还考虑到发展的实际情况、考虑船和环境。在选择桥型和初步设计时应考虑到将尽量多地水域留给航道,先将航道中通航船舶所具有的船撞(水平)力

图12　防撞外钢围与桥墩之间并联串联着柔性耗能复合防撞圈

Fig. 12　Between the outer steel gate and the pier, there are series and parallel connection many flexible consume-energy anti-collision rings

计算出来，设计桥墩（包括防撞装置）具有足够的水平抗力，设计防撞装置有足够的柔性，万一撞上时对船反力小而不致泄漏。达到既保护桥又保护船和环境的目的。

从必要条件到充分条件当中的空间，就是规范需要发展与修订的地方。

按照现行的铁路和公路桥梁设计规范去衡量已有的桥梁，由于情况不断地变化，很多桥梁已经不符合要求，需要增设防撞装置。按照交通部的要求，应该对管内桥梁进行评估[7]，有计划地建设必要的防撞设施。

参考文献

[1] 中华人民共和国交通部综合规划司. 新中国交通五十年统计资料汇编（1949—1999）[M]. 北京：人民交通出版社，2000.

[2] TB10002. 1—2005，铁路桥涵设计基本规范[S].

[3] JTG D60—2004，公路桥涵设计通用规范[S].

[4] 陆宗林，陈国虞，张澄. 统一我国两个桥涵设计规范中船撞力公式的探讨[A]. 第十七届全国桥梁学术会议论文集（C1247—1252）. 人民交通出版社，2006.

[5] 陈国虞，张澄，倪步友，王礼立，黄德进，张忠伟. 怎样实现桥墩柔性防撞[A]. 第十六届全国桥梁学术会议论文集[C]. 北京：人民交通出版社，2004，75－81.

[6] 陈国虞，王礼立. 船撞桥及其防御[A]. 北京：中国铁道出版社，2060.

[7] 廖娟，陈国虞. 杭州内河92座桥梁防撞评估与增设防撞装置建议[A]. 第十九届全国桥梁学术会议论文集[C]. 北京：人民交通出版社，2010，1362－1369.

发表于：城市道路与防洪，2011(6).

Published at：Urban Roads Bridges & Flood Control, 2011(6).

桥梁防船撞理念

Aspects of anti-collision on ship with bridge

陈国虞

(上海海洋钢结构研究所,上海 201204)

CHEN Guoyu

(Shanghai Marine Steel and Structure Research Institute, Shanghai 201204, China)

摘　要　丹麦科威公司(COWI)的弗赖德逊(A. G. Frandsen)于1988年撰文,提出“几座当代大桥的防撞设计理念”。他对1991年至2000年10年时间的22座大桥的防撞理念进行分析评论,使读者阅后能得出桥梁防船撞设计理念。结合中国最近几年的实践,提出五点桥梁防撞理念,即“桥隧比选、一跨过江(主槽无墩)、应保尽保、交通管制、对只抗撞而不保护船舶和环境的桥梁设计应予改进”。

关键词　桥梁防船撞　防撞理念　桥隧比选　一跨过江　应保尽保

Abstract: A. G. Frandsen from COWI (Denmark) wrote an article in 1988, entitled aspects of several contemporary bridges anti-collision design. The aspects of these 22 bridges anti-collision design were analyzed in that article, in order to make readers understand the design concept. In this paper, five concepts are presented combing with domestic practical experience in the last few years, which are bridge-tunnel comparison, one span cross the river and no piers in main channel, protection be given which is required, transport controlling, improvement of anti-collision design which the ship and the environment protection are ignored.

Keywords: anti-collision on ship with bridge; aspects of anti-collision; bridge-tunnel comparison; one span cross the river; protection be given which is required

1 引言

船舶撞击桥墩,自从航道中建设桥墩以来,便时有发生。由于近百年来水运事业的发展,船愈来愈大、愈来愈快,航道上的船也愈来愈多。这样,船撞桥的事例也日渐被重视。另一方面,桥也越建越多,不但跨过江河和海峡,也从陆岸通向离岛,也有连接两个大陆的大桥,这样的桥下跨越洲际航线,通过的船很大。

为此,国际桥梁和结构工程协会(IABSE)已于1983年、1991年和1998年召开国际会议探讨船撞桥问题,发表综合性文章;美国各州公路和运输工作者协会(AASHTO)于1991年和2009年两次发表防船撞设计指南,并将其中要旨写入高速公路设计规范中。

2 防撞实例

弗赖德逊曾对22座当代桥梁的防护理念进行了评介,本文作者增加介绍几例,其中瑞典特雍(Tjorn)新桥、美国阿克拉荷马州阿肯色河新桥和美国的阳光大桥新桥是撞塌后重建的;湛江海湾大桥和象山港大桥桥梁防撞装置,作者曾亲自参与修建。表1为对这29座桥的理念评析。

表1　当代大桥防撞设施理念评析

Table 1　**Evaluation and analysis of contemporary bridges anti-collision design aspects**

序号	桥　名	国　家	年　份	主跨通航净空(宽×高)/m	防撞措施	防撞设计理念评析
1	奥兰松桥	丹麦—瑞典	2000	隧道+490×57	桥用人工岛	90%的船走平行的跨隧道主航线
2	跨越东京湾公路桥	日本	1998	隧道	隧道侧人工岛	主航道隧道
3	上海长江隧桥	中国	2000	隧道6970+730	桥跨辅航道	主航道隧道
4	港珠澳大桥	中国	在建	隧道+3桥	主航道隧道	主航道隧道
5	江阴公路桥	中国	1998	1 385×50	—	一跨过江
6	香港青马桥	中国	1997	1 377×62	人工岛	主航道无墩
7	大海带东桥	丹麦	1998	1 624×65	人工岛	主航道无墩
8	第二赛文桥	英国	1996	456×40	通航管理	深槽无墩
9	诺曼底桥	法国	1995	856×50	—	一跨过江
10	明石海峡大桥	日本	1998	1 990×65	—	深槽无墩
11	海尔根特桥	挪威	1991	425×45	强墩	深槽无墩
12	斯卡松特桥	挪威	1991	530×45	—	深槽无墩
13	伽玛伐斯哥桥	葡萄牙	1998	420×45	强墩	深槽无墩
14	南岸桥	瑞典	1997	1 210×40	—	一跨过江
15	湄南河桥	泰国	1987	450×41	—	主槽无墩

续表

序号	桥　名	国　家	年　份	主跨通航净空（宽×高）/m	防撞措施	防撞设计理念评析
16	泰尔玛纪念桥	美国	1990	335×56.4	—	主槽无墩
17	特雍新桥	瑞典	1981	366×45（原278）	取消上承拱形式用斜拉桥	一跨过江
18	阳光大桥新桥	美国	1987	364×60（原242×44）	加大通航净空，主墩人工岛，边墩防撞墩，不分开两桥建设	一跨过江
19	香港汀九桥	中国	1997	448+475×64	人工岛	主航道无墩
20	象山港大桥	中国	2012	688+2×262+2×820+4×60	中线两侧各818 m柔性防撞	航线中线两侧818 m柔性防撞
21	联合桥	加拿大	1997	250×49	两侧各500 m人工岛及护柱	航道中线两侧500 m
22	湛江海湾大桥	中国	2007	468×48	主塔柔性防护，两侧封航养殖	480 m航道以外养殖，显示航道边缘
23	大海带西桥	丹麦	1997	2×110×18	限航小船	限航小船
24	伊丽莎二世皇后桥（达脱福）	英国	1991	450×53	大沉井桥墩	抗撞
25	新格兰泰桥	土耳其	1993	75开启	航道侧两个主墩	抗撞
26	新悉尼莱尼欧桥	美国	2000	381×56.4	人工岛	抗撞
27	港城桥（弗莱特唯特曼）	美国	1995	385×41	大人工岛	抗撞
28	达姆岬桥	美国	1989	396×53.4	海豚式防撞墩	墩外墩
29	阿肯色河新桥	美国	2005	38.1+61.3+100.6	两桥改一桥，三柱墩加固	单侧墩外墩

3　桥梁防撞理念的评析

3.1　桥隧比选

为了达到彼岸，可桥可隧，中国60年来进行过三十多次桥隧比选。众所周知，上海崇启长江隧桥（见图1）和港珠澳（珠江口）隧桥（见图2）两个通道的比选结果是桥隧结合，主航道修建隧道，辅航道修建桥梁，这其中的原因显而易见。两桥的辅航道分别建有1座和3座桥梁，桥墩迎船面做成尖形，并应设置柔性防撞装置。

主航道航行船舶吨位大，建设桥梁需净空高、跨度大，建造费用接近建设隧道，还不如建设隧道更安全。桥梁的建设费用大于轮渡线，略小于隧道。现在还在进行桥隧比选的有琼州海峡、台湾海峡、渤海湾口等处。

丹麦和瑞典之间的奥兰松大桥所跨区的航线有一条平行的航线，90%的船走隧道顶

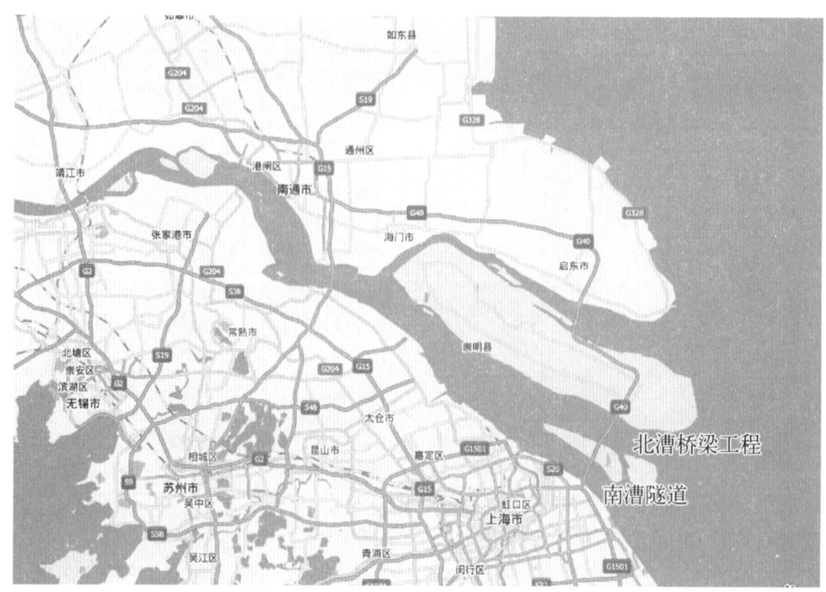

图 1　上海崇启长江隧桥位置图(崇明越江通道工程：南漕隧道,北漕桥梁工程)

Fig. 1　The location plan of Shanghai Chongming-Qidong Yangtze River Tunnel Bridge

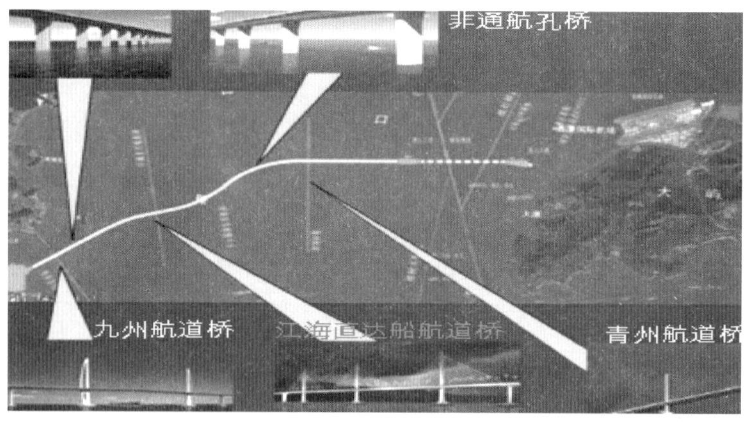

图 2　港珠澳(珠江口)隧桥的一隧三桥布置图

Fig. 2　The location plan of Hong Kong-Zhuhai-Macao (Pearl River Estuary) Tunnel Bridge

上的那条航线,只有 10% 的船走奥兰松大桥桥下通过;东京湾公路桥更是一条与隧道相连的桥,只有小船才从桥下过,防撞装置不贵(但不保护船)。

宜桥则桥,宜隧则隧,不但节省投资,而且高效安全,隧道剩下的部分再加装防船撞装置就不贵了。

3.2　“一跨过江(主槽无墩)”理念

主槽一般也是深槽。江河的槽线会变动,江河一处横截面会有多槽,有深有浅,而且会在历年洪水之后变动,会交替。“一跨过江,江中无墩”在弗赖德逊的论文中占了 14 项,显然是重点,也是30年来全世界桥梁建设的共识,是该作者推荐的样式,也是解决江中设置桥墩过多引起船撞桥问题的主要方向。

中国长江一跨过江的桥梁非常多,例如西陵长江公路大桥、宜昌长江公路大桥、阳逻长江公路大桥、鄂东长江大桥、南京长江第四大桥、润扬长江大桥、江阴长江大桥等都是。

要“一跨过江,主槽无墩”,通常选择的桥型和跨度的建设费用要高一些,但要具体衡量决定,如黄石长江大桥与鄂东长江大桥相比,前者于1995年12月通车,江中设6墩,实践结果是不利于航运,已经发生撞毁船舶的事故,到2010年9月便被一跨过江的鄂东长江大桥所取代,如图3所示。规范规定寿命为100年[2]的大桥仅15年便被取代了,怎让人不为之叹息。

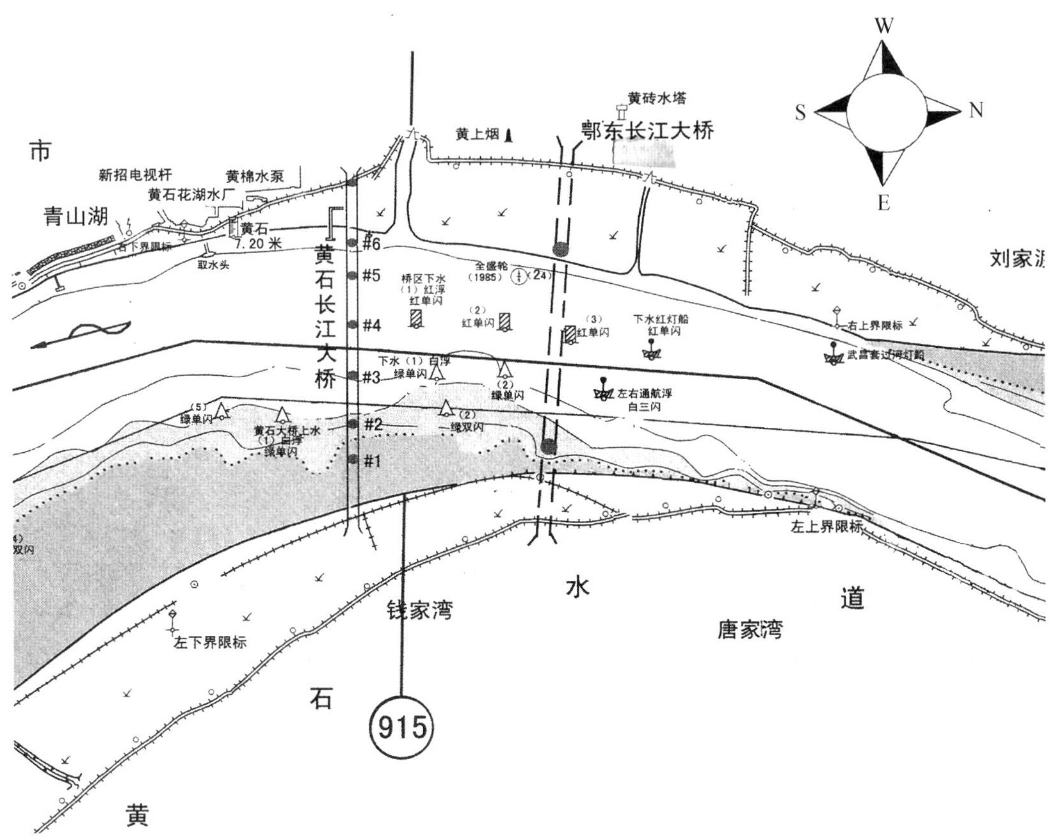

图3 在黄石长江大桥上游926 m处建成鄂东长江大桥

Fig. 3 At the upstream 926 m activate the Edong Bridge

还有一个极端的例子:石板坡长江大桥于1981年建成通车,如图4所示,5号和6号墩之间为上行桥孔,6号和7号墩之间为下行桥孔,两跨跨度为156 m + 174 m,江心6号桥墩正对长江主流,建桥前论证该墩船撞事故概率最大,乃在桥的上游设立了导航站,30年来并未发生船舶撞击6号桥墩事故。此例说明,水运船员和航行管理部门对陆路交通(桥梁)高度重视,竭尽全力避免了船撞桥事故发生。按照我国公路桥梁规范的规定,此桥寿命为100年[2],以后的70年谁能保证不被船撞上。

图 4　船舶驾驶员对水中(江中 6 号墩)非常谨慎

Fig. 4　The navigator are very cautious on the obstruction (6# pier) in the water way

下面一个是尽量把通航水面还给航道的好例子：某桥可行性设计时只有 2 个通航孔，经过航运部门提出，增加了 2 个通航孔，现按不同水深设置不同宽度的 4 个通航孔(见图 5)，供大小船舶分道行驶，将通航水面尽量多地还给航道[3,6]。

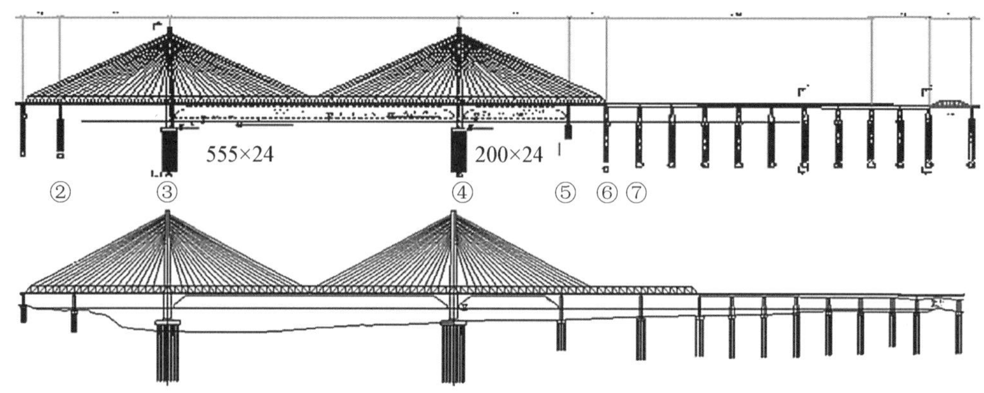

图 5　某长江大桥桥型立面图(包括水中全部桥墩)

Fig. 5　The vertical view of one bridge in Yangtze River (include all the piers in water)

3.3　"应保尽保"理念

应当说，"应保尽保"理念是一种目标和追求，实际上并不能保证 100% 地达到。周恩来总理对发展"两弹一星"时，曾提出了"严肃认真，周到细致，稳妥可靠，万无一失"的 16 个字，其中最后 4 个字"万无一失"也是一种目标和追求，不是考核指标。在周总理十六字方针的指导下，中国卫星发射的成功率不断升高，到 2011 年，中国的火箭发射成功率达到 94.7%。

"应保尽保"理念就是对凡是有可能被船撞的桥墩均设置防撞设施。因为桥梁及其连接线上任一座桥涵或线路的断毁都会使全线不通，所以主墩以外的辅助墩、边墩、水中引桥都要考虑防船撞的问题。

中国近年有几个例子。杭州湾跨海大桥对通航孔设置了防撞装置外，通航孔两边 7

个墩也作了直接式柔性防撞的施工设计(未施工);杭州湾跨海大桥部分水中引桥的前面还补充设置了部分链条拦阻船舶的装置(此装置全部预算为4.4亿元)[4],如图6所示;平潭跨海大桥在通航孔两侧设置了绳索拦阻系统[5]和水中锚泊拦阻船等,如图7所示。

图6　杭州湾跨海大桥的浮链拦船装置

Fig. 6　The chain hold back system at the Over sea bridge of Hangzhou Bay

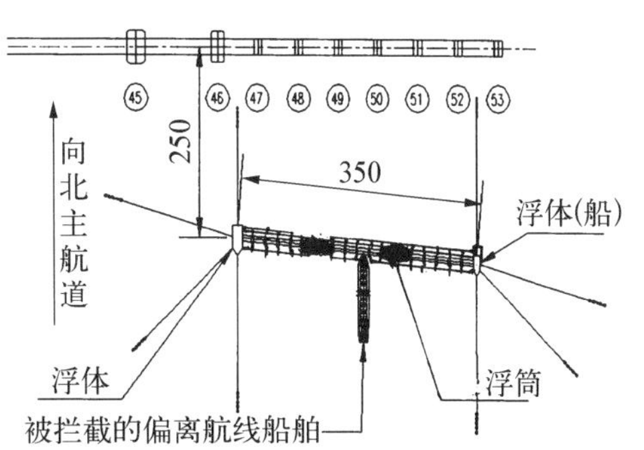

图7　平潭跨海大桥的绳索拦阻系统

Fig. 7　Nylon wire deformation energy lets the ship stop

表1中还有两个很容易懂的例子。加拿大的联合桥和中国新建的象山港大桥分别通航37 000 t和50 000 t级大船,前者在航道中线两侧各500 m设计人原要求设置人工岛和护柱(后来没有建设);象山港大桥在中线两侧各818 m每边5个墩均已建成了柔性防撞装置。设计人的理念是航船偏航有一定距离,故将可能偏航范围内的桥墩均予以保护。

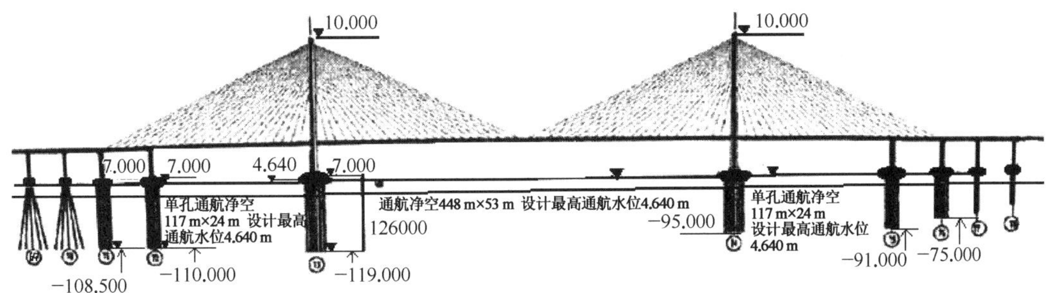

图8　象山港大桥10个墩防撞装置简图

Fig. 8　The sketch of Xiangshan Harbor Bridge with the anti-collision device at 10 piers

3.4　"交通管制"理念

用交通管理方法限航小船,这个理念是行之有效的。在表1中,英国的第二塞尔大桥,有6 500 t级的船舶通航456 m的主跨,船走深槽,其余两侧水浅,限制大船行驶,若大船通过将搁浅,船政部门认为不必要再设置防撞装置。

在中国,这个理念也有多处实践。如广东珠江的白鹅潭至二沙头的江面有8座桥梁,只限小船通航,针对通航的几百吨小船建有防撞装置(图9);上海市黄浦江长55 km,限航小船和疏浚等工程船,在苏州河通入黄浦江处建有拦船装置,如图10所示。

图 9　广州解放桥的防撞桩群

Fig. 9　Anti-collision peg bevy at Guangzhou Liberate Bridge

图 10　苏州河口钢丝绳变形耗能拦船装置[3]

Fig. 10　Steel wire block nets lets the ship stop at the bayou of Shanghai Suzhou River

3.5　其他理念和装置

表 1 中英国伊丽莎白二世皇后桥，设计为大沉井桥墩，航船对桥墩是撞不坏的，但对船舶的保护是欠考虑的，属于抗撞型；土耳其的新格兰泰桥是一座 75 m 跨度的开启桥，由于两侧开启机构加强了桥墩，船也是撞不坏该桥墩的，所以没有设置防撞装置，也属于抗撞型。我们提倡，在保护桥的同时，也保护船，从而使环境得到保护。在撞不坏的桥墩的前方加装一些保护船的柔性装置。我们对天兴洲大桥等曾提出过类似的建议。

有些防撞方法虽有一定的作用，例如桥墩外的防撞墩，在美国有两次被撞后减轻损失的例子，但到底还是有损失，不如我们推荐的柔性防撞装置在万一撞上后仍能将船拨开，回归航线。美国有些设计人员喜欢使用桥墩外的防撞墩，称为海豚（Dolphin），但实际效果并不好。除了防撞墩被撞塌，船仍然撞向桥（如 1987 年美国的外通道桥 5 号墩，海豚墩被撞坏后船仍撞向桥）外，美国 2002 年被撞塌的阿肯色河桥恶性事故，也是装有墩外墩的（单侧），更是明显的实例，这也说明光装海豚式墩外墩是不够用的（见图 11）。美国阳光大桥虽然装了 36 个海豚式墩外墩，也是仅作为 4 种桥梁防船撞措施中的一种。

广东湛江海湾大桥除了主墩用柔性防船撞装置保护桥和船之外，主墩外的其他桥墩用养殖标志法，养殖外线在 480 m 主航道边上（见图 12），养殖的设施、标志和晚上的锚泊指示灯成行排列，也可供航船作为驾驶指引。

4　总结

防撞装置多种多样，但防撞理念归纳起来并不多，大致如：宜隧则隧，宜桥则桥；将尽量多的水面留给船舶，尽量使用一跨过江，实现主槽无墩；采用柔性防撞装置在保护桥的同时也保护船，从而使环境也得到保护；主墩和侧边应保均保；配以合适的交通管制，就可以做到消除桥毁船沉的恶性船桥相撞事故。对于只加强桥墩而不考虑船的方法，建议加以改进。

图 11　被撞塌的美国阿肯色河桥的墩外墩

Fig. 11　The bridge on Arkansas River (with anti-collision pier out of the bridge pier) collapse by ship collision at 2002

图 12　湛江海湾大桥桥墩采用养殖标志法（引自“图读湛江”）

Fig. 12　Except used the soft anti-collision device at the main pier tower to protect the bridge and ship, at the side piers used the cultivation to sign out the route

参 考 文 献

[1] 弗赖德逊 AG. 几座当代大桥的防撞设计理念[C]. 丹麦,国际桥梁和结构工程协会,1998.

[2] JTG D60—2004. 公路桥涵设计通用规范[S]. 北京：人民交通出版社,2004.

[3] TB10002. 1—2005. 铁路桥涵设计基本规范[S]. 北京：中国铁道出版社,2005.

[4] 徐左正,等. 水闸拦阻系统[C]. 上海市苏州河河口水闸工程建设纪实. 上海：上海科学技术出版社,2007.

[5] 陈国虞,倪步友,张澄,等. 跨海湾(河湾)桥非通航孔柔性拦船防撞装置[J]. 广东造船,2011,30(1)：38－41,31.

[6] 陈明栋,陈明,陈国虞,等. 安庆长江铁路大桥防船撞研究(船撞速度选择)[J]. 重庆交通大学学报(自然科学版),2009,28(2)：103－207.

发表于：国际船桥相撞及其防护学术研讨会论文集[M]. 北京：中国铁道出版社,2014：24－30.

Published at: Proceedings of International Symposium on Ship-Bridge Collision and its Protection[M]. China Railway Press, 2014: 24－30.

第二部分

船对桥的撞击力
The impact force between ship and bridge

桥墩船撞力(正撞、侧撞)计算方法及其半经验公式研究

The force of ship collision (positive collision and side collision) with bridge pier and research of its half empirical formulas

陈国虞[1]　王礼立[2]
(1. 上海海洋钢结构研究所 201204　2. 宁波大学 315211)
CHEN Guoyu[1], WANG Lili[2]
(1. Shanghai Marine Steel and Structure Research Institute 201204
2. Ningbo University 315211)

摘　要　首先提出研究桥梁船撞力的方法和判断标准,列举了欧美亚各洲的研究者提出的公式、线图和实例,指出一些公式过于简单或已经被淘汰。总结我国学者研究结果,认为欧美常用的和我国规范中的公式都是同源的半经验公式。其次概括了船撞桥墩的相遇角度情况,归纳为4种类型,提出计算侧撞力的方法,以及船舶偏航后可能撞到边墩的船撞力计算方法。最后提出船撞力半经验公式仅适用于桥梁开始设计的时段,到有了桥梁初步设计图之后,可利用动态数值方法计算船撞力。计算后或需加强桥墩和装设防撞装置,以达到万一撞上也不造成毁坏的目的。

关键词　船撞力判断标准　正撞力　侧撞力　半经验公式　动态数值计算

Abstract: Originally this paper puts forward the method and the judgment standard for the studies of the force of ship collision with bridge, enumerating the formula, line graph and the data of local bridges of the researchers in Euro-American and Asia. Point out some formulas had been eliminated due to his too simple. After sum up we consider all the half empirical formula is all affine formula, include used by the researcher in Euro-American and insertion in the railway and highway criterion of our country. Then, this paper also sums up the angel of encounter on ship collision with bridge, reduce to 4 cases, putting forward the method that compute of side collision. And also give the method of the leeway ship would leeway how many meters from the route and collision how many piers. At last, puts forward the half empirical formula only used at the starts step of bridge design, when we have the diagram of the pier, we can make use of the dynamic calculation. After compute we may be need to strengthen the pier or to build the equipment to anti-collision. Then, we can meet the purpose on a bare possibility to protect the bridge at the same time protect the ship and the circumstance.

Keywords: judgment standard of the force of ship collision with bridge, force of positive collision, force of side collision, half empirical formula, dynamic numerical value calculation

1 研究方法与判定标准

具有高动量的运动中的船舶与桥墩碰撞时,会产生巨大的碰撞力。船舶碰撞力计算过程非常复杂,同时船舶碰撞力大小,在碰撞过程中是随时间变化的。影响船撞力大小的因素很多,主要有:船首形状和结构、船首刚性,船舶排水量、附连水的质量、船舶尺寸、船舶碰撞时的速度,桥墩的几何形状、强度以及弹性塑性性能等。

确定船舶撞击力的方法有多种:最主要的有半经验公式估算法,动态有限元模拟数值计算法和实验法等,上述三种方法均在实际工程中得到了应用。在桥梁工程的可行性研究阶段多使用半理论、半经验的公式计算法,求得准静态的船撞力,供桥梁设计人作桥型比选或选择防撞设施的参考;到了桥梁的初步设计和施工图设计阶段,以工程设计图建立计算模型,使用动态数值计算方法;实验法常用于对计算方法、模型设置等方面的验证,由于实验法需要先做仔细的设计和计算之后进行,且费时耗资巨大,仅在有条件时采用之。

经过对文献记载的半理论、半经验公式进行研究和梳理,认清它们的根源和简化之处,才能摆对他们的位置,正确地处理和应用这些半理论、半经验公式。

2 文献记载的桥墩船撞力的半经验公式

目前,欧洲、美国和亚洲都有专家在研究船撞桥的问题,列出的文献有 300 多篇,(1991 年北欧作者列出西文 153 篇[1~2],近 20 年又增加一些;我国作者 2006 年选录了中文文献 102 篇[6],2011 年增补为 194 篇)其中涉及船撞墩力的研究亦颇多。

国际桥梁和结构工程协会(IABSE)在 1991 年 9 月的“综述”及其 4 月的草稿中选录了多种计算船撞力的公式或例子,有的是计算实例,有的是线图,其中 9 月的“综述与指

南”中有公式或线图等 14 个例子。现先讨论其中的 6 个公式,其中后面 3 个两变量公式经常被使用着。

有些公式偏于简单,如式中只有一个变量:“多大载重量的船便有多大船撞力”[1],船的速度和其他因素都不考虑,太简化了;有的原理有缺陷,如:“多大的动能便有多大的力”[2],实际上,同一个动能可以由不同质量和速度得来,经典力学理论认为不同的速度得到相同的动能时,仍可有不同的撞击力。

2.1 已被淘汰的公式

2.1.1 单变量公式

(1) 索尔和斯文森(Saul 和 Svensson)在 1981—1983 年,对沃以信(Woisin)公式在应用于大船时,给出修正值后的沃以信公式为:

$$P_{max} = 0.88(DWT)^{1/2} \pm 50\%$$

式中 P_{max} 为船舶有效冲击力的最大值(MN);DWT 为船舶公称载重量。

(2) 挪威公共道路局的船舶对桥和浮桥碰撞力公式:

$$P = 3.5(DWT)^{1/3}$$

式中 P 为静态等效碰撞力(MN);DWT 为船舶公称载重量。

2.1.2 能量决定力的公式

1991 年 4 月,由拉森(O. D. Larsen)编写,代表小组向委员会提出的“综述与指南”[2]中,有一个以船的动能为主要参数的船首碰撞力公式:

$$P_{bow} = P_0[5.0EL]$$

式中 P_{bow} 为船首最大碰撞力(MN);P_0 为 210(MN);L 为船的长度 L_{pp} 的函数,当不同的 L 值时,公式还有一个姐妹式子;E 为船舶动能的函数。此公式在 1991 年 9 月“综述与指南”[1]公布时已被删去。连同上述两个单变量公式,人们淘汰了 3 个公式。

2.2 5 个常用公式

2.2.1 在北欧的“综述与指南”中有 3 个常用公式

在北欧的“综述与指南”中,能够将船的速度 v 和船舶质量 W,一起作为参变量代入的公式只有 3 个:

(1) 敏诺斯基-捷勒-沃以信(Minorsky-Gerlach-Woision)公式:

$$P = 0.024(vD_{max})^{2/3}$$

式中:P 为撞击力(MN),v 为船速(m/s),D_{max} 为船的满载排水量(t)。

公式中用到船的满载排水量,运输船舶一般公称的是船的载重量,所以欧洲的综述告诉你,一个从船的载重量到满载排水量的简单系数,下面为桥梁工程师列出一张简表供参考:

表 1　　运输船舶从载重量估算排水量用的参考数据

Table 1　　**The reference data for calculate the ship's displacement from deadweight**

船种	序号	船　名	船长 L/m	载重量 DWT/t	排水量 D/t	比值 D/DWT
干货船	1	3 000 t 沿海货船	95.0	3 203	4 600	1.44
	2	5 000 t 多用途船	100.6	5 527	7 254	1.31
	3	7 000 t 远洋干货船	124.0	7 228	10 904	1.51
	4	12 000 t 江海直达货船	153.0	12 000	20 000	1.67
	5	15 000 t 经济干货船	149.9	15 572	20 881	1.34
	6	28 000 t 多用途货船	182.8	28 450	38 242	1.34
集装箱船	7	700 TEU	147.5	12 300	18 466	1.50
	8	1 700 TEU	179.7	20 700	30 166	1.46
	9	3 108 TEU	220.5	27 251	42 210	1.55
	10	5 600 TEU	280.0	69 285	93 885	1.36
	11	8 500 TEU	334.0	99 500	136 690	1.37
	12	14 100 TEU	366.0	155 000	197 511	1.27
散货船	13	5 000 t 沿海散货船	114.9	6 399	8 670	1.35
	14	20 000 t 散货船	164.0	20 400	26 485	1.30
	15	27 000 t 运木散货船	169.0	27 635	33 852	1.22
	16	35 000 t 浅吃水散货船	189.0	36 665	45 141	1.23
	17	52 300 t 散货船	190.0	52 104	62 078	1.19
	18	175 000 t 散货船	289.9	170 800	193 227	1.13
油船	19	5 000 t 级油船	107.4	5 263	7 235	1.37
	20	10 000 t 级油船	115.0	9 927	12 548	1.26
	21	13 000 t 级油船	142.0	13 144	16 964	1.29
	22	15 000 t 级油船	163.3	15 786	21 020	1.33
	23	25 000 t 级油船	178.6	24 774	32 319	1.30
	24	30 000 t 级油船	171.0	32 397	39 830	1.23
	25	40 000 t 级油船	187.8	42 196	53 144	1.26
	26	63 000 t 级油船	224.6	62 200	76 250	1.23
	27	90 000 t 级油船	243.8	90 261	105 160	1.17
	28	110 000 t 级油船	243.0	110 296	126 622	1.15

注：1. 表中船长为船的全长 L_{oa}，但表中大型集装箱船为船的垂线间长 L_{pp}；

2. 表中仅包括 4 种运输船，其他桥下通过船舶应另行予以考虑；

3. 表中通过桥下的船舶适用于沿海港口和我国内河通航部分，对连岛和海峡桥梁通过的船舶应对各桥单独讨论。

（2）索尔-诺特-格林那（Saul SveIsson-Knott-Greiner）公式：

$$P_{max} = 0.88(DWT)^{1/2}(v/8)^{2/3}(D_{act}/D_{max})^{1/3}$$

式中：P_{max} 为最大撞击力，DWT 为船的载重量，v 为撞击时的船速(m/s)，D_{act} 为撞击时的排水量(t)，D_{max} 为船只满载排水量(t)。

(3) 美国各州公路和运输工作者协会(AASHTO)的公式，经 1994 年[3]修正为：

$$P_s = 1.2\chi 10^5 v(DWT)^{1/2}$$

式中：P_s 为船只的等效正面静撞击力(N)，DWT 为船只的载重吨数(t)，v 为船只的撞击速度(m/s)。

2.2.2 在中国现行桥梁设计规范中有两个公式

(1) 公路桥梁设计规范[4]附录四：通航河流中的桥梁墩台所受的船只撞击力，如无实际资料时，可按附表 4 采用。

漂流物撞击力可按下式估算：

$$P = Wv/(gT)$$

式中：P 为漂流物撞击力(kN)，W 为漂流物重力(kN)(应根据河流中漂流物情况，按实际调查确定)，v 为水流速度(m/s)，T 为撞击时间(s)(应根据实际资料估计，在无实际资料时，一般用 1 s)，g 为重力加速度 9.81(m/s^2)。

在本公式中"T——撞击时间(s)，应根据实际资料估计"的后面有一句话："在无实际资料时，一般用 1 s。"因为这个数值在实际中，从 0.4 到 4.5 大范围地变化(见表 2)，所以这句话是不能用的。

在钢船头撞水泥墩的情况下，作者根据商用动态计算程序(其中有应力应变时间和应力传播时间，能计算出结构物的响应时间——给出时程曲线)求出一个时间，并收集了一些其他作者的时间数据，如表 2，供读者参考。

表 2　钢船头撞混凝土桥墩(全部能量交换)过程的时间举例

Table 2　The example of seconds about steel ship collision with concrete bridge pier (entirely energy exchanged)

序	船　名	总长/m	船宽/m	型深(吃水)/m	DWT/t	D/t	v/(m/s)	时间/s	备注
1	300 t 级渔船	44	7.2	3.6		427	4.0	0.55	※2
2	500 t 级江海联运货船	42	9.2	(1.9)	500	700	4.0	0.40	※1
3	2 000 t 级江海集装箱船	64	12.6	(3.5)	1 650	2 350	6.0	0.60	※1
4	1 000 t 级沿海货船	65	10.8	5.35	1 020	1 774	4.0	0.90	※2
5	3 000 t 级沿海油船	101	13.8	(3.49)	空船压载	2 966	4.0	1.10	※2
6	3 000 t 级沿海油船	101	13.8	(5.87)	满载	5 332	4.0	1.45	※2
7	5 000 t 级油船	107	15.	7.5	5 263	7 235	4.0	1.86	
8	5 000 t 级散货船	107	17.6	9.0	6 900	9 400	4.0	1.90	
9	万吨级多用途船	137	22.4	11.0	10 475	17 000	4.0	1.90	
10	万吨级散装货船	140	22.0	12.2	13 189	19 000	4.0	2.46	
11	40 000 t 级油船	150	30.0	17.0	40 000	50 500	5.05	3.28	※2

续表

序	船　　名	总长/m	船宽/m	型深(吃水)/m	DWT/t	D/t	v/(m/s)	时间/s	备注
12	50 000 t 级油船	197	32.3	19.2	50 000	62 500	4.0	3.00	
13	50 000 t 级散装货船	182	32.3	17.2	52 300	62 500	3.0	4.50	※1

※1. 商用动态程序。当撞击力下降到峰值的1/3~1/4时,认为撞击过程结束。

※2. 不同的程序。此表中该数据从各家用不同的程序计算的结果汇集而成,仅供参考。

※3. 如有防撞钢围和防撞圈。时间会延长;如有斜面能滑动船头,时间会延长。而且滑动会消耗能量(本表所选仅为正撞)。

(2)铁路桥梁设计规范[5]第3.4.6条墩台承受船只或排筏的撞击力可按下式计算:

$$F = \gamma v \sin\alpha [W/(C_1 + C_2)]^{0.5}$$

式中:F 为撞击力/kN;γ 为动能折减系数/($s/m^{0.5}$),当船只或排筏斜向撞击墩台(指船只或排筏驶近方向与撞击点处墩台面法线方向不一致)时可采用0.2,正向撞击(指船只或排筏驶近方向与撞击点墩台面处法线方向一致)时可用0.3;v 为船只或排筏撞击墩台时的速度,m/s。此项速度对于船只采用航运部门提供的数据,对丁排筏可采用筏运期的水流速度;α 为船只或排筏驶近方向与墩台撞击点处切线所成的夹角,应根据具体情况确定,如有困难,可采用 $\alpha=20°$;W 为船只重或排筏重/kN,见参考表[6];C_1、C_2为船只或排筏的弹性变形系数和墩台圬工的弹件变形系数,缺乏资料时可假定 $C_1 + C_2 = 0.0005$ m/kN(取为一个固定的常数也是不对的,见[6]中的附录参考表)。

由于铁路桥梁规范给出的公式考虑的因素最多,所以作者推荐使用这个公式,但要找到正确的数值代入该公式是很不容易的。

首先,作者用试验方法研究了动能折减系数 γ,在落锤下进行了约40次不同速度不同材料结构的碰撞,在模拟船撞桥的速度和结构做实验时,有明显的声音,但没有大的火花,绘出全部能量消耗图中,碰撞表面的能量损耗部分的份额较小。因此认为动能折减系数 γ 应加大[14]。

其次,船只或排筏撞击墩台时的速度 v,需要找出代表船航经桥位时,经常采用的速度,需要考虑该桥墩在河流横断面的位置,需要考虑丰水期的墩前流速等[15],不能按想像简化处理。

对于船只或排筏驶近方向与墩台撞击点处切线所成的夹角 α,正撞时应该是90°,其他的时候"应根据具体情况确定",根据具体情况确定在实践中并不困难。

对于船只重或排筏重 W,有了表1和考虑附连水质量的方法可以算出。——船吸附着一些水共同运动,船撞桥时这部分水以附加质量(乘上一个系数)计入,此系数为1.02~1.10,快些的船取1.02,一般取1.04,较慢的船(例如快靠码头)取1.10。

对于船只或排筏的弹性变形系数和墩台圬工的弹件变形系数 C_1、C_2,由于 C_2 比 C_1 小得多,很多人将 C_2 忽略不计。在撞击系统中有防撞装置时还应该有防撞装置的弹件变形系数 C_3,下面补充论述。船头的弹性变形系数 C_1,同样只要认可计算软件中的应力应变曲线,便可以得出,下面列一个简表供参考,如表3所示。

表3　　计算出的船头平均弹性系数 C_1

Table 3　　The calculated average elastics coefficient C_1 for the ship bow

序号	船　型	排水量 /t	撞击速度 /m·s^{-1}	最大力 /MN	变形 /m	船头平均弹性系数 C_1/m·kN^{-1}
1	79.54 m 客船	5 102	5.35	9.23	2.29	0.000 250
2	5 000 t 级多用途船	9 839	5.0	46.8	5.40	0.000 120
3	万吨级散货船	18 917	5.0	56.5	6.85	0.000 120
4	万吨级集装箱船	17 670	3.0	16.5	0.77	0.000 047
5	3.5 万吨级散货船	45 807	5.0	97.5	9.11	0.000 093
6	4 万吨级油船	50 500	6.7	148.0	10.50	0.000 071
7	5 万吨级散货船	62 500	3.0	99.0	6.97	0.000 070
8	6.5 万吨级油船	76 189	5.0	290.0	6.44	0.000 022

注：由于动态力的局域性，船头刚度亦与动态参数(例如速度)有关。

2.3　在北欧的"综述与指南"中，还有 8 个以一船一桥为对象的研究计算结果

例如：

(1) 1966 年，奥尔豪森(Olnhausen)研究出：40 000 t 油船撞向 50 000 t 货船时的冲击力为 145 MN。

(2) 1978 年，丹麦大海峡工程研究出：250 000 t 的满载油船以 16 节航行时，撞击力为 250 ~ 700 MN。

(3) 跨越英吉利海峡桥的研究，得出：270 000 DWT 的油船冲击力为 500MN + 30% 的动力影响。

(4) 对于英国泰晤士河达特福(Dartfort)桥，假设 65 000 DWT 的船，5 m/s 航速的撞击力为 350 MN。

(5) 新奥尔良附近跨越密西西比河的芦苓(Luling)桥，假设 40 000 DWT 船的撞击力为 270 MN。

(6) 诺尔斯基(Dot Norske Veritas)为丹麦大海峡桥估算出 2 000 ~ 400 000 DWT 的船，5.1 m/s 航速的撞击力如图 1 中 M_1，M_2 两条曲线所示。

在北欧的"综述与指南"中，还有 2 个实际碰撞的计算研究结果。

(1) 哥本哈根一艘 10 600 DWT 的船以 8 m/s 的速度撞向德洛典(Drogden)灯塔的力，乔士登菲尔德(Qstenfeld)估算出为 70 MN，而奥尔豪森(Olnhausen)估算出为 35 MN。

(2) 古易斯(Kuese)报道了一艘 30 000*DWT* 货船与很波特桥的碰撞力为 60 MN。

2.4　欧洲学者对半经验公式的总结

北欧的"综述与指南"的上述结果，及其综合出的图 14 条曲线，是到目前为止最详尽的碰撞力图表，根据此图不但能够按照其中一条曲线，得出目标船舶在与该曲线依据的速度相同时的撞击力，而且可以看出不同研究者对一艘船不同速度时给出的撞击力。更可以进一步看出，对同一艘船同一速度不同作者给出的不同撞击力。

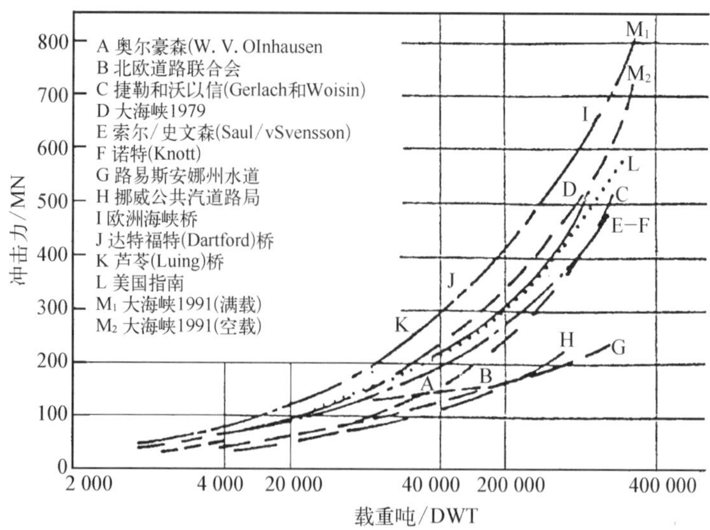

图 1　不同来源的船舶冲击力设计值

Fig. 1　The force of ship collision with bridge calculated from difference authors

2.5　我国对半经验公式的使用

在我国,半经验公式估算出的船撞力比较正确,这是因为一开始我国便淘汰了那些误差比较大的、原理不正确的公式。我国公开出版的书籍(2006 年)提供了一些使用半经验公式时相关的数据表[6],所以用 5 个常用的半经验公式计算出来的结果比较接近,比较可信。提供给桥梁工程师在初始的阶段使用,也就更有价值了。

现在举广东湛江海湾大桥(2002 年)作为一个例子,说明当正确选择代入的参数时,5 个常用的半经验公式计算出来的结果比较接近。

对湛江港选用的代表船型,50 000 t 载重量的散货船,主墩塔在航向两面端为有圆角和斜面,以该船型的参数代入,取值如表 4,最大正撞力计算结果如下。

表 4　**湛江海湾大桥选用的代表船型 50 000 t 载重量的散货船速度 3 m/s 撞墩的力**

Table 4　**The force of 50 000 t bulk cargo (it is the typical ship of Zhanjiang bay bridge) collision with the bridge**

公　式	取　值	最大正撞力/MN
中国公路规范公式	v = 3 m/s　T = 2.5 s	84
中国铁路规范公式	v = 3 m/s　C_1 = 0.000 07　γ = 0.3	89
敏诺斯基—捷勒—沃易荪公式	v = 3 m/s　D = 62 500 t	79
索尔—诺特—格林那公式	v = 3 m/s　DWT = 50 000　D_{act}/D = 0.8	86
美国公路规范公式	v = 3 m/s　DWT = 50 000	80

经过比较后,中外 5 个公式计算出的最大正撞力相差不大,建议取 84 MN 作为使用值。

我国自 1994 年以来,对几十座桥梁进行防撞装置设计和研究,有几十组数据,这些数据分别来自 3 个课题组。而且是从两种不同的方法得来的:半经验公式估算法,一般是在方案阶段讨论桥型时进行的;数值模拟计算方法,一般是在有了图纸之后进行的。半经验公式估算出的可看作是一个准静态的力,供讨论桥型桥跨时参考。有了图纸之后,用数值计算得出的力的时程曲线,就比较具体了。

现在将几十组数据中的部分,列如表5:

表5　**500~50 000*DWT* 的船撞力举例(选自3个课题组2个方法)**

Table 5　**The force of ship collision with bridge of 500~50 000*DWT* (from 3 research groups by two methods)**

序	桥　名	船　名	相撞速度/(m/s)	撞击力/MN	备　注
1	湛江海湾大桥　主墩塔	50 000*DWT* 散货船 有柔性防撞装置	3.00 3.00 3.00	84.0 98.5 44.7	② ① ①
2	典型计算	40 000*DWT* 油　船	4.00	~148.0	③①
3	苏通长江大桥	50 000*DWT*	5.99 4.30	160.7 115.4	③② ③②
4	厦门东通道	50 000*DWT* 5 000*DWT*	3.10 3.10	82,6 25.1	③② ③②
5	象山港公路桥　主墩	50 000*DWT* 有柔性防撞装置	4.00 4.00	150.0 72.0	① ①
6	杭州湾跨海大桥	3 000*DWT* 1 000*DWT*	3.00 5.00	19.0 15.0	① ①
7	安庆铁路长江大桥　主墩	12 000*DWT* 5 200*DWT*	4.16 3.33 3.33	53.4 42.8 20.8	② ② ②
8	南澳大桥	5 000*DWT* 3 000*DWT*	3.90 1.80 3.80	32.0 14.0 19.5	③① ③① ③①
9	双碑嘉陵江大桥	1 650*DWT*	6.00	25.5	②
10	宁波外滩大桥	500*DWT*	4.00	3.4	①

注:1. 模拟数值计算峰值;2. 多个半经验公式计算结果;3. 搜集来的数据。

在我国利用半经验公式初估船撞力的问题相对地简单,因为需要代入各个半经验公式的船舶参数、撞击时间参数和船头刚度参数均已发表,经过正确地选择代入的参数之后,几个公式得出的船撞力非常地接近。对这几个双变量公式的每个相撞速度有一条曲线,举3 m/s和4 m/s为例,如图2所示。

这两条曲线的实用性在于:我国沿海及内河深水港并不多,500 t到50 000 t的船可以涵盖航行船舶的大部分;还在于:我国交通部规定进入大多数港口限速8 kn(上海港、湛江港、宁波港、平潭海峡水道等),遇到桥梁和

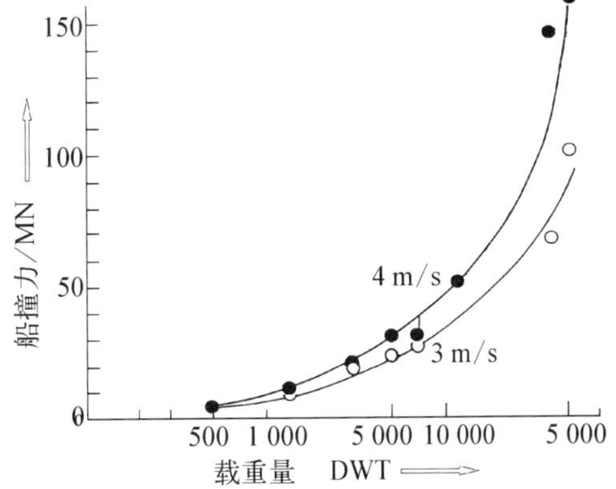

图2　3 m/s~4 m/s相撞速度时的船撞力

Fig. 2　The force of ship collision with bridge pier, when the ship with velocity 3~4 m/s

其他海洋工程建筑物要减速，因此通过桥梁的船舶大多数航速在 3 ~4 m/s。

3 防撞装置降低船撞力的研究

防撞装置一般采用降低刚性、延长撞击过程时间的办法，以降低船撞力。这是符合冲击动力学原理的。例如一位夜行者，第一次撞上电线杆觉得非常痛，第二次又撞上觉得不怎么痛，摸一摸，原来第一次撞上的是钢柱，第二次撞上的是木柱子。刚度小了，力也就小了。

从可以体现刚度的半经验公式——铁路桥梁设计规范船撞力公式的物理意义谈起，得出有防撞装置时计算最大正撞力的近似方法[10]。公式的推导：

当有一艘质量为 m 速度为 v 的船，船头正撞桥墩时。设撞后船头被镶住不动，船的速度由 $v \to 0$，船的动能由 $(1/2)mv^2 \to 0$，这个动能（ΔE）引致船头、桥墩和防撞装置三者的变形，简单地认为通过三者的力是一样大的，它引致桥墩、船头和防撞装置三者的变形（位移），依次称为 L_1、L_2、L_3：

在力与变形的“$F—L$”图上，设其为线性做功，即：$\Delta E = 1/2(FL)$，得到：

$$1/2(mv^2) = 1/2[F(L_1 + L_2 + L_3)]$$

现将斜率的倒数（1/斜率）称为 C，即 $C = L/F$, $L = FC$，对桥墩、船头和防撞装置三者的 C 分别称为 C_1、C_2、C_3，则上式可写为：

$$\begin{aligned} 1/2\ (mv^2) &= 1/2\ (FL_1 + FL_2 + FL_3) \\ &= 1/2\ (FFC_1 + FFC_2 + FFC_3) \\ &= 1/2[F^2(C_1 + C_2 + C_3)] \end{aligned}$$

移项得到：

$$F = v[m/(C_1 + C_2 + C_3)]^{0.5} \tag{1}$$

将式中 m 用船的重量 W（满载排水量 · 附连水系数）表示，考虑撞击能量耗散系数写作 γ，即得到铁路规范中角度折减前有防撞装置的最大正撞力公式[1]：

$$F = \gamma v[W/(C_1 + C_2 + C_3)]^{0.5} \tag{2}$$

C 的物理意义：当桥墩的刚性大于船头的刚性几十倍，变形也小几十倍，这样桥墩吸收的能量很小，经过计算认为将其忽略不计时（$C_2 = 0$）误差可接受。如果这时也没有采用防撞装置，则式中只有 C_1，C_1的割线意义表示如图 1，这是将一艘 40 000 t 载重量的油船，撞桥时的变形时程曲线与力的时程曲线整合而得的“力-撞深”曲线。图中的直线斜率的倒数就是 C_1。

从物理意义比较明确、公式参变量比较多和采集公式数据的可能性几方面来说，这是现有各公式中比较好的一个。但仍有一些缺陷如：第一，此式以最高点以下的面积与全部变形能($0.5mv^2$)相对应,实际上到达最高点后能量还在交换;第二,此式认为相撞力是一个通过船、桥都不变的力,实际上船头在变形,船头各处受力并不相同;如考虑到应力波的传递则还会有波长与元件的关系、界面影响等。故“比较好”只是在一定程度上而言的。

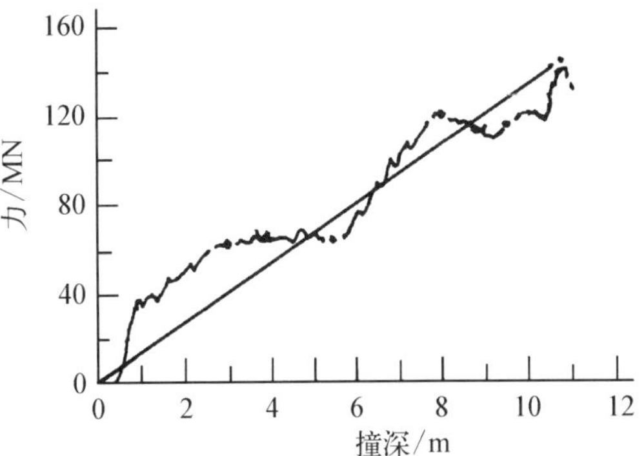

图3 40 000 t 油船“力-撞深”曲线的割线(斜率 $=1/C_1$)

Fig. 3 The secant (slope $=1/C_1$) of “force-destroy” curve of 40 000 t oil tanker

船若直接撞到碰垫上,碰垫受力和变形,适用厂商提供的“力-变形”图,若多个防撞圈(或碰垫)一齐用,则多了一个联系各防撞圈的钢围,它也参加变形。如果钢围刚性足够大,钢围和防撞圈组成的防撞装置的变形规律便可用防撞圈的规律来代表。

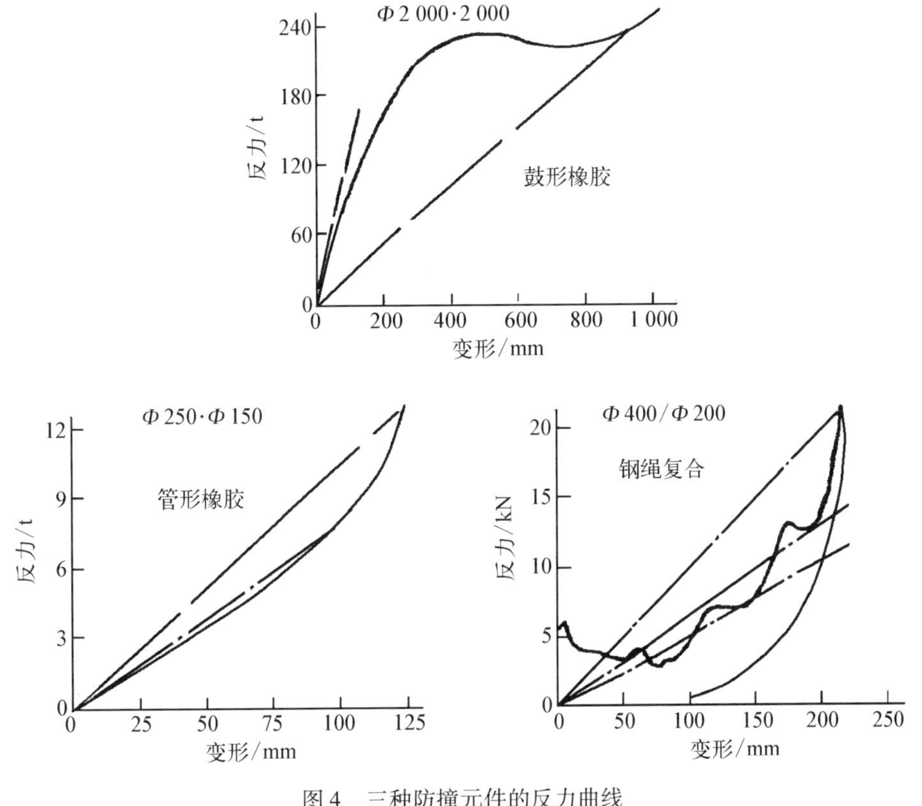

图4 三种防撞元件的反力曲线

Fig. 4 The “force-deformation” curves of three type elements for anti-collision

上图是两种碰垫和复合防撞圈的 3 幅“F—L”曲线,鼓形碰垫用于防撞时由于曲线太硬——凸曲线,反力大变形小;管形碰垫解决了这个问题,得到了凹曲线,即初撞便后退;此两种碰垫均为弹性的橡胶,变形过程吸能很小。钢丝绳复合防撞圈是凹曲线且吸

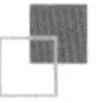

能很多,"吸能比"很大,做到了又软又吸能。此三曲线图上可以看出割线斜率 $1/C$ 代表刚柔程度的意义，由图中看出,钢丝绳复合防撞圈反力斜率小,尤其是开始阶段更小。

加上防撞装置后,撞击系统的刚性下降,撞击力就下降了。

4　半经验公式是同源的

——半经验公式分析研究的总结[9]

现在进一步对前面 5 个公式常用公式的原理进行讨论,经过此番讨论要求对这些公式的应用有更彻底的认识。

应该指出：现有各种有关规范中的船桥撞击力的半经验计算公式,包括我国现行公路规范公式、铁路规范公式、美国指南(ASHHTO)公式、和北欧"综述"公式(此式亦载于 *Eurocode 1, Part 2.7*[7])等,本质上都是建立在船撞桥(或船撞船)的刚体或弹性体的整体碰撞的简单理论基础上、再作若干修正的准静态半经验公式。

就我国现行的两个船桥撞击力计算公式而言,如下的公路规范公式本质上源自刚体整体运动的动量原理或冲量原理($Ft = mv$)

$$F = \frac{W}{g}\frac{v}{t} = \frac{mv}{t} \tag{1}$$

而如下的铁路规范公式则本质上源自计及船桥整体弹性柔度的动能原理[8]

$$F = \gamma v \sin\alpha \sqrt{\frac{W}{C_1 + C_2}} \tag{2}$$

式中 F(MN)为压缩撞击力,W(MN)和 $m(=W/g)$ 分别为船舶的重量和质量,v(m/s)为船舶的撞击速度,t(s)为撞击历时,α 为船舶与墩台撞击面的夹角,C_1 和 C_2(m/MN)分别为船舶和桥墩的弹性柔度,即单位力作用下产生的变形(刚度的倒数),而 γ($s/m^{1/2}$)为动能折减系数,用以计及船舶动能没有全部由桥墩所吸收。

当采用式(1)来计算撞击力时,最大的困难在于如何在各种不同的船桥撞击情况下正确确定撞击历时 t。在实践上,设计者不得不采用经验值(参看 6.2 节),而这些经验值实际上既缺乏理论依据也缺乏足够的实验验证。由小型实验测得的数值由于没有满足动态相似律也难以被广为接受。实际上,在式(1)基础上进行修正的各种试图从来未获成功。其根本原因在于式(1)本质上是刚体整体运动的准静态分析,不可能用来分析船桥相撞的冲击动力学问题。

于是,更多的设计者倾向于采用式(2)。其实,式(2)和式(1)是内在相通的,并无本质差别。事实上,如果用 U 来表示船桥相撞时发生的相对位移,则式(1)中 t 的平均值可以通过 U 除以撞击速度 v 来计算,即 $t = U/v$, 从而式(1)可相应地改写为:

$$F = \frac{W}{g}\frac{v}{t} = \frac{mv}{t} = \frac{mv^2}{U} \tag{1a}$$

对于弹性系统,上式在物理上表示:船的动能($mv^2/2$)与撞击力做功($FU/2$)相等,正是动能原理的具体表现。而对于弹性系统,位移 U 与作用力 F 成正比, $U = CF$, 正比系数 C 即弹性系统的弹性柔度(刚度 K 的倒数)。这样, $t = U/v = CF/v$, 式(1)可进一步改写为:

$$F = v\sqrt{mK} = v\sqrt{\frac{m}{C}} = v\sqrt{\frac{W}{gC}} \tag{2a}$$

如果再考虑到斜撞击时撞击角 α 的影响($\sin\alpha$),把弹性系统的弹性柔度 C 取为船的柔度 C_1与桥的柔度 C_2之和, $C = C_1 + C_2$,以及假设船的总动能中只有$\beta(=\gamma g^{1/2})$ 部分被桥吸收,则上式就与式(2)完全相同了。

显然,美国指南(ASHHTO)公式

$$F = 1.2 \times 10^5 v\sqrt{DWT} \tag{3}$$

可以看作式(2)的简化特例[8],此处 DWT 是船的载重(吨),与质量等价。

然而,采用式(2)时船的动态柔度怎么确定;桥的动态柔度又怎么确定;撞击条件不同时动能折减系数 γ 又怎么确定;各有什么依据。问题并未解决。

可见,采用式(1)时如何确定撞击历时 t 的难题现在只不过转化为采用式(2)时如何确定 C_1、C_2和 γ 的难题了。实践上,设计者又不得不采用经验值(参看[6]的附录),而现行推荐的这些经验值,实际上同样既缺乏理论依据也缺乏足够的实验验证。

也有人曾经对于源自动能原理的公式,如式(1b),尝试进行一些修正和改进。代表性的有:敏诺斯基-捷勒-沃以信(Minorsky-Gerlach-Woisin)公式和索尔-诺特-格林那(Saul Svensson-Knott-Greiner)公式。采用本文统一的符号时,前者具有如下形式

$$F = 0.024(vD_{max})^{2/3} \propto (vm)^{2/3} \tag{4}$$

后者具有如下形式

$$F = 0.88(DWT)^{1/2}(v/8)^{2/3}(D_{act}/D_{max})^{1/3} \propto v^{2/3}\sqrt{m} \tag{5}$$

式中 D_{max}是船的满载排水量(吨),D_{act}是撞击时船的实际排水量(吨),DWT 是船的载重量(吨),都可以换算为船的质量 m。

对于这类半经验公式,可以通过引入一个新系数 $\Gamma = \gamma/C^{1/2}$ 来加以讨论和理解。对照式(2)可知 Γ 综合反映了动能折减系数 γ 与系统弹性柔度 C 的影响。不难设想,对于不同质量 m 的船舶在不同撞击速度 v 下,Γ 理应具有不同数值,即 Γ 一般应是 m 和 v 的函数, $\Gamma = \Gamma(m, v)$, 则源于动能原理的式(1b)可改写为如下更一般的形式:

$$F = \Gamma(m, v)v\sqrt{m} \tag{6}$$

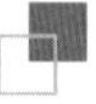

函数 $\Gamma(m, v)$ 的一种可能形式是以幂函数关系分别依赖于 m 和 v,即有:$\Gamma(m, v) = \xi m^r v^s$,此处 ξ 是常系数。于是,式(6)可表为:

$$F = \xi m^{r+1/2} v^{s+1} \tag{6a}$$

显然,当 $r = 1/6$ 和 $s = -1/3$ 时,上式化为敏诺斯基-捷勒-沃以信(Minorsky-Gerlach-Woisin)公式(4),而当 $r = 0$ 和 $s = -1/3$ 时,上式化为索尔-诺特-格林那(Saul Svensson-Knott-Greiner)公式(5)。可见,该两式都可以理解为式(2)中的 γ 和 C 以幂函数关系分别依赖于 m 和 v 时的某种简化特例,只是 r 和 s 各自取了特定的经验值。

其实,在式(2)或式(1b)基础上进行修正的各种试图并未能在普遍的条件下获得广泛适用和真正的成功。根本原因还在于这些公式本质上是船桥整体运动的准静态分析,不可能用来正确分析船桥相撞的冲击动力学问题。

由此可见,我们完全没有必要再停留在对这些准静态经验公式进行孰优孰劣的讨论上,也完全没有必要再停留在对这些准静态经验公式进行修正改进[12]的尝试上,因为船桥相撞问题本质上是一个冲击动力学问题。出路是采用冲击动力学分析。

5 侧撞力[11]

5.1 船撞墩的可能角度

国际桥梁和结构协会(IABSE)《航行船舶与桥梁结构的相互影响　综述与指南》认为:“船只行驶速度可分解为:计算纵向动能平行于船轴线的分量和计算横向动能垂直于船轴线的分量”;“如果船只完全停止,其碰撞总动能将耗尽;如果船只仅仅转向,碰撞能量应以碰撞前后船只动能的矢量分析来确定”[7]。这一点,共识者较多,但具体分析时可能有些差异。要是防撞装置按“动能耗尽”来设计,设计出来的防撞设施将硕大无比,且造价大,影响了防撞设施的普遍采用[9]。

采用横向分速度计算能量的方法时,如何对待奇点极值,是一个需要重视并合理解决的问题。现在分析船撞墩的各种可能情况[13]:

第一种情况:直航前进的船大都是船头部位碰撞桥墩,其分速度夹角为 γ。γ 决定于船的 B/L,通常速度较高的船设计成 $B/L \leqslant 1/7$,这时夹角为 8.1°;速度较慢的船、货驳等,设计成 $B/L \approx 1/5$,这时夹角为 11.3°;拖船、渡船设计成 $B/L \approx 1/4$,这时夹角为 14°。横向分速度分别为原向航速的 0.14、0.2 和 0.25 倍,其能量 $(1/2)mv^2$ 分别为原能量的 0.02、0.04 和 0.06 倍,相撞情况如图 1 所示。图中有剖面线的是桥墩,它的周围两头尖的部分是防撞设施。

第二种情况:该船除了前进速度外,尚有横漂和转弯,所以碰到了平行中段,有点像船靠码头的情况。此时船不能维持纵轴方向(主龙骨方向)前进。由于此时船的横向速度比前进的速度小得多,算出的能比用直航速度算出的能小得多。相撞情况如图 6 所示。

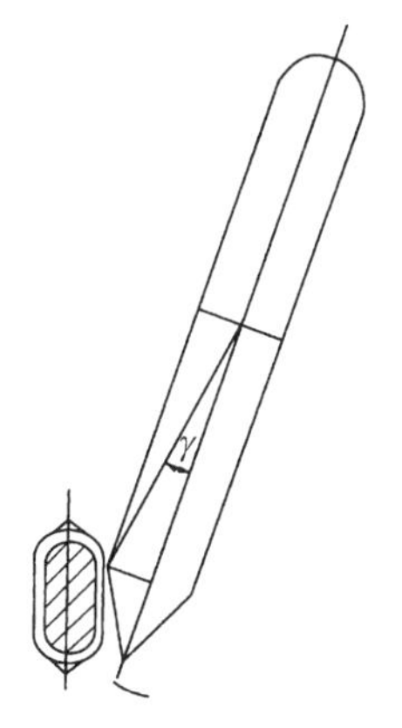

图5　前进中船首部撞墩

Fig. 5　The bow of a going ship collision with the bridge pier

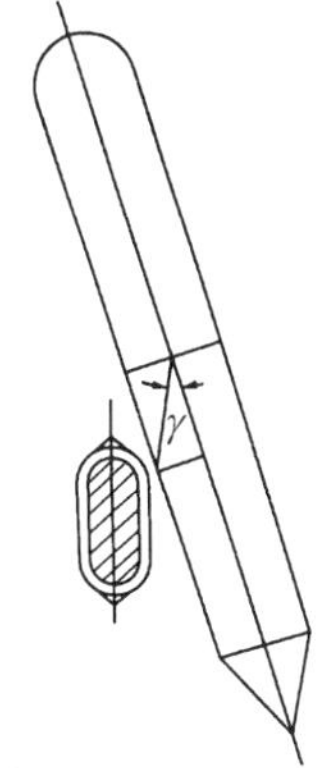

图6　横漂船和船侧碰撞

Fig. 6　The driven ship and ship side collision with the pier

第三种情况是一种极端情况,即船正对桥墩开过来,如图7所示。如果相撞后顶住不动,则船与墩交换全部动能(船舶具有的最大的动能值)。但因设计的防撞设施外箍板作成尖型,两相遇瞬间即滑开变成第一种情况。由此可以理解为:以横向分速度计算能量时,正撞后不动的情况,是“能量—角度”曲线上的一个奇点,此时横向速度分量为0,而能量交换最大。笔者建议用保证率的办法处理此奇点,即认为此种状态的概率非常小,置于保证率之外。

现在有一种钢板格子变形消能的防撞装置,它的特点是钢板变形吸能值较大,但每次撞后要修理,且对尖船头会镶住,增加船对桥墩交换的能量。

第四种情况也是一种极端情况,横漂的船正好顶在船的重心上(如果不是顶在重心,则船的惯性力会使船转动,变为第2种情况),这时的碰撞能是以全部横漂速度 v_H 计算的,$(1/2)mv_H^2$。瞬间之后。

由于水流合力与船的重心不重合,船头即慢慢旋转,实现“船到桥头自然直”,变为顺流而下,见图8。

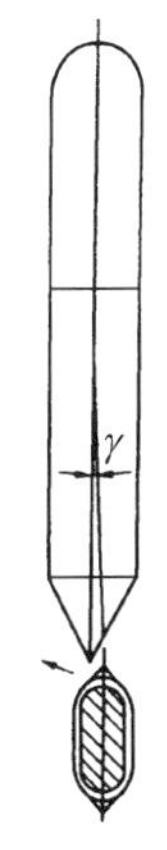

图7　船以正方向撞墩后滑开

Fig. 7　Ship slide out after frontispiece collision with the pier

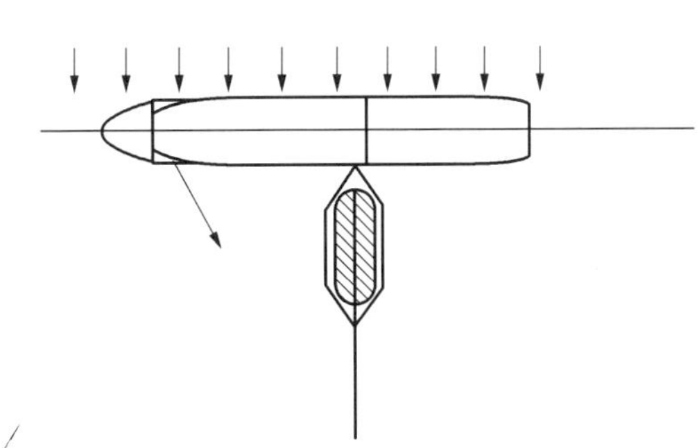

图8　横漂船重心正好撞在墩上

Fig. 8　The center gravity of transverse driven ship collision with the pier

所有船与墩相撞均离不开上列四种情况[9]。除了横漂船和极端情况外,只有2种情况,一是船撞墩的正面与墩的尖头斜面接触;二是船头撞在墩的侧面。

5.2 墩的大小和跨距与角度的关系

船驶近桥,如果航道的宽度和弯度合乎规定;如果航线上有一定的能见度;如果船没有失去动力或失去控制;如果船员没有因故而不能履行职责(醉酒、瞌睡、眩晕……);则船是不会撞到桥墩上去的。

如果驾驶员因各种原因之一而未能操纵舵机,如图9,船从正确航向(图中 $R-Q$ 段)进入偏航段,不操舵的最大偏航角即该航线这时的风流压偏角(自然条件作用的总和)。

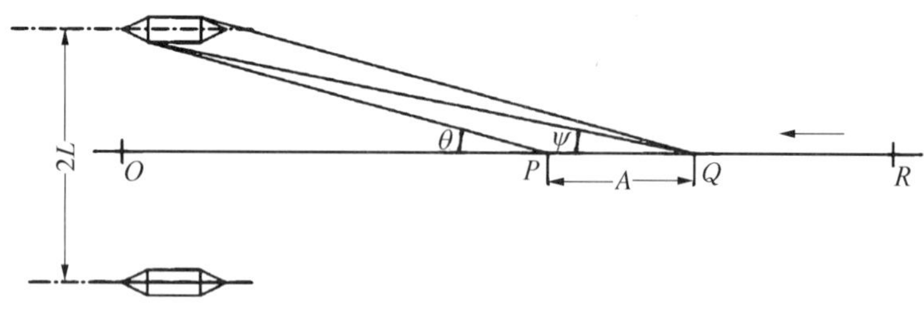

图9 船从航线偏离而撞墩的几何位置

Fig. 9 The geometry position of a departure route ship collision with the pier

A 为在这角度下的桥墩投影长度,在 $Q-P$ 段以 θ 角度偏航会撞到桥墩,调整角度小于 Ψ 便不会撞,如果以3 m/s船速驶过 A 段只有半分钟左右,驾驶员(或领航员)纠正便可,如果这时 $2L$ 比较大,使 $\mathrm{tg}^{-1}(L/OP)$ 大于失舵时的风流压偏角,也是撞不上的(L 为航线中心与桥墩的距离,$O-P$ 段用能见度或失舵距离代入,可得到定量数值)。

算例:如桥墩跨距内侧为400 m,航线中心线与桥墩中心重合,风流压偏角为13°代入,则 $O-P$ 距离为870 m,即当 P 点达到870 m以近,失舵漂流,风流压偏角为13°,船将从墩边过,桥跨愈宽允许失舵的距离愈长,此期间可纠偏(如有别的制约因素,要增加考虑)。

我们常说,正撞的概率比较低,如图10所示:当船距墩1 000 m时,如果发现船头对准桥墩中线,只要转向1° 便可避开桥墩。

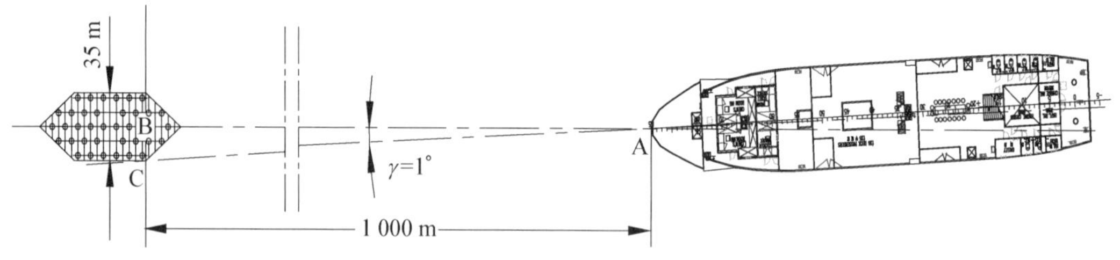

图10 正面撞墩示意图

Fig. 10 A sketch map of ship frontispiece collision with the pier

侧面撞墩概率大些,例如:船长200 m,船宽32 m,墩宽35 m,风流压偏角为13°,船长加墩长投影在墩前的弧长为55.4 m,加半船宽和半墩宽为88.9 m,当船驶近到1 000 m

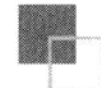

时,约在墩前占5°。所以说,侧撞概率比正撞大几倍。

5.3 船舶航行时“风流压偏角”分析

船舶在航道上航行,由船舶本身的特性(船舶类型、船舶尺度、主机功率、导航设备、舵机性能)决定船舶操纵性,适航性;还有航道条件(风况、雾天能见度、水流状态)以及船舶航行密度的影响;在航道上有横跨桥梁时,更受桥梁建筑等因素的制约。允许船舶穿过桥孔的通航条件,除了一般通航条件外,还需另加桥梁的条件(桥梁通航净空尺度、桥墩位置、水流变化、沿岸风力)才能保证航行安全,顺利通航,避免不幸的船舶撞击桥梁的航行事故发生。

船舶在航道上航行,一般是按航道中心呈蛇形航迹左右摆动前进,实船满载情况,船舶下沉量较大。受水流流态、流向、流速左右较大;空载情况,干舷增高,则受风向、风速影响较大。在海湾河口地区,水流除径流作用外,还受沿岸潮汐变化的影响。因此船舶航行产生风流压偏角是正常的事,在航行中,船舶导航驾驶人员控制船舶航向必须将舵角控制在一个合理值的范围,保持船舶航行的稳定性。

船舶在航道上航行,可能产生船舶航行的风流压偏角,同时;桥梁桥墩建设时,桥墩中心线与水流流向也会产生夹角(应不大于标准[4]所允许值),这两个角度的瞬时综合结果,组成了偏航船舶与桥墩瞬时撞击的撞击角的。这是随机因素变化的夹角,也是有一定变化范围的,因为桥墩中心线与水流流向的夹角是较稳定的,船舶航行的风流压偏角对一定的航道平常也有一定数值,但在发生撞击事故时也可能有一些意外的变化。

这两个角度相加时,对内河可分上水、下水,每种分左墩、右墩共4种情况;对港湾亦应按涨潮、退潮,左墩、右墩4种情况。简化计算港湾4种情况的最大侧撞角时,可用绝对值相加,因为桥孔下面通过船舶是双向的,一向相减时另一向便相加。用公式表示:

$$\theta_{\text{侧撞角}} = |\alpha_{\text{风流压偏角}}| + |\beta_{\text{桥法线偏角}}|$$

根据研究的桥,对以下各方面进行讨论:桥位、轴线与航线,桥墩(或桥塔)所处的河槽位置,风压方向与船撞桥的关系,流压、雾天、进出港航道宽度和上下游直线段讨论(桥位上下游各应有4倍船长的直段[4])……。

实际通过船舶较少则船撞墩的概率正比减少,可参考美国规范对撞塌年频率进行计算[8]。

5.4 我国主要港口航道满载船舶风流压偏角经验值

船舶在航道上航行的风流压偏角究竟为多少度?在国内外有关航道、港务、航运专家经长期研究、观测、试验有了一个比较符合实际的认识,也编写进入了规范[3]。

此外,2001年12月,长江航运规划设计研究院和西南水运工程科学研究所分别作了桥墩形状和过桥航迹的水工模型试验,后者就是在各种情况下通过模型测定流压偏角(蔡汝哲等,西南水运工程科学研究所,桥孔通航船摸试验研究报告 长江航道规划设计研究院印 2001年12月)。

我国主要港口航道满载船舶风流压偏角经验值见表6。

表 6　我国主要港口风流压偏角经验值[3]

Table 6　The experience value of wind and current pressure drift angle at our main ports

港口航道名称	折算横风横流	风流压偏角/°	备　注
大连港大港航道	6 级风 0.38 km	5	
大连鲇鱼湾	6 级风 2.0 km	15	无航道
秦皇岛航道	6 级风 0.51 km	3～4	
天津港进港主航道	6 级风 0.57 km	5～7	
青岛港大港航道	6 级风 1.07 km	5～8	
连云港航道	6 级风 0.9～1.15 km	8～9	
	0.9 km	5～6	
湛江港斗龙村航道	7 级风 2.0 km	13	
八所港航道	6 级风 1.32 km	10	
	6 级风 无流	2～3	
上海港进口航道	6 级风 流速极小	3	船流夹角
	6 级风	20	空　船
石臼港航道	6 级风 0.6 km	7	
汕头港	6 级风 1.5 km	10	

注：本表由交通部水规院根据实测及调查所得。

5.5　其他国外风流压偏角资料

（1）美国陆军工程兵团对巴拿马运河和苏伊士运河观测结果，建议：当仅有岸吸力时为 2°，一般有横向风流影响取 10°。

（2）日本“港湾深水航道规划”（和管野一，《港湾及海岸工学》）指出：航道上航行船舶风流压偏角最大不超过 10°。

（3）苏联列宁格勒水运学院和敖德萨工学院资料论述船舶偏离和漂流决定于风向、风速、流速、船舶类型和船舶速度，建议风流压偏角最大值不超过 25°（指船舶空载状态）。

（4）国际海运伦敦航运会议第二次油轮会议报告，对船舶受横流影响的压偏角，可按下式计算：

$$\alpha = tg^{-1}（横向流速/航速）$$

如 $\tan\alpha \leq 0.25$，即横流为 2.0 kn 船舶至少为 8.0 kn 时，$\alpha = 14°$

（5）鹿特丹港航道流速 1 kn，风流压偏角为 10°

（6）哥德堡港航道流速 1 kn，风流压偏角为 7.2°

5.6　湛江港风流压偏角实测结果

湛江海事局大力配合湛江海湾大桥的防撞设计，对通过桥下的 50 000 t 级到 2 000 t 级的 8 艘船舶，进港出港 10 个航次（其中进港 4 次出港 6 次；10 次中遇到涨潮 6 次，平潮 2 次，退潮 2 次）进行风、流压偏角的测量，得到平常风和平常水流条件下，10 次风、流压偏角的最大值为 3°，现将这组最新数据列表如表 7。

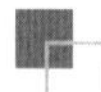

表 7　　2004 年桥位处实测风、流压偏角(湛江海事局测定)

Table 7　　The value of wind and current pressure drift angle at the bridge position measured at 2004 (measured by the Zhanjiang Maritime Bureau)

序	月-日-时	船　名	船的尺度/m			总吨/t	风	流		船速/kn	航向/航迹向/(°)	风流压偏角/(°)
			长	宽	吃水(实)		风级/风向	流向	流速/kn			
1	08-22-23	雪　林	245	32	65	41 699	2~3/东南	323	0.8	7.9	141/142	1
2	08-31-11	马里奇	225	32	13.1	36 042	2/东	325	1.0	6.5	323/322	0
3	09-04-19	马里奇	225	32	7.1	36 042	微/—	325	1.0	9.5	143/141	2
4	08-28-09	加力士 GALAXY	220	32	7.5	32 976	4~5/东	320	1.5	8.0	145/143	2
5	09-02-21	玛　丽	190	31	11.5	26 831	2~3/偏东	323	1.5	8.8	320/322	2
6	09-04-08	华　鲲	182	28	5.4	20 990	2~3/东南	平潮	0.2	4.9	326/323	3
7	08-27-09	嘉　宏	189	23	10.8	17 677	2~3/东	325	0.5	6.0	325/325	0
8	08-31-06	嘉　宏	189	23	6.6	17 677	2/南	143	1.5	7.0	142/142	0
9	09-06-09	飞　马	112	19	6.3	5 369	2~3/偏南	145	0.5	6.2	141.5/143	1.5
10	08-30-17	海明星	88	13	5.8	1 998	4~5/偏南	平潮	平潮	6.9	144/142	2

设计时可按照:风流压偏角和桥法线偏角两个角的绝对值之和作为船对桥墩的侧撞角的最大值,用此角的角度函数乘正撞力便得出侧撞力。

6　船撞力半经验公式的应用

6.1　在桥梁设计的哪个阶段应用船撞力半经验公式

确定船舶撞击力的方法有多种:包括经验公式估算法,有限元动态模拟分析法和实验法,上述 3 种方法均在实际工程中得到了应用。但依据这 3 种方法的特点,它们应用的阶段和作用是不相同的。

半经验公式,使用起来比较简单,只需要知道桥梁所跨越的航线航行什么样的船,就可以进行初步的估算。

使用的必要性在于:进行桥型、桥跨讨论时,需要考虑船撞力的大小。

当通行的船舶非常大、船撞力很大,以至选用一跨过江的桥梁时,船撞墩的水平力就不存在了。

当桥梁设计刚刚开始,桥墩还不知道有没有,当然不需要进行数值计算,也没有条件进行数值计算。因为数值计算需要有具体的结构才能计算他们的刚度、强度。

6.2　准静态船撞力与数值计算时程值(各个瞬时的力)的应用

当桥梁设计刚刚开始,水中桥墩还不知道有没有,当然不需要进行数值计算,也不能进行数值计算。这时用到的是半经验公式(或查曲线)得出的准静态船撞力,以之进行桥型、桥跨的选择和讨论,这时没有对应的瞬时的力。

到了初步设计阶段,有了桥墩,才有船撞,有了船撞才能进行船撞力的数值计算,计算的结果,桥墩的响应(强度和位移等)是不是超过动态下材料的允许值,如果超过则要加强桥墩,这需要进行反复计算。直到不超过动态下材料的允许值为止。这时,不需要用到半经验公式估出的准静态船撞力。

参 考 文 献

[1] 国际桥梁和结构工程协会(IABSE),交通船只与桥梁结构的相互影响(综述与指南). 同济大学,1991-09.
顾翔、交通部公路规划设计院鲍卫刚译. 同济大学张乃华校,1993-03.

[2] 国际桥梁和结构工程协会(IABSE). O. D. 拉尔森编写,(小组向委员会提出)交通船只与桥梁结构的相互影响,1991-04;广东虎门技术咨询公司. 陈守容,张乃华译,岑国基校. 1995.

[3] 美国各州公路和运输工作者协会(AASHTO)2009:公路桥梁船撞设计指南(第二版)上海海洋钢结构研究所、宁波大学、重庆交通大学等译. 同济大学陆宗林校,2010.

[4] 中华人民共和国交通部. 船舶或漂流物的撞击作用. 公路桥涵设计通用规范 JTG D60—2004. 北京:人民交通出版社,2004.

[5] 中华人民共和国铁道部. 墩台承受船只或排筏的撞击力 TB10002. 1—2005 铁路桥涵设计基本规范 4.4.6 节 北京:中国铁道出版社,2005.

[6] 陈国虞,王礼立. 船撞桥及其防御. 北京:中国铁道出版社,2006.

[7] Vrouwenvelder A. C. W. M., *Design for Ship Impact According to Eurocode 1, Part 2.7, Ship Collision Analysis*, A. A. Balkema, Rotterdam, 1998, 123-134.

[8] 王礼立,张忠伟,黄德进,姚小虎,陈国虞. 船撞桥的钢丝绳圈柔性防撞装置的冲击动力学分析. 洪友士主编.《应用力学进展》——祝贺郑哲敏先生八十华诞. 北京:科学出版社,2004:172-180.

[9] 王礼立,杨黎明,陈国虞,陆宗林. 船桥相撞的冲击力分析. 第二届国际自动化和工程控制会议论文集,2011(7):5850-5853.

[10] 陈国虞. 有防撞装置时计算船撞桥的力——铁路桥梁规范中船撞力公式的延伸修订,铁道标准设计,2004(1).

[11] 陈国虞,沈文玮. 船对桥墩的侧撞力. 中国土木工程学会桥梁及结构工程分会. 第十五届全国桥梁学术会议论文集. 上海:同济大学出版社,2002:228-232.

[12] 钱铧. 桥梁船舶碰撞的简化分析. 同济大学,2002.

[13] 陈国虞. 关于“船撞桥”问题的几点浅见. 上海造船,1995(3).

[14] 陈国虞,倪步友. 铁路规范船撞力公式中动能折减系数的实验厘定. 上海:城市桥梁养护管理与检测维修加固技术交流研讨会论文集,2008:88-95.

发表于:桥梁工程与技术,2011(5).

Published at: Bridge engineering and technology, 2011(5).

船桥碰撞过程引发的冲击动力学论题

Impact dynamics topics motivated by the ship-bridge collision process

王礼立[1] 陈国虞[2] 杨黎明[1]
(1. 宁波大学机械工程和力学学院,宁波 315211;
2. 上海海洋钢结构研究所,上海 201204)
WANG Lili[1], CHEN Guoyu[2], YANG Liming[1]
(1. Mechanical Engineering and Mechanics Faculty,
Ningbo University, Ningbo 315211 China;
2. Shanghai Marine Steel Structure Research Institute, Shanghai 201204, China)

摘 要 对船桥撞击过程引发的几个冲击动力学论题进行了分析。研究表明:(1) 为降低船撞力,应采用柔性(低的结构动态广义波阻抗)防撞装置;(2) 撞击力所做的功,通过应力波传播转化为内能(变形能)与动能之和;而变形能中的不可逆部分愈高,防撞装置发挥的整体作用愈大,则愈有利于防撞装置发挥缓冲耗能作用。如何让船舶尽早结束撞击并带走尽量多的剩余动能,应是防撞装置设计的关键点;(3) 黏性耗能可缓冲撞击过程、延长撞击历时,有利于防撞装置发挥整体作用,进而为船舶在低应力下转向滑离,从而带走尽可能多的剩余动能创造条件。因此,船撞桥防护装置的设计应该建立在如下的科学设计理念上:(i) 低波阻抗意义上的冲击柔性,(ii) 缓冲撞击过程意义上的黏性耗能,(iii) 防撞装置能及早发挥整体作用,化撞击集中力为分布载荷,以及(iv) 让船尽早滑离而带走尽量多的剩余动能。以钢丝绳防撞圈为主要元件的柔性耗能防撞装置是这一防撞理念的工程应用实例,其有效性已为工程实践和实船撞击试验证实。

关键词 船桥碰撞 冲击动力学 冲击力 能量转换 动态响应

Abstract: Some impact dynamics topics motivated by the ship-bridge collision process are analyzed in this paper. It is shown that (1) in order to reduce the impact force a flexible (i. e. with low structural dynamic generalized wave impedance) crashworthy device should be applied. (2) The work done by the impact force is transformed via wave propagation into the internal energy (deformation energy) and kinetic energy. The larger the irreversible part of the former is, as well as the greater the overall role played by the crashworthy device is, the better the buffer role played by the crashworthy device will be. Moreover, how to make the ship as soon as possible to end the collision and carry away as much as possible the remaining kinetic energy should be a key point. (3) Viscous dissipation of energy can buffer the collision process, prolong the dissipation duration, and help the crashworthy device to play an overall role, and create the condition for turning ship away to end the collision. Thus the scientific design idea of crashworthy device should be based on (i) impact flexibility in terms of low structural wave impedance, (ii) viscous dissipation in terms of damping collision process, (iii) let the crashworthy device plays an integral role as soon as possible so that the intense impact concentrated force could be changed into a weaker distributed load, and (iv) let ship turns away as soon as possible, and thus takes away the remaining kinetic energy as much as possible. As an engineering application example, such design idea is reflected in the new flexible crashworthy device consisting of hundreds of steel-wire-rope coils. Its validity has been confirmed by the engineering practice and the real ship collision tests.

Keywords: ship-bridge collision; impact dynamics; impact force; energy transformation; dynamic response

船桥相撞的危害性已经人所共知[1~3]。

如何避免或减轻船舶与桥梁相撞的灾难性后果,是当前具有广泛意义的国际性课题,日益引起各国学术界、工程界和管理部门的共同关注。

就实际工作而言,不论对于船舶设计师还是桥梁设计师,首先是如何科学地认识、分析和确定船桥撞击力 F_{cq},舍此就谈不上如何加强防护等等,这里用下标 c 代表船和 q 代表桥来指船与桥撞击界面处的总撞击力。

为什么船桥撞击力 F_{cq} 的确定会成为一个问题呢?困难在哪里呢?

从发展历史来看,主要由于人们对它有一个由浅入深的认识发展过程。关键点在于:在分析船桥撞击力 F_{cq} 时,是把船桥相撞过程看作一个准静态平衡过程来处理,只考虑其最终平衡结果而不计及其时间过程;还是把它看作一个随时间 t 变化的、冲击动力学过程来处理。

冲击动力学理论与固体静力学理论的主要区别是什么呢?

概括地说,在研究冲击载荷下结构和材料的动态响应时,通常应计及两种基本的动力学效应以区别于静力学分析,即结构惯性效应和材料应变率效应[4]。对结构惯性效应的考虑实质上导致了对结构中各种形式的波传播的研究,不论是精确的还是简化的,并促进了"结构冲击动力学"的发展;而对材料应变率效应的考虑则导致了对材料的各种类型的应变率相关的(率型)本构关系和失效准则的研究,促进了"材料冲击动力学"的发展。

下面我们就相关的主要论题作一讨论。

1　影响船桥撞击力 F_{cq} 的主要因素

对于船桥撞击力 F_{cq} 的一切分析研究，最终归结为到底有哪些主要影响因素，以及它们如何定量地影响船撞力 F_{cq}。只有掌握了这一点，我们才能进而提出科学的防撞措施。

就我国现行的两个船桥撞击力计算公式而言，如下的公路规范公式[5]本质上源自刚体整体运动的动量原理或冲量原理（$Ft = Mv$），以本文统一的符号表示时为：

$$F_{GL} = \frac{W}{g}\frac{v}{t_d} = \frac{Mv}{t_d} \tag{1}$$

而如下的铁路规范公式[6]则本质上源自船和桥作为整体但计及其结构弹性柔度的动能原理：

$$F_{TL} = gv\sin\alpha\sqrt{\frac{W}{C_{u1}+C_{u2}}} = \frac{g}{\sqrt{g}}v\sin\alpha\sqrt{\frac{M}{C_{u1}+C_{u2}}} = \frac{g}{\sqrt{g}}\sin\alpha v\sqrt{K_{u12}M} \tag{2}$$

两式中 F(MN)为压缩撞击力（下标表示不同公式的出处，如 GL 表示公路规范，TL 表示铁路规范等），W(MN)和 $M(=W/g)$分别为船舶的重量和质量，v(m/s)为船舶的撞击速度，t_d(s)为撞击历时，α 为船舶与墩台撞击面的夹角，$\gamma(\mathrm{s/m^{1/2}})$为动能折减系数，用以计及船舶动能没有全部由桥墩所吸收，而 C_{u1} 和 C_{u2}(m/MN)分别为船舶和桥墩的结构弹性柔度，即单位力作用下产生的位移（结构刚度 K_u 的倒数），K_{u12} 是如下定义的组合刚度：

$$K_{u12} = \frac{1}{C_{u1}+C_{u2}} = \frac{1}{\frac{1}{K_{u1}}+\frac{1}{K_{u2}}} = \frac{K_{u1}K_{u2}}{K_{u1}+K_{u2}} \tag{3}$$

此处 C 和 K 中的下标 u 表示这里的结构柔度是以位移与载荷之比定义的（单位 m/MN）；下文中凡是结构柔度以变形（应变）与载荷之比定义时（单位 $\mathrm{MN^{-1}}$），则以下标 ε 表示，以示区别。

国际上常用的船撞力公式如美国指导规范（ASHHTO）公式[7]和欧洲统一规范公式[8]等，都可以归类于式(2)类型的公式，只是取了不同的经验系数[9]。

对比式(1)和式(2)可见，两者都以撞击速度 v 和船舶质量 M 为影响船撞力 F_{cq} 的主要因素，而且两者相同地给出 F_{cq} 正比于 v，但在船舶质量 M 的定量影响程度上则各不相同。

用式(1)来计算撞击力时，最大的困难在于如何正确确定撞击历时 t_d。下面我们分别从准静态分析和冲击动力学分析两个不同的角度来讨论一下撞击历时。

从准静态力学的角度来分析 t_d 时，设以 U 表示船桥以 v 相撞时的相对位移，则 t_d 的平均值可表为 $t = U/v$，从而式(1)可改写为：

$$F_{cq} = \frac{W}{g}\frac{v}{t_d} = \frac{Mv}{t_d} = \frac{Mv^2}{U} \tag{4a}$$

对于弹性系统,上式意味着:船的动能($Mv^2/2$)与撞击力做功($FU/2$)相等,正是动能原理的表现形式之一。而且对于弹性系统,位移 U 与作用力 F 成正比,$U = C_u F$,正比系数 C_u 即弹性系统的弹性柔度(刚度 K_u 的倒数)。这样,由于 $t_d = U/v = C_u F/v = F/(K_u v)$,式(4a)可进一步改写为:

$$F_{cq} = v\sqrt{MK_u} = v\sqrt{\frac{M}{C_u}} = v\sqrt{\frac{W}{gC_u}} \tag{4b}$$

当计及斜撞击时撞击角 α 的影响($\sin\alpha$),把系统的弹性柔度 C_u 取为船的柔度 C_{u1} 与桥的柔度 C_{u2} 之和,$C_u = C_{u1} + C_{u2}$,再假设船的总动能中只有 $\beta(=\gamma g^{1/2})$ 部分被桥吸收,则上式就与铁路规范公式(式 2)完全相同了。在这个意义上,式(2)和式(1)是内在相通的,只是表现形式不同而已。

再从冲击动力学的角度来分析 t_d,即从波传播的角度来分析:考虑一个等截面积 A_0、长 L_0 的杆状结构以速度 v^* 轴向撞击另一个相同材料但更长的等截面积弹性杆状结构,按照弹性应力波传播理论[4],撞击界面处的质点速度为 $v = v^*/2$,而撞击历时 t_d 等于应力波以弹性波速 $C_o(=\sqrt{E/r_0})$ 在撞击杆中传播一个来回的时间($t_d = 2L_0/C_o$),如果再考虑到此撞击杆的质量 $M = p_0 L_0 A_0$,则有:

$$t_d = \frac{2L_0}{C_0} = \frac{2M}{r_0 C_0 A_0} \tag{5}$$

式中 ρ_0 为材料原始密度,E 为杨氏弹性模量。把式(5)代入式(1)得

$$F_{ID} = \frac{Mv^*}{t_d} = r_0 C_0 A_0 v = R_w v \tag{6a}$$

式中 $\rho_0 C_0(=\sqrt{r_0 E})$ 称为波阻抗,只依赖于材料特性;而 $R_w = \rho_0 C_0 A_0$ 称为广义波阻抗,计及了结构尺寸效应。如果引入结构的线密度 $m = \rho_0 A_0$ 和以载荷与应变之比定义的结构刚度 $K_\varepsilon = EA_0$,则结构的广义波阻抗还可以表示为 $R_w = m(K_\varepsilon/m)^{1/2} = \sqrt{mK_e}$,从而式(6a)可改写为

$$F_{ID} = r_0 C_0 A_0 v = mC_0 v = m\sqrt{\frac{K_e}{m}}v = \sqrt{mK_e}v = R_w v \tag{6b}$$

在式(6)中已经把 F 的下标写为 ID 以表示是由冲击动力学(Impact Dynamics)观点导出的。事实上,按照应力波传播理论进行严格推导,将得出与式(6)完全相同的结果[3,4,9]。

对比式(4)和式(6),可以看出准静态分析和冲击动力学分析对于船撞力主要影响因素的异同。为方便起见,把式(4)和式(6)的对比简单归纳如下式所示:

$$F_{\mathrm{cq}} = \sqrt{MK_u}v \tag{4}$$

$$F_{\mathrm{ID}} = \sqrt{mK_e}v = R_w v \tag{6}$$

由此可见：

(a) 两种分析一致给出：船撞力正比于撞击速度 v。因此，限制船舶在邻近桥梁时的航速应是首要的防护措施之一；

(b) 两种分析都给出：船撞力正比于结构刚度的平方根，因此采用柔性防护应是首选；反之，如果片面追求桥梁/防撞装置的高刚度高强度，则船撞力反而更大，不论对桥还是对船都更加不利；

(c) 准静态分析式(4)表示船撞力正比于结构质量 M 的平方根，而冲击动力学分析式(6)表示船撞力正比于结构线密度 m 的平方根，并且线密度 m 总是与结构刚度 K_ε 组合在一起以结构广义波阻抗 R_w 的形式出现，即最终表现为：船撞力正比于结构广义波阻抗。

关于撞击质量 M 如何影响船撞力，有必要作进一步的讨论。人们常常凭直觉或日常经验认为：撞击质量 M 应该直接影响撞击力。想不通"船撞力怎么会与船舶总质量 M 无关"呢？这需要根据不同情况来分析。如果船桥相撞是一个可以忽略应力波传播过程的准静态过程，而且关心的是撞击的最终结果的话，则正如式(4)所示，船的总质量 M 无疑是一个重要影响因素。但对于应力波传播起主导作用的撞击早期过程，外加载荷和撞击能量都是通过应力波传播而逐步作用于波阵面后方区域的，撞击的初始峰值起着关键作用；这时船的总质量不会在撞击一开始就发挥总体作用，而是随应力波在船中传播才逐步发挥愈来愈大的作用，因而总质量 M 并不直接影响瞬态初始撞击力。

事实上，不难通过一个简化实例对这一动态过程作一定量说明。考虑一个质量为 M 的刚体 B_{s}(模拟船)轴向撞击一弹性长杆 B_{b}(模拟桥)。应力波分析表明(例如参考文献[4]的公式(3-5))[4]，这时撞击界面处的撞击应力和质点速度一开始达到最大值 F^*，然后遵循如下的指数规律衰减：

$$F = F^*\exp\left(-\frac{r_0C_0A_0}{M}t\right) = F^*\exp\left(-\frac{M_t}{M}\right) \tag{7a}$$

$$v = v^*\exp\left(-\frac{r_0C_0A_0}{M}t\right) = v^*\exp\left(-\frac{M_t}{M}\right) \tag{7b}$$

式中 v^* 是初始撞击速度，$F^*(=-\rho_0C_0A_0v^*)$ 是相应的初始峰值撞击力，$M_t(=\rho_0C_0A_0t)$ 代表 t 时刻杆中应力波波阵面所扫过的那部分杆的质量，无量纲质量因子 $R_m(=\rho_0C_0A_0t/M)$ 则代表波阵面所扫过部分的质量 M_t 与撞击物总质量 M 之比，它是随时间增大的。上式表示，应力波和质点速度波的波剖面表现为一强间断波阵面前沿(峰值)及随后的呈指数衰减的波尾。从这里可以定量地理解总质量 M 在应力波传播过程中所扮演的作用：撞击一开始($t=0$)的初始最大撞击力取决于撞击速度和波阻抗，与 M 无关；但此后通过时间相关的无量纲质量因子 $R_m(=\rho_0C_{we}At/M)$，总质量 M 对于应力波剖面指数衰减的快慢有影

响,但随时间其影响又逐渐减弱。

对于刚度 K 的影响也有必要作点补充讨论。式(4)和式(6)都表明,结构刚度愈大,撞击力愈大。基于这一分析,人们已经愈来愈倾向于设计建造“柔性”防护装置。但怎么来评价防护装置的柔性呢?是不是具有一定结构柔度的防护装置都是“柔性”防护装置呢?都能降低撞击力呢?对此,我们从基于应力波理论的式(6)出发来评价:

(1) 首先,就船撞力的冲击动力学分析而言,柔性防护装置的“柔度”应该更严格地理解为“结构广义波阻抗 R_w”,或简称为“冲击柔度”,而并非一般结构静力学意义上的柔度($1/K$)。这样,“柔性防护装置”实际上应该指“结构广义波阻抗 R_w”低的防撞装置;

(2) 其次,“结构广义波阻抗 R_w”的高低是相对而言的,严格地说,只有防护装置的“结构广义波阻抗”R_{ws}小于船的“结构广义波阻抗”R_{wb}时,才能发挥降低撞击力的作用;

(3) 再次,结构广义波阻抗包含的有关材料参数都应该是计及应变率效应的,即指高应变率下的“结构动态广义波阻抗”。

强调这三点,不仅有利于正确认识和科学设计“柔性”防护装置,同时也是对今后柔性防护装置(包括其元件)进一步研制发展提出的新挑战。

特别应该指出,式(6)是为了说明应力波效应而把船舶简化为“均质等截面杆”时得出的理论解,式中的广义波阻抗 $R_w(=\rho_0 C_0 A_0)$ 所包含的 $\rho_0 C_0$ 取决于材料特性,而 A_0 反映了结构特性。实际的船舶结构要复杂得多,如何确定实际船舶在冲击载荷下等效的“结构广义波阻抗”,是一个设计师们面临的新课题。对于给定的船型,在采用计及应力波效应的动态数值模拟计算时,已经隐式地包含了船舶“等效结构广义波阻抗”的分析。目前尚未见到为改进船舶抗撞功能而主动对其“等效结构广义波阻抗”进行分析研究和设计的报道,这应是一个有待深入研究的新课题。

综上所述,在应力波传播起主导作用的船桥撞击过程中,撞击一开始的峰值撞击力主要取决于撞击速度 v 和动态结构广义波阻抗 R_w,船的总质量(重量)则随着应力波的传播和相互作用而逐渐产生影响。为降低船撞力,应该采用以低于船的“结构动态广义波阻抗 R_w”为特征的“柔性防护装置”。

2 影响船桥相撞过程中能量交换的主要因素

从能量/动量交换的角度看,船桥相撞的过程是一个船与桥在短历时内进行能量/动量传递和交换的动力学过程。

按照传统的弹性系统准静态力学分析,不论是我国公路规范公式(1)还是铁路规范公式(2),实质上都如式(4a)所示那样,把船桥相撞的动量/能量交换关系归结为船的总动能($Mv^2/2$)转化为撞击力所做的功($FU/2$),而相应的能量守恒关系则表现为:船的总动能最终转化为船和桥的总变形能(内能)。以 50 000 t 船舶为例,如果船速以 4 m/s 计,则相应的总动能高达约 300 MJ。对于这么巨大的动能,如果其全部或大部分要由被撞桥梁的局部受损区在短历时内来承受,又不至于导致安全事故,那无疑是一个极其严峻的挑战!

从冲击动力学的观点来分析这一能量/动量交换关系时，与上述的准静态力学分析相区别，应强调以下两点动力学效应。

(1) 其一是：能量传递和交换不是整体结构在瞬时立即完成的，而是通过应力波的传播过程逐渐发生的，具体的能量转换形式则需要考察跨过波阵面的能量守恒关系，并视不同材料和结构特性而异。

(2) 其二是：没有理由预先限定撞击的终态必定对应于“船的总动能最终转化为船和桥的总变形能（内能）”；恰恰相反，既然这是一个经由应力波传播进行能量交换的过程，我们可以期望或设法在交换了总撞击能量中尽可能低的百分比后就能结束（脱离）撞击。这从根本上对于船和桥的安全防护都将是极有利的。下面对这两点分别作进一步分析。

首先应该强调，式(1)和式(2)等准静态公式都已暗中假定船的总质量 M 作为整体参与了能量交换，完全忽略了时间相关的波传播过程。事实上，一旦考虑到波传播过程[4]，不论是船还是桥，都不是立即整体地参与到能量交换中去的（对照式(7)中的 $m_t(=\rho_0 C_{we} A t)$），而只是波阵面后方的那部分质量参与了动量/能量交换，波阵面前方的那部分质量仍然保持其初始状态。换句话说，只有随着应力波向更远范围的传播，参与到能量交换的质量才随之增加。容易理解，波速 C 愈快，参与能量交换的质量范围就愈大，而波速（$C=\sqrt{\dfrac{1}{r_0}\dfrac{\mathrm{d}s}{\mathrm{d}e}}$）快慢则取决于材料动态特性[4]。所以，从冲击动力学的角度来看，撞击过程中能量/动量的吸收和转换与应力波效应和材料应变率效应密切相关。

具体地说，当经由应力波以波速 D 传播而发生能量交换时，应该满足如下的跨过波阵面的能量守恒条件（见参考文献[4]的式(2-61)和式(2-62)）[4]：

$$\mp\Delta(\sigma v)=\rho_0 D\Delta e+\frac{1}{2}\rho_0 D\Delta(v^2) \tag{8a}$$

$$\rho_0\Delta e=\frac{1}{2}(\sigma^-+\sigma^+)(\varepsilon^--\varepsilon^+) \tag{8b}$$

此处应力 σ 以拉为正，质点速度 v 以坐标正向为正，e 是材料单位质量的内能（或 $\rho_0 e$ 是单位体积的内能），Δ 表示跨过波阵面的相关量的差值，并以上标 - 和 + 分别表示波阵面前方和后方的各量。式(8a)等号左边的负号对应于右行波，正号对应于左行波。式(8a)的物理意义是：在应力波以波速 D 传播的过程中，当波阵面在 $\mathrm{d}t$ 时间传播过 $\mathrm{d}X(=D\mathrm{d}t)$ 距离的质量时，应力 σ 所做的功转化为两部分能量：内能（即变形能）和动能（正是动能部分在准静态分析中被忽略了）；而式(8b)的物理意义是：内能即变形能。

为方便计，下面讨论波阵面前方处于静止的零应力状态（$\sigma^+=v^+=\varepsilon^+=e^+=0$）的情况，则式(8)化为：

$$\mp\sigma^- v^-=\rho_0 De^-+\frac{1}{2}\rho_0 D(v^-)^2=\frac{1}{2}D\sigma^-\varepsilon^-+\frac{1}{2}\rho_0 D(v^-)^2 \tag{9a}$$

$$\rho_0 e^- = \frac{1}{2}\sigma^- \varepsilon^- \tag{9b}$$

对于线弹性系统，弹性波速 $D = C_e = (E/\rho_0)^{1/2}$。当把跨过波阵面的动量守恒条件 $\sigma^- = \mp \rho_0 C_e v^-$ 和连续性条件 $v^- = \mp C_e e^-$ 分别代入式(9a)等号右边动能项中的$(v^-)^2$，即可证明式(9a)中的动能项刚好等于内能项[8,9]，即：

$$\frac{1}{2}\rho_0 C_e (v^-)^2 = \frac{1}{2}(-\sigma^-)(-C_e \varepsilon^-) = \frac{1}{2}C_e \sigma^- \varepsilon^- \tag{10}$$

换句话说，如图 1 所示，由波阵面扫过的那部分质量所吸收的总能量中，动能形式和内能形式的能量相等，各占总能量的一半。在传统的准静态分析中，认为撞击力所做的功都转化为变形能(内能)，而没有考虑到不可忽略的、与内能等量的动能，这正是用准静态分析来研究冲击动力学动态问题中的能量交换时之不足之处。

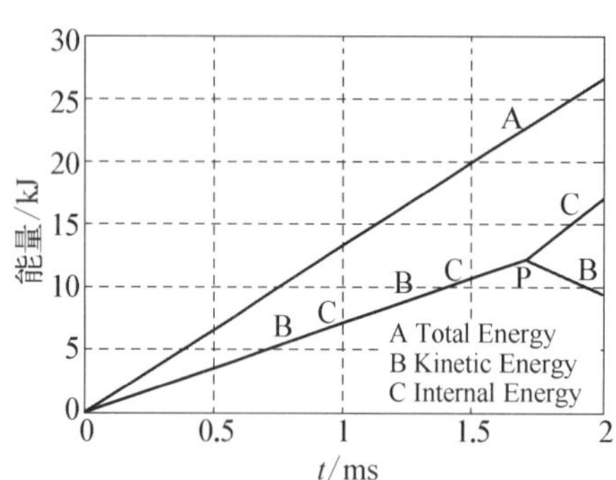

图 1　跨过弹性波波阵面的能量分配随时间的变化

Fig. 1　Energy allocation across the elastic wave front changes with the time

图 1 中的 P 点对应于弹性波传播到达固定端，由于固定端边界条件对应于位移和质点速度为零，受此条件的约束，动能被释放而转化为变形能。此后，随着反射波在固定端的反射传播，动能随时间进一步减少，而变形能则随时间进一步增大。

对于弹性-线性硬化塑性情况，设弹性模量为 E 和塑性线性硬化模量为 $E_p (\ll E)$。撞击引起的应力波将“分裂”成两部分[4]：以较快的弹性波速 $C_e (= (E/\rho_0)^{1/2})$ 传播的弹性前驱波，和后随的以较慢塑性波速 $C_p (= (E_p/\rho_0)^{1/2} \ll C_e)$ 传播的塑性波。对于弹性前驱波，如前所述，动能和内能各占总吸收能量的一半。对于后随的塑性波，经过与推导式(10)相类似于的分析和数学运算后可以发现[9,10]，由于塑性变形的不可逆性，塑性波的比内能$(\rho_0 e^-)_p$不再与塑性波的动能$(\rho_0 (v^-)^2/2)_p$相等，其差值为：

$$(\rho_0 e^-)_p - \left(\frac{1}{2}\rho_0 (v^-)^2\right)_p = (1 - C_{wp}/C_{we})\sigma_y (\varepsilon - \varepsilon_Y) > 0 \tag{11}$$

可见通过塑性波传播进行能量传递时，所吸收的总能量中内能(变形能)部分大于动能部分，内能(变形能)部分中包括可恢复的弹性应变能和不可恢复(耗散)的塑性应变能。

应该强调：对于具有弹塑性特征的大多数金属材料，如上所述，撞击引起的应力波将“分裂”成以较快的弹性波速 $C_e (= (E/\rho_0)^{1/2})$ 传播的弹性前驱波，以及后随的以较慢塑性波速 $C_p (= (E_p/\rho_0)^{1/2} \ll C_e)$ 传播的塑性波。由于塑性波速通常比弹性波速小一个量级，撞击过程结束时塑性波到达的区域有限，这就是为什么撞击造成的塑性区常常集中在高度局域化的小范围。然而,如果一个防撞装置只有局域化的小范围发挥耗能作用,不论从技术角度,还是从经济角度,都是不可取的。显然,一个科学而经济的防撞设计应该追求防撞装置发挥整体的吸能/耗能作用。这时不仅防撞装置整体起到了吸能/耗能作用,而且还起到了把局域化的高强度集中撞击力转化为较弱的分布载荷的作用。

从以上分析可见,任一防撞装置的能量吸收功能中,一般包含可恢复能量和不可恢复能量(耗能)。如果吸收的全部是弹性的可恢复能量,能量形式只会随着具体边界条件而转化,而不会有任何耗散。例如当边界条件为零应力条件(自由端)时,可逆变形能将被释放而转化为动能。显然,任一高效的防撞装置,不仅应该起到降低撞击力的作用,把较强的集中撞击力转化为较弱的分布载荷,而且应该让防撞装置整体(而不是局域化范围)起到耗散撞击能量的作用,从而能够通过防撞装置尽可能地减少传递给桥梁的撞击能量。

其实,如本节一开头所说,更为重要的是:船桥相撞时应尽最大可能使船和桥及早脱离接触,以尽可能减少撞击过程所交换的能量,此乃保护船桥安全的上上之策。犹如坦克装甲板设计成能使“反坦克弹”发生迅速“滑弹”那样,如果能在船桥相撞时让船舶尽可能早地滑离防撞装置,从而使得船舶总动能中尽可能少的百分比参与撞击过程的能量交换,应该成为我们的追求目标。还应该注意,船舶滑离防撞装置的过程在冲击动力学分析上相当于处理具有移动冲击载荷边界条件的复杂问题,使得应力波效应扮演主导作用的历时进一步延长而更加不可忽略。

图2给出这样的一个已应用于广东湛江海湾大桥的实例[11,12]。该柔性耗能防撞装置以钢丝绳防撞圈为主要元件,其外钢围在迎撞面的一侧设计成90度夹角的楔形结构,使得船轴线与外钢围迎撞面的碰撞角 ϕ 为45度夹角。由于撞击力的方向一般不通过船的质心,必然对船施加了一个力矩,从而促使船的转动而改变航行方向,沿着外钢围滑开。动态数值计算表明:在大约时间 $t=4.4$ s时,撞击力 $F(t)$ 几乎降为零,表明船与防撞装置脱离,撞击完全结束。

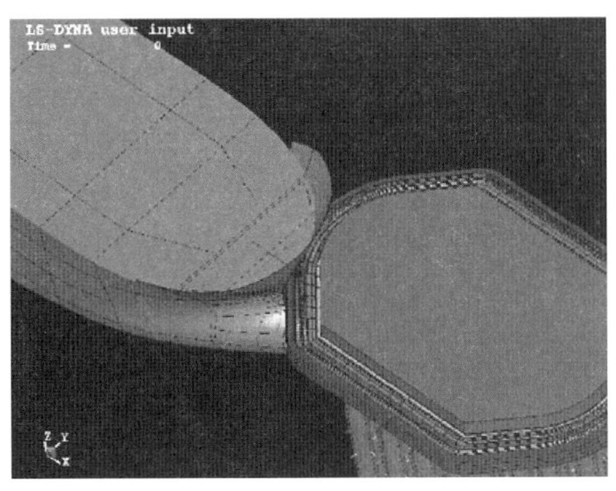

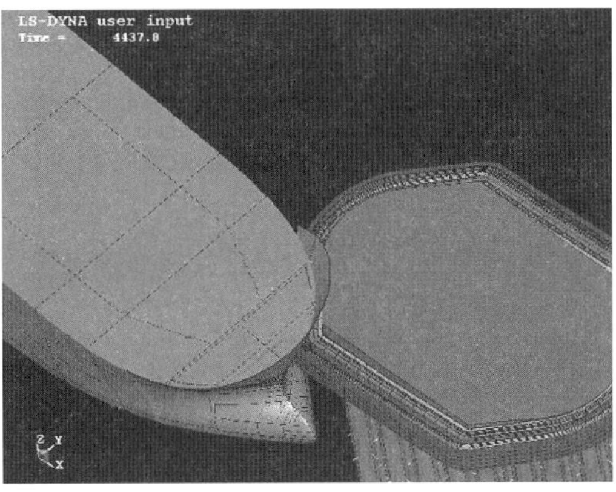

图2 撞击角 $\phi=45°$时船和桥墩相对位置:(左)撞击开始($t=0$),(右)撞击结束($t=4.4$ s)

Fig. 2 Ship-bridge collision in the case of $\phi=45°$: showing the relative position of ship and pier (left) at the beginning ($t=0$) of collision and (right) at $t=4.4$ s indicating the ship turned-away

相应地，撞击过程中系统的能量分配及其随时间的变化如图 3 所示。图中曲线 C 代表系统的总能量（撞击前的船舶总动能），曲线 A 代表系统的动能，曲线 B 代表系统的内能（变形能）。显然，在撞击过程中船舶的动能减少，转变为系统的动能和变形能，其中，大部分转换为船和防撞装置的变形能（曲线 B），另一部分转变为曲线 D 所代表的滑动能。A、B、D 三曲线之和与 C 曲线之差反映了计算中的沙漏能，在本例中几乎可以忽略不计。

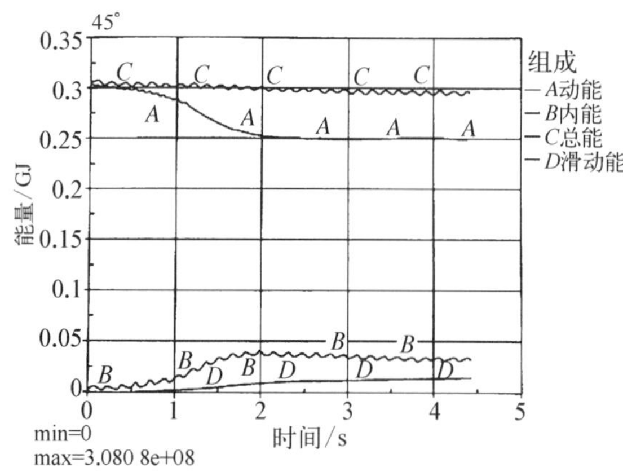

图 3　撞击角 $\phi=45°$ 时系统能量-时间曲线：A—动能，B—内能（变形能），C—总能，D—滑动能

Fig. 3　Curves of energy vs. time calculated in the case of $\phi=45°$: curve A—kinetic energy, B—internal (deformation) energy, C—total energy and D—sliding energy

本例表明，采用这一新型柔性耗能防撞装置后，船舶动能在撞击前后的变化不大（约 50 MJ），仅占船舶总动能（307 MJ）的约 16%。这意味着船在转向并脱离碰撞后把大部分冲击能量以剩余动能形式带走了（占船舶初始动能的 80% 以上）。这是避免船桥两败俱伤的关键所在。对变形能的具体计算还表明，其中防撞装置所吸收的达到约 22 MJ，船舶变形所吸收的达到约 8.5 MJ，分别占船舶初始动能的 7.2% 和 2.8% 左右，都不高，且前者大于后者，说明防撞装置发挥了“吸能/耗能器”的作用，既保护了桥，也保护了船舶免遭严重破坏。

从以上分析可见，撞击过程中的能量交换的形式和多少以及参与能量转换的质量的多少，都随波传播过程而变化发展。撞击力所做的功，通过应力波传播通常转化为内能（变形能）与动能之和，其可逆部分的能量形式视反射边界条件的不同可相互转换；而变形能中的不可逆部分愈高，防撞装置愈能发挥整体吸能/耗能作用，则愈有利于防撞装置发挥缓冲耗能作用。在船桥相撞过程中如何让船舶尽可能早地滑离防撞装置，带走尽可能多的剩余动能，从而尽可能地减少撞击能量交换，乃是防撞装置设计的关键性要点之一。

3　黏性耗散在船桥相撞过程中的作用

从上一节能量转换的角度来看，弹性系统在撞击过程中只吸收能量而并不耗散能量，其所吸收的能量都是可恢复的。由此不难想象，如果防护装置具备耗能特性，能经由防护装置耗散掉尽可能多的冲击能量，显然更有利于桥梁和船舶的安全。

就耗能类型而言，通常可划分为塑性耗能和黏性耗能两类。前者通过结构/材料的不可逆塑性变形起到耗能作用，后者则通过结构/材料的不可逆黏性流动起到耗能作用。

由钢结构为主组成的弹塑性防撞装置（如目前常用的钢套箱结构等）是塑性耗能防

撞装置的典型代表。对于这类耗能防撞装置,有以下三点值得注意:

(1) 首先,由于钢的波阻抗高,并且只有在超过屈服强度的高载荷下才会发生塑性耗能,所以从冲击动力学角度看,难以实现真正的低撞击力,即相对于船舶结构而言的低波阻抗意义上的“柔性防撞”。

(2) 其次,钢的塑性波速通常比其弹性波速小一个量级,因此钢结构防撞装置在经受船撞时,容易形成高度局域化的塑性变形区,不能充分发挥整个防撞装置的作用。尤其是一旦形成高度局域化的塑性变形撞击区,船头容易镶住在局部撞击区而难以滑离,于是船舶总动能将自始至终、百分之百地参与撞击过程的能量交换,这对船桥安全防护是最不利的。

(3) 再次,塑性耗能伴有不可逆的塑性残余变形,防撞装置每经受一次撞击就要进行修复,更换已发生残余变形的元件,不能重复使用。

鉴于塑性耗能防撞装置上述三点先天性的不足之处,人们遂倾向于探索基于不可逆黏性流动的黏性耗能防撞装置。那么黏性流动耗能机制对于船桥相撞过程的应力波传播和相应的能量交换有什么样的影响呢?

我们先来考察一下黏性耗能特性对于应力波传播和撞击力的影响。为了便于从原理上对黏性效应加以揭示和说明,考虑一个简化的“短弹性杆 B_s-黏弹性阻尼层 B_d-长弹性杆 B_b”组成的具有黏性耗散的非弹性系统,即短杆 B_s 以速度 v 撞击前端带有阻尼层 B_d 的长杆 B_b,如图 4 所示。黏弹性阻尼层的动态力学响应采用图 4(b)所示的三单元黏弹性模型来描述,即由一个弹性模量为 E 的弹簧元件和一个 Maxwell 元件并联组成,后者由弹性模量为 E_M 的弹簧元件和松弛时间为 θ_M 的黏壶元件串联组成。相应的黏弹性本构关系由下式描述[4]:

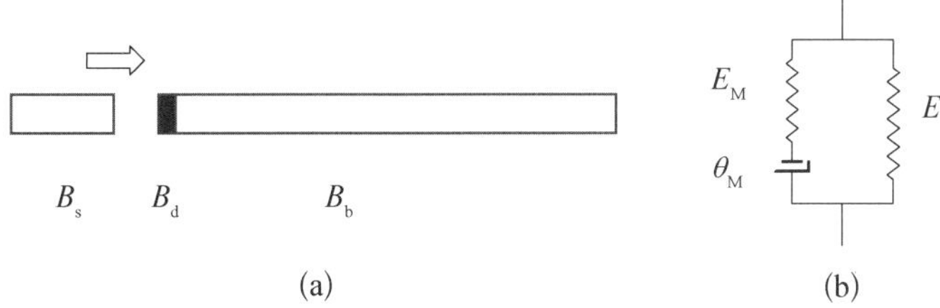

图 4　黏弹性耗能系统示意图

Fig. 4　Schematic of a visco-elastic energy-dissipating system

(a) 杆-阻尼层-杆的撞击系统,(b) 三单元黏弹性模型

(a) a bar-damping layer-bar impact system,

(b) a three-elements visco-elastic model

$$\sigma = E_{\varepsilon} + E_M \int_0^t \varepsilon \exp\left(-\frac{t-\tau}{\theta_M}\right) d\tau \tag{12a}$$

或其微分形式:

$$\frac{\partial \varepsilon}{\partial t} - \frac{1}{E_a + E_M}\frac{\partial \sigma}{\partial t} + \frac{E_a \varepsilon}{(E_a + E_M)\theta_M} - \frac{\sigma}{(E_a + E_M)\theta_M} = 0 \tag{12b}$$

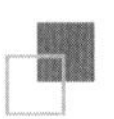

下面我们采用动态 LS - DYNA 数值计算对相关的应力波传播特性和撞击力进行分析。

数值计算中,钢制有限长杆 B_s 的有关材料参数取为：密度 $\rho_0 = 7.85 \times 10^3$ kg/m^3，弹性模量 $E = 210$ GPa，泊松比 $v = 0.3$ 因而波速 $C_{we} = 5.17$ km/s 及波阻抗 $\rho_0 C_{we} = 40.6$ MPa · s/m。杆 B_b 的材料设为三种：(a) 刚体($\rho_0 C_e = \infty$)，(b) 与撞击杆 B_s 相同的钢，(c) 混凝土，有关材料参数为 $\rho_0 = 2.50 \times 10^3$ kg/m^3，$E = 25$ GPa，$v = 0.17$，因而 $C_e = 3.16$ km/s 及 $\rho_0 C_e = 7.9$ MPa · s/m。黏弹性阻尼层的有关材料参数则参照我们过去对于有机玻璃动态力学特性的实验研究结果[4]，取为密度 $\rho_0 = 1.19 \times 10^3$ kg/m^3。三单元黏弹性模型中并联弹簧的弹性模量 $E = 2.94$ GPa，并联 Maxwell 元件的串联弹簧 $E_M = 3.07$ GPa，而串联黏壶的松弛时间 $\theta_M = 95.4$ μs，从而有特征波速 $C_w = ((E + E_M)/\rho_0)^{1/2} = 2.25$ km/s 以及瞬时波阻抗 $\rho_0 C_w = 2.68$ MPa · s/m。这时，钢杆 B_s 波阻抗与黏弹性阻尼层波阻抗之比 $n_{s-d} = 15.1$。此值愈高意味着黏弹性阻尼层的冲击柔性愈低，而其耗散特性则主要由黏弹性松弛时间 θ_M 来刻画，这可以通过以下的算例来理解。

撞击杆 B_s 与黏弹性阻尼层 B_d 撞击界面处撞击力的计算结果汇总在图 5a 中，而相应的没有黏弹性阻尼层时的计算结果则给出在图 5b 中(曲线 1,2,3)，以供比较。

由图 5 可见以下几点主要结果：

(1) 不论有没有黏弹性耗能阻尼层，撞击力的高低依赖于杆 B_s 与杆 B_b 的波阻抗之比，在上述三种不同情况中，以 B_b 为刚性材料时为最高，而以 B_b 为混凝土材料为最低。这意味着桥墩的波阻抗低，则撞击应力就低。此结果与本文第 1 节的分析一致。

(2) 不论上述 B_b 三种不同情况中的哪一种，添加了低波阻抗的黏弹性耗能阻尼层后，撞击应力都显著地、甚至于成倍地降低。

(3) 伴随着黏性能量耗散，不论是加载波还是卸载波，都不再像无黏弹性耗能阻尼层的弹性波那样(图 5b 中曲线 1,2,3)显示无缓冲的“瞬态响应”，而显示一种低应力下伴随阻尼耗散的缓冲迟滞过程，从而使低应力下的撞击历时大大延长。在图 5b 中，黏性效应导致的应力波作用历时延长了近一个量级，使得应力波传播效应更加不可忽略。这种在应力波传播过程中的缓冲迟滞效应对于船桥相撞而言，从开始撞击到随后的脱离撞击都将起到十分有益的缓冲作用。

上述原理性分析说明，采用低波阻抗黏性耗能防护装置既可以明显降低撞击力，同时还可以缓冲撞击过程、延长撞击历时。不难想象，只要在防撞装置设计中能使船偏离航向，那么在低撞击力下延长撞击历时将给船舶提供足够时间转变其航行方向，从而创造条件让船舶带走尽可能多的剩余动能，更加有利于桥梁和船舶的安全。

下面我们再来考察一下黏性耗能特性对于撞击能量转换与分配的影响。

由于黏弹性波传播的复杂性，其传播过程中的能量转换与分配已难以用类似于式(10)和式(11)那样的解析式来描述。下面借助于一个实例的数值计算来分析。考虑一长为 3 米的黏弹性杆，一端受恒速 v 撞击，另一端为固定端(位移和质点速度为零)。材料参数与前面讨论图 4 中黏弹性阻尼层 B_d 时所采用的相同。

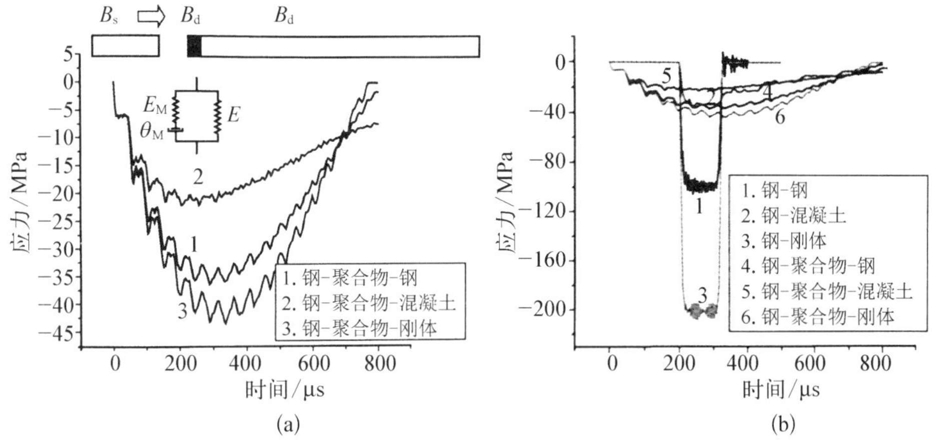

图 5　撞击应力的计算结果

Fig. 5　Impact stresses calculated

（a）三种不同情况下的撞击力，即杆 B_b 材料分别为(1)钢，(2)混凝土和(3)刚体；
（b）具有黏弹性耗能阻尼层时和没有黏弹性耗能阻尼层时上述三种情况计算结果的比较
（a）Impact stresses calculated for three cases of bar B_b material：(1) steel，(2) concrete and (3) rigid.
（b）Comparisons of impact stresses calculated with and without visco-elastic damping layer

图 6 给出了通过黏弹性波传播所吸收的总能量中内能与动能的分配。

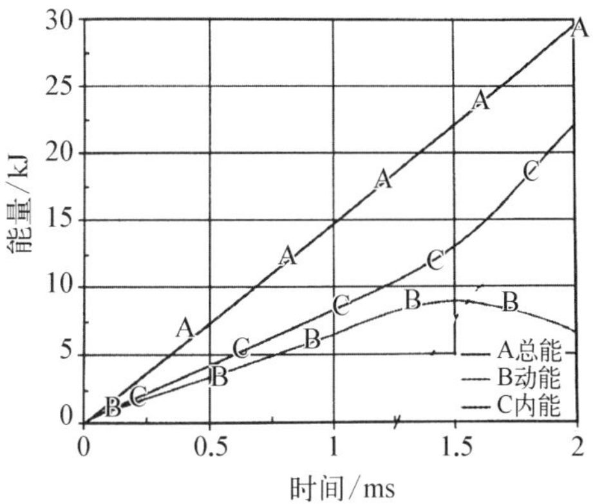

图 6　黏弹性波能量分配计算结果

Fig. 6　Energy allocation calculated for visco-elastic waves

如令此黏弹性材料的松弛时间 $\theta_M = \infty$，就化为相应的弹性波问题，那就是图 5 所示结果。对两者进行对比，可看到黏弹性波与弹性波在能量转换与分配中的差别。

由图可见，与弹性波时内能总等于动能(图 5)的情况不同，在黏弹性材料的情况下，黏弹性杆所吸收的总能量中内能(曲线 C)大于动能(曲线 B)，并且由于耗散特性，其差别随时间增加。在本算例中，时间约为 1.7 ms 时入射波到达固定端。受到固定端位移和质点速度为零的约束，这时动能开始释放并转化为内能。此后动能随时间继续减少，而内能随时间进一步增大。这是一种由于固定端边界条件所引起的能量形式的内部转换。

在分析了黏性耗能对于撞击力和撞击能量转换的影响之后，现在可以设想一下如下两种不同情况的物理图像：一条船分别撞击一个弹簧和一个图 4b 所示黏弹性元件。当撞击在弹簧元件上时，撞击力的时程曲线将如图 5b 中的曲线 1,2,3 所示那样，加载和卸载都呈现无延迟的瞬时响应，而且卸载后，弹簧吸收的能量没有耗损，会全部释放。但当撞击黏弹性元件时，撞击力的时程曲线将如图 5a 所示那样，加载和卸载都呈现延迟的非瞬时响应(见图5b中的对比),特别是即使载荷开始卸降了,变形还会继续;并且由于在加-卸载过程中有能量耗损,黏壶阻尼器所吸收的能量在卸载后只会释放一部分。人如果跟着船舶一起撞击这两种元件,在撞击弹簧元件时会有一种突发的冲击感,而在撞击黏壶阻尼器时则会有一种延迟的缓冲感。这种缓冲效应不仅有利于降低和缓冲船桥相撞开始时的撞击力,而且有利于缓冲船桥脱离撞击时的卸载载荷,以免船舶转头太快时有可能造成船尾对桥的二次撞击。

还应该指出,黏性耗能防撞装置与塑性耗能防撞装置相比,由于黏弹性波的传播速度与弹性波相同,有助于防撞装置整体发挥耗能作用;而塑性波的传播速度比弹性波小一个量级,容易形成高度局域化的塑性变形区,不利于发挥防撞装置的整体耗能作用。

当然,由于黏弹性波传播的应变率相关性,黏性耗能防撞装置的设计远比无黏性防撞装置复杂得多。黏性效应显著与否主要与刻画冲击条件下黏性效应的"高频松弛时间"θ_2的数值大小有关,见式(12)。事实上,表征黏弹性材料黏性特性的任一松弛时间参数$\theta_j(j=1, 2, 3\cdots)$,各自都只对应一个有效的应变率(或时间)影响区,此"有效影响区"不论以时间表示还是以应变率表示,均为大约4.5个量级[4]。与此相对应地,就黏弹性波的传播而言,存在一个由θ_2起主要作用的,或即以"有效传播时间" $t_{eff} = \theta_2$,或"有效传播距离" $X_{eff} = C_v\theta_{22}$ 占统治地位的辖区。超出这一"有效传播时间"或"有效传播距离"占统治地位的辖区,θ_2就不再发挥显著的影响作用。因此,如果防撞装置的等效松弛时间选择得不适当,甚至于可能在某些情况下,设计者会在数值计算中发现黏性耗能不大,黏性缓冲效应不明显。这时就要调整防撞装置的等效松弛时间。如何调整和制造出具有不同松弛特性的防撞装置,是今后需要进一步研究解决的课题。

综合以上分析可知,船撞桥防护装置的设计应该建立在低波阻抗意义上的冲击柔性和缓冲撞击过程意义上的黏性耗能的设计理念上。一方面可以降低船撞力,另一方面由于黏性耗能机制可以缓冲撞击过程、延长撞击历时,有助于防撞装置发挥整体作用。并为船舶在低应力下转向滑离创造条件,从而带走尽可能多的剩余动能。达到既保护桥又保护船,并尽可能使防护装置能够反复使用的目的。图2所示的以钢丝绳防撞圈为主要元件的柔性耗能防撞装置正是按照这一防撞理念研发的工程应用的实例。实船撞击试验证实了这一防撞理念是正确和有效的[13]。

4 总结

对于船桥撞击过程中相关的几个冲击动力学论题进行了分析,得出以下几点主要结论:

(1) 在应力波传播起主导作用的船桥撞击过程中,撞击一开始的峰值撞击力主要取决于撞击速度v和结构动态广义波阻抗R_w,船的总质量则随着应力波的传播和相互作用而逐渐产生影响。为降低船撞力,应该采用以低于船的"结构动态广义波阻抗R_w"为特征的"柔性防护装置"。

(2) 在船桥撞击的能量交换过程中,其能量交换的形式和多少以及参与能量转换的质量的多少,都随波传播过程而变化发展。撞击力所做的功,通过应力波传播而转化为内能(变形能)与动能之和,其可逆部分的能量形式视反射边界条件的不同可相互转换;而变形能中的不可逆部分愈高,防撞装置发挥的整体作用愈大,则愈有利于防撞装置发挥缓冲耗能作用。在船桥相撞过程中如何让船舶尽可能早地滑离防撞装置,带走尽可能多的剩余动能,从而尽可能地减少撞击能量交换,应是防撞装置设计的关键性要点。

(3) 兼备柔性和黏性耗能特性的防护装置,一方面可以降低船撞力,另一方面黏性耗能机制可以缓冲撞击过程和延长撞击历时。这既有助于让防撞装置发挥整体作用,达到整体发挥吸能/耗能作用,并把较强的撞击集中力转化为较弱的分布载荷;又为船舶在低应力下转向滑离创造条件,从而带走尽可能多的剩余动能。达到既保护桥又保护船,并尽可能使防护装置能够反复使用的目的。

(4) 概而括之,船撞桥防护装置的设计应该建立在如下的科学设计理念上:(i) 低波阻抗意义上的冲击柔性,(ii) 缓冲撞击过程意义上的黏性耗能,(iii) 防撞装置能及早发挥整体作用,化撞击集中力为分布载荷,以及(iv) 让船尽早滑离而带走尽量多的剩余动能。图2所示的以钢丝绳防撞圈为主要元件的柔性耗能防撞装置正是这一防撞理念的工程应用实例,其有效性已为多年的工程实践和大型实船撞击试验证实。

参 考 文 献

[1] Jones N. Structural Aspects of Ship Collisions[C]. In Jones N and Wierzbicki T, Editors. Structural Crashworthiness. Butterworths Publishers, London and Boston, 1983. pp. 308 - 337.

[2] 陈国虞,王礼立. 船撞桥及其防御[M]. 北京: 中国铁道出版社,2006.

[3] 陈国虞,王礼立,杨黎明,陈明栋. 桥梁防撞理论和防撞设施设计[M]. 北京: 人民交通出版社,2013.

[4] 王礼立. 应力波基础[M],第二版. 北京: 国防工业出版社出版,2005.

[5] 中华人民共和国交通部. 公路桥涵设计通用规范[S](JTG D60—2004),2004.

[6] 中华人民共和国铁道部. 铁路桥涵设计基本规范[S](TB10002.1—2005),2005.

[7] AASHTO. Guide Specifications and Commentary for Vessel Collision Design of Highway Bridges. American Association of State Highway and Transportation Official, Washington D. C., 2009.

[8] Vrouwenvelder A C W M, Design for Ship Impact According to Eurocode 1, Part 2.7, Ship Collision Analysis. Rotterdam: A A Balkema, 1998: 123 - 134.

[9] 王礼立,杨黎明,陈国虞,陆宗林. 船桥相撞时撞击力和能量转换的冲击动力学分析,武汉: 第二十届全国桥梁学术会议论文集(下),2012: 921 - 935.

[10] Lili Wang, Liming Yang, Changgang Tang, Zhongwei Zhang, Guoyu Chen and Zonglin LU, On the Impact Force and Energy Transformation During Ship-Bridge Collisions, International Journal of Protective Structures, v. 3, No. 1 (2012), 105 - 120.

[11] 王礼立,张忠伟,黄德进,姚小虎,陈国虞. 船撞桥的钢丝绳圈柔性防撞装置的冲击动力学分析. 见: 洪友士. 应用力学进展——祝贺郑哲敏先生八十华诞. 北京: 科学出版社,2004: 172 - 180.

[12] Wang Lili, Yang Liming, Huang Dejin, Zhang Zhongwei and Chen Guoyu. An Impact Dynamics Analysis

on a New Crashworthy Device against Ship-Bridge Collision, *International Journal of Impact Engineering*, 2008, 35(8): 895 - 904.

[13] 杨黎明,吕忠达,王礼立,陈国虞,陆宗林. 桥梁抗船撞柔性防护方法及实船撞击实验,武汉：第二十届全国桥梁学术会议论文集(下),2012: 948 - 954.

发表于：振动与冲击,2015(3): 14 - 22.

Published at: Journal of Vibration and Shock, 2015(3): 14 - 22.

CCES Proceeding of the 17th symposium of bridges Beijing 2006.

计算船撞力选择撞击速度时考虑墩位流速的方法

The method of determine the force of the ship collision with the pier on consider with the water flow velocity at every piers

陈国虞[1]　陈明栋[2]　郑丹[2]

（1. 上海海洋钢结构研究所，上海，201204；2. 重庆交通大学，重庆，400074）

CHEN Guoyu[1], CHEN Mingdong[2], ZHENG Dan[2]

（1. Shanghai Marine Steel and Structure Reseach Institute;
2. Chongqing Jiaotong University）

摘　要　进行桥墩防撞设计时，船舶撞击速度是计算船撞力的重要参数之一。它直接影响到船撞力的大小和桥梁的设防标准。在分析各国船舶撞击桥墩的速度选取方法的基础上，研究了实际发生船撞时的速度和船舶偏航时船撞速度沿横向的变化趋势，指出了目前世界各国使用的5种方法存在的不足，提出了考虑船撞速度沿桥轴线方向的分布及船舶意外失速等因素综合影响下的撞击速度的计算方法。通过在某长江铁路大桥船撞研究中的应用实例，说明按照各桥墩所在位置选取的不同撞击速度计算船撞力的方法较为合理，可作为防船撞研究和设计的参考。

关键词　防船撞　船撞力　撞击速度　流速　墩前流速

Abstract: How to select the impact speed is the most important factor to determine the force of the ship collision with the pier. It will directly influence the standard on anti-impact force in the bridge design. In this paper, the existed methods of determining impact speed in all countries and the examined examples of ship collision with pier are analyzed. Based on the limitation of existing method, a new way to determine impact speed is proposed. This can consider the water flow velocity of every pier along bridge axial and other influence of ship accident. Through application in one Yangtze Railway Bridge, the reasonableness of the method is examined, which can provide references for bridge design on river, channel, and also on harbor and estuary.

Keywords: anti-collision, force of the ship collision with the pier, impact speed, water flow velocity, flow velocity in front of the pier

1 引言

进行桥墩防撞设计时,船舶撞击各个桥墩的速度是一个在综合考虑了各种因素之后选取的、用以计算桥墩抵受水平力的强度和防撞装置强度与刚性的重要的参数之一[1-2]。在桥梁可行性研究阶段,撞击速度选择的合理性将直接影响到船撞力计算结果和桥梁防船撞的设防标准。目前,国内、外现有的几种船舶撞击速度计算方法中,有的认为各个桥墩的撞速应按距航道中心距离进行正比折减;有的则认为发生意外船撞时,船舶速度不会降低等。近年来研究发现,以上方法虽计算简便,但速度划分过于单一,其结果代表性较差。而最主要问题是没有结合桥区水域的实际情况分析船撞速度,导致了速度选择不尽合理,其结果直接影响到计算船撞力的大小和桥梁设防标准。本文通过船撞速度计算方法的分析研究,指出美、欧、日三种方法的不足,提出在选用沿桥轴线方向各墩的撞击速度时,应该先求出船撞墩最可能发生的速度,并直接计入水面流速影响的方法。本文并结合某长江铁路大桥防撞研究实例,分析比较了本文推荐的方法选择的船撞速度对船撞力计算结果的影响。

2 现有船撞速度选取方法

2.1 美国高速公路桥梁设计指南的方法[3]

美国(AASHTO)指南中指出,航道上船舶的航行速度应能反映诸如风、水流、能见度、迎面来船以及航道的几何尺度等典型条件。对于选择船只的"典型"航速,该指南规定,船撞速度在航道范围内为正常速度;航道范围以外,船撞速度随桥墩距航道中线的距离而正比下降,即撞速呈线性地降低(见图1),该方法用于天然航道上的桥梁难以反映"美国指南"所述(如风、水流、能见度、迎面来船以及航道的几何尺度等)诸因素:

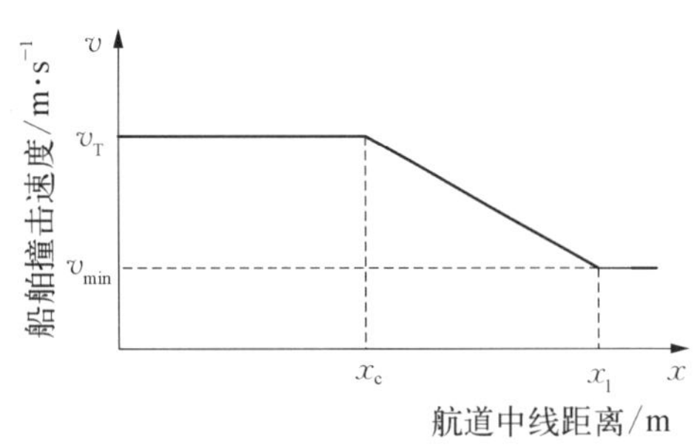

图1 美国(AASHTO)指南选用设计撞击速度分布图

Fig. 1 Design impact velocity profile by AASHTO guide

图中 v 为设计船舶撞击速度(m/s),v_T 代表船舶正常航行速度(m/s),v_{min} 为最小设计撞击速度(m/s)(不得小于桥位的年平均水流速度),x 为至航道中线距离(m),x_c 为航道边缘至航道中心线距离(m),x_l 为航道中心线至3倍船长距离(m)。美国设计指南对船舶撞击速度的选取,主要是依据船舶

实际通过桥区的统计资料。其具体规定是,主航道内船舶撞击速度按正常航行速度选取;主航道以外即偏离航道较远的船舶碰撞桥墩时,航行速度较主航道范围逐渐减小,最小按漂流速度计算。因此,偏航于主航道边缘的船只航速接近于主航道的航速;偏航于3倍船长处的船舶撞击速度,按顺随水漂流速度计算。

目前该方法被我国的深圳湾西部通道桥、南澳大桥等大型桥梁的防撞研究中用来确定船舶撞击速度。但不少专家认为,该方法假设的船撞速度沿航道横向距离航道中线正比降低的假设与船撞桥的实际发生船撞桥的情况并不相符,如美国阿肯色河桥[4-5]、广东九江大桥[6]等桥梁,被撞塌的桥墩都远离航道中线,而船舶与桥墩相撞时船舶航速并未下降。按照该种假设,船舶如偏航到河道边缘的堤岸航速就等于流速,船不会撞堤岸了。众多实例证明,美国指南选择相撞速度方法应用于船舶撞击力计算的正确性和合理性是有待商榷的。

2.2 欧洲规范方法[7]

2006年欧洲(包括英国)颁布BS EN1991－1－7结构规范,制定出了指导船撞速度的选择标准:内河船舶3 m/s,港湾区1.5 m/s;海船5 m/s,港湾区采用2.5 m/s。分析可见,欧洲规范方法规定的是单一速度,难以满足不同航道和不同桥梁船舶撞击分析和设计的需要。

2.3 日本对于船撞桥速度的选用[8,9]

日本学者藤井(Y. Fujii)较早地提出船撞桥墩几何概率模型(1974年)[8],但是在日本桥梁防撞设计中,对船撞墩速度的选取却是各不相同。例如:岩井・聡(Akira Iwai)[9]提出当船通过桥下时,船速应为流速的2倍,因此1988年4月建成通车的濑户跨海大桥,选择的船速为7～8 m/s,远远超过其他方法所得出的速度;但是同在日本,名古屋跨港大桥进港航道的船撞桥墩速度却较小,如表1所示。

表1　名古屋跨港大桥进港航道的船撞桥墩速度选择
Table 1　Design impact velocity of approach channel at Nagoya bridge

速　度	船的航速/(m/s)	船头撞墩速度/(m/s)	船侧撞墩速度/(m/s)
1 000 t船	4.1	2.1	1.4
5 000 t船	1.0	1.0	0.7

从船撞桥墩事故实例可知,当航速为4.1 m/s时,船头撞墩的速度一般会超过2.1 m/s,因此该船撞墩的速度选得偏小。又如岩黑岛桥2号桥墩[8],在航道侧和水流方向均在墩上设置直接式钢丝绳拦阻装置,并在钢丝绳装置两侧各设置多个橡胶碰垫,橡胶碰垫从来预定给慢速靠帮用的(YOKOHAMA公司的橡胶碰垫提供的使用速度为0.3～0.5 m/s)。可见由于缺少统一的规范或指南,日本船撞桥墩速度的选取方法并不一致。

2.4 罗列不同船速计算出的船撞力[10]

这种方法就是罗列出各种航船、各种航速下的船撞力,向桥梁设计方提出多张计算结果表,由桥梁设计方自行选择。如2001年我国嘉兴到慈溪的杭州湾跨海大桥的撞击力标准论证中就采用了该方法。业主拿到这些计算结果还需要委托对口的研究机构有桥梁专业知识的技术人员和船舶运输专业技术人员联合通过可信的研究和论证,得到各种情况下最有代表性的典型船舶和航速,才能选用。

2.5　以偏航开始的线速度作为相撞速度的方法

简称为“失舵不失速”方法。如美国阿肯色河桥[4-5]、广东九江大桥[6]等桥梁,被撞塌的桥墩都远离航道中线,且相撞时船舶航速并未下降。其中美国阿肯色河桥被撞的桥墩距离航道中线为 101.6 m,事后调查,撞桥时驾驶员可能正发眩晕症;广东九江大桥被撞的桥墩距离航道中线为 130 m,桥塌下后螺旋桨继续转动了一段时间,并没有人去关机或减速。

这种航向偏离而航速不减的工况,在研究船撞桥中,称为“失舵不失速”,即船舶舵效失去控制的短时间内(机械或人为的原因),航速并没有下降。桥墩受船舶撞击的线速度维持偏航前的线速度,只是方向有了改变。此方法曾用于湛江海湾大桥防撞计算[11]。

3　航道中心的船舶速度

防撞装置设计时选择的船舶撞击速度是取船舶在航道内正常行驶速度(不是最大速度,是万一发生撞击时最可能的速度)。由于迷航而导致的侧撞应首先考虑风流压偏角。偏航会造成对桥墩的侧撞力加大。事实证明偏航多是非主观原因,所以船机的静水速度不会降低,只是方向改变了;由于驶入航道外面河流边缘,水流速度改变会对船撞墩的速度产生少许影响(下水撞速减少、上水撞速增加)。

首先求出不偏航时航道中心速度的下限,办法是: 统计出长江有桥以来对船舶航行速度的规定(即长江干流关于航行安全的法定文件中对于航速的规定)。共得 10 项,采用编年序,见表 2。

表 2　**长江船舶航行速度规定表**
Table 2　**ship speed regulation table of Yangtze river**

序号	航　段	限速/(km · h^{-1})		文　件　名
		上　行	下　行	
1	武汉长江大桥	≥4	≥14	国务院批准 1963 - 02 - 05
2	九江长江大桥	≥4	顺流转逆流船队能前进	航政监字 79 - 068 号
3	重庆长江大桥	≥4	≥14	重府发 1980 - 57 号
4	南京长江大桥	≥4	顺流转逆流船队能前进	宁政发 1986 - 71 号
5	黄石长江大桥	≥4	≥8(低水位)≥14(高水位)	长督法字 96 - 289 号
6	铜陵长江公路大桥(否则分拖或助航)	≥4 ≥5(洪期)	≥14	长督法字 96 - 290
7	长江桥区水域	≥4	≥12	长海体法 2001 - 484 号

续表

序号	航　段	限速/(km·h⁻¹)		文　件　名
		上　行	下　行	
8	重庆大佛寺长江桥	≥4	≥14	长江海事局 2002 第二号通告
9	长江江苏段(严禁淌航)	≥4	≥4	交海发 2003－171 号
10	忠县长江大桥	≥4	≥14	长江海事局 2005－08－16 通知

由表 2 可以得出以下几点结论。

(1) 航运主管部门对船舶航速规定的目的是要保证船舶有良好的操纵性,所以各年发布的规定中对长江航船只有速度下限的要求,没有上限要求。从驾驶专业得知船舶只要舵叶上有流速,船舶就是有舵效的(这一点也体现在历年颁布的规定中)。规定中对下行的航速是要求舵面上有正向流速,即船速要大于水流速度。

(2) 内河航行法规一般也规定了驳船队的航速,众多规定都有:"顺流转逆流时,拖船(包括推船)的动力应能使驳船队前进"的规定。如果该拖船功率不足,应采取"分拖或助拖措施"(拖船单船速度对防撞力的大小并不起控制因素)。

综上所述,根据船舶驾驶的需要,为保证船舶航行中的可操纵性(主要是舵的可操作性)我国长江航运规定,船舶上行最低航速为 4 km/h,即 1.11 m/s,下行最低航速为 14 km/h,即 3.9 m/s。

其次,根据长江航道中船舶的通常航速观测和调查的结果(见图 2)为:轮船上行航速通常为 12 km/h,即 3.33 m/s;轮船下行航速为 15 km/h,即 4.16 m/s。

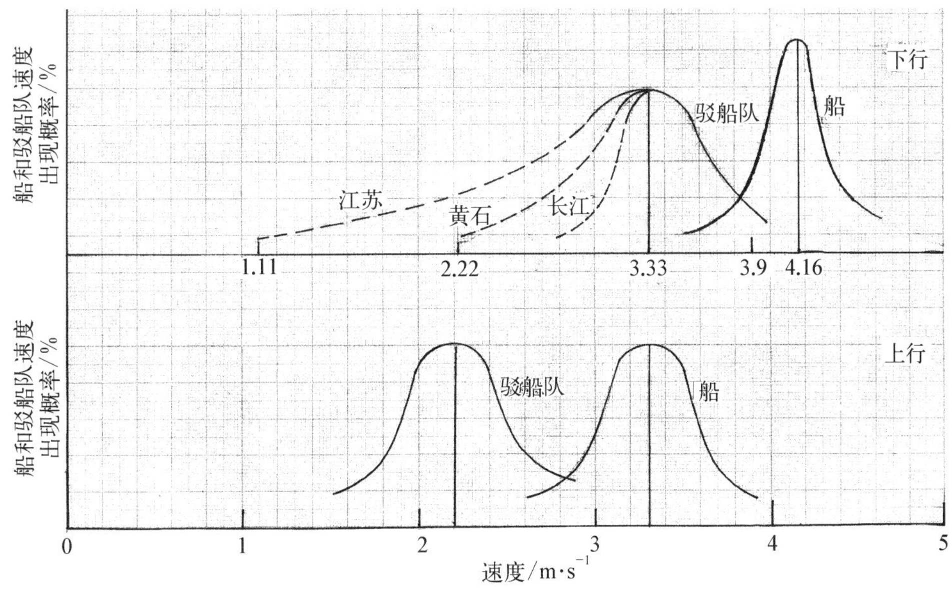

图 2　长江船和驳船队航速分布(观测和调查)

Fig. 2　ships and barges train speed distribution of Yangtze river (observation and survey)

同样,根据航速的调查结果,洪水期间当流速过大,航行管理部门会通知停航或封航,封航前下水船舶的航速会等于5 m/s和大于5 m/s。

船队航行速度比轮船低,上行航速约为8 km/h,即2.22 m/s;下行航速约为12 km/h,即3.33 m/s。

最小、最大速度均不取,选择最可能发生的速度。因此,本桥船对墩的撞击速度选择为4.16 m/s。

4 考虑河道流场综合影响的船撞速度计算方法

综上所述,船撞速度的合理选取对桥梁防船撞设计至关重要。而目前各国船撞速度的计算及选取方法均不够成熟,船撞速度的选取方法存在方法单一、缺乏依据的等问题,难以满足不同航道、不同桥梁船舶撞击分析和设计的需要。

研究认为,发生船撞时船舶的撞击速度应该为代表船舶在经过桥区时的正常航速。要表达船舶在桥区的实际航行速度,应区别船舶在设计航道中的正常航行航速和发生意外偏航后在一定桥孔范围内出现的航速,即应按照各个需要设防桥墩在水域中的分布情况,根据航道流场实际的横向分布来确定船桥碰撞时最可能发生的速度。

通常,诱发船撞的原因除气候条件、操作失误及机械故障等因素外,航道的水流条件(如流速较大时)的影响尤为重要。特别是上游地区的山区河流,河道流速对船撞通常起着至关重要的作用。船舶撞速选取的合理方法应该是将船舶速度分解为静水航速和水流速度,合成的对岸航速就是需要确定的船撞速度。根据船撞桥研究中"失舵不失速"的观点,发生船撞桥时船舶的静水航速可以认为是不改变的,原因是发生事故瞬间内船舶通常来不及减速或停机,船舶还将保持原有动力。但是一般情况下,河道流速在横向(顺桥向)的分布是呈抛物线状,即主航道(主通航孔)区域流速较大,航道边缘及外侧的(辅通航孔)的流速较小。船撞桥墩计算选取速度时,应根据船舶所航行水域的水流速度依次进行调整(折减或增加),得到船舶行驶到各桥墩时不同的航行速度,采用该船撞速度计算船撞力才是合理的。

具体计算法如下。

(1) 根据调查分析方法得到典型船舶在桥区(主通航孔)航行的正常航速,由此作为通航船舶通过桥梁水域的典型速度。

(2) 然后根据实际测量或数值计算方法得到建桥后桥区水域流速沿桥轴线分布数据,计算出桥区水域的流速差值。逐一对各桥墩附近水域的流速进行调整(折减或增加),得到船撞桥的典型航速的分布曲线,即:

$$V(x) = V_0 - v_0 + v(x)$$

式中$V(x)$,桥墩处船舶典型航速;$v(x)$为距离航道中心x处的流速;V_0和v_0分别为桥区正常航速和航道中心的流速。根据以上步骤,便可得到沿桥梁各墩位船撞速度的横向分布。

5 应用实例

5.1 项目简介

某铁路长江大桥桥型为钢桁梁双塔斜拉桥,如图3所示。由于两岸接线高程和通航净高的要求,桥面距常水位高度约达40 m,主塔墩及过渡墩的墩身均在50 m左右,通航水位距承台较高,不利于抵抗船舶撞击[12]。

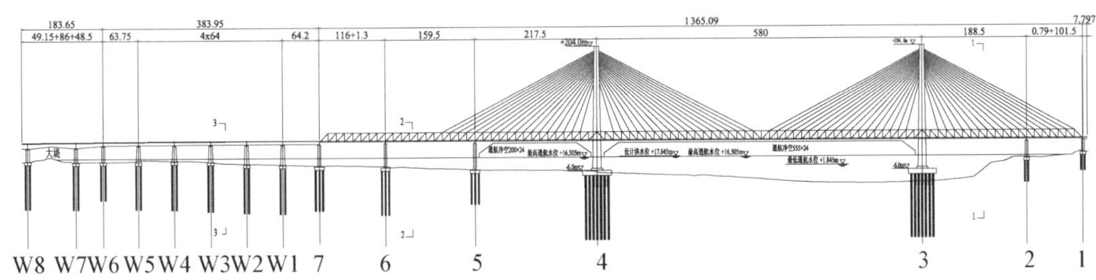

图3 某铁路长江大桥桥型立面图(尺寸单位: m)

Fig. 3 General drawing (including all piers in water) of one Yangtze river bridge (unit: m)

根据通过桥区船舶船型、流量数据、航运量发展预测调查,经过统计分析和交通部主管部门批复,防撞设计船舶为主通航孔为16×3 000 t驳船队和10 000 t级江海轮,北侧217.5通航孔为9×2 000 t驳船队和10 000 t级江海轮,159.5 m通航孔为4×3 000 t驳船队和5 000 t级江海轮,113 m通航孔和其余水中桥墩按3 000 t江海轮设防。由于船舶撞击桥墩时其撞击力主要由自航单船的质量确定,因此各桥墩的防撞设计船舶吨位如表3所示。

表3 某铁路长江大桥水中各桥墩撞击典型船舶

Table 3 Typical ship used for impact design of one railway Yangtze river bridge

桥 墩	3#	4#	5#	6#	7#	W1～W7
撞击船级/t	10 000	10 000	10 000	5 000	3 000	3 000
撞击典型船舶	12 000 t 多用途船	12 000 t 多用途船	12 000 t 多用途船	5 200 t 成品油船	3 000 t 供油船	3 000 t 供油船

5.2 撞击速度确定

根据长江航道中船舶的通常航速的调查结果为: 轮船上行航速通常为12 km/h,即3.33 m/s;轮船下行航速为15 km/h,即4.16 m/s。船队航行速度比轮船低,上行航速约为8 km/h,即2.22 m/s;下行航速约为12 km/h,即3.33 m/s。因此,选择在航道中心船对桥墩的撞击速度为: 下行4.16 m/s,上行3.33 m/s。

2006年10月28日,长委长江下游水文水资源勘测局对桥区河段进行了水文测验工作。测时水位5.32 m,测时流量16 700 m^3/s。所测得桥位流速分布如图4所示。

从图中可以看出,桥位轴线各点流速很有规律: 江心流速大,江边流速小;河流弯道的小半径一侧河槽深流速大,大半径一侧河漕浅流速小。这与内河航运船长、大副熟知的

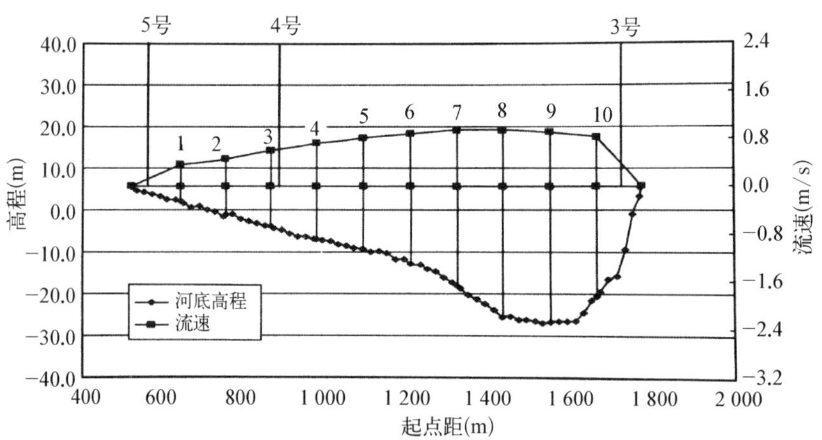

图 4　某铁路长江大桥桥位实测流速和水深

Fig. 4　Actual measurement velocity and depth at bridge location of one railway Yangtze river bridge

谚语"下水靠江心,上水靠江边,又快又省油"相符。

根据图 4 可知,桥位轴线上的各点中 8#点流速最大,为 1.03 m/s;1#点最小,为 0.40 m/s。根据图 3 可以确定安庆铁路长江大桥各桥墩附近的典型流速,以及考虑流速折减后的船桥撞击速度如表 4:

表 4　某铁路长江大桥桥墩处典型流速[12]

Table 4　**Typical velocity of pier location of one railway Yangtze river bridge (m/s)**[12]

(单位: m/s)

桥墩		3#	4#	5#	6#	7#	W1	W2	W3	W4	W5 ~ W7
流速		0.86	0.85	0.54	0.40	0.32	0.26	0.20	0.14	0.07	0.00
撞击速度	上行	3.16	3.15	2.84	2.70	2.62	2.56	2.50	2.44	2.37	2.30 *
	下行	3.99	3.98	3.67	3.53	3.45	3.39	3.33	3.27	3.20	3.13 *

注: * 由于测量流速时非最高通航水位,因此 W5, W6 和 W7 此时均位于岸上

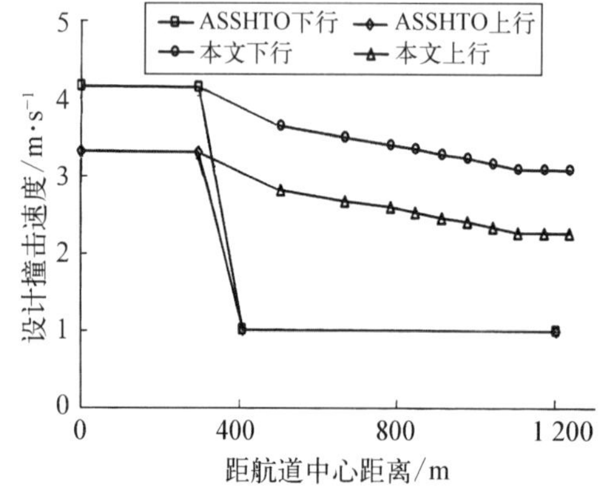

图 5　安庆铁路长江大桥船舶撞击速度沿桥向分布图

Fig. 5　Impact velocity distrubition along bridge direction of Anqing railway Yangtze river bridge

根据前述分析,可以分别按照美国(ASSHTO)指南推荐的船速折减方法和本文考虑流速折减的方法得出船舶撞击速度沿桥向分布比较图,如图 5 所示。图中原点表示桥梁主跨的中心。

由图 5 可知,美国(ASSHTO)指南方法较高地估计了随着船舶远离航道时,船舶撞击速度的折减,因此有可能低估远离主航道各桥墩的船舶撞击风险,降低桥梁的安全系数。

5.3　船舶撞击速度及船撞力确定

得到防撞典型船舶和撞击船速后,船舶

撞击力按照中国铁路规范公式[13]计算,计算公式为:

$$F = \gamma V \sin\alpha[W/(C_1 + C_2)]^{1/2}$$

式中: F(kN)为撞击力;γ(s/m)为动能折减系数,当船只斜向撞击墩台时可采用0.2,正向撞击时可用0.3;V(m/s)为撞击速度;α 为船只或排筏驶近方向与墩台撞击点处切线所成的夹角,应根据具体情况确定,如有困难,可采用 $\alpha = 20°$;W(kN)为船重;C_1、C_2(m/kN)分别为船和桥墩的弹性变形系数。根据上述分析,根据上述分析,选择了参数如下表所示的典型船进行船舶撞击力计算。

表5　**典型船舶参数表**

Table 5　**Parameter table of typical ship**

船吨位级别	10 000 t 级	5 000 t 级	3 000 t 级
型　船	12 000 t 多用途船	5 200 t 成品油船	3 000 t 供油船
长×宽×深/m	136.0×22.4×11.0	103.3×16.8×16.8	91.8×14.0×7.1
连附水质量/kN	220 000	92 444	54 375
变形系数 C_1+C_2	0.000 12	0.000 21	0.000 23

根据上述分析可以得出水中各桥墩的设计船撞力。

表6　**某铁路长江大桥水中各桥墩船舶撞击力**

Table 6　**Ship impact force of pier in water of one railway Yangtze river bridge**

桥　墩		3#	4#	5#	6#	7#	W1	W2	W3	W4	W5～W7
美国方法撞击力(kN)	上行	42.8	42.8	12.8	6.3	4.6	4.6	4.6	4.6	4.6	4.6
	下行	53.4	53.4	12.8	6.3	4.6	4.6	4.6	4.6	4.6	4.6
不失速方法撞击力(kN)	上行	42.8	42.8	42.8	21.0	15.4	15.4	15.4	15.4	15.4	15.4
	下行	53.4	53.4	53.4	26.2	19.2	19.2	19.2	19.2	19.2	19.2
本文方法撞击力(kN)	上行	40.6	40.5	36.5	17.0	12.1	11.8	11.5	11.3	10.9	10.6
	下行	53.4	53.4	47.1	22.2	15.9	15.6	15.4	15.1	14.8	14.4

由表6可以看出,本文考虑桥区水流速度变化,所得出的船撞力与美国(ASSHTO)指南方法比较,在航道中心附近的主桥墩变化不大,但对远离航道的桥墩相差2～3倍。可见,美国(ASSHTO)指南方法低估了远离主航道各桥墩的船舶撞击风险,降低了桥梁的设防标准,可能使桥墩得不到有效的防护。

同时,采用本文提出的方法还可以考虑内河航道枯、洪水期时,由于水位、流速变化对船撞力大小的影响,可以更为准确地评估船桥相撞的风险。

6　总结

本文在分析国内、外现有船桥撞击中撞速确定方法及其在应用中的问题的基础上,考虑河道和其他广阔水域流速分布及船舶意外失速综合影响，提出了一种船撞桥速度的计算方法。该方法先选取最可能发生的速度，用以计算航道两侧的桥墩，再分析船舶在偏航后撞击航道边上的桥墩，计及航道流场中流速的横向分布，提出了偏离航道桥墩的船撞速度新的计算方法。通过在安庆长江铁路大桥船撞研究中的应用，说明选取的撞击速度较为合理，且计算取值有依据、方法简便，可为内河和其他广阔水域船撞桥的设计和研究提供参考。

鸣谢

本文作者感谢交通部长江航务管理局、安庆海事局等单位的同志们两年来对本课题从事航速调研等方面的大力支持。

参 考 文 献

[1] 陈国虞，王礼立. 船撞桥及其防御[M]. 北京：中国铁道出版社，2006.

[2] 国际桥梁和结构工程协会. 交通船只与桥梁结构的相互影响（综述与指南）[M]. 顾翔，鲍卫刚译，1993.

[3] AASHTO 2009. Guide Specification and Commentary for Vessel Collision Design of Highway Bridges[S]. American Association of State Highway and Transportation Officials, Washington D. C.

[4] Vrouwenvelder AW. Design for Ship Impact according to Eurocode [S], Ship Collision Analysis. 1998.

[5] 陈国虞，张澄. 从美国阿肯色河桥被撞塌谈起[J]. 中国水运，2002(12).

[6] 邵旭东，占雪芳，廖朝华. 从美国阳光大道桥被撞重建看现有桥梁防撞风险评估[J]. 公路，2007(8).

[7] 杜旭升. 6.15 九江大桥船撞事故引发的思考[J]. 中国海事，2007(9).

[8] Fujii Y, Some factors affecting the frequency of accidents in marine traffic[J], Journal of navigation 1974 (27), 29 - 235.

[9] 岩井・聪. 关于船舶对桥梁的安全措施[J]. 中国航海杂志，1986. 12.

[10] 交通部上海船舶运输科学研究所，杭州湾跨海大桥船舶撞击力计算及防撞方案研究[R]. 2001.

[11] 曹映泓主编. 湛江海湾大桥[M]. 北京：人民交通出版社，2008.

[12] 上海海洋钢结构研究所. 重庆交通大学. 南京至安庆铁路安庆长江大桥防撞力标准和防撞设施方案研究报告[R]. 2009 - 7.

[13] TB 2010002. 1—2005，铁路桥涵设计基本规范[S]. 北京：中国铁道出版社，2005.

发表于：广东造船，2010(3)：38 - 41，31.

Published at: Guangdong Ship building, 2010(3): 38 - 41，31.

防御船舶撞击桥梁的设计中的风流压偏角

The deviation angle pressed by wind and current for the design of bridge anti-collision

陈国虞

(上海海洋钢结构研究所,上海 201204)

CHEN Guoyu

(Shanghai Marine Steel and Structure Research Institute, Shanghai 201204, China)

摘　要　在防御船舶撞击桥梁设计中,风流压偏角主要用于估算船舶侧撞桥墩的角度;其次,当船驶近桥发生偏航时,偏航距离是多少,撞到旁边的哪一个桥墩,需要讨论该航线此时的风流压偏角(自然条件作用的总和)。主要讨论船在各港口进入偏航段不操舵的最大偏航角。求出风流压偏角,才能正确地设计航线边上哪几个桥墩会受到船舶撞击,才能准确地进行防船撞设计。

关键词　桥梁防船撞设计　偏航　风速和风向角　流速和流角　风流压偏角

Abstract: The deviation angle pressed by wind and current has two main uses for the design on ship collision with bridge. First is to estimate the side impact angle of ship collision with the bridge, for calculate the side impact force. And the second is for estimate the yaw distance and to calculation how many side piers need to protect. So we need to discuss the deviation angle pressed by wind and current (the sum of total nature conditions). This paper discusses the ship sail in to the deviation leg, fined out the maximum deviation angle pressed by wind and current. Then, we can accurately to design the anti-collision devices for the side piers.

Keywords: the design on ship collision with bridge; yaw; the velocity and direction of wind; the velocity and direction of current; the deviation angle pressed by wind and current

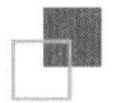

1 前言

不同的船舶在不同的航线上,有不同的风流压偏角。同样的风,对上层建筑大的船舶(例如客船)影响就大;同样的横流,对水中体积大的、方形系数大的影响就大。风流压偏角需在每一条航线的多种风、流情况和多种代表船型进行测定。

风流压偏角的第一个用途是用来决定船舶失舵时撞向桥墩的角度,以计算船舶对桥墩的侧撞力。

风流压偏角的第二个用途有两个很容易懂的例子:加拿大的联合大桥通航孔为200 m×49 m,通航37 000 t级船舶,设计要求在航道中线两侧各500 m处设置人工岛和护柱以防船撞,其理念是航船偏航有一定距离,将可能偏航的范围均予以保护(最终并没有设置,改用强制性领航),如图1所示。

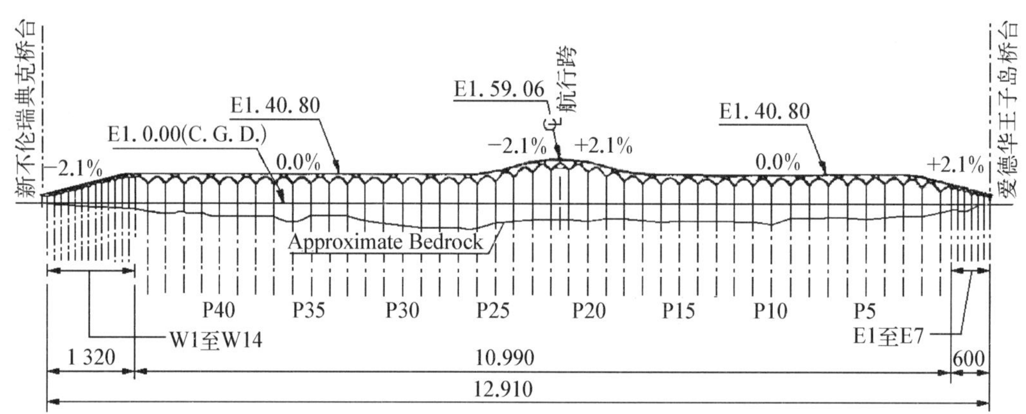

图1 加拿大联合大桥立面图

Fig. 1 The vertical sketch of Confederation Bridge at Canada

中国新建的象山港大桥,通航50 000 t级大船,在中线两侧各818 m处设置了10个柔性防撞装置。其理念也是航船偏航有一定距离,将可能偏航的范围均予以保护。至2013年初,象山港大桥的航道中线每边5个墩的柔性防撞装置均已设置完成(见图2)。

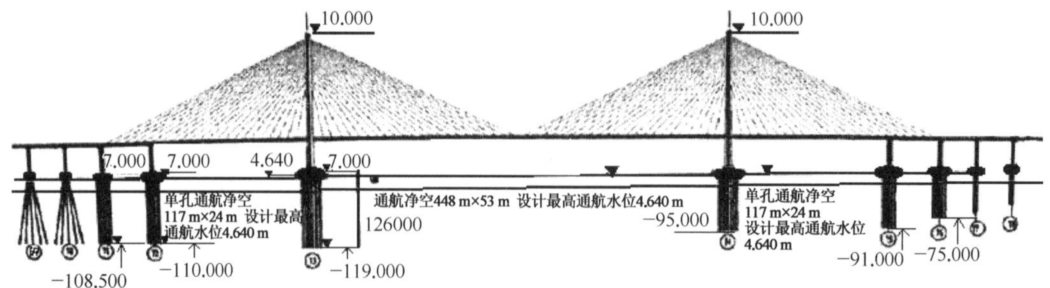

图2 象山港大桥10个墩的防撞装置简图

Fig. 2 The sketch of Xiangshan Harbor Bridge with the anti-collision device at 10 piers

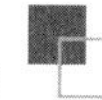

那么,怎样选定设计的风流压偏角和偏航角度呢?这需要分析下面几个关系。

2 墩的大小和跨距与角度的关系

船驶近桥,如果航道的宽度和弯度合乎规定,如果航线上有一定的能见度,如果船没有失去动力或失去控制,如果船员没有因故(醉酒、瞌睡、眩晕等)而不能履行职责,则船是不会撞到桥墩上去的。如果驾驶员因各种原因之一而未能操纵舵机(见图3),船从正确航向(图中RQ段)进入偏航段,不操舵的最大偏航角即为该航线此时的风流压偏角(自然条件作用的总和)。

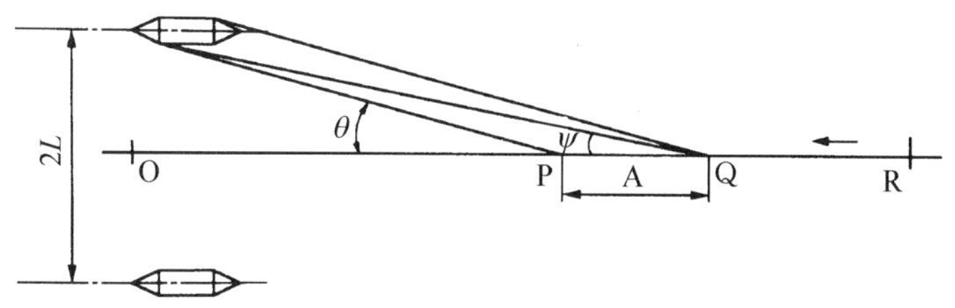

图3 船从航线偏离而撞墩的几何位置

Fig. 3 The geometry position of a departure route ship collision with the pier

A为在这个角度下的桥墩投影长度,在QP段以θ角度偏航会撞到桥墩,调整角度至小于ψ便不会撞。设偏航开始时距墩100 m,如果以3 m/s的船速驶过A段只有半分钟左右的时间,驾驶员(或领航员)纠正便可;如果这时$2L$比较大,使$\arctan(L/OP)$大于失舵时的风流压偏角,也是撞不上的(L为航线中心与桥墩的距离,OP段用能见度或失舵距离代入,可得到定量数值)。

算例:如桥墩跨距内侧为400 m,航线中心线与桥墩中心重合,将风流压偏角13°代入,则OP距离为870 m,即当P点达到870 m以近,失舵漂流,风流压偏角为13°,船将从墩边过,桥跨愈宽允许失舵的距离愈长,此期间可纠偏(如有别的制约因素,要增加考虑)。

我们常说,正撞的概率比较低。如图4所示,当船距墩1 000 m时,如果发现船头对准桥墩中线,只要转向1°便可避开桥墩。

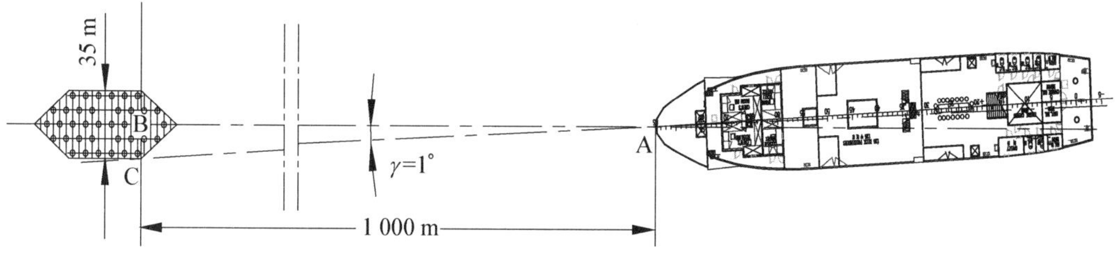

图4 正面撞墩示意图

Fig. 4 A sketch map of ship frontispiece collision with the pier

侧面撞墩的概率则大一些。例如,船长 200 m,船宽 32 m,墩宽 35 m,风流压偏角为 13°,船长加墩长投影在墩前的弧长为 55.4 m,加半船宽和半墩宽为 88.9 m,当船驶近到 1 000 m 时,约在墩前占 5°。所以说,侧撞概率比正撞大几倍。

3 船舶航行时"风流压偏角"分析

船舶在航道上航行,基本上由船舶本身的特性(船舶类型、船舶尺度、主机功率、导航设备、舵机性能)决定船舶操纵性和适航性。船舶能否安全航行,要考虑航道条件(风况、雾天能见度、水流状态)以及船舶航行密度的影响;在航道上有横跨桥梁时,更受桥梁建筑等因素的制约。允许船舶穿过桥孔的通航条件,除了一般通航条件外,还需另加桥梁的条件(桥梁通航净空尺度、桥墩位置、水流变化、沿岸风力)才能保证航行安全,顺利通航,避免船舶撞击桥梁的不幸航行事故发生。

船舶在航道上航行,一般是按航道中心呈蛇形航迹左右摆动前进。实船满载情况下,船舶下沉量较大,受水流流态、流向、流速左右较大;空载情况下,干舷增高,则受风向、风速影响较大。在海湾河口地区,水流除径流作用外,还受沿岸潮汐变化的影响。因此,船舶航行产生风流压偏角是正常的事。在航行中,船舶导航驾驶人员为控制船舶航向必须将舵角控制在一个合理的范围内,以保持船舶航行的稳定性。

船舶在航道上航行,可能产生船舶航行的风流压偏角。同时,桥梁桥墩建设时,桥墩中心线与水流流向也会产生夹角(应不大于标准[4]所允许的值)。这两个角度瞬时综合的结果,组成了偏航船舶与桥墩瞬时撞击的撞击角。这是随机因素变化的夹角,也是有一定变化范围的,因为桥墩中心线与水流流向的夹角是较稳定的,船舶航行的风流压偏角对一定的航道平常也有一定数值,但在发生撞击事故时也可能有一些意外的变化。

这两个角度相加时,对于内河,可分上水、下水和左墩、右墩共 4 种情况;对于港湾,亦应考虑涨潮、退潮和左墩、右墩共 4 种情况。简化计算港湾 4 种情况的最大侧撞角时,可用绝对值相加,因为桥孔下面通过船舶是双向的,一向相减时另一向便相加。用公式表示为

$$\theta_{\text{侧撞角}} = |\alpha_{\text{风流压偏角}}| + |\beta_{\text{桥法线偏角}}|$$

根据所研究的桥梁情况,本文对以下各方面进行讨论:桥位、轴线与航线,桥墩(或桥塔)所处的河槽位置,风压方向与船撞桥的关系,流压、雾天、进出港航道宽度和上下游直线段(桥位上下游各应有 4 倍船长的直段[4])等。

实际通过船舶较少则船舶撞上桥墩的概率正比减少。

船舶在航道上航行的风流压偏角值究竟为多少度?在国内外有关航道、港务、航运专家经长期研究、观测、试验有了一个比较符合实际的认识[3],也被编写进了规范。

4 中国主要港口航道满载船舶风流压偏角经验值

2001 年 12 月,长江航运规划设计研究院和西南水运工程科学研究所分别做了桥墩

形状和过桥航迹的水工模型试验，后者就是在各种情况下通过模型测定的（参见西南水运工程科学研究所蔡汝哲等撰写，2001 年 12 月由长江航道规划设计研究院印制的《桥孔通航船摸试验研究报告》）。

中国主要港口航道满载船舶风流压偏角经验值见表 1。

表 1 **中国主要港口风流压偏角经验值**[3]

Table 1 **The experience value of wind and current pressure drift angle at our main ports**

港口航道名称	横风/横流/km·h^{-1}	风流压偏角/(°)	备　注
大连港大港航道	6 级风/0.38	5	
大连鲇鱼湾	6 级风/2.0	15	无航道
秦皇岛航道	6 级风/0.51	3~4	
天津港进港主航道	6 级风/0.57	5~7	
青岛港大港航道	6 级风/1.07	5~8	
连云港航道	6 级风/0.9~1.15	8~9	
连云港航道	/0.9	5~6	
湛江港斗龙村航道	7 级风/2.0	13	
八所港航道	6 级风/1.32	10	
八所港航道	6 级风/无流	2~3	
上海港进口航道	6 级风/流速极小	3	船流夹角
上海港进口航道	6 级风/	20	空船
石臼港航道	6 级风/0.6	7	
汕头港	6 级风/1.5	10	

注：本表由交通部水规院根据实测及调查得到。

5　其他国外风流压偏角资料

(1) 美国陆军工程兵团根据对巴拿马运河和苏伊士运河的观测结果建议，当仅有岸吸力时为 2°，一般有横向风流影响时取 10°。

(2) 日本“港湾深水航道规划”（和管野一《港湾及海岸工学》）指出，航道上航行船舶风流压偏角最大不超过 10°。

(3) 苏联列宁格勒水运学院和敖德萨工学院资料论述，船舶偏离和漂流决定于风向、风速、流速、船舶类型和船舶速度，建议风流压偏角最大值不超过 25°（指船舶空载状态）。

(4) 国际海运伦敦航运会议第二次油轮会议报告，对船舶受横流影响的压偏角，可按下式计算：

$$\alpha = \arctan(\text{横向流速}/\text{航速})$$

如 $\tan\alpha \leqslant 0.25$，即横流为 2.0 kn、船舶至少为 8.0 kn 时，$\alpha = 14°$。

(5) 鹿特丹港航道流速为 1 kn,风流压偏角为 10°。

(6) 哥德堡港航道流速为 1 kn,风流压偏角为 7.2°。

6 湛江港风流压偏角实测结果

湛江海事局大力配合湛江海湾大桥的防撞设计,对通过桥下的 50 000 t 级到 2 000 t 级的 8 艘船舶进出港 10 个航次(其中进港 4 次、出港 6 次,10 次中遇到涨潮 6 次、平潮 2 次、退潮 2 次)进行风流压偏角测量,得到平常风和平常水流条件下 10 次风流压偏角的最大值为 3°,如表 2 所示。

表 2　**2004 年桥位处实测风流压偏角**

Table 2　**The value of wind and current pressure drift angle at the bridge position measured at 2004**

序	月-日-时	船名	船的尺度/m			总吨/t	风	流	船速/kn	航向/航迹向/(°)	风压偏角/(°)
			长	宽	吃水(实)		风级/风向	流向/流速/kn			
1	08-22-23	雪林	245	32	65	41 699	2~3/东南	323/0.8	7.9	141/142	1
2	08-31-11	马里奇	225	32	13.1	36 042	2/东	325/1.0	6.5	323/322	0
3	09-04-19	马里奇	225	32	7.1	36 042	微/—	325/1.0	9.5	143/141	2
4	08-28-09	加力士	220	32	7.5	32 976	4~5/东	320/1.5	8.0	145/143	2
5	09-02-21	玛丽	190	31	11.5	26 831	2~3/偏东	323/1.5	8.8	320/322	2
6	09-04-08	华鲲	182	28	5.4	20 990	2~3/东南	平潮/0.2	4.9	326/323	3
7	08-27-09	嘉宏	189	23	10.8	17 677	2~3/东	325/0.5	6.0	325/325	0
8	08-31-06	嘉宏	189	23	6.6	17 677	2/南	143/1.5	7.0	142/142	0
9	09-06-09	飞马	112	19	6.3	5 369	2~3/偏南	145/0.5	6.2	141.5/143	1.5
10	08-30-17	海明星	88	13	5.8	1 998	4~5/偏南	平潮/平潮	6.9	144/142	2

实测结果说明在没有台风的航行情况下风流压偏角为 3°。

7 总结

设计时,可将风流压偏角和桥法线偏角两个角的绝对值之和作为船对桥墩侧撞角的最大值,用此角的角度函数乘正撞力便得出侧撞力,也可据之计算偏航到桥位处时偏离航线中心的距离。

参 考 文 献

[1] IABSE. 交通船只与桥梁结构的相互影响(综述与指南)[S]. 国际桥梁和结构工程协会,丹麦,哥本哈根: 1991-09.

[2] OD 拉尔森. 交通船只与桥梁结构的相互影响[S]. 国际桥梁和结构工程协会,1991-04.

[3] AASHTO. 公路桥梁船撞设计指南[S]. 第 2 版. 华盛顿: 美国各州公路和运输工作者协会,2009.

[4] TB10002.1—2005. 铁路桥涵设计基本规范[S]. 北京: 中国铁道出版社,2005.

[5] JTG D60—2004. 公路桥涵设计通用规范[S]. 北京：人民交通出版社，2004.

[6] 陈国虞，王礼立. 船撞桥及其防御[M]. 北京：中国铁道出版社，2006.

[7] Vrouwenvelder A C W M. Design for Ship Impact According to Eurocode 1, Part 2. 7 [C]//Ship Collision Analysis, A. A. Balkema, Rotterdam, 1998：123－134.

[8] 王礼立，张忠伟，黄德进等. 船撞桥的钢丝绳圈柔性防撞装置的冲击动力学分析[C]//洪友士. 应用力学进展——祝贺郑哲敏先生八十华诞. 北京：科学出版社，2004：172－180.

[9] 王礼立，杨黎明，黄德进等. 船桥相撞的冲击力分析[J]. 国际工程冲击，2008，35(8)：895－904.

[10] 陈国虞. 有防撞装置时计算船撞桥的力——铁路桥梁规范中船撞力公式的延伸修订[J]. 铁道标准设计.

[11] 陈国虞，沈文玮. 船对桥墩的侧撞力[C]. 中国土木工程学会桥梁及结构工程分会. 第十五届全国桥梁学术会议论文集. 上海：同济大学出版社，2002：228－232.

[12] 陈国虞. 关于"船撞桥"问题的几点浅见[J]. 上海造船，1995，(3).

[13] 陈国虞，倪步友，李玉节，等. 船舶与桥墩撞击力的实验室和实船试验与数值模拟计算比较研究——兼论船撞力半经验公式[J]. 中国造船，2013，(增刊2).

[14] 陈国虞，陈明栋，郑丹. 计算船撞力选择撞击速度时考虑墩位流速的方法[J]. 广东造船，2010，(3)：38－41，31.

发表于：国际船桥相撞及其防护学术研讨会论文集[M]. 北京：中国铁道出版社，2014：31－35.

Published at：Proceedings of International Symposium on Ship-Bridge Collision and Its Protection. China Railway Press, 2014：31－35.

第三部分

怎样实现桥梁柔性防撞
How does the flexible anti-collision device implement

柔性消能防撞装置的技术特点

The specialty of flexible energy-dissipating crashworthy device

陈国虞[1] 张澄[1] 倪步友[1] 王礼立[2] 黄德进[2] 张忠伟[2]

(1. 上海海洋钢结构研究所,上海 201204;
2. 宁波大学机械工程和力学学院,宁波 315211)

CHEN Guoyu[1], ZHANG Cheng[1], NI Buyou[1],
WANG Lili[2], HUANG Dejin[2], ZHANG Zhongwei[2]

(1. Shanghai Marine Steel & Structure Research Institute, Shanghai 201204, China;
2. Mechanical Engineering and Mechanics Faculty,
Ningbo University, Ningbo 315211, China)

摘　要　湛江海湾大桥使用的柔性消能防御船撞桥墩的装置[21]已经建成。被广东的专家称为世界首创[16],其实现方法已经公开[14],为了桥梁设计工作者选用柔性消能防撞装置,特将其技术特点如:防撞元件的黏滞性;黏滞性高耗能防撞元件的实验曲线;从防撞元件到防撞装置;黏滞性防撞元件降低撞击力的理论;数值计算时实验曲线的拟合;外钢围所用材料的动载性能以及这些技术特点使柔性消能防撞装置得到多方面应用。

关键词　柔性消能防撞　黏滞性　长圈型防撞钢围　复合消能防撞圈　实验曲线的拟合　钢的动载性能

Abstract: In June 2007, the gulf bridge in Zhanjiang of Guangdong province have been used the flexible deplete energy equipment for anti-collision about ship with bridge pier[21]. The specialist of bridge and director of communication department of Guangdong province also consider it is the first try in the world[16]. It's construction method has been open[14]. For the designer of bridge to choose the flexible deplete energy equipment, now we mention some of the technical characteristics as follow: The meaning of viscous damping in the anti-impact parts; the experimental curve of the viscous high deplete energy rings; from the anti-impact parts to the anti-impact equipment (the synchronism in several rings); the theory about reduce the force of collision with viscous high deplete energy parts; when we go to numerical calculation, how to adapting the experimental curve in; the dynamic strength in the outer steel gate for impact; . . . , and also show: these technical characteristics can let the flexible deplete energy equipment used to the high way and the industry fields.

Keywords: flexible deplete energy for anti-collision, viscous damping, long ring shape type steel gate for anti-impact; composite flexible deplete energy ring for anti-collision, dynamic strength of steel

1 前言

湛江海湾大桥使用的柔性消能防御船撞桥墩的装置[21]已经于2007年6月在桥墩旁边合龙完毕。在2002年4月16日有广州、北京、上海、武汉和湛江的专家参加的会议上，湛江海湾大桥使用的防撞装置被称为世界首创[16]，这种中国式的防撞装置其实现方法已经公开[14]（ZL2005200422387长圈型防撞钢围和ZL2005200422372复合消能防撞圈）。本文为了桥梁设计工作者采用柔性消能防撞装置，特将其技术特点如：防撞元件从弹性、弹塑性发展到黏滞性；黏滞性高耗能防撞元件的实验曲线；从防撞元件到防撞装置；黏滞性高耗能防撞元件降低撞击力的理论和实践；数值计算时实验曲线的拟合；外钢围和桥墩所用材料的动载性能以及这些技术特点使防撞装置得到的其他方面应用加以简述。以便桥梁设计工作者据以设计、校核。

2 防撞元件从弹性、弹塑性发展到黏滞性

黏滞性高耗能防撞元件是在弹性的、弹塑性的防撞元件已应用之后发展研制的。弹性防撞元件不消耗能，回弹时可能造成撞击对象（例如船）的损坏；弹塑性的防撞元件消耗能量，但不能恢复撞前形状，防撞装置被撞一次修一次。黏滞性高耗能复合防撞元件与弹性外钢围等组成的防撞装置，被撞后消耗掉大部分撞击能量并能够恢复，多次使用。

黏滞性高耗能防撞元件的表现有点像湿面团，力的上升和下降回线包围的面积就是消耗掉的能量，其比例较大。制造黏滞性高耗能防撞元件可以有气体、液体和固体的方法。用集束钢丝绳外包橡胶制成复合的固体黏滞性高耗能防撞元件，使用可靠，维修方便。

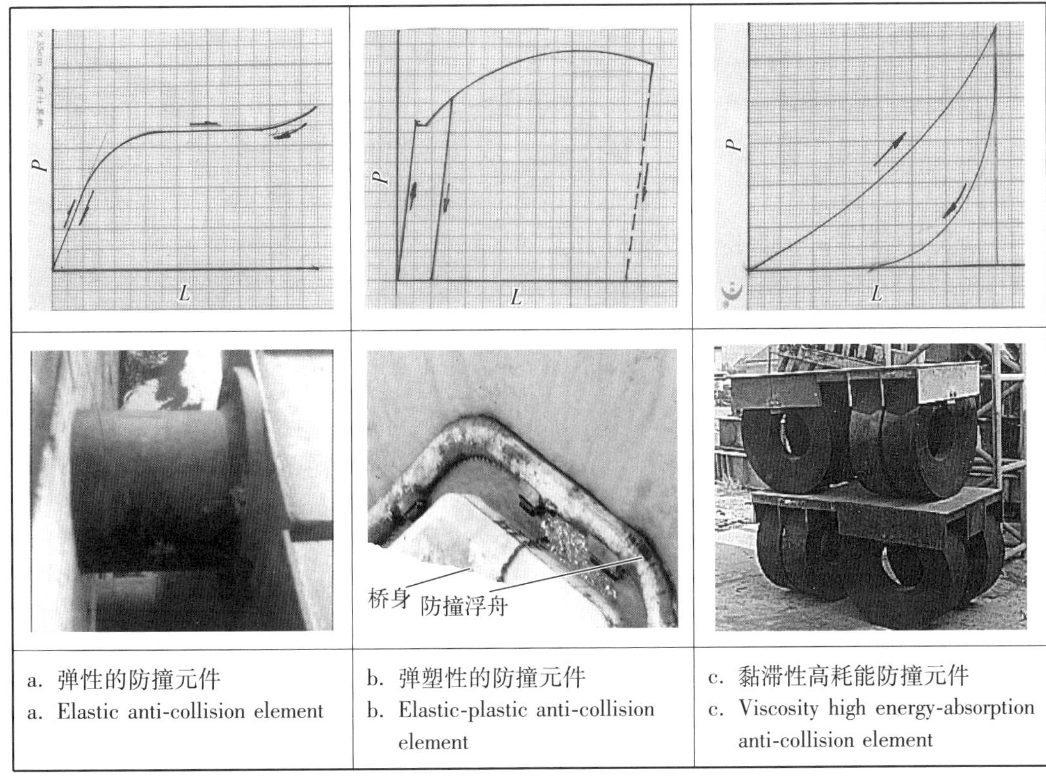

a. 弹性的防撞元件
a. Elastic anti-collision element

b. 弹塑性的防撞元件
b. Elastic-plastic anti-collision element

c. 黏滞性高耗能防撞元件
c. Viscosity high energy-absorption anti-collision element

图 1　三类防撞元件及其力学特征
Fig. 1　Three types anti-collision element and these mechanical characteristics

3　黏滞性高耗能防撞元件的实验曲线

此实验曲线有几个特征：首先，其上升曲线基本上是一条凹曲线，前半段变形大而力较小（与凸曲线比较）；其次，消耗的功很大，占的比率很高（60%以上）；再次，回程不到0，要想别的办法使其恢复形状；最后，冲击开始接触时，有一个消耗能量的小峰值。

对于第3点，我们在防撞圈的外面复合橡胶，橡胶处于弹性状态，帮助钢丝绳圈恢复形状；外钢围设计得比较强，在它处于弹性状态时也能帮助钢丝绳圈恢复形状。

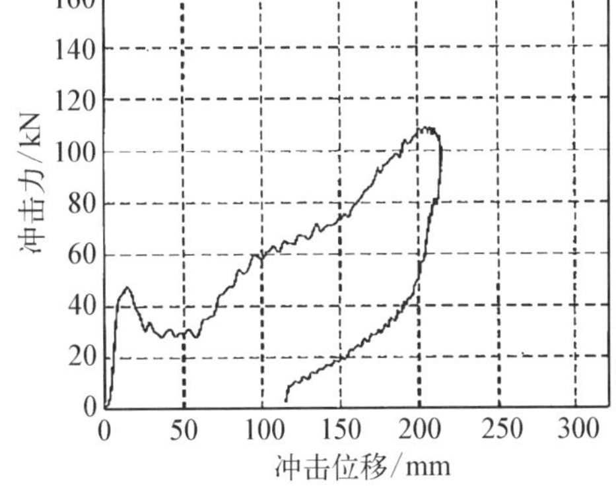

图 2　黏滞性高耗能防撞元件的实验曲线
Fig. 2　Test curve of the viscosity high energy-absorption anti-collision element

4　从单个防撞元件到防撞装置

为了得到较大的能量消耗，将众多的防撞圈串联和并联起来；为了使众多的防撞圈共同起作用,也为了帮助钢丝绳圈恢复形状,外钢围应设计得比较强,使它在工作时尽量处于弹性状态。

先用动态有限元方法计算出外钢围内各个防撞圈的变形和受力的同期性,再用 4 个圈、6 个圈的模型分别试验验证。设计足够强的外钢围用同样的计算方法,证明 700 个防撞圈在 1.7 s 内都受力和变形。这时的外钢围的截面惯性距达到比来撞船的船头稍强。

从两方面来校核外钢围的强度和刚性,从而得到外钢围内各个防撞圈的变形和受力的同期性。一方面将外钢围的设计工程图用动态有限元方法计算出外钢围内各个防撞圈的变形和受力,考核其同期性是否符合要求;另一方面用船舶设计开底泥驳的方法,当外钢围设计成浮体时,当中的月亮井就是泥驳的开底泥舱(泥驳的舱底板打开,就是一个大的月亮井),泥驳一边受撞会整体移动,当外钢围设计得与泥驳的周边一样强,一边受撞时便会整体移动,外钢围内的防撞圈便会同期变形和受力(湛江海湾大桥防撞装置的外钢围宽度最宽处达到 2.8 m)。

外钢围的截面尺寸、强度和刚性都可以进行设计,如图 3 所示的变截面外钢围可以改善桥墩与船的相遇角,从而有利于拨开船头,使船的动能尽量多地保留在船上,尽量少地参与交换。

图 3 黏滞性防撞装置图

Fig. 3 The viscosity high energy-absorption anti-collision device

5 黏滞性高耗能防撞元件能降低撞击力

先从原理上分析,霍布金生试验机上用钢杆冲击 3 种不同材料的杆件,中间加黏滞性阻尼和不加阻尼,共 6 种工况,冲击界面应力值如图 4 和表 1。

然后,用一个实例可以看出降低的程度。选 50 000 t 散货船撞击湛江海湾大桥的桥墩作为例子(撞击系统由船、防撞装置和桥墩组成,如图 5 所示),数值计算的模型将撞击系统分为 7 个部分,共 130 897 个单元,其中从船头经过防撞舱壁直到平行中段都照船的工程图详细划分,如图 6 所示,7 个部分的单元属性和材料模型如表 2 所示。

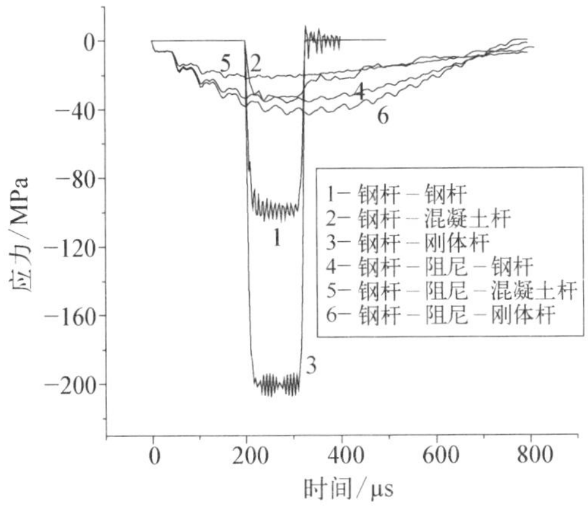

图4 6种工况计算比较

Fig. 4 Calculation comparison of six working conditions

表1 加黏滞性阻尼和不加阻尼冲击界面应力值

Table 1 Interface impact stress with or without viscosity damping

序号	碰撞工况	应力/MPa
1	钢-钢	100
2	钢-混凝土	34
3	钢-刚体	200
4	钢-阻尼-钢	35
5	钢-阻尼-混凝土	21
6	钢-阻尼-刚体	42

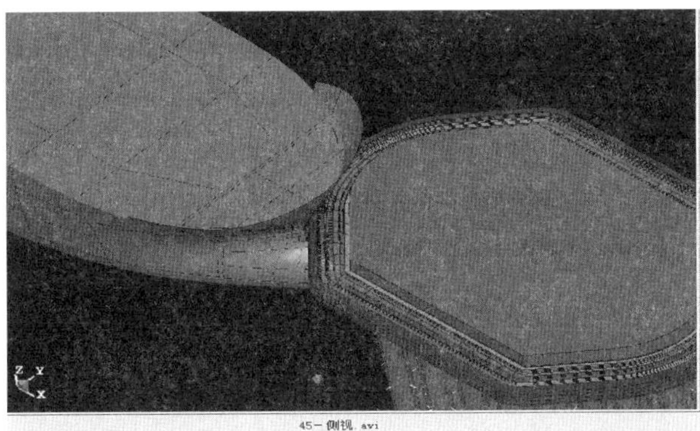

图5 50 000 t散货船撞击湛江海湾大桥的桥墩

Fig. 5 50 000 t bulk carrier impacts the pier of zhanjiang bay bridge

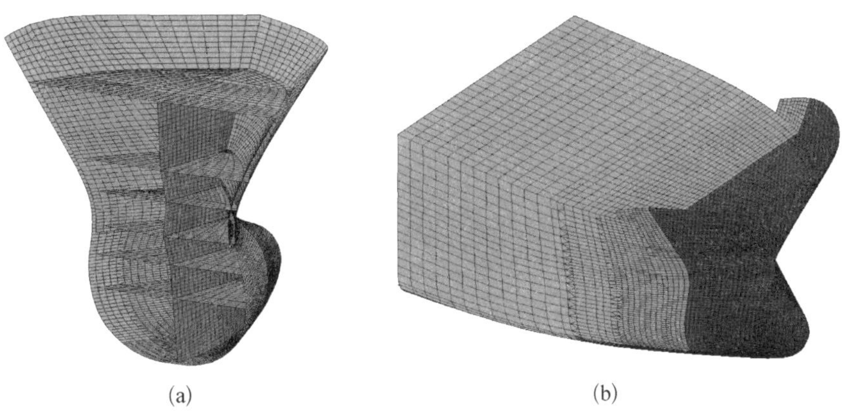

图6 从船头经过防撞仓壁直到平行中段划分图

Fig. 6 From the front after a collision silo wall until parallel middle figures

a. 从船头到防撞舱壁　　b. 从船头到平行中段

a. From the bow to anti-collision silo wall　　b. From the bow to parallel in the middle

表 2 冲击系统 7 个部分(130 897 单元)的单元属性和材料模型

Table 2 The element properties and material models of seven impact systems (130 897 elements)

序号	部　分	单元个数	单元属性	材 料 模 型
1	船	29 137	壳单元	考虑应变率效应的弹塑性模型
2	防撞装置	84 868	壳单元	考虑应变率效应的弹塑性模型
3	L 型钢	76	梁单元	考虑应变率效应的弹塑性模型
4	钢绳绳圈	1 216	离散单元	非线性黏弹性模型
5	桥墩	6 621	实体单元	线弹性材料
6	桩	5 580	实体单元	线弹性材料
7	土弹簧	2 536	离散单元	线弹性材料

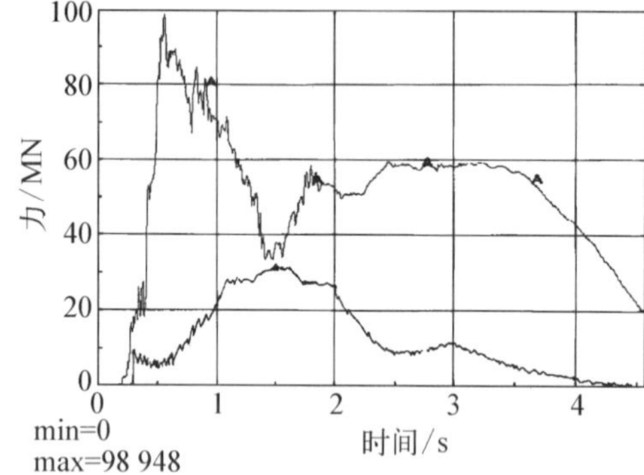

图 7　黏滞性防撞装置降低船撞力图(湛江海湾大桥)

Fig. 7　After using viscosity anti-collision device, the impact force decrease (Zhanjiang bay bridge)

将装设了黏滞性防撞装置和没有装设防撞装置两种情况的计算结果放在一张图上(见图 7),图中 A 曲线是没有防撞装置的。从图中可以看出:

第一,装设了黏滞性防撞装置后,曲线的前半段形状为凹曲线,变性大、力上升慢;

第二,力的峰值小了,峰值到来的时间也晚了;

第三,整个撞击过程的时间短了,能量交换小了。

6　数值计算时黏滞性防撞元件实验曲线的拟合

对采用钢丝绳圈防撞装置的船撞桥问题进行数值模拟时,都要用到钢丝绳圈的力-位移的物理模型,但在 LS - DYNA 中没有可供选用的非线性黏弹性本构模型。

关于应变率相关的非线性黏弹性本构关系,朱兆祥、王礼立和他们的合作者近二十年来曾对典型的工程塑料(包括环氧树脂、有机玻璃(PMMA)、聚碳酸酯(PC)、尼龙、ABS、PBT 等)进行过一系列实验研究[9],表明在准静载荷到冲击载荷(应变率为 10^{-4} 到 $10^{3}\ s^{-1}$)的范围内,其非线性黏弹性本构关系可以令人满意地用如下的 ZWT 方程来描述:

$$\sigma = f_e(\varepsilon) + E_1\int_0^t \dot{\varepsilon}\exp\left(-\frac{t-\tau}{\theta_1}\right)d\tau + E_2\int_0^t \dot{\varepsilon}\exp\left(-\frac{t-\tau}{\theta_2}\right)d\tau \tag{1a}$$

$$f_e(\varepsilon) = E_0\varepsilon + \alpha\varepsilon^2 + \beta\varepsilon^3 \tag{1b}$$

此处 s 表示应力，e 应变，$\dot{\varepsilon}$ 应变率，t 时间；$f_e(\varepsilon)$ 描述非线性弹性平衡响应，E_0、α 和 β 是对应的弹性常数；第一个积分项描述低应变率下的黏弹性响应，E_1 和 q_1 分别是所对应的马克斯威尔(Maxwell)单元的弹性常数和松弛时间；而后一个积分项描述高应变率下的黏弹性响应，E_2 和 q_2 则分别是所对应的 Maxwell 单元的弹性常数和松弛时间。

我们尝试将 ZWT 方程推广应用到钢丝绳圈。对于外径为 D 的钢丝绳圈，如以 u 和 $v(=\mathrm{d}v/\mathrm{d}t)$ 表示外径两点间的位移和速度，则钢丝绳圈受压时的名义应变为 u/D，名义应变率 $\dot{\varepsilon}=v/D$；于是上式可改写为以力 F(N)与位移 u(mm)之关系表示的如下形式：

$$F = K(u)u + K_2\int_0^t v(\tau)\exp\left(-\frac{t-\tau}{\theta_2}\right)\mathrm{d}\tau \tag{2a}$$

经与试验数据拟合，发现钢丝绳圈在冲击动载下的力-位移曲线的确可以相当满意地用式(2)来描述，拟合曲线与试验曲线的比较如图 8 所示，相应的黏弹性特性参数为：

$$K(u) = 61.3 - 0.596u + 2.99\times10^{-3}u^2,\ K_2 = 395(\mathrm{N/mm}),\ q_2 = 1.673(\mathrm{ms}) \tag{2b}$$

这说明钢丝绳圈在受到冲击载荷时的动态响应可以分为两部分，一部分为非线性弹性响应，另一部分是 Maxwell 体所表示的线性黏弹性响应，体现了钢丝绳圈的阻尼耗散作用。

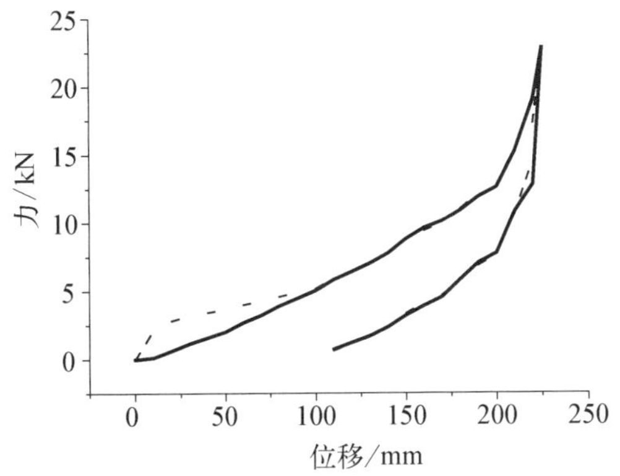

图 8　拟合曲线与试验曲线的比较
（实线—试验曲线，虚线—拟合曲线）

Fig. 8　Comparision of test curve and fitted curve (solid line-test curve, dotted line-fitted curve)

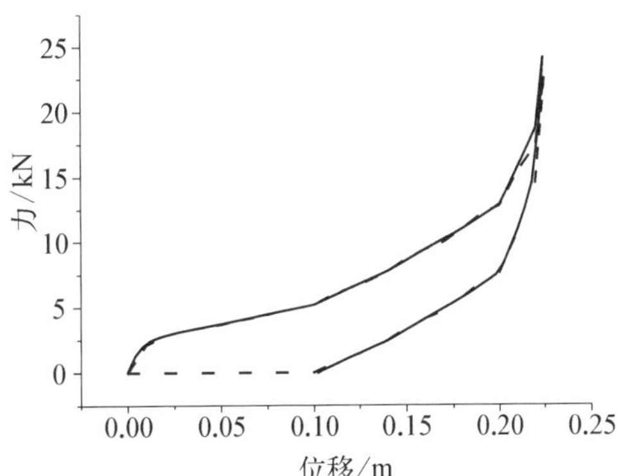

图 9　计算曲线与拟合曲线的比较
（实线—计算曲线，虚线—拟合曲线）

Fig. 9　Comparision of calculated curve and fitted curve (solid line-calculated curve, dotted line-fitted curve)

我们通过把非线性弹簧和 Maxwell 体的组合，定义出描述钢丝绳圈特性所需的 ZWT 计算模型。由此采用 LS-DYNA 程序所得的计算曲线与建模拟合曲线的对比如图 9 所示。可见无论在加载段还是在卸载段,所采用的计算模型都能很好地反映出钢丝绳圈的力-位移特性,这对下一步的柔性耗能防撞装置的仿真计算具有重要意义。

通过多次计算,我们体会,在进行数值计算时,如果不能将黏滞性的实验曲线拟合进去,计算结果是不正确的。

7 数值计算中受撞击材料考虑在不同撞击速度(应变率)时的力学性能(弹塑性力学模型)

在船撞桥的计算中,相关的材料有低碳结构钢、普通低合金结构钢、橡胶和混凝土;相关的结构有钢丝绳圈、纤维增强橡胶、复合钢丝绳圈和钢结构等,结构件除了与材料性质有关外尚与结构的几何形状有关,故在研究中按其工件形状单独讨论(或单独试验标定)。

对于钢材,取杨氏弹性模量 $E=2.1\times10^5$ MPa,泊松比 $\mu=0.28$,密度 $\rho=7.85$ g/cm^3,并采用著名的考帕-塞门斯(Cooper-Symonds)公式作为钢材在计及应变率效应时的弹塑性本构关系。以有效应力 σ_{eff}和有效塑性应变 $\varepsilon_{\text{eff}}^{\text{p}}$表示时,该公式有如下形式:

$$\sigma_{\text{eff}} = \left[1+\left(\frac{\dot{\varepsilon}}{C}\right)^{1/p}\right](\sigma_0+\beta E_p\varepsilon_{\text{eff}}^{\text{p}}) \tag{3}$$

其中 σ_{eff}是按材料力学第四强度理论(Von-Mises 准则)的有效应力。其他符号的名称和取值分别列如表 3:

表 3 考帕-塞门斯公式的取值
Table 3 Cooper-Symonds parameter

序号	参数名称、符号	单 位	低碳钢	高强度低合金钢	备 注
1	钢号举例		A_3, q235, CSC - A、B、D、E	16Mn, q355, CSC - AH36	GB712
2	初始屈服点,σ_0	MPa	235	355	
3	应变硬化参数		0.8	0.8	
4	塑性硬化模量,E_{p}	GPa	3	3	
5	应变率参数,C	s^{-1}	40.5	40.5	
6	应变率参数,p		5	5	
7	应变率,$\dot{\varepsilon}$	s^{-1}	50	50	
8	有效塑性应变,$\varepsilon_{\text{eff}}^{\text{p}}$				
9	动态屈服点,$\sigma_{动0}$	MPa	480	725	当 $\varepsilon_{\text{eff}}^{\text{p}}=0\%$
10	动态屈服点,$\sigma_{动4\%}$	MPa	676	922	当 $\varepsilon_{\text{eff}}^{\text{p}}=4\%$

$C = 40.4\ s^{-1}$、$p = 5$，取值来自诺曼·琼斯著《结构冲击》书中所给材料系数表（见表4）。

表4 不同材料的系数
Table 4 **Cooper-Symonds parameter of different materials**

材　　料	C/s^{-1}	p
软　　钢	40.4	5
铝合金	6 500	4
α_钛（Ti50A）	120	9
304 不锈钢	100	10

当取$\dot{\varepsilon} = 50$时，采用此系数代入考帕-塞门斯公式，计算得到低碳钢CSC－A的动态屈服点$\sigma_{动0} = 480$ MPa；普通低合金钢CSC－AH36动态屈服点$\sigma_{动0} = 725$ MPa。

用上述公式，得出钢在各种恒应变率下的"应力-应变"如图10所示：但使用者应注意，工程实践中，往往一次冲击过程里，应变率是在不断变化的。

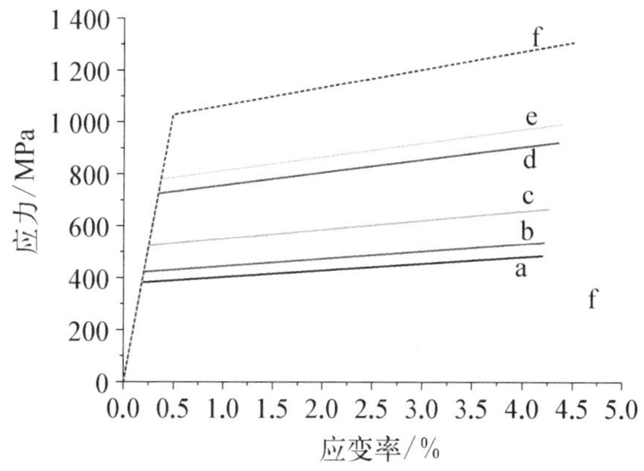

图10 考虑应变率效应的钢的弹塑性本构关系（式(3)）
Fig. 10 Elastic-plastic constitutive relation of steel with strain rate effect (eq. 3)

图中各曲线对应的应变率（1/s）：a—10^{-4}，b—10^{-2}，c—10^{0}，d—50，e—10^{2}，f—10^{3}。

上述公式计算出的结果与图11——L·D·索柯洛夫用低碳钢试验的结果大致相符。大致相符指的是：当变形速度提高时，弹性系数提高，屈服点提高，屈服以后的应变硬化系数提高。至于定量的验证，还有待于不同应变率下、不同材料的大量实验数据。

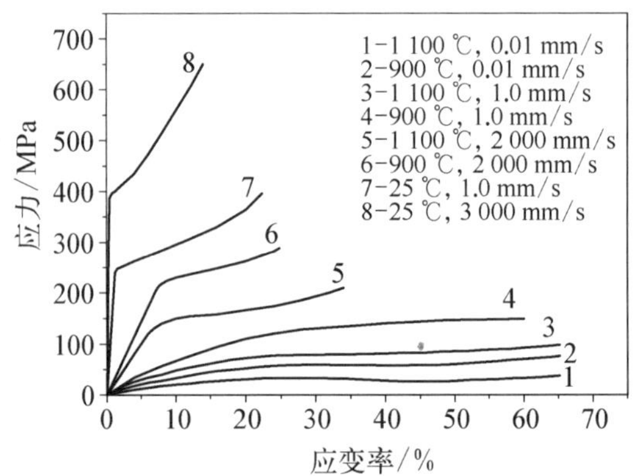

图 11 q235 低碳钢工程屈服点和断裂强度与加载时温度、速度的关系

Fig. 11 The relationship of yield stress, fracture strength and loading temperiture, loading velocity of q345 mild steel

至于混凝土的抗拉性能，对动载较为敏感，动载下的抗拉性能用“动载倍增因子 *DIF*”表示：

$$DIF = ft/ft_s$$

其中：ft 是动态$\dot{\varepsilon}$时的抗拉性能

ft_s 是静态$\dot{\varepsilon}_s$时的抗拉性能

综合 10 家的试验结果，用纵坐标为“动载倍增因子 *DIF*”；横坐标应变率$\dot{\varepsilon}$，在图上得到一条比较离散的凹折线。

动载倍增因子成折线关系，可以用两段直线表示，直接应用线图中对应于某一$\dot{\varepsilon}$的 *DIF* 中值便可(图略)。

由上述可知，无论是钢结构还是混凝土结构，都应该考虑应变率效应。例如，对于外钢围，不计及应变率效应的话，将会报告提前屈服，变形被加大，断裂限提前到来。不坏也会报告成坏。

8 在其他方面的推广应用

在公路急弯和匝道等场合，应用高耗能的防撞圈构成的防撞装置可以减少碰撞后的翻车或避免二次碰撞造成的翻车。其装置如图 12 和图 13 所示。

应用高耗能的防撞圈与钢板构成的防撞装置(见图 14)，可以作码头的护舷，装在坞门的旁边可以避免船只进出时碰伤。

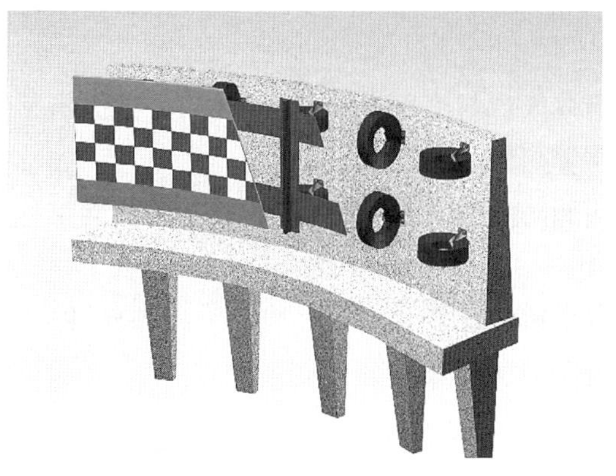

图 12　公路急弯用的防撞栏

Fig. 12　anti-collision barrier for highway

图 13　公路匝道用的防撞墩

Fig. 13　anti-collision barrier for highway

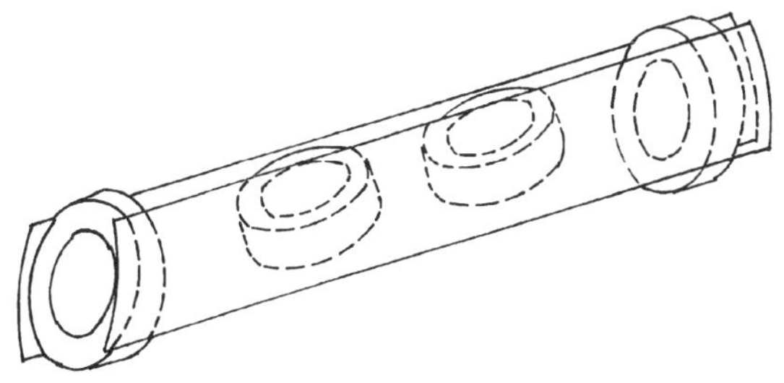

图 14　码头用的高耗能护舷

Fig. 14　high energy absorption fender for wharf

9　总结

自从试制出柔性钢丝绳防撞圈[1]以来，已经过了 12 年，现在已经工业化批量生产大型（ϕ800 mm）橡胶与钢丝绳复合的防撞圈。前后两种柔性耗能防撞圈都得到国家专利授权。

回顾了人类历史上使用过的各种桥墩防撞设施，提出了对桥墩防撞的理想——“三不坏”桥墩防撞装置，并以武汉长江大桥为例提出了柔性防撞装置方案。[2-8]

参考美国撞塌的桥梁，研究中外各种桥梁防撞的规范要求。分析了世界上曾采用过的 14 种船撞力计算方法，反对采用过分简化的公式，推荐能考虑船和桥、质量和速度、撞击角度，并能计及撞击系统各部分的刚性的公式，将这公式延伸，顺理成章地考虑到有防撞装置时撞击力的降低。[9-13,20]

近 20 年来，我国在建设跨越通航河流、海湾、河口的桥梁时，考虑到通航的需要，尽量将桥墩建在浅水、岸边，或是用一跨过江。这时，桥的墩塔比较强大一般是撞不垮的，这时的防撞装置主要保护船；只有在水域、航道宽度足够宽时，为了节省投资，在比较深的水中

建桥墩，这时就需装设柔性防撞装置，降低船撞力，以求在保护桥的同时也保护船当然也是保护环境[14-17]。

在建设湛江海湾大桥的防撞装置的过程，研究人员与工程实践相结合，工程界提出了非常宝贵而可行的三级防撞理念："小撞不坏、中撞可修、大撞不倒"[16,21]。

研究人员集中力量，解决怎样实现柔性高耗能防撞的问题，这种方案被广东桥梁工程界认为世界首创。在方案的数值计算中尽量应用冲击动力学的方法[14-18]。

经过6年的理论与实践结合的过程，经过多个单位在多个问题上的修改和补充，终于使"柔性消能防撞不再是梦想"而在2007年6月于特大桥梁中建成使用[21]。

参考文献

[1] 陈国虞等. 水中桩柱用钢绳柔性冲击吸能器试验研究[J]. 交通部上海船舶运输科学研究所学报，1995(2).

[2] 陈国虞. 长江中游桥墩防撞——防撞要求的分析[J]. 航海科技动态，1995(3).

[3] 陈国虞，林树人. 长江中游桥墩防撞(续1)——防撞设施的种类及其特点[J]. 航海科技动态，1995(4).

[4] 陈国虞，倪步友等. 长江中游桥墩防撞(续2)——钢绳柔性吸能防撞器试验研究[J]. 航海科技动态，1995(5).

[5] 陈国虞. 桥墩防撞设施的选择. 中国水运，1995(9).

[6] 陈国虞. 关于"船撞桥"问题的几点浅见[J]. 上海造船，1995(3).

[7] 陈国虞. 三不坏桥墩防撞装置的设计[M]. 船撞桥论文选. 上海海洋钢结构研究所，2000.

[8] 陈国虞. 桥墩防撞设施的历史及其功能——"三不坏"桥墩防撞装置的诞生[M]. 科学中国人十年优秀论文选，北京：科学中国人杂志社，2002.

[9] 陈国虞，张澄. 从美国阿肯色河桥被撞塌谈起[J]. 中国水运，2002(12)：45-45.

[10] 陈国虞. 船对桥的正撞力[C]. 第15届全国桥梁学术会议论文集. 上海：同济大学出版社，2002：222-227.

[11] 陈国虞，沈文玮. 船对桥的侧撞力[C]. 第15届全国桥梁学术会议论文集. 上海：同济大学出版社，2002：228-232.

[12] 陈国虞. 有防撞装置时计算船撞桥的力——铁路桥梁规范中船撞力公式的延伸修订[J]. 铁道标准设计，2004(1).

[13] 王礼立，陈国虞等. 船撞桥的钢丝绳圈柔性防撞装置的冲击动力学分析[M]. 应用力学进展. 北京：科学出版社，2004.

[14] 陈国虞等. 怎样实现桥墩柔性防撞[C]. 第十六届全国桥梁学术会议论文集，北京：人民交通出版社，2004：75-81.

[15] 陆宗林，陈国虞等. 一种新型的柔性吸能防撞装置[C]. 中国公路学会2004年全国桥梁学术会议论文集. 北京：人民交通出版社，2004.

[16] 陈冠雄. 挑战新高——广东省公路桥梁建设综述(上)[J]. 桥梁，2005(6)：20.

[17] 陈国虞，张澄，倪步友，王礼立，黄德进，张忠伟. 怎样实现桥墩柔性防撞[J]. 桥梁，2005(6)：58.

[18] 陈国虞，王礼立. 船撞桥及其防御[M]. 北京：中国铁道出版社，2006.

[19] 陈国虞,张澄,王礼立等. 桥墩防撞问题研究的进展[C]. 第十七届全国桥梁学术会议论文集. 北京:人民交通出版社,2006.

[20] 陆宗林,陈国虞,张澄. 统一我国两个桥涵设计规范中船撞力公式的探讨[C]. 第十七届全国桥梁学术会议论文集. 北京:人民交通出版社,2006.

[21] 曹映泓,柔性消能防撞不再是梦想[J]. 桥梁,2007(2):84.

发表于:桥梁,2007(4):58-62.

Published at: Bridge, 2007(4): 58-62.

桥墩柔性防船撞装置结构设计研究

Research on structural design of flexible anti-ship-collision devices

王建强[2]　赵彦龙[1]　杨祥磊[1]　赵振宇[1,2]　陈国虞[3]

（1．西安中交土木科技有限公司，西安，中国，710075；

2．中交第一公路勘察设计研究院有限公司，西安，中国，710075；

3．上海海洋钢结构研究所，上海，中国，201204）

WANG Jianqiang[2], ZHAO Yanlong[1], YANG Xianglei[2], ZHAO Zhenyu[1,2], CHEN Guoyu[3]

(1. CCCC Civil Engineering Science & Technology Co., Ltd., Xi'an 710075, China;

2. CCCC First Highway Consultants Co., Ltd., Xi'an 710075, China;

3. Shanghai Marine Steel and Structure research Institute, Shanghai 201204, China)

摘　要　以健跳港特大桥防船撞项目为例，提出了桥墩柔性防护装置的设计方法。利用显式动力分析软件 LS－DYNA 针对桥墩柔性防船撞装置结构性能进行优化，对比分析防撞圈数量、钢板厚度、外钢围舱室间距对防船撞装置性能产生的影响。同时，提出一种利用非线性离散梁单元模拟黏滞性防撞圈的方法，并提出了一种浮力的简化模拟方法。最后，以实际项目为例，验证了柔性防船撞装置的设防效果。

关键词　船撞桥　柔性防船撞装置设计优化　数值模拟

Abstract: This paper presents the design method of flexible bridge pier protection device rely on anti-ship-collision project of Jiantiao Bridge. The performance of flexible anti-ship-collision device is optimized by using the dynamic FEM software LS－DYNA in this paper. The factors influenced the device's properties such as number of anti-collision rings, thickness of the steel plate and cabin distance has been analyzed. A fitting method of viscosity anti-collision ring by nonlinear discrete beam element has been established. A simplified simulation method of buoyancy is put forward. Finally, the actual project is taken as an example to verify the protected effect of flexible anti-ship-collision device.

Keywords: ship-bridge collision, flexible anti-ship-collision device, numerical simulation

1 引言

船撞桥事故多由于天气、环境和人为因素所导致,航道部门的管控可降低事故风险,但仍无法避免,事故一旦发生,损失惨重。在武汉长江大桥被撞的70次记录中,除3次撞到钢梁外,其余均撞在桥墩上。桥墩的安全防护技术愈发受到重视。

桥墩防船撞设施的设计指导思想正在从刚性、半刚性向柔性转变。柔性防船撞技术可在撞击发生时改变船身方向、减小撞击力、延长撞击时间、消耗撞击能量[1]。

国内桥梁设计规范中将船舶撞击视为偶然水平静力荷载,采用半经验公式计算。船桥相撞是一个在短时历程中包含巨大能量交换的动态过程,本质上是一个复杂和困难的冲击动力学问题[2],很难用简化的物理公式来对防护设施的作用进行有效的评估。与花费巨大的船撞桥实验相比,动力数值仿真技术花费少、理论成熟,目前多被研究者采用。

桥墩柔性防船撞技术的关键点在于建立一套成熟可靠的设计方法。本文依托健跳港特大桥防船撞工程提出了一套基于动力数值仿真技术的防船撞装置设计和优化方法。

2 桥墩柔性防船撞装置设计方法

2.1 结构特点及防护原理

柔性防船撞装置主要由外钢围、内钢围及防撞圈组成,如图1所示。外钢围需要有足够的局部刚度和整体刚度,防止撞击造成的局部塌陷,并使所有防撞圈共同受力,从而传递、分散撞击力和拨转船舶航行方向;防撞圈提供防撞设施整体协同作用所需要的柔性,延长撞击时间;内钢围支撑防撞圈,扩大受力面积。

图1 柔性防船撞装置结构

Fig. 1 Structure of flexible anti-ship-collision device

2.2 设计原则

根据柔性防船撞装置防护原理及结构特点,设计者总结出以下方案设计时应遵循的原则:

(1) 对撞击船舶进行耗能缓冲,使桥墩承受的撞击力控制在安全范围内;

(2) 各水位条件下,撞击船舶不能触及墩壁,球艏不能触及桩基;

(3) 防撞设施不能影响航道的正常通航;

(4) 通过合理的结构设计,减少船舶的损伤;

(5) 制造、安装、维修经济易操作;

(6) 经久耐用、功能可靠。

2.3 设计内容

柔性防船撞装置设计包含以下内容和注意事项。

1) 确定船撞力

采用国内外常用的船撞力计算公式计算健跳港主墩典型船舶撞击力,并采用有限元仿真方法进行真实模拟。计算结果表明,由于所采用的半经验公式所处背景和角度不同,各规范计算值相差甚大,为了更接近于工程真实状况,可采用数值模拟结果作为防撞装置设计依据。

2) 确定防御范围

防撞装置外形尺寸应能保证在各种水位条件下船舶均不触及墩壁或桩基,装置不脱离承台。

3) 防撞圈布置

防撞圈是柔性防船撞装置的核心元件,发挥缓冲耗能的作用。防撞圈的合理布置对整个装置的防撞性能具有重要影响。

防撞圈布置应遵循: ① 具有一定刚度,避免外钢围发生局部变形;② 具有一定柔度,使装置协同运动;③ 应有足够的个数吸收撞击过程中的部分能量。

4) 结构设计

箱体结构设计。柔性防船撞装置结构设计应注意: ① 装置随水位上下浮动,需要与承台预留一定间隙;② 为防止装置随水位上下浮动而导致承台及装置磨损,需要在装置与承台间设置减摩材料;③ 装置的外钢围迎接撞击,并具有导向功能,外侧必须光滑;④ 为实现箱体外侧与船舶更大的接触面积,外钢围外侧呈一定角度;⑤ 箱体由分隔板分成小舱室,通过型钢提高强度;⑥ 钢围宽度应满足构造、强度和维护需求;⑦ 内、外钢围分为多个独立的水密分块,分别运输至施工地进行拼接。

5) 浮动性设计

柔性防船撞装置的浮动性设计应注意: ① 设置独立水密舱,保证局部破损后装置不会沉没;② 装置与桥墩留有一定的水平间隙,并设置减摩材料,避免装置与桥墩磨损和卡滞;③ 通过添加混凝土块将内、外钢围出水高度调整一致;④ 浮力储备应大于装置破舱而损失的浮力。

6）耐久性设计

装置钢围外侧表面采用了电弧喷锌铝伪合金防腐层和铝-锌-铟牺牲阳极防腐的双重防腐方案。

7）制造安装

柔性防船撞装置的制造施工主要分为4个部分：① 原材料采购；② 防撞装置制作；③ 防腐涂装；④ 运输和安装。柔性防船撞装置在承台施工时将限位装置和反力支架的预埋部分预埋在承台上，待承台施工完成后，拆除围堰，安装制造完成的柔性防撞装置。

8）装置维养

发生局部变形或破损时，可就地进行局部修正；对于影响装置功能的破损需局部切除、焊接、修补；定时检查防腐涂层，并及时修补。装置大面积受损难以修复时，直接更换受损分块。

9）优化设计

采用数值模拟辅助手段，优化结构，提出最优方案。

3 数值计算及关键技术参数

采用显式动力分析软件 LS - DYNA 分析桥墩柔性防船撞装置在船舶撞击下的作用效果，对比分析防撞圈数量、钢板厚度、外钢围舱室间隔距离对防船撞装置性能产生的影响，对装置结构优化设计提供参考依据。

3.1 有限元模型

有限元模型包括承台、防船撞装置以及典型船舶。为了独立分析防船撞装置本身的力学性能，节约计算成本，承台采用刚性壳单元模拟。防船撞装置是按照实际工程图中的真实尺寸进行建模。船舶全尺寸模型按照船舶设计图纸建立，并验证了碰撞区域的刚度和碰撞力范围真实可靠。防船撞装置和船舶材料模型选用考虑应变率效应的 Cowper-Symonds 材料本构模型，防撞圈采用非线性离散梁单元。通过在防船撞装置和船舶底部添加浮力弹簧的方法实现了浮力和重力对整个碰撞响应过程的影响效果。整体模型如图2所示。

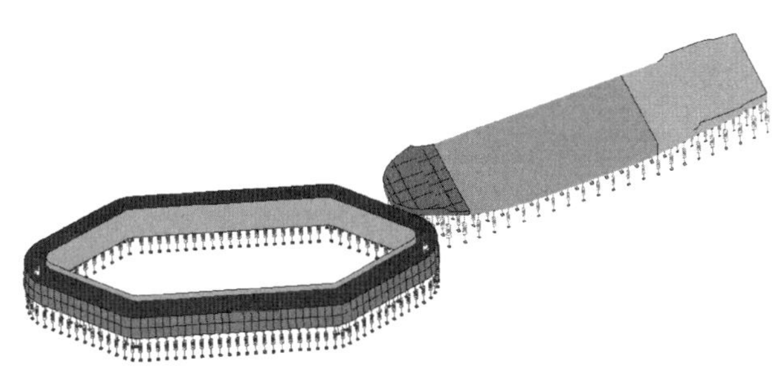

图2　船撞桥有限元模型

Fig. 2　FEM model of ship-bridge collision

3.2 防撞圈模拟

柔性防船撞装置主要结构由内、外钢围和防撞圈组成。其中,防撞圈是一类具有黏性阻尼耗散特性的非线性力学元件[2],建立一个能够反映出防撞圈力学性能的本构模型是柔性防船撞装置有限元分析中最为关键的部分。中交一公院根据对防撞圈实验数据的分析研究,最终采用 LS－DYNA 模型库中具有应变率相关性的单自由度离散梁模型对防撞圈材料本构进行了数值拟合。图 3 为该模型的典型加载卸载状态[3]。

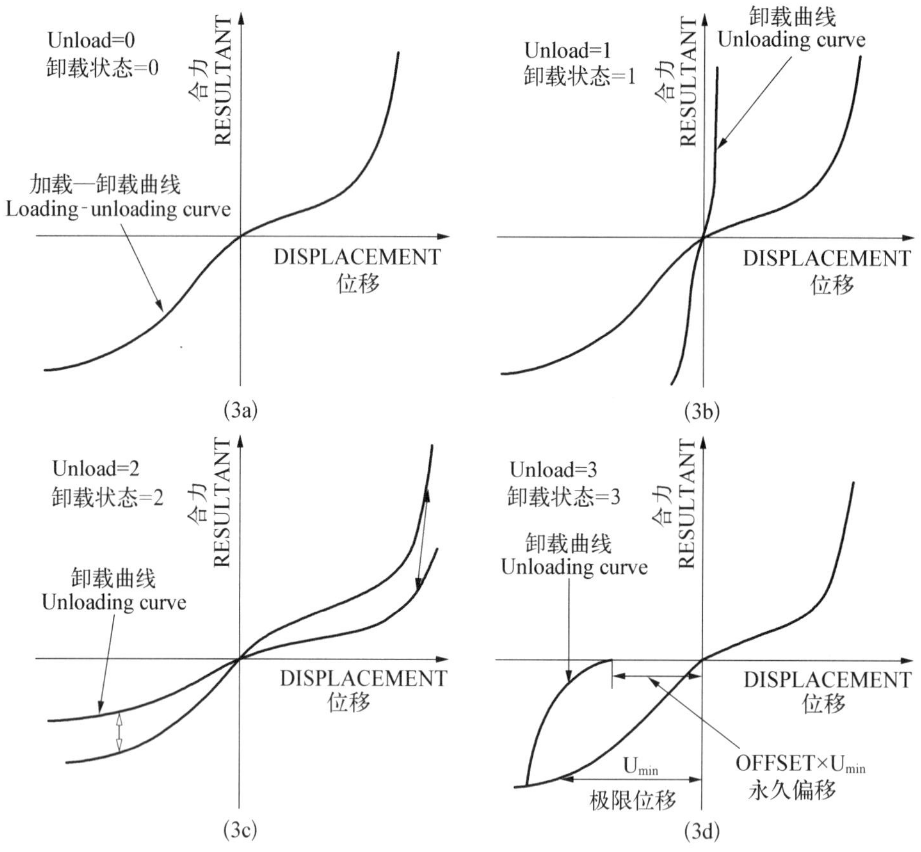

图 3　材料本构加载卸载状态

Fig. 3　Curve: loading and unloading behavior of material property

通过材料参数控制可以选择适合的加载卸载状态。为验证该模型的有效性,以 ϕ800 型(外径为 800 mm)复合高耗能防撞圈动态压缩试验数据作为数值分析拟合结果的评判依据。ϕ800 型复合高耗能防撞圈压缩受力时程试验和数值模拟结果如图 4 所示。

对比试验和数值模拟结果可以看出,数值拟合结果与试验结果十分吻合。

未验证该方法在船撞装置模拟的实际效果,分别使用非线性离散梁单元和非线性弹簧单元模拟防撞圈并进行整船撞击数值分析,防撞装置撞击撞模拟效果如图 5 所示。

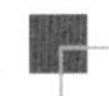

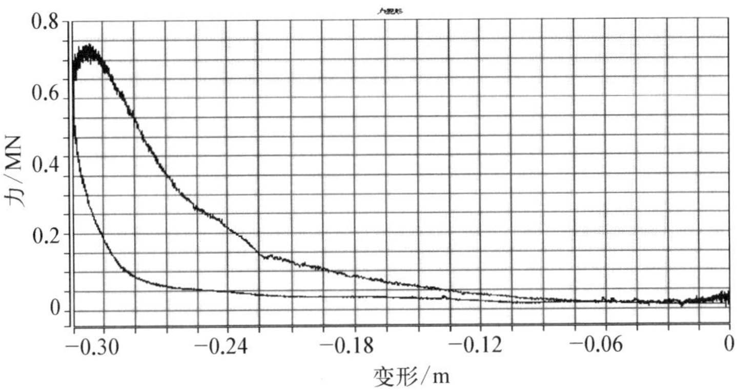

（a）试验结果

（a）Experimental result

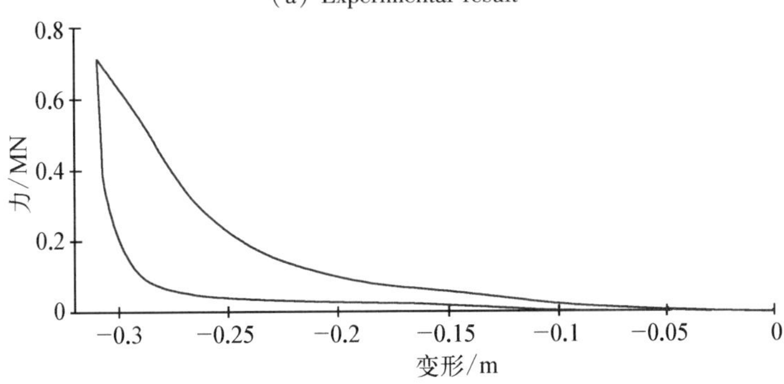

（b）拟合结果

（b）Simulation result

图 4　ϕ800 型复合高耗能防撞圈压缩试验及仿真结果

Fig. 4　Curve: compression test and simulation results of ϕ800 compound type of high energy consumption anti-collision ring

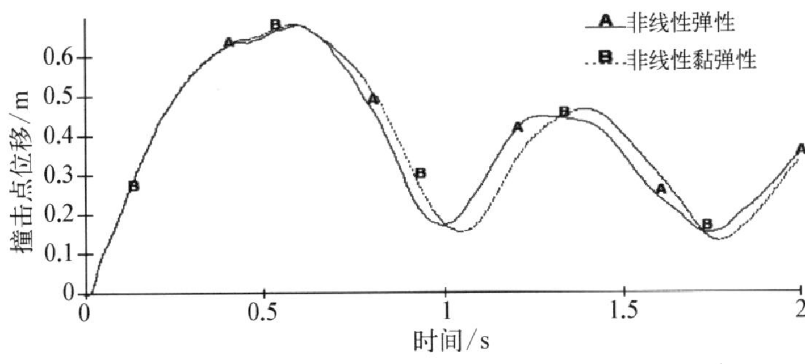

（a）撞击处位移

（a）Displacement of the impact point

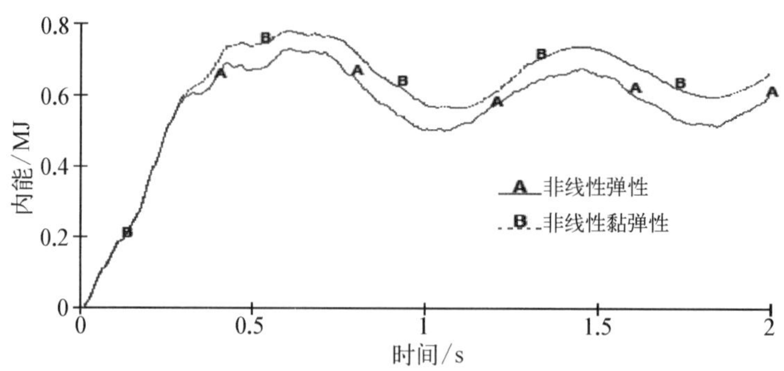

(b) 装置内能变化
(b) Device internal energy change

图5 撞击模拟效果
Fig. 5 Curve: impact simulation result

根据装置撞击处位移曲线可以看到,在撞击力加载阶段,非线性离散梁单元与非线性弹簧单元具有相同的加载过程,在撞击力卸载阶段,使用非线性离散梁单元模型的位移曲线出现了明显的滞后,表现出了其黏性阻尼特征。从两种模拟方法装置内能的变化情况看,使用非线性离散梁单元后,内能增长12.7%,更多的能量被吸收,达到了预想效果。

结果表明,非线性离散梁单元可以很好地还原防撞圈的真实力学性能。

3.3 浮力模拟

利用在浮体(船舶和防船撞装置)底部添加弹簧单元的方法,模拟“船撞桥”有限元数值仿真中浮力和重力的共同作用效果。该方法可以反映“船撞桥”这一动态仿真过程中浮体的真实受力状况以及运动轨迹,避免使用复杂的流固耦合方法,在保证计算精度的情况下缩短了计算时间。通过设置浮力弹簧刚度模拟重力和浮力的组合作用效果,图6为某桥防撞装置添加浮力弹簧前后的撞击效果对比。

图6为未考虑浮力和考虑浮力后的撞击效果。从图中可以看出,未添加浮力弹簧时,撞击效果明显失真,添加浮力弹簧后撞击效果趋于真实。

3.4 防撞圈布置

工程初期对防撞圈布置个数进行了初步的理论计算,通过仿真验算发现有较大的优化空间,因而首先对有限元模型中的防撞圈个数进行删减并计算。图7为防撞圈数量变化对照组的动能曲线。

防撞圈数量减少后,动能折损由20.2%减少为17.7%,装置整体刚度变弱,更容易产生整体位移而减少局部的塑性变形,变形能较之前更少,将更多的外部能量留在了船舶本身。

图8为防撞圈个数删减前后的撞击力曲线。减少防撞圈个数后,撞击力峰值降低5.8%,撞击力平均值降低13.2%。由于防撞圈数量减少,装置整体刚度变小,更容易被撞装置产生整体位移。减少防撞圈数量工况的撞击力曲线中两次波动较为明显的峰值显示了装置与船的相对加速度减小。

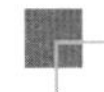

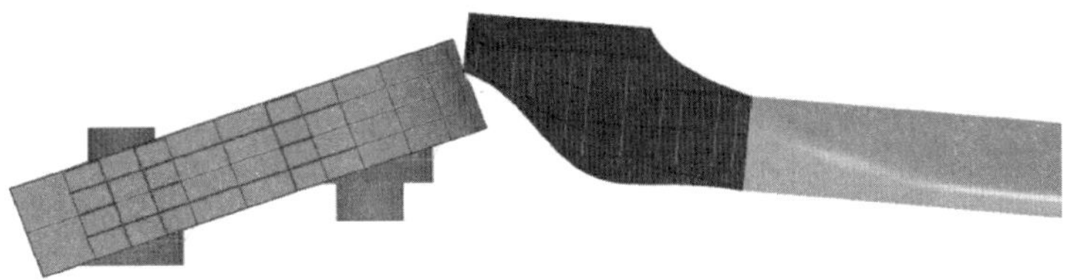

（a）未考虑浮力重力

（a）Buoyancy and gravity not be considered

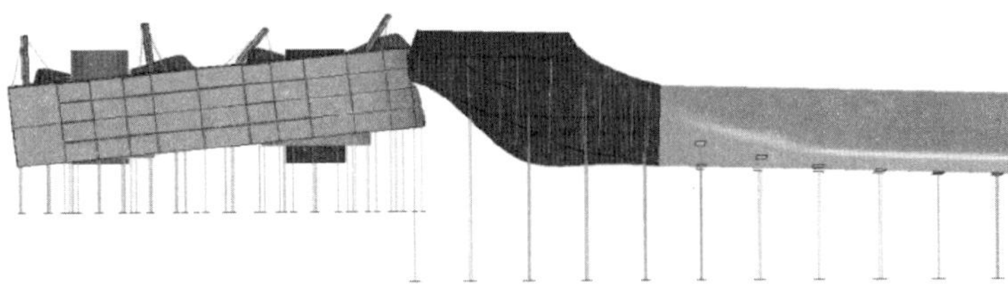

（b）考虑浮力重力

（b）Buoyancy and gravity be considered

图6　添加浮力弹簧的对比效果

Fig. 6　Buoyancy spring simulation effect

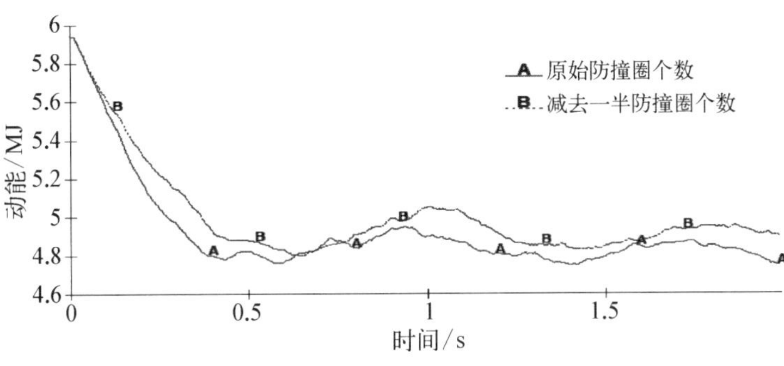

图7　动能变化

Fig. 7　Curve：change of kinetic energy

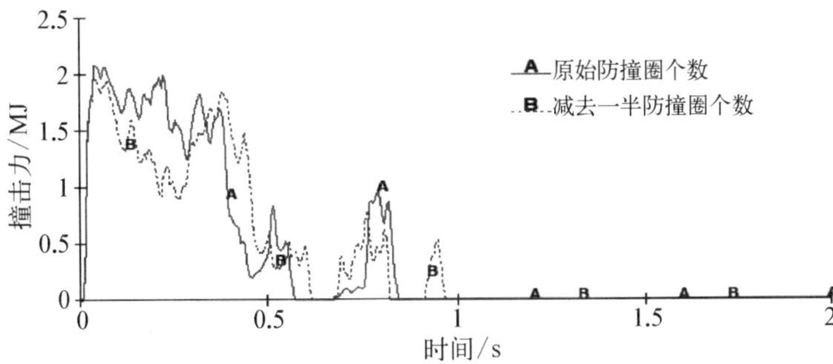

图8　撞击力曲线

Fig. 8　Curve：impact force

图 9 为防撞圈数量变化对照组的防撞圈变形情况。减少一半防撞圈数量后，撞击过程中防撞圈变形量增大，作用时间变长，是由于单位长度钢围范围内，防撞圈数量变少，多个防撞圈的整体刚度降低。

从上述调整防撞圈个数方案的结果可以看出，调整防撞圈个数可以简单直接地改变装置整体刚度。防撞圈最大变形量未达设计极限，且仍有富余，说明减少一半数量防撞圈可行。

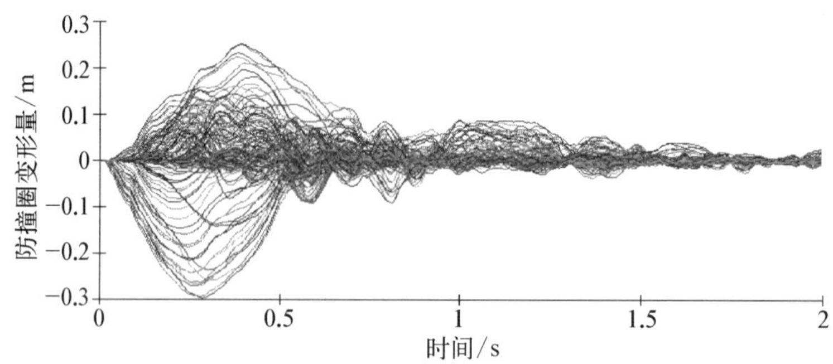

（a）未减少防撞圈个数
（a）Original number of anti-collision ring

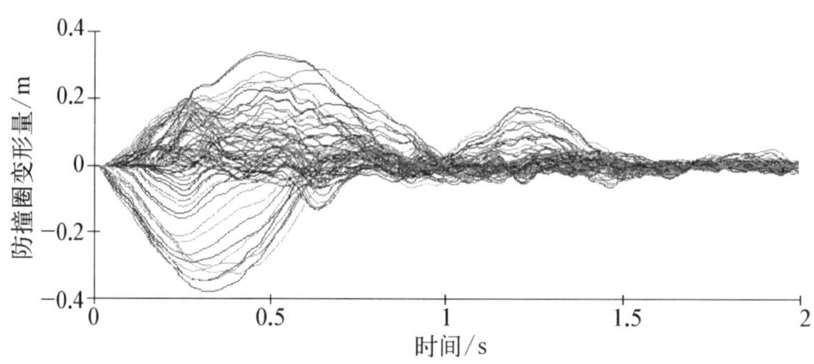

（b）减少防撞圈个数
（b）Reduced number of anti-collision ring

图 9　防撞圈变形量
Fig. 9　Curve：deformation of anti-collision ring

3.5　钢板厚度

为了分析外钢围刚度对装置防撞效果的影响，调整外钢围的钢板厚度。表 1 为钢板厚度递减的 4 种工况。

图 10 为工况 1 和工况 4 中防撞装置变形情况，可以清晰直观地看出，在板厚很薄的条件下，会出现外钢围明显的局部破坏，容易将船头嵌入变形处，不利于导向。

表 1　**各工况中防船撞装置钢板厚度**

Table 1　**Thickness of steel plate in different cases**

工　况	外层钢板厚度/mm	内部钢板厚度/mm
1	$5t$	$4t$
2	$4t$	$3t$
3	$3t$	$2t$
4	$2t$	t

注：t 表示单位厚度，单位为毫米（mm）

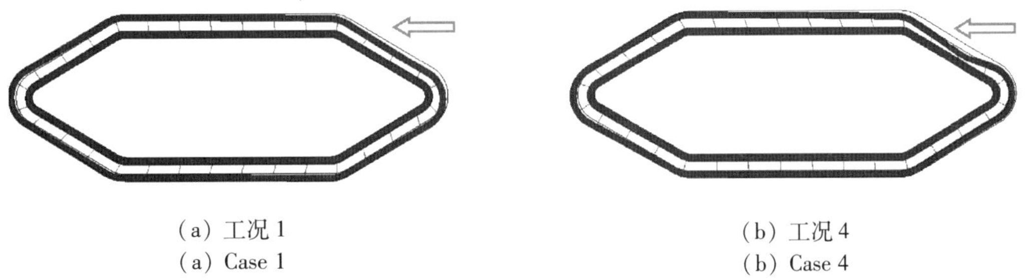

（a）工况 1　　（b）工况 4

（a）Case 1　　（b）Case 4

图 10　防撞装置变形

Fig. 10　Deformation of anti-collision device

表 2　**能量转化**

Table 2　**Simulation result of energy exchange**

工　况	动能折损/%	内能/J	滑移能/J
1	17.70	4.62E+5	4.19E+5
2	20.63	7.99E+5	6.03E+5
3	21.81	8.64E+5	6.03E+5
4	29.27	1.21E+6	5.29E+5

表 2 为四种工况下的能量转化。从表中可以看出随着钢板厚度减小，撞击处钢板更容易屈服，变形能逐渐增大。其中，以工况 4 中装置的变形能增加幅度明显，视其为装置破坏状态。

图 11 为调整钢板厚度各工况的撞击力曲线。随着钢板厚度减小，撞击力逐渐呈现出

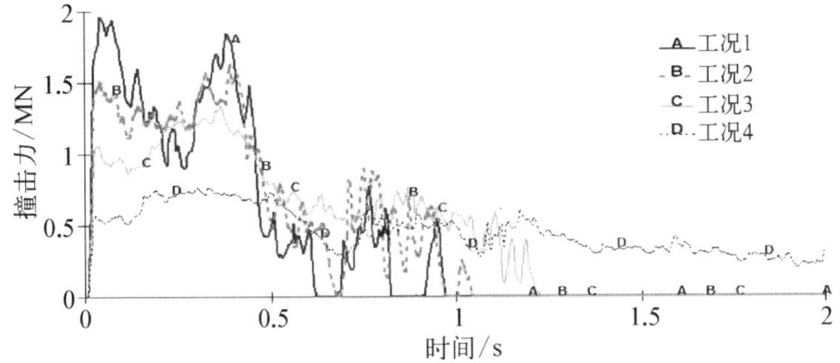

图 11　撞击力曲线

Fig. 11　Curve: impact force

平稳的趋势,峰值力逐渐降低,力作用时间变长,薄壁结构特性随着钢板厚度减小体现得越为明显,外钢围更容易出现局部破坏。

图 12 为各个板厚工况下装置撞击处的位移。装置撞击处位移随装置钢板厚度减小递增,工况 4 曲线可以看出,装置变形后无回弹。

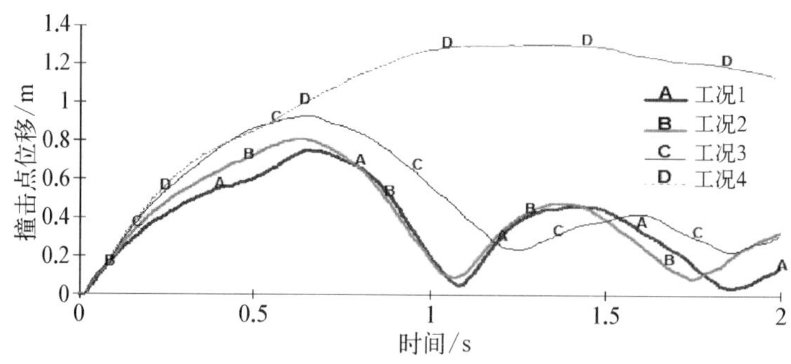

图 12 撞击处位移

Fig. 12 Curve: displacement of the impact point

表 3 防撞圈变形量

Table 3 Simulation result of anti-collision rings' deformation

工 况	防撞圈最大压缩量/mm	防撞圈最大拉伸量/mm
1	0.306	0.298
2	0.369	0.323
3	0.356	0.315
4	0.318	0.257

表 3 为各个钢板厚度工况下防撞圈变形量。后三种工况,防撞圈变形量随钢板厚度减小递减,然而撞击处位移随钢板厚度减小递增,说明后三种工况随钢板厚度减小装置局部变形增大而整体位移减小,协同性减弱。值得注意的是,在调整钢板厚度时应注意钢板厚度的不同工艺要求和使用环境限制。

3.6 舱室间隔距离

调整外钢围舱室间隔距离同样也是调整外钢围刚度的方法,以 d 为单位舱室间隔距离分别取 d, $2d$ 和 $10d$ 的不同间隔距离作对照。图 13 为外钢围舱室间隔距离变化对照组的撞击力曲线。

结果显示,钢围舱室间距增大,对削弱撞击力峰值作用明显。

调整钢板厚度和舱室间隔均为调整装置局部刚度的方法。结果表明,装置局部刚度影响能量吸收和撞击峰值力,装置整体刚度影响防撞圈协同作用及装置导向。两者看似矛盾,实存最优匹配关系。

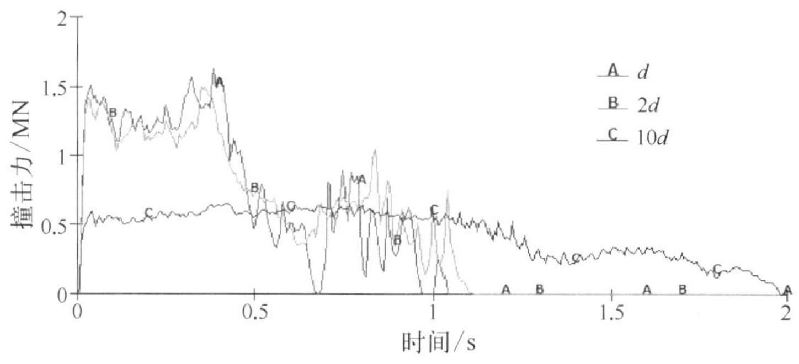

图 13　撞击力曲线

Fig. 13　Curve: impact force

4　健跳港特大桥桥墩柔性防护技术

4.1　工程概况

健跳港位于台州市三门县城东 25 km 处，全长 17 km。拟建健跳港特大桥跨越健跳港，其桥位处水面宽约 550 m，水深大于 5 m，局部最深 9 m。拟在船撞风险较大的 33 号和 34 号主墩进行船撞安全防护。桥区最高通航水位 5.49 m，最低通航水位 -3.12 m。通航代表船型 500 t。设防桥梁桥型方案如图 14 所示。

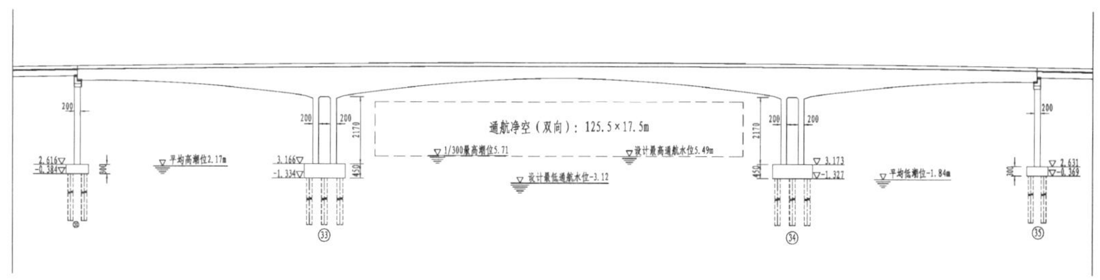

图 14　工程桥型图

Fig. 14　Bridge map

4.2　结构设计

为保证在各种水位条件下船舶均不触及墩壁或桩基、装置不脱离承台，结合健跳港桥区的通航水位以及典型船舶构造，防船撞装置高度设计为 4 m，同时在承台上搭建支撑架、设置限位装置，最终实现各水位安全防护。船舶与桥墩在各水位的相遇情况见图 15 所示。

根据装置整体和局部刚度协调性计算，最终确定防撞圈个数为 120 个。根据通航水位、代表船舶、桥墩下部构造和所需满足的其他设防要求，设计者提出柔性防船撞装置设计方案，如图 16 所示。

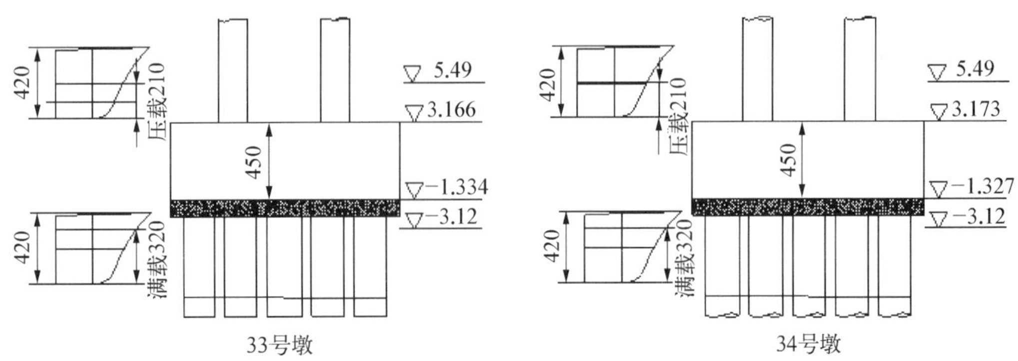

图 15　船桥相遇情况图

Fig. 15　Ship bridge position

根据设防需求及结构设计要求，装置与承台间设置减摩材料来实现装置随水位浮动时于承台间的摩擦；内外钢围通过双层布置的防撞圈进行连接；箱体由分隔板分成小舱室，通过型钢提高强度，保证箱体局部和整体强度；分别于承台上安装三角支架和限位装置在极限水位时为这个箱体提供支撑的必要条件。装置结构示意如图17 所示。

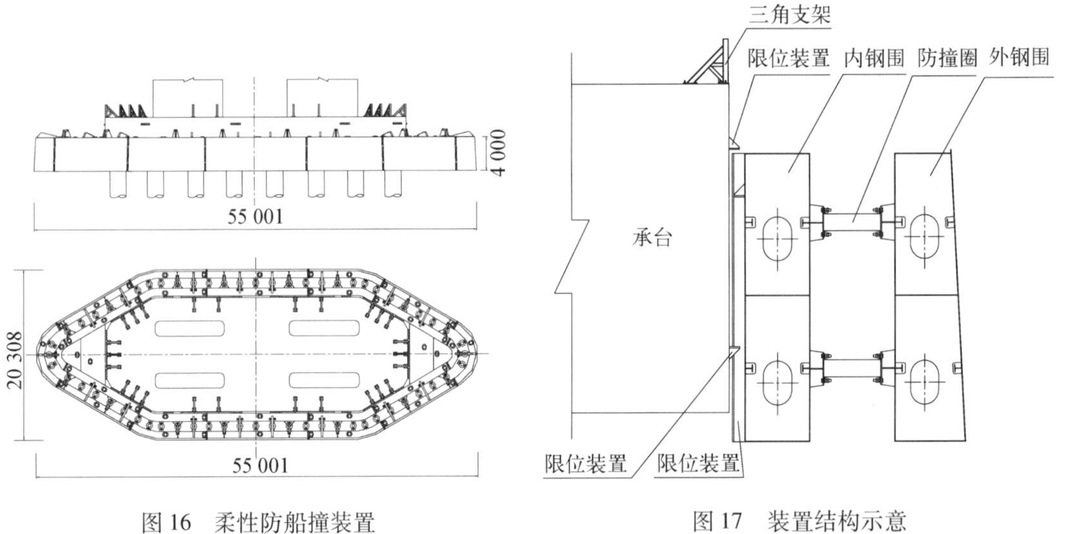

图 16　柔性防船撞装置

Fig. 16　Anti-ship-collision device

图 17　装置结构示意

Fig. 17　Device structure sketch

4.3　防护性能验证

4.3.1　计算工况

设计者采用裸墩和设防后两种状态多种撞击角度进行设防效果计算（见图 18），考虑航道夹角及风流压偏角，此处将下述侧撞工况作为典型工况进行描述。

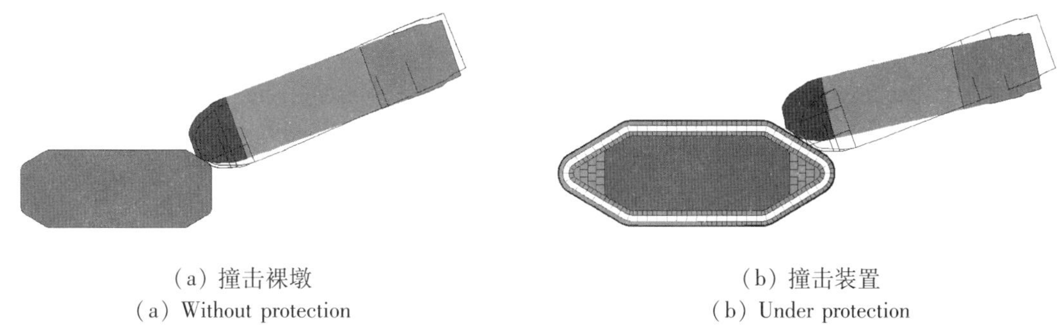

（a）撞击裸墩
（a）Without protection

（b）撞击装置
（b）Under protection

图 18　典型工况计算模型

Fig. 18　Typical condition simulation model

4.3.2　能量转化对比

撞击过程的能量转化能够直观地说明装置防撞的机理，撞击过程中动能及装置内能变化如图 19 所示，计算结果见表 4。

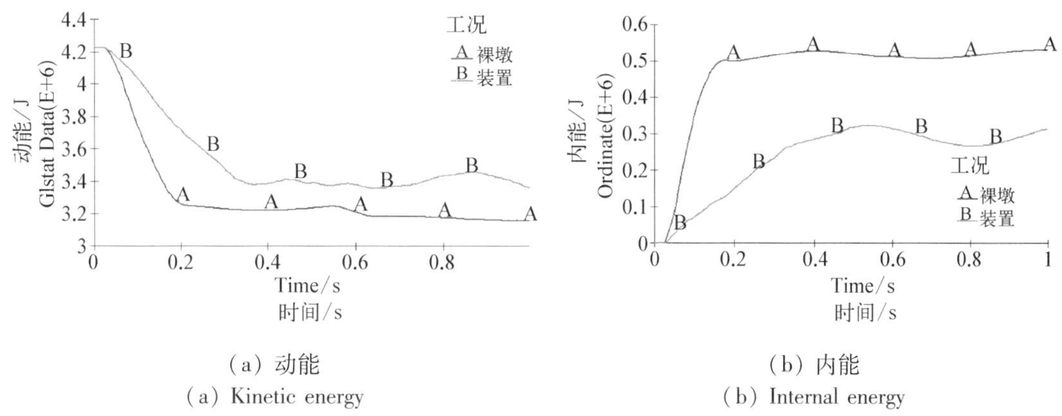

（a）动能
（a）Kinetic energy

（b）内能
（b）Internal energy

图 19　能量变化对比

Fig. 19　Curve：comparison of energy

表 4　**能量变化计算结果**

Table 4　**Simulation result of energy exchange**

工　况	总能量/J	动能衰减/J	动能折减/%	船舶变形能/J
撞击裸墩	4.23E+6	1.07E+6	25.3	0.53E+6
撞击装置	4.23E+6	0.84E+6	19.8	0.33E+6

从上述计算结果中可以看出，在有防撞装置的情况下，动能衰减较无防撞装置的情况少，大部分动能未参与撞击过程的能量交换，装置可反复多次使用，船舶变形能相对减少，达到保护船舶的目的。

4.3.3 撞击力对比

撞击力为防撞装置设防效果判定的关键指标,撞击裸墩和撞击装置过程中撞击力时程如图20所示,计算结果见表5。

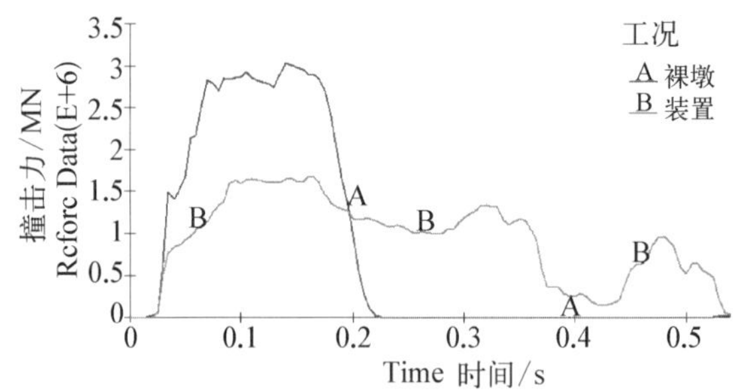

图20 撞击力对比

Fig. 20 Curve: comparison of impact force

表5 撞击力计算结果

Table 5 Simulation result of impact force

平均撞击力/MN			等效撞击力/MN		
有防撞装置 A	无防撞装置 B	相差/% (B-A)/B	有防撞装置 A	无防撞装置 B	相差/% (B-A)/B
0.95	1.97	51.78	1.64	3.00	45.33

相较于直接撞击承台,有防撞装置的情况下,峰值撞击力小,撞击力作用时间长,撞击力时程曲线平缓,具有较好的缓冲效果。在有防撞装置的情况下,桥墩上所受到的平均撞击力比无防撞装置桥墩所受到的撞击力至少51.78%,等效撞击力减至少45.33%,达到了保护桥墩的目的。

4.3.4 协同作用

当防撞装置受撞击时,防撞圈元件发挥作用的数量多少关系到整个防撞装置是否整体发挥作用。图21反映了防撞圈共同作用效果。

防撞圈协同作用趋势满足撞击力作用趋势,在最大撞击力时刻,防撞圈变形达到峰值。0.2 s左右全部防撞圈参与作用,同期性良好。防撞圈最大变形量为防撞圈设计性能参数中最大变形量的50%,在其允许变形范围内。

4.3.5 外钢围应力分布

通过钢围应力分布可判断装置是否发生破坏,图22为撞击力峰值时刻外钢围的应力分布。

考虑应变率效应下的钢材本构特征,本计算中动态屈服应力定为580 MPa,整个撞击过程中,外钢围应力均在屈服点以下,未发生破坏。

4.3.6 导向效果分析

导向性也是评价装置设防效果的重要指标,表6为导向效果计算结果。

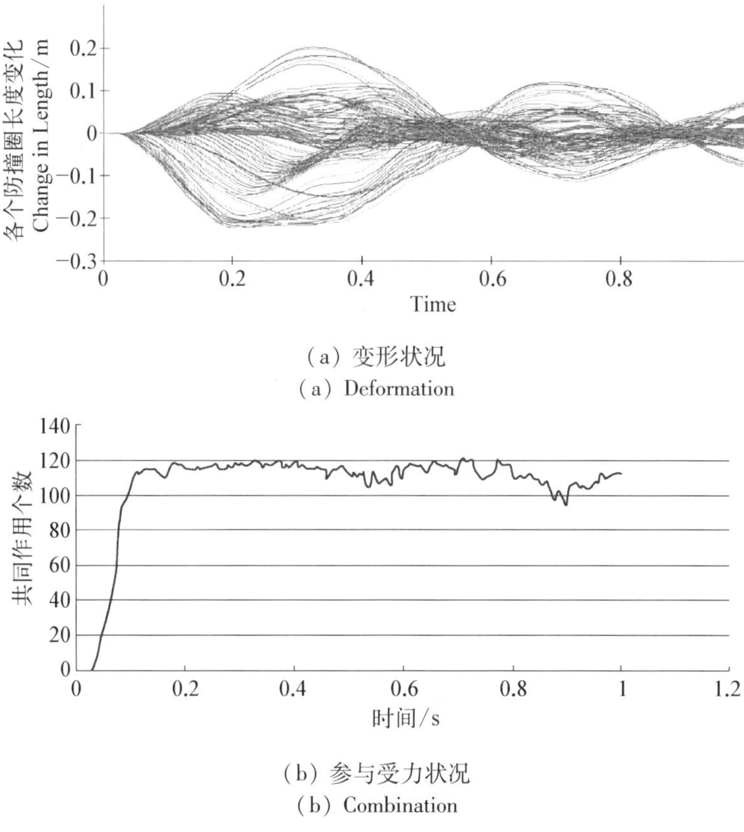

（a）变形状况

（a）Deformation

（b）参与受力状况

（b）Combination

图 21　防撞圈变形曲线

Fig. 21　Curve: deformation of anti-collision rings

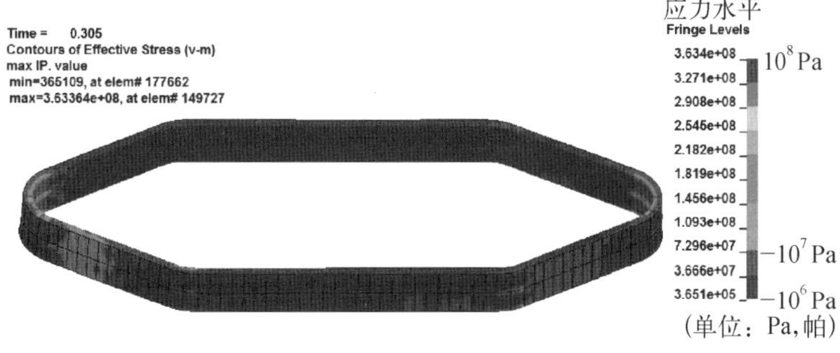

图 22　外钢围应力分布

Fig. 22　The stress distribution of device

表 6　**船舶导向对比**

Table 6　**Comparison of ship orientation**

工　况	船头偏移量/m	距离质心/m	偏转角度/°
撞击裸墩	3.88	31.5	7.02
撞击装置	4.28	31.5	7.74

在有防撞装置的情况下,船头偏移角度大于无防撞装置时,由于撞击接触面装置角度与承台角度相同,说明防撞装置有利于促进船舶的导向。

4.3.7 设防性能结论

(1) 与船舶撞击裸墩相比,由于柔性防撞装置能降低撞击力并将船头拨开,船舶初始动能(4.23 MJ)参与能量交换由 25.3% 降至 19.8%;

(2) 与船舶撞击裸墩相比,安装柔性防撞装置后等效撞击力降低了 45.33%,达到保护桥墩的目的;

(3) 各防撞圈同时受力,协同作用性能良好;

(4) 设置防撞装置有利于船舶导向。

5 总结

(1) 提出了桥墩柔性防船撞装置的设计和优化方法;

(2) 相对于普通弹簧单元,非线性离散梁单元本构模型可以更好地表现出防撞圈黏滞性耗能特性,方法可操作性强;

(3) 通过添加浮力弹簧可以有效模拟浮力和重力的组合作用,避免计算结果失真;

(4) 柔性防船撞装置整体和局部刚度直接影响设防效果,通过结构的合理设计安排,可以使装置达到最优的刚度要求;

(5) 有限元模拟计算显示,健跳港特大桥主墩设置柔性防撞装置后,可以有效降低船舶与桥梁撞击的作用力,保证桥梁安全。

参 考 文 献

[1] 陈国虞,王礼立,杨黎明,陈明栋. 桥梁防撞理论和防撞装置设计[M]. 北京:人民交通出版社,2013.

[2] 陈国虞,王礼立. 船撞桥及其防御[M]. 北京:中国铁道出版社,2006.

[3] LS-DYNA 关键词用户指南[Z]. 利弗莫尔:利弗莫尔软件技术公司,2007:971.

发表于:国际船桥相撞及其防护学术研讨会论文集[M].
北京:中国铁道出版社,2014:154-160.

Published at: Proceeding of International Symposium on Ship-Bridge Collision and its Protection. China Railway Press, 2014-154-160.

防撞装置多个防撞圈同期作用数值分析及试验验证

The numerical analysis and experiment of synchronism on multi-anti-collision rings within the anti-collision device with outer steel gate

黄德进[1]　王礼立[1]　倪步友[2]　陈国虞[2]

（1. 宁波大学机械工程和力学学院，宁波　315211；
2. 上海海洋钢结构研究所，上海　201204）

HUANG Dejin[1], WANG Lili[1], NI Buyou[2], CHEN Guoyu[2]

(1. Mechanical Engineering and Mechanics Faculty, Ningbo University, Ningbo 315211, China; 2. Shanghai Marine Steel & Structure Research Institute, Shanghai 201204, China)

摘　要　采用一个将模拟桥墩及浮于其周围的防撞装置横置的模型（用 ϕ300 mm 防撞圈），测定其冲击试验时防撞圈受压、受拉和受剪三个工况的力和功，绘出时程曲线，以便求出外钢围包络下的多个防撞圈在防撞时的贡献。试验前对该模型的作用过程进行动态数值分析，并与试验结果进行对比，所得出的结论提供给防御 50 000 t 船撞击桥梁的防撞装置初步设计作参考。

关键词　船桥碰撞模拟试验　多个防撞圈共同作用　同期性　外钢围　动态数值分析

Abstract: A bridge pier and his impact defend device model (with many ϕ300 mm anti-collision rings) be held horizontally, by impact test, determine the forces and works in pressed, tension or in shear, draw out its time travel curves, for determine the contributions of the anti-collision rings envelope by the outer steel gate. Before test people carry through the dynamic numerical analysis and contrast with the result of test. The conclusion should be consult for the primary design of the defend impact device to 50 000 t ship.

Keywords: modeling test for ship-bridge collision, combined action of multi-anti-collision rings, synchronism, outer steel gate, dynamic numerical analysis

1 前言

进行动态有限元数值模拟和模型试验的目的：通过动态有限元数值模拟，对钢绳柔性防撞装置在船—桥撞击过程中各钢绳防撞圈元件同时发挥作用的所谓“同期作用历时”进行数值分析，并对钢绳防撞圈的刚度（或其倒数，即柔度）对于“同期作用历时”的影响作分析讨论。

为了更合理有效地解决船—桥撞击的安全防护问题，人们提出了船、桥和防撞装置三者都不损坏的“三不坏”的设计思想[1]。以此思想为指导，陈国虞等开发了以柔性钢绳防撞圈为元件，通过并联和串联的形式相组合的新型吸能防撞装置[2]。从冲击动力学的观点出发[3-4]，当船撞击防撞装置的瞬间，一般会有一个先由少数防撞圈元件发挥作用，再发展到全部防撞圈元件都发挥作用的时间过程。如果以发挥作用的防撞圈数目 N 与构成防撞装置的防撞圈总数 N_T 之比值定义为“有效作用系数”f_{eff}（它是时间的函数），则有

$$f_{eff}(t) < 1, 若\ t < T_{tq}$$

$$f_{eff}(t) = 1, 若\ t \geqslant T_{tq}$$

此处 T_{tq} 是从撞击开始时刻 T_0 到全部防撞圈元件都发挥作用的时刻 T_q 所经历的时间（$T_{tq} = T_q - T_0$），本文将其定义为“同期作用历时”。不同的防撞元件和不同的防撞装置设计显然会有不同的“同期作用历时”，人们当然期望这一过程的历时 T_{tq} 愈短愈好。

鉴于钢绳防撞圈与其他防撞元件相比具有较大的柔性，从定性上不难想象理应具有较短的 T_{tq}。从定量上则应由落锤试验和动态有限元数值分析作进一步研究分析。本文重点致力于用动态有限元方法对同期作用历时作数值分析并与试验作对比。

2 动态数值模拟

冲击高应变率条件下的结构动态响应与静载条件下的结构响应相区别，通常应计及两种基本效应，即惯性效应与应变率效应[3,4]。前者导致各种形式的，精确的或简化的，波传播的研究；后者则导致各种类型的应变率相关的本构关系与失效准则的研究。问题在于这两种效应常常耦合在一起出现。

相应地，在以下研究钢绳防撞装置在撞击初期的同期作用历程时，一方面必须考虑到应力波效应，另一方面必须考虑到钢绳防撞圈在冲击载荷下具有与静载下不同的力-位移特性。为此，我们采用动态有限元程序进行数值模拟以计及应力波效应，并且计算中所用的钢绳防撞圈的力-位移特性是以落锤试验实测数据为依据的。

2.1 计算模型的建立

与落锤试验相对应,在数值模拟中取防撞装置的简化模型如图 1 所示。防护围子用 H 型钢(宽 120 mm,高 112 mm,壁厚 6 mm)建造,并且设为各向同性弹性材料。

2.2 初始和边界条件

初始条件：参照落锤试验,初始条件设为一个重 500 kg 的方形钢块以初速 $v=4$ m/s 垂直撞向桥墩,如图 1 ~ 3 所示。

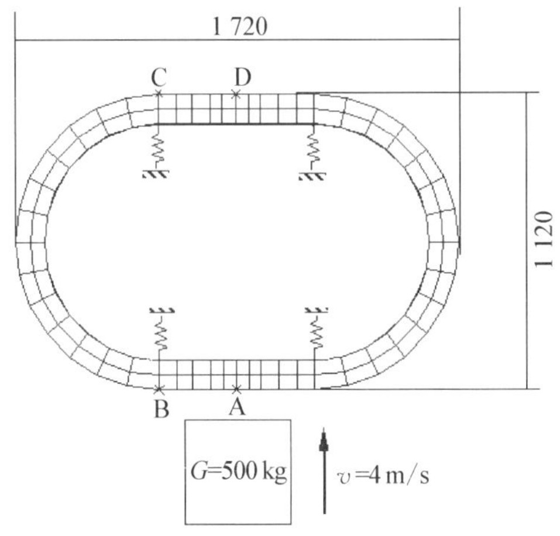

图 1 钢绳防撞装置计算模型(尺寸单位：mm)

Fig. 1 The calculation model of steel wire anti-collision device

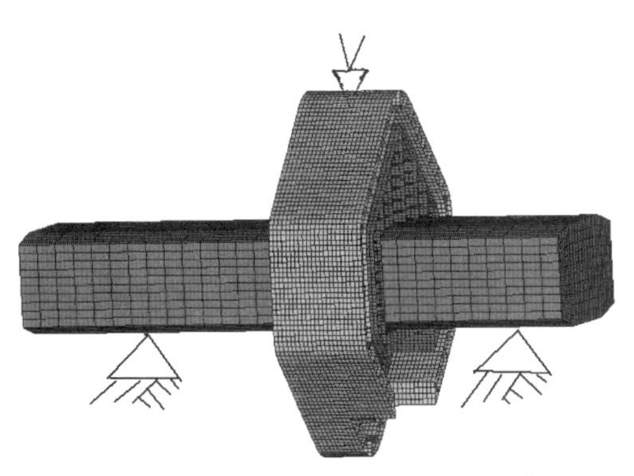

图 2 钢绳防撞装置试验模型效果图

Fig. 2 The test model effect picture of steel wire anti-collision device (with outer steel gate)

图 3 钢绳防撞装置模型试验照片

Fig. 3 The test picture of steel wire anti-collision device model (with outer steel gate)

边界条件则取以下三种边界条件进行对比：

(1) 外钢围没有约束,以便单独分析应力波在外钢围中传播的影响;

(2) 外钢围在图 1 所示 4 个约束处给定,刚度系数为 $K=100$ kN/m;

(3) 外钢围在图 1 所示 4 个约束处给定：刚度系数为 $K=50$ kN/m,以考察不同刚度

(柔度)的影响。

2.3 数值模拟结果及讨论

在第一种条件下(即外钢围没有约束),计算得出的图 1 中 A、B、C、D 四点的垂直位移如图 4 所示。相应地,撞击处 A 点的应力-时间曲线见图 5。

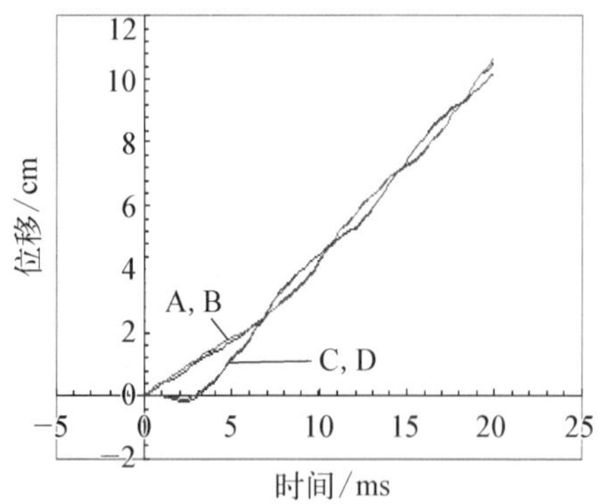

图 4 第一种条件下外钢围 A、B、C、D 四点的位移-时间关系

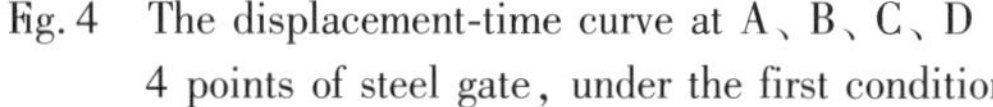

Fig. 4 The displacement-time curve at A、B、C、D 4 points of steel gate, under the first condition

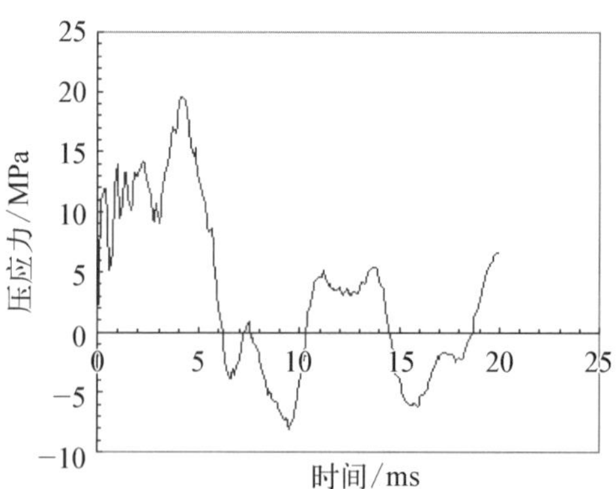

图 5 第一种条件($K=0$)下 A 点的压应力-时间曲线

Fig. 5 The stress-time curve at point A, when $K=0$ under the first condition

由图 4 可见,外钢围中 A 点与 B 点,C 点与 D 点的垂直位移基本接近。这显然是由于各自的位置很接近,应力波传播的影响就不太明显。但是在撞击的初期,由于应力波传播效应,C 点(D 点)的动态位移响应就明显落后于 B 点(A 点),要滞后大约 6 ms。直到 6.8 ms 左右,A(B)点与 C(D)点的位移-时间曲线才基本趋于一致。如果忽略这两组曲线间的相位差,则在 $T_{tq}\approx 6.8$ ms 后,外钢围已可被视为以平均恒速整体运动。

由图 5 可见,在撞击初期,撞击处 A 点受到冲击压力,在 4.8 ms 时达到最大值 19.3 MPa。此后由于弯曲波的作用,处于拉压应力交替的弯曲震荡过程中。

下面再考虑钢绳防撞圈的作用。不难想象,在 T_{tq}大约为 $10^0\sim10^1$ ms 量级的情况下,钢绳防护圈对 T_{tq}的作用主要取决于其初始刚度。因此,在计算中钢绳防护圈的作用可以用一个与钢绳防撞圈初始刚度相同的弹簧元件来表征。

这样,在第二种边界条件下,外钢围在图 1 所示 4 个约束处给定,其刚度系数取为 $K=100$ kN/m。计算得出的图 1 中 A、B、C、D 四点的位移-时间曲线如图 6 所示。相应地,撞击处 A 点的压应力-时间曲线则如图 7 所示。

由图 6 可见,虽然 A 点与 B 点,C 点与 D 点的位移仍然各个基本接近,但由于在第二种条件下,外钢围在这四个点处受到初始刚度系数为 $K=100$ kN/m 的钢绳防护圈的约束,在初始阶段,C、D 点的位移-时间曲线比 A、B 要滞后 5 ms 左右,直到大约 40 ms 后四者才趋于一致,即 $T_{tq}\approx 40$ ms。此外,在 22.3 ms 时 A、B 曲线达到最大值,最大值为 4.58 cm,而 C、D 曲线则在 17.5 ms 和 31.7 ms 时达到两个峰值,分别为 3.78 cm 和 3.82 cm。

A、B、C、D 位移-时间曲线的振荡在 60 ms 后趋向减弱。

由图 7 可见，A 点处的冲击压应力，一开始也在约 5 ms 时出现约 20 MPa 的峰值。但由于钢绳防撞圈的约束作用，在 26 ms 时出现第二个峰值，达到其最大压力值 27.9 MPa。

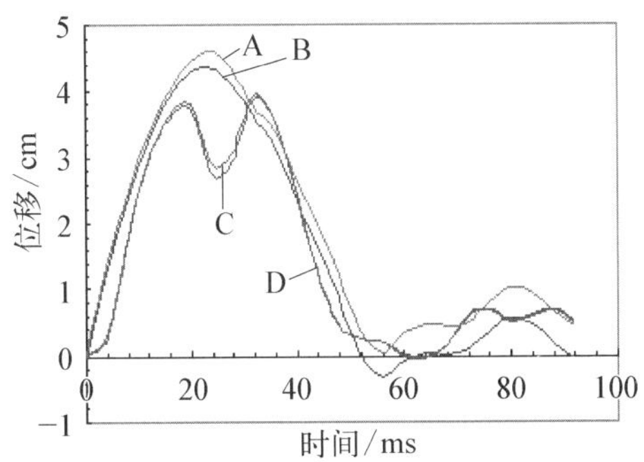

图 6　第二种条件下外钢围中 A、B、C、D 四点的位移-时间关系

Fig. 6　The displacement-time curve at A, B, C, D 4 points of steel gate, under second condition

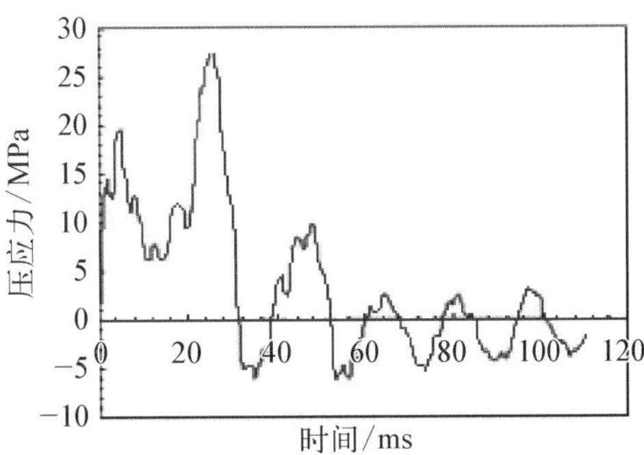

图 7　第二种条件($K=100$ kN/m)下 A 点的压应力-时间曲线

Fig. 7　The stress-time curve at point A, when $K=100$ kN/m under the second condition

为了了解钢绳防撞圈刚度对于同期作用历时的影响，在第三种计算条件下仍然取外钢围在图 1 所示四个点处受到约束，但其刚度系数为 $K=50$ kN/m。计算得出的 A、B、C、D 四点处的位移-时间曲线如图 8 所示。相应地，撞击处 A 点的应力-时间曲线则如图 9 所示。

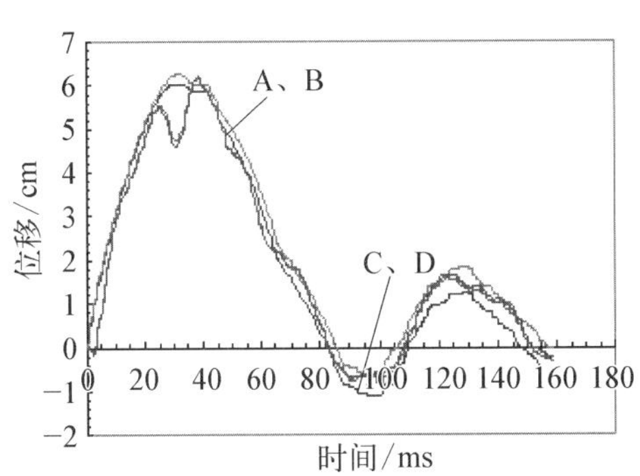

图 8　第三种条件下外钢围中 A、B、C、D 四点的位移-时间关系

Fig. 8　The displacement-time curve at A, B, C, D 4 points of steel gate, under third condition

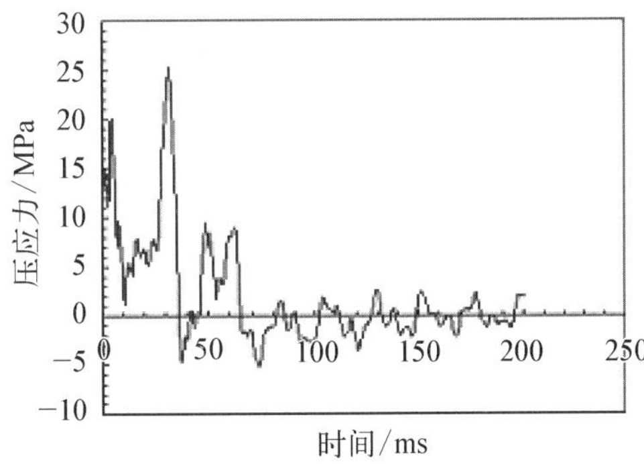

图 9　第三种条件($K=50$ kN/m)下 A 点的压应力-时间曲线

Fig. 9　The stress -time curve at point A, when $K=50$ kN/m under the third condition

对比图 8 与图 6 可见，钢绳防撞圈的初始刚度系数从 $K=100$ kN/m 减为 $K=50$ kN/m 时，在撞击初始阶段 C、D 点的位移-时间曲线比 A、B 点的滞后值从 5 ms 降到 2 ms 左右；但同期作用时间仍约 40 ms，即 $T_{tq}\approx 40$ ms 后四者才趋于一致。此外，在 27.73 ms 时A、B 曲线达到最大值，最大值为 6.22 cm。C、D 曲线在 22.15 ms 和 38.4 ms 时达到两个峰值，分别为 5.37 cm 和 6.21 cm。A、B、C、D 在 80 ms 后趋向于在

0 值左右、上下振荡。

由图 9 则可见，A 点处的冲击压力一开始也与图 7 所示类似，在约 5 ms 时出现约 20 MPa 的第一个峰值，然后由于钢绳防撞圈的约束作用出现第二个峰值。但与图 7 相比可见，随着钢绳防护圈的初始刚度系数从 $K=100$ kN/m 减为 $K=50$ kN/m，其第二个峰值出现的时间延到 32 ms，而其最大压力的数值降为 24.9 MPa。

2.4 计算分析结论

（1）考虑到船桥撞击过程中的应力波传播，一般而言，在船撞击防撞装置的初期，会有一个先由少数防撞圈元件发挥作用、再发展到全部防撞圈元件都发挥作用的时间过程。在设计新型防撞装置时，应该力求使这一过程的历时，即所谓“同期作用历时”T_{tq}愈短愈好。

（2）对于本文所研究的钢绳柔性防撞装置模型，同期作用历时大约为 40 ms。这对于以秒计的船桥撞击过程而言，是可以忽略不计的。

（3）本数值模拟还表明，防撞元件的初始刚度的减小，有利于最大撞击压力出现时间的推迟，也有利于降低最大撞击压力值。

（4）“同期作用历时”对于防撞装置的合理设计是有意义的。它既取决于防撞元件的刚度，也还取决于防撞装置的具体结构。在设计防撞装置时，建议通过数值模拟进行分析，以便通过对比来选定最优设计。

3 多个柔性防撞圈共同作用系数试验

2001 年 11 月 12 日试验使用的 F300 mm 防撞圈额定冲击能为 2 400 J。实测试验时施加 2 370 J，吸能率为 71.5%。

3.1 共同作用系数试验验证布置

共同作用系数试验验证布置如 10 和图 11 所示。

图 10 右图是各种组合的总和，当只有 1、2 时是并联；有 1、2、3、4 时是正反两面并联；只有 1、7 时是串联；只有 1、2、7、8 是串并联；只有 5、6 时是剪切；有 1、2、3、4、5、6 时是串联、并联和剪切。

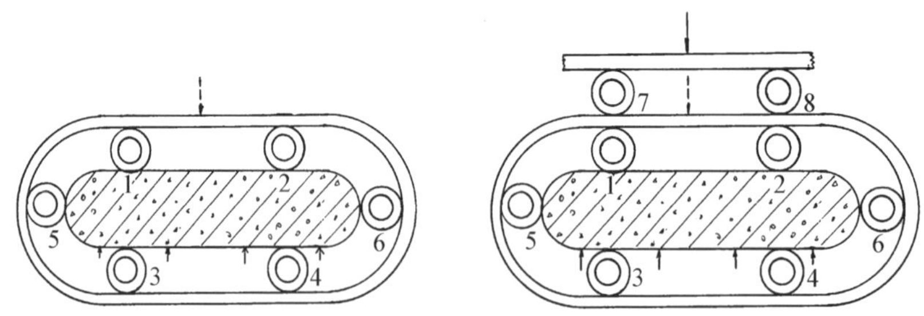

图 10 同期作用系数试验验证试样设计

Fig. 10 The samples for test of coefficient synchronism

图 11　同期系数试样照片

Fig. 11　The photo of samples for test of coefficient synchronism

3.2　共同作用系数试验结果

共同作用系数试验结果如表 1 所示。

表 1　作用系数试验结果

Table 1　The result of synchronism coefficient test

试验项目	设计值/J	试验值/J
单个(平均值)	2 000	2 164
两个串联	3 800	5 014
两个并联四个剪切	8 200	8 278
四个并联两个剪切	9 800	10 449

因为表 1 中的设计值是根据表 2 的系数设计出来的。试验结果与设计值比较吻合，由此证明设计所依据的共同作用系数是正确的。

表 2　三种受力状态下的同期系数

Table 2　The synchronism coefficients under three stress conditions

同期系数名称	系数值
串联	0.95
并联	0.95
剪切	0.55

3.3　多个防撞圈多次重复试验

为了判明多次受撞时，经过恢复的防撞圈的吸能能力是否变化，特制作正反均为两个

并联加两个剪切共6个(图10的1、2、3、4、5、6)防撞圈的试样进行多次冲击,其结果如表3。

表3 受压和剪切两次受力状态下多个防撞圈重复试验的吸收功

Table 3 The repeat test on test works of multi-anti-collision rings under two force conditions

摘　要	设计值/J	试验值/J
1. 正反四个并联受压,两个剪切	9 800	10 022
2. 正反四个并联受压,两个剪切	9 800	10 091
3. 正反四个并联受压,两个剪切	9 800	10 230

从表3看出,三次试验的结果非常接近,吸能能力不下降。

3.4 F800钢丝绳柔性吸能防撞圈(未复合)1:1分段试验

1:1分段的选取体现了整体方案的特征:

(1) 取1:1的防撞圈实样,钢围子也按实际的抗弯截面设计,分段有8个防撞圈;

(2) 具有两层;

(3) 每层分为相互垂直的两向布置;

(4) 用钢板构架模拟外钢围将两层防撞圈联系起来。

1:1分段的实样如图12所示。

图12 具有8个防撞圈与钢围子组成的分段

Fig. 12 The section component with 8rings and the outer steel gate

试验结果的冲击总功如表4,由于落锤不够大,两层分段试验的变形和吸能均未达到设计值。

表4 4个和8个钢丝绳防撞圈与钢围子组成的分段试验值

Table 4 The test result of section component with 8 rings and the outer steel gate

摘　要	设计值/J	试验/J
1. 两层组合的分段(8个防撞圈)	120 000	113 700
2. 单层分段(4个防撞圈)	60 000	86 090

3.5 F800复合柔性吸能防撞圈1:1分段试验

2003年3月3日试验使用的F800 mm防撞圈每个额定冲击能为50 000 J。实测试验时施加57 996 J,吸能率为78.4%。

1:1分段的选取体现了整体方案的特征:

(1) 取1:1的防撞圈实样,试验分段有4个和8个防撞圈两种;

(2) 试验分段具有一层和两层两种;

(3) 每层分为相互垂直的两向布置;

(4) 用钢板构架将两层防撞圈联系起来,如图13所示。

试验分段吸收能量可达86%。

图13 有4个单层F800复合柔性吸能防撞圈1:1的分段

Fig. 13 The 1:1 section component with F800 × 4 composite anti-collision rings and the outer steel gate

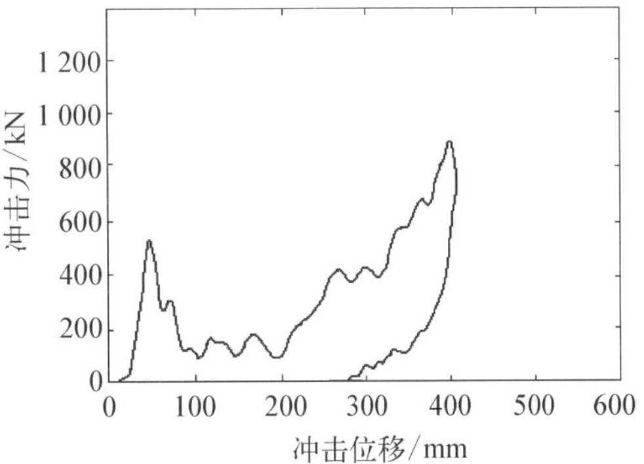

图14 4个防撞圈分段的力——位移图

Fig. 14 The displacement-time curve of the 1:1 section component with F800 ×4 composite anti-collision rings and the outer steel gate

3.6 双层F800复合柔性吸能防撞圈1:1分段试验

双层F800复合柔性吸能防撞圈1:1试验分段实样如图15所示。冲击试验现场如图16所示。

图15 双层,有8个F800复合柔性吸能防撞圈1:1分段试验试样照片

Fig. 15 The photo of 1:1 section component with F800 ×8 composite anti-collision rings in double deck with the outer steel gate

图 16　F800 复合柔性吸能防撞圈 1∶1分段冲击试验现场

Fig. 16　The test site photo of 1∶1 section component with F800 ×8 composite anti-collision rings in double deck with the outer steel gate

由于单个圈的额定能量增大，对于 8 个防撞圈的分段，现用的落锤试验机的功率不够，不能打到额定位移值，也不能发生 8 个防撞圈所需要的能量。

在本次试验具体情况下吸收能量可达 73.6%。

4　总结

4 个和 8 个防撞圈组成的分段冲击试验得到以下几点结论：

（1）钢结构能够使多个复合柔性吸能防撞圈同期发挥作用；

（2）所选用的紧固件能够使复合柔性吸能防撞圈发挥作用；

（3）多个复合柔性吸能防撞圈能够串联、并联发挥作用；

（4）多个复合柔性吸能防撞圈能够获得比较大的能量吸收率，本次试验达到 73.6% ~86%。

参考文献

[1] 陈国虞. 三不坏桥墩防撞装置的设计[C]. 上海海洋钢结构研究所船撞桥论文集，2000.

[2] 陈国虞，倪步友. 水中桩柱用钢绳柔性冲击吸能器试验研究[J]. 交通部上海船舶运输科学研究所学报，1995(2).

[3] 王礼立. 应力波基础[M]. 2 版. 北京：国防工业出版社,2005.

[4] 王礼立,张忠伟,黄德进,等. 船撞桥的钢丝绳圈柔性防撞装置的冲击动力学分析[C]. 洪友士. 应用力学进展——祝贺郑哲敏先生八十华诞. 北京：科学出版社,2004：172－180.

发表于：国际船桥相撞及其防护学术研会论文集[M].
北京：中国铁道出版社,2014：146－153.

Published at：Proceedings of International Symposium on Ship-Bridge Collision and Its Protection. China Railway Press，2014：146－153.

第四部分

柔性防船撞的实验基础及实船验证

The experimental basis and test validation of flexible anti-collision technology

水中桩桩用钢绳柔性冲击吸能器试验研究

Experimental study on steel rope-flexible impact energy absorber for structures in waterways

陈国虞　倪步友

（交通部上海船舶运输科学研究所）

CHEN Guoyu, NI Buyou

(Shanghai Ship & Shipping Institute, Ministry of Communication)

摘　要　船撞桥的研究最近20年来已形成一个学科。国际桥梁和结构工程协会在1991年于列宁格勒会议上汇总了这一领域的153篇文章。按该汇总报告的，作者开发了一种新的钢绳冲击吸能器。

在制造这种吸能器时，应用了3种技术：钢绳紧密对垒排列；选择合理的钢绳结构和高强度钢绳；钢绳端部压套。这样便得到高的吸能率，而且在多次冲击后不会松散。

测定了动态特性，诸如最大冲击功、吸收功、吸能率、变形量恢复等，这些参数对于设计防撞设备是必需的。这些吸能器的吸能率为橡胶吸能器的2~3倍。

给出用这些吸能器装配成吸能设施的方法，当它们串联和并联时的能量计算，能将船头折反离开的钢圈的构造以及使防撞设施浮在与船舶水线相当位置的办法。

关键词　圈航运安全　船撞桥　吸能　冲击　柔性　钢绳

Abstract: During the last 20 years, the study on ship collision with bridge has been become an engineering discipline. In the conference of IABSE held in 1991 at Leningrad, 153 papers of this area were published. Based on these view points, the authors developed a new impact energy absorber made by steel rope loops.

For manufacturing the absorber, three techniques were applied: the tight tier of rope loops, the selection of reasonable configuration and strength of rope, and the use of ferrules to rope ends. In this way, its high efficiency of absorbing impact energy was obtained and it can still work well after impact many times.

The dynamic characteristics of the absorber, such as the maximum impact power, the rate of absorbed energy, the recovery of deformation displacement, etc., which are the parameters needed for the design of anti-impact equipment, is given in the paper. Its absorbed energy efficiency is about 2 ~ 3 times of rubber absorber.

This paper describes the way how to assemble the absorbers to be an anti-impact device, the calculation of absorbed energy when absorbers placed in series or in parallel, the configuration of steel hoop that can repel ship bow and the method to make the anti-impact equipment floating near the ship waterline.

Keywords: shipping safety, collision between ship and bridge, energy absorbing, impact, flexibility, steel rope

1 前言

在 1991 年 9 月于列宁格勒召开的国际桥梁和结构工程协会(IABSE)年会上,Ole Damgaard Larsen 总结了 1983 ~ 1991 年近 10 年有关船撞桥的研究,分析了 1964 年至 1990 年间共 19 例典型船撞桥事故。他应用大量论文提出建桥和防撞的指南,并认为船撞桥的研究已发展成为一个学科。

由 O Larsen 主持的分委会提出船撞桥的研究应考虑:桥的安全,桥上车和人的安全,船只的安全和事故对环境污染的影响等 4 个方面。

该指南综合应用了欧洲和日本的研究者建立的碰撞公式对不同船舶碰撞力的计算值,有较大的参考意义,但试验验证需继续进行。

该指南中分析航行船只和漂流船只的特点,提出“船只行驶速度可分解为计算纵向、横向动能用的平行于船轴和垂直于船轴的两个分量”。在垂直分量的作用下,航向偏转后船继续前进,前进方向保有余下的速度及其代表的能量。

碰撞方向的能量被防撞设施吸收,防撞设施应作成碰撞后能使航向改变,在改变后的航向上继续前进(其原理类似坦克装甲将弹头折滑而出),极力避免将船卡住,因为船若停止,将交换全部动能,其值较大。

本文讨论的防撞设施,由吸能防撞器组装而成,能满足上述要求。作者还对吸能防撞器元件的吸能能力进行了实际标定,如标定最大冲击能,冲击系数等。

2 吸能防撞器原理特点

按中华人民共和国专利 ZL93224217.0 吸能防撞器由钢丝绳制成,其原理已于 1994 年 10 月 30 日公布。吸能防撞器选用受压时内摩擦大的钢绳结构品种;采用紧密对垒排列的绕层方式;用铝合金压接技术紧固其绳端,使其在多次冲击载荷下绳圈不会失效,钢绳内摩擦能够消耗掉撞击能量,它的消耗能量比率高达70%~86%,为橡胶防撞器的2~3倍(在同一试验机上作的橡胶防撞器消耗能量为30%)。

在额定的大冲击之后吸能防撞器即回复,其外形可恢复至80%左右,由图5中可读出。试验表明多次重载之后仍有较高的吸能率,恢复过程甚快,约200 ms左右即完成大部分变形恢复,此恢复的时间亦可在图5中的横坐标读出。

图1a是制作过程中未压接前的紧密排列钢绳圈,b、c、d是撞击恢复后的外形。综上所述,本文选用1∶1实用的钢绳柔性吸能防撞器作试验是直接而现实的。

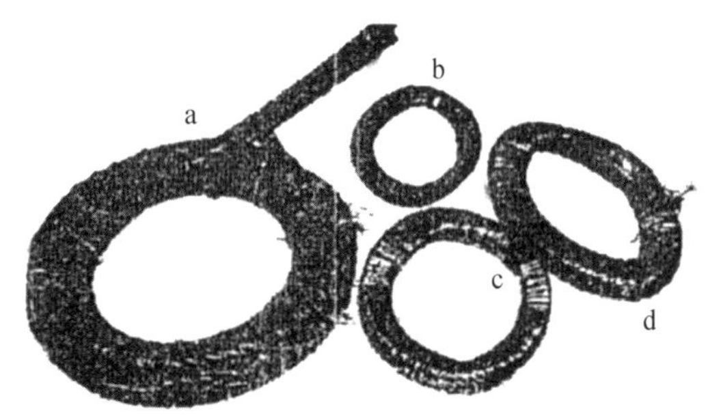

图1 ϕ550 吸能防撞器

Fig. 1 ϕ550 energy absorption anti-collision element

3 试验设备的选择

我们已具备用实际速度直接撞击作动态试验[1]、用实际设计能量值撞击的条件。

我们有一些列的冲击试验机。其打击速度从1.85 m/s至10 m/s,其上限速度相当于20 kn船舶撞向水中墩柱。其能量对单个吸能防撞器来说也已够大。

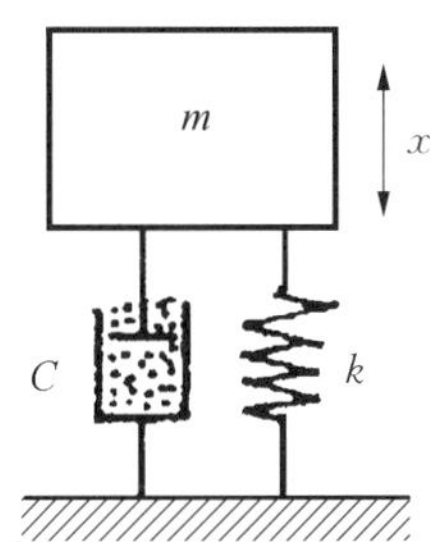

图2 单自由度系统

Fig. 2 Single degree of freedom system

在冲击机中绘出力和变形的图有两种方法:一种方法使用专用的X-Y仪,X轴为变形量,通常用光栅传感输入;Y轴为力,通常用压电传感器,最近几年也有用电阻丝传感器的。使用这种原理的设备很多,如莱比锡产的PSWO型和美国产的300 J冲击试验机,以及国内设计配套的霍布金生压杆试验机等[2,3,4]。作者所用的第二种方法则可免去光栅传感器,他的原理见文献[6]:在落锤与防撞器碰撞期间,可用图2所示的单自由度系统来分析,它的运动方程为:

$$m\ddot{x} + c\dot{x} + kx = mg$$

式中:m——落锤质量,kg;

c——防撞器阻尼,Ns/m;

k——防撞器刚度,N/m;

g——重力加速度,9.8 m/s^2。

安装在落锤上的加速度计可以测量得到落锤的“加速度-时间”的曲线$\ddot{x}$,而落锤的速度$\dot{x}$和位移x可由$\ddot{x}$积分而得

$$\dot{x} = \int \ddot{x} \mathrm{d}x$$

$$x = \int \dot{x} \mathrm{d}x$$

在落锤与防撞器碰撞期间，落锤的速度就是防撞器的上面部分的位移速度，落锤的位移就是防撞器上部的位移。

防撞器受到的冲击力：

$$F = mg - m\dot{x}$$

用防撞器上部的位移为横坐标，对应时刻的力为纵坐标，即可得到图 3 所示的防撞器动态特性曲线（在单一传感器和数据处理系统中实现）。

实验证明，不论作准静态标定或动态试验（过程时间 200 ms 左右）在试验过程中防撞器保持垂直变形，不歪斜不倾倒，符合原定单自由度系统假设。

实验中选用的设备和仪器如方框图所示，其中的波形记录仪的采样频率应足够高，应保证曲线有 200～400 个取样点，使曲线准确而光滑。

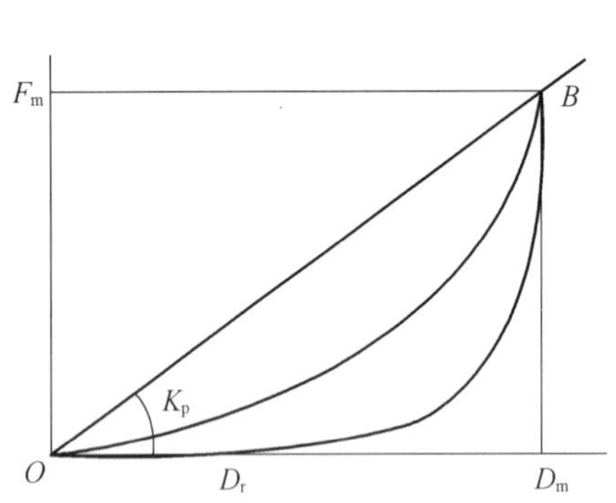

图 3　防撞器的动态特性曲线

Fig. 3　Dynamic characteristic curve of anti-collision element

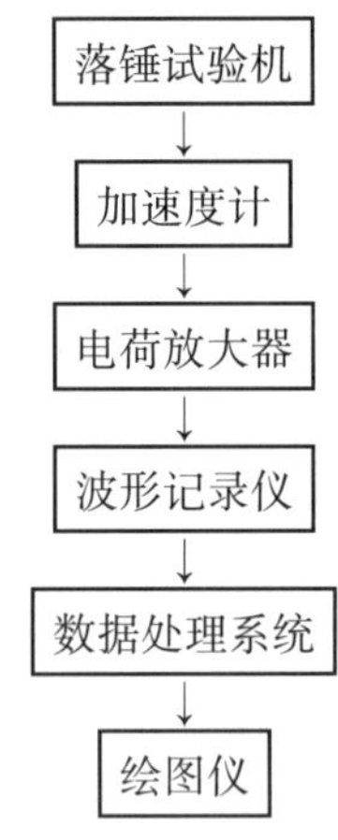

图 4　试验设备方框图

Fig. 4　Block chart of experimental device

4　试验系统能给出的参数

试验系统和数据处理系统在绘出动态特性曲线的同时，将几个重要参数计算好并打出：

1）最大冲击力 F_m（单位 N），防撞器在冲击作用下产生的最大抗力，是弹性力和塑性力（阻尼力）之和。

2）最大冲击位移 D_m（单位 mm），防撞器在一定冲击条件下达到的最大变形量，其极限值是防撞器的额定变形量。

3）残余位移 D_r（单位 mm），即恢复后位移残余值，是冲击结束或冲击力为 0 时防撞器的残余变形量。

4）最大冲击能量 W_m（单位 J），它的大小等于动态力与压缩变形关系曲线的加载段

(从 O 至 B)与水平坐标轴所围成的面积(O, B, D_m, O)。防撞器受到的最大冲击能量等于落锤对防撞器所做的功。

5）防撞器吸收的能量 W_a(单位 J),它的大小等于动态力与压缩变形关系曲线围成的面积(O, B, D_r, O)。

6）剩余冲击能量 W_r(单位 J),它的大小等于动态力与压缩变形关系曲线恢复段与水平坐标轴围成的面积(B, D_r, D_m, B)。它是防撞器释放出的冲击能量：

$$W_r = W_m - W_a$$

7）能量吸收系数 S_f,它的大小等于防撞器吸收能量与最大冲击能量之比：

$$S_f = W_a/W_m$$

8）参考刚度 K_p(单位 N/m),在动态力和压缩变形曲线中的坐标原点(O)到最大位移点(B)的直线的斜率,在理想的单自由度系统中 $K_p = K$。

9）阻尼系数 C(单位 Ns/m),它是单自由度运动方程式中的阻尼系数。

$C = (W_a - K_p D_r^2/2) \Big/ \int_0^{t_r} \dot{x}^2 \mathrm{d}t$ 式中 t_r 是与 D_r 对应的时刻。

图 5 是加速度曲线及其一次、二次积分所得到的速度和位移曲线,它们所用的时间横轴是一致的。

图 6 是“力-变形”曲线,图中封闭的面积是防撞器吸能,这部分面积愈大愈好。

使用实际撞击的速度去作动态吸能试验之前,在万能试验机上先做准静态吸能曲线测定,图 7 是准静态标定的结果,用这两种标定结果与吸能防撞器的设计值(见表 1)相比较,可以看出设计值、准静态标定值和动态标定值三者比较相近。

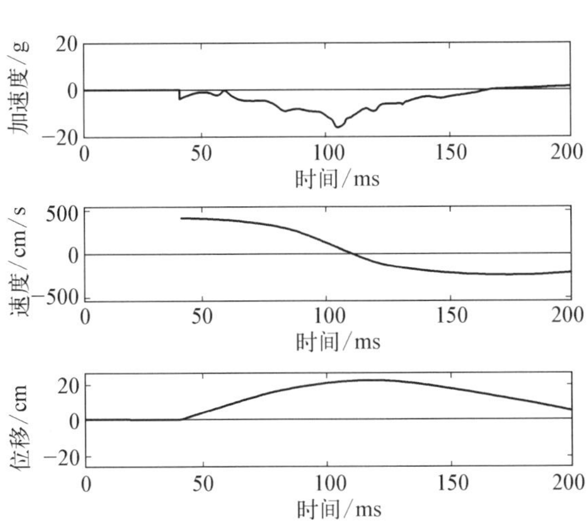

图 5　试验数据处理所得曲线

Fig. 5　The curve by test data processing

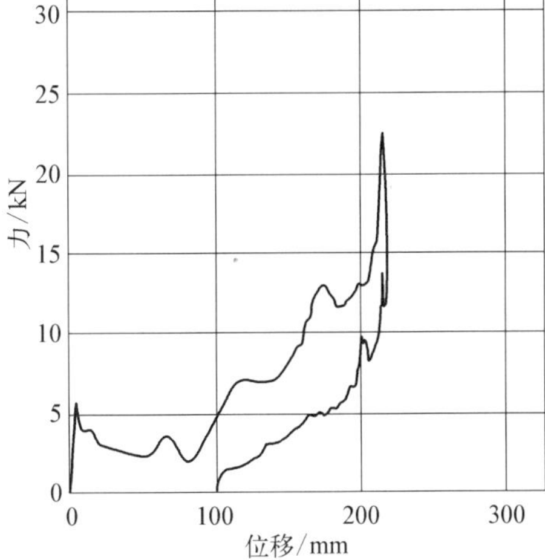

图 6　一次撞击的“力-位移”曲线

Fig. 6　The “force-displacement” curve by one impact test

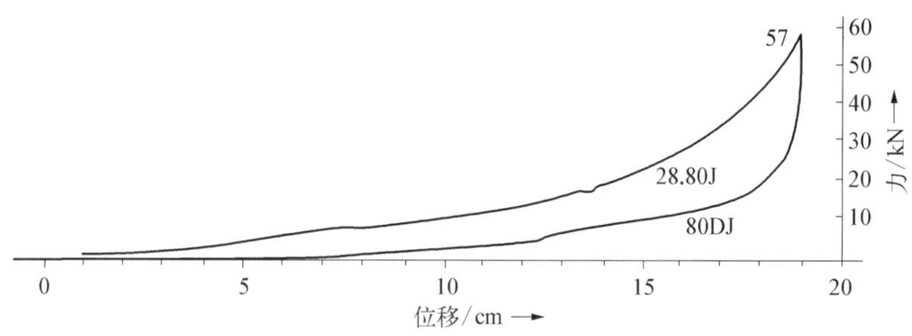

图 7　吸能防撞器准静态标定曲线

Fig. 7　Quasi static calibration curve of energy absorption anti-collision element

5　试验结果

表 1 为中、大型水中墩柱用吸能防撞器系列参数。表 2 为该系列吸能防撞器准静态和动态撞击试验结果。其中动态标定每种防撞器选录 2 中撞击速度。

试验发现在额定撞击荷载下多次撞击(十次左右),其最大吸能值不下降。

表 1　防撞器系列参数

Table 1　The series of anti-collision element

序	项目名称	单位	防撞器设计编号(与表 2 共用)			
			1	2	3	4
1	防撞器外径	mm	440	550	550	750
2	层数—圈数		3 ~ 6	3 ~ 6	3 ~ 6	3 ~ 6
3	钢绳直径	mm	22	34.5	43	60.5
4	钢绳强度数	N/mm^2	1 810	1 810	1 670	1 670
5	钢绳金属面积	mm	204.3	446.1	697.1	1 366.3
6	钢绳单重	kg/m	1.92	4.19	6.55	12.87
7	防撞器重量	kg	13.2	41.0	66.2	141.4
8	设计最大冲击功	J	2 000	3 500	5 500	1 000

表 2　防撞器系列参数(续)

Table 2　The series of anti-collision element

标定种类	项目名称及符号	单位	防撞器设计编号(与表 1 共用)		
			1	2	3
准静态标定	最大撞击能量,W_m	J	2 050	3 212	5 689
	吸收能量,W_a	J	1 344	2 340	3 641
	吸收系数,S_F	%	65.5	73	64
	最大反力,F_m	kN	43.5	63.5	76.2
	位移恢复	%	70	60	60
	参考刚度,K_p	kN/m	181	265	318

续表

标定种类	项目名称及符号	单位	防撞器设计编号(与表1共用)					
			1		2		3	
动态标定	撞击速度,v	m/s	3.86	4.23	5.26	6.95	6.43	8.29
	最大撞击能量,W_m	J	1 123	1 486	2 375	3 875	3 297	5 271
	吸收能量,W_a	J	740	919	1 688	3 130	2 839	4 401
	吸收系数,S_F	%	63	61	71	81	86	83
	最大反力,F_m	kN	11.6	22.5	22.0	59.3	32.4	52.2
	位移恢复	%	67	78	83	67	65	78
	参考刚度,K_p	kN/m	55.5	67.9	69.5	173	70.1	167
	阻尼系数,C	Ns/m	717	560	911	579	1 767	153.5
	阻尼比,η		0.14	0.10	0.14	0.06	0.28	0.16

6 防撞装置的设计

1）按照1991年的指南,将各种因素考虑进去,可得到某桥墩最大冲击功要求。按照桥墩试样布置防撞器组成的防撞装置。防撞器可以并联、串联组合,不论串联和并联,吸能都是叠加的,上下并联时位移不变,反力在上下两处,每处反力不变;水平串联时位移加倍,反力不变。例如某桥墩截面为4.5 m×13 m,周边布置1 000个吸能防撞器得到10^7 J的最大冲击功。

2）防撞器固定在钢箍上,钢箍两头尖中间直,钢箍的截面设计借鉴船的边龙骨,由于支反力的支点是均布的,且支反力开始受撞时甚小(柔性支撑特点),故钢箍能使防撞器受力均匀。

3）钢箍连接好的防撞装置放在橡胶浮筏上,浮筏设计成单圈或双圈视钢绳防撞器串联或并联而定,组合比重为0.8~0.9,浮筏内填逼空泡沫塑料,不会因局部受损而减少浮力。

4）钢丝绳和钢箍在水中用海洋平台水舱不干性涂料喷刷,保护期涂层内保持银亮表面。

7 总结

1）对所设计的钢绳柔性吸能防撞器系列进行试验研究,其动态吸能值与设计值相吻合与准静态吸能值也相近,本文介绍了其中3种防撞器。它们相差≤10%。

2）对某桥墩用一层吸能防撞器得吸能能力10^7 J。可采用加倍吸能量的串联、并联方法。

3）对多次撞击及其吸能 进行了试验,发现多次撞击中的各次的吸能系数在60%~

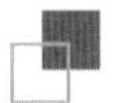

86%之间,由于在同一试验机上所作的橡胶防撞垫[6]2~3倍。

参 考 文 献

[1] 胡时胜.材料动力学实验技术.冲击动力学进展[M].合肥:中国科技大学出版社,1992.
[2] 王绍祖.船体钢室温冲击断裂时的启裂与失稳[J].船舶工程,1985(2).
[3] 胡时胜,王礼立.一种用于材料高应变率试验的装置[J].振动与冲击,1986(1).
[4] 吴用舒等.硬聚受醋泡沫塑料动态压缩特性的一次试验测量[J].振动与冲击,1986(1).
[5] 岩井·聪.关于船舶对桥梁的安全措施[J].中国造船,1986(2).

发表于:交通部上海船舶运输科学研究所学报,1995(2).

Published at: Journal of SSSRI, 1995(2).

黏滞性高耗能柔性防撞圈的研制和试验

The manufactory and examination on viscosity high consume energy flexible composite anti-collision rings

倪步友[1] 倪士强[1] 陈国虞[2]

（1. 上海士强起重索具有限公司，上海 200135；

2. 上海海洋钢结构研究所，上海 201204）

NI Buyou[1], NI Shiqiang[1], CHEN Guoyu[2]

(1. Shanghai Shiqiang Lifting Cable Co., Ltd., Shanghai 200135, China

2. Shanghai Marine Steel and Structure research Institute, Shanghai 201204, China)

摘　要　黏滞性高耗能柔性防撞圈的试验研究已有18年，从单个防撞圈到多层串联、并联；从小防撞圈到防御50 000 t实船用的ϕ800 mm防撞圈；从裸钢丝绳圈到复合防撞圈；从没有外钢围的防撞圈性能测定到有外钢围的1∶1防撞装置实用分段的性能测定试验。以上述黏滞性高耗能复合钢丝绳柔性防撞圈为主要元件的柔性防撞装置所进行的陆上车辆撞击试验和海上防船撞实船试验。一系列的试验研究和实船试验证实，以防撞圈为主要元件的柔性防撞装置，能减低船撞力，延长撞击历时，化集中撞击力为分布载荷，使船头尽早转向，带走比较多的动能，从而达到柔性防撞装置的最高效果——“三不坏”。即船与桥墩相撞时，桥、船和防撞装置三者都不坏。柔性防撞装置已成功应用到能通过50 000 t海船的湛江海湾大桥和象山港大桥。

关键词　黏滞性　桥梁防船撞　柔性防撞装置　防撞圈　高耗能复合钢丝绳防撞圈

Abstract: This paper mention the process of the study of the flexible equipments on anti-collision with ship and bridge in China at the last 18 years. From one anti-collision ring only to many rings with in series and in parallel, from the small ring to the rings can applied to anti the 50 000 t big ship, from the nakedness steel wire ring to the composite anti-collision rings, from determination the characters without outer steel gate to determination the characters of 1 : 1 subsection of the anti-collision flexible equipments. This paper also mentioned the process of these flexible equipments on ground vehicle and real ship test. These full scale studies proofed this flexible equipments can be reduced the force of ship collision with bridge, can be extend the time of impact, change the concentrate force to distributed load, lets the ship bow turn back to the correct route and at same time carries out the most kinetic energy of the ship. So that it achieved the best effects of the anti-collision equipments, "three destroy" bridge, ship and the defend equipment cannot be destroy. The flexible equipments for anti-collision with ship and bridge have been used to the Zhangjiang Bay Bridge for the 50 000 t ships.

Keywords: viscosity, anti-collision of ship with bridge, flexible equipments on anti-collision, anti-collision rings, high consume energy composite anti-collision rings

1 黏滞性耗能理论依据

桥墩防船撞装置无非是受撞时桥墩受力和受撞时桥墩不受力两大类。不论是哪一种类型,均应选择柔性防船撞元件能较多地消耗船舶动能。防撞元件受力变形时,能够消耗能量,变形的大小与耗能的多少有密切关系。防撞元件的变形从小到大,可以有弹性-弹塑性-塑性-黏滞性等阶段,后面的阶段耗能越来越大。钢丝绳柔性防撞圈是高耗能的,这一点可从动态"冲击力-冲击位移"试验曲线得到证明。

高耗能的复合钢丝绳柔性防撞圈的"动态冲击力-冲击位移"曲线的上升段是一条凹曲线,前半段变形大而受力较小(与凸曲线比较),上升曲线与下降曲线包围的面积代表消耗掉的能量,黏滞性防撞圈消耗的能占作用于防撞圈的能的60%以上。它能有效地延长撞击历时,减低船撞力,充分发挥黏滞性柔性防撞元件的缓冲消能作用。由黏滞性高耗能防撞圈元件与内外钢围组成的防撞装置,既能减低船撞力又能发挥整体作用,使船撞力集中载荷化为分布载荷,使船头尽快转向、滑离,还能够带走尽可能多的剩余动量,在船桥相撞时,达到桥、船、防撞装置"三不坏"的目的。

2 黏滞性柔性高耗能复合钢丝绳防撞圈元件的特性

工业上常用的钢丝绳的制件,在受到外力而变形时,能在体积较小的元件产生较大的耗能效应。用于航天器上的耗能减震元件,已被上海船舶运输科学研究所成功用在空压机机座上,放在南京路沈大成糕团店的顶层晒台。钢丝绳防撞元件不同于钢丝绳减震元件,它希望个体小而耗能大。这就需要特别定制钢丝绳,并选择合适的钢丝绳结构,还要配合以钢丝绳防撞圈元件的特殊加工工艺。

首先,选用符合要求的线接触钢芯结构的无油钢丝绳,以保证全部绳内丝间钢对钢的摩擦,追求尽量多的线接触摩擦;其次,钢丝绳绕成防撞圈时用紧密排列,这样就要求防撞圈的径向横截面内钢丝绳呈三角形堆垒,便于约束钢丝绳,减少非摩擦变形;第三,用铝合金椭圆箍将钢丝绳两头压紧,并用细钢丝将钢丝绳圈扎紧,限制非摩擦的变形,迫使钢丝绳内部钢丝在受外部作用力时产生丝间摩擦,导致内部消耗发热;第四,增大钢丝绳丝间的摩擦系数,采用钢丝之间钢对钢的干摩擦,要求生产表面无油的钢丝用以捻制钢丝绳;最后,将密排钢丝绳圈外面用高温硫化氯丁橡胶包覆,制成高耗能柔性复合防撞圈,外层复合的氯丁橡胶既可防海水腐蚀,也有助于防撞圈恢复形状,达到多次使用的目的。

图 1 是钢丝绳绕成防撞圈在受拉、压力变形时,测定其“力-变形”图,分析图中各阶段的抗力和功耗。图 2 是批量生产的复合防撞圈。

(a) 受压时变形和能量测试

(a) Determination the characters on deformation and absorb energy, when the ring as pressed

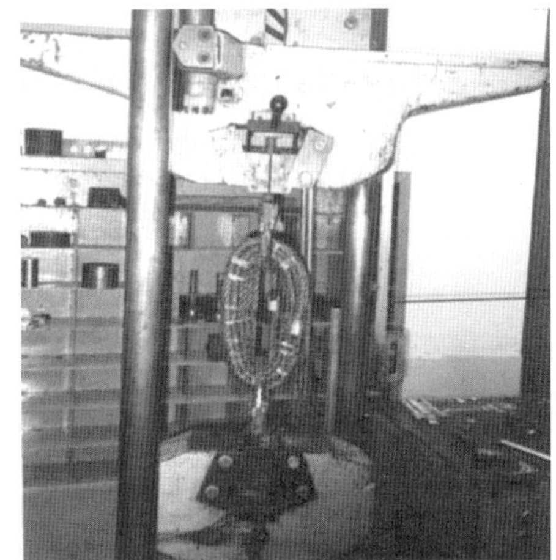

(b) 受拉时变形和能量测试

(b) Determination the characters on deformation and absorb energy, when the ring as tensile

图 1　密排钢丝绳元件拉压准静态试验

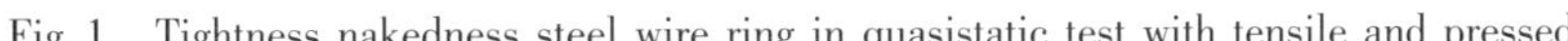

Fig. 1　Tightness nakedness steel wire ring in quasistatic test with tensile and pressed

图 2　复合防撞圈系列批量生产

Fig. 2　The composite anti-collision rings in batch production

3 复合高耗能防撞圈准静态拉压曲线

3.1 ϕ400 型复合高耗能防撞圈准静态拉压曲线(典型化)

图 3 为 ϕ400 型复合高消耗能防撞圈准静态拉压曲线。

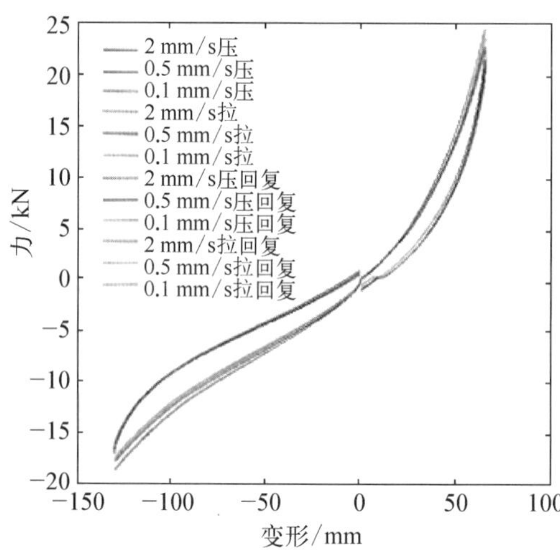

图 3 ϕ400 型复合高消耗能防撞圈准静态拉压曲线
(本图由宁波大学周风华提供)

Fig. 3 The curve of quasistatic tensile and pressed test of ϕ400 type high consume energy composite anti-collision rings (Drawing by Professor Zhou Fenghua of Ningbo University)

3.2 ϕ600 型复合高耗能防撞圈的准静态拉压曲线

图 4 为 ϕ600 型复合高耗能防撞圈准静态拉、压曲线。

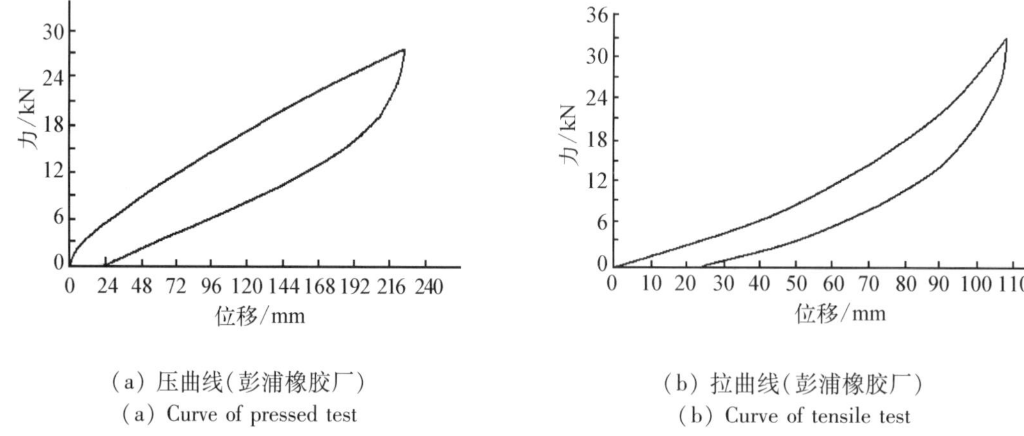

(a) 压曲线(彭浦橡胶厂)
(a) Curve of pressed test

(b) 拉曲线(彭浦橡胶厂)
(b) Curve of tensile test

图 4 ϕ600 型复合高耗能防撞圈准静态拉、压曲线

Fig. 4 The curve on quasistatic pressed and tensile test of ϕ600 type composite anti-collision ring

3.3 ϕ800 复合高耗能防撞圈的准静态拉压曲线

图 5 为 ϕ800 型复合高耗能防撞圈准静态拉、压曲线。

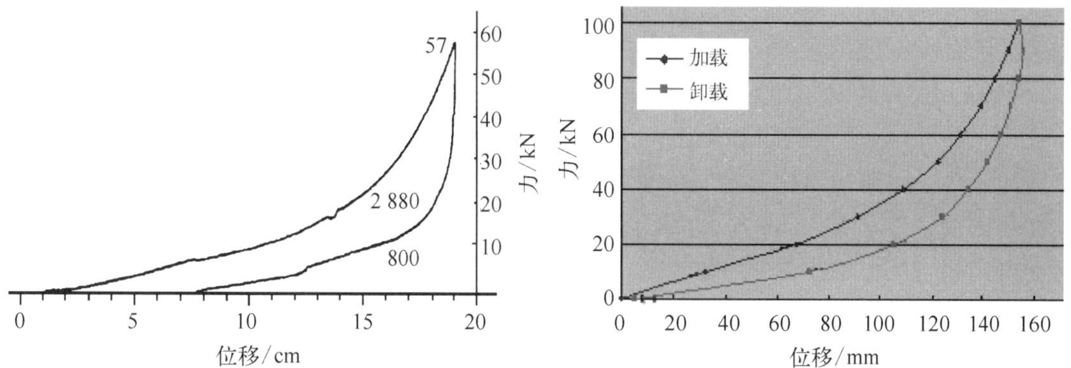

(a) 压曲线(莱比锡试验机,702 所)
(a) Curve of pressed test (Leipzig machine, 702 Institute)

(b) 拉曲线(德国申克试验机,东海水产所)
(b) Curve of tensile test (Schenck machine, East-sea Marine-lives Institute)

图 5 ϕ800 型复合高耗能防撞圈准静态拉、压曲线

Fig. 5 The curve on quasistatic pressed and tensile test of ϕ800 type composite anti-collision ring

3.4 ϕ800 型复合高耗能防撞圈动态压曲线

图 6 为复合高耗能防撞圈动态压曲线。

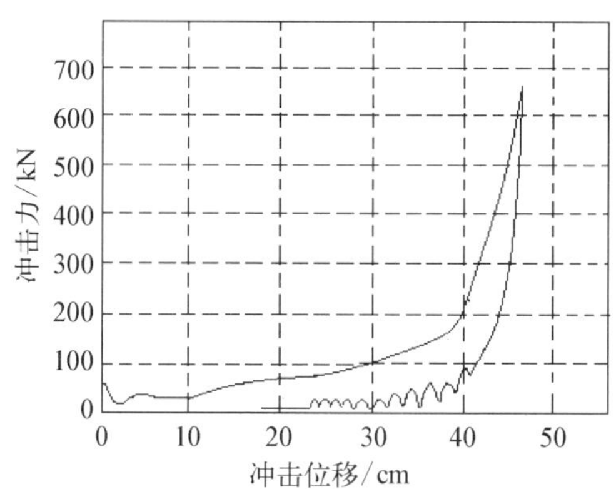

(a) ϕ800 mm 圈的动态压曲线(702 所)
(a) Curve of dynamic pressed test of ϕ800 mm ring (702 Institute)

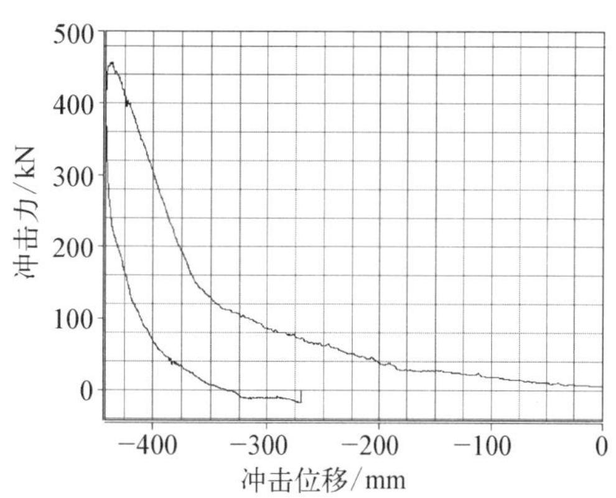

(b) ϕ800 mm 圈的动态压曲线(彭浦橡胶厂)
(b) Curve of dynamic pressed test of ϕ800 mm ring (Pengpu Rubber Factory)

图 6 复合高耗能防撞圈动态压曲线

Fig. 6 Curve of dynamic pressed test of high consume energy composite anti-collision ring

4 黏滞性高耗能柔性防撞圈与外钢围组成防撞装置试验

要对付来撞的大船,必须使成百上千个防撞圈一齐作用,使用外钢围可以达到这个目的。有的人对于船舶撞击外钢围外部时与外钢围该部分相连的防撞圈共同受压的现象想得通,而对位于撞击点对面外钢围拉防撞圈则想不通。实际上,其原理也很简单:若背面防撞圈中孔允许位移为 0 ~ 400 mm,外钢围设计的刚性和强度使得它在该处变形小于400 mm 时,外钢围就会拉防撞圈使其变形,达到多个防撞圈同期作用的结果。

涉船的专业人员可以将外钢围想象成一艘疏浚用的开底泥驳,将船底门打开、拆掉,把桥墩放进去,来船撞击开底泥驳的外边,中空开口井内的钢构件(运动)可以拉动固定在桥墩与船之间的防撞圈。

先用试验直观地证明之。可以用下面几个试验设计,分别求出多圈受压、多圈受拉和多圈受剪时的抗力和变形。图 7(a)的试样,其外钢围和模拟桥墩都是由钢制作的(用 ϕ300 mm 防撞圈)。

(a) 用外钢围测定防撞圈同期性的试样

(a) The sample with outer steel gate and rings used to determination the synchronism

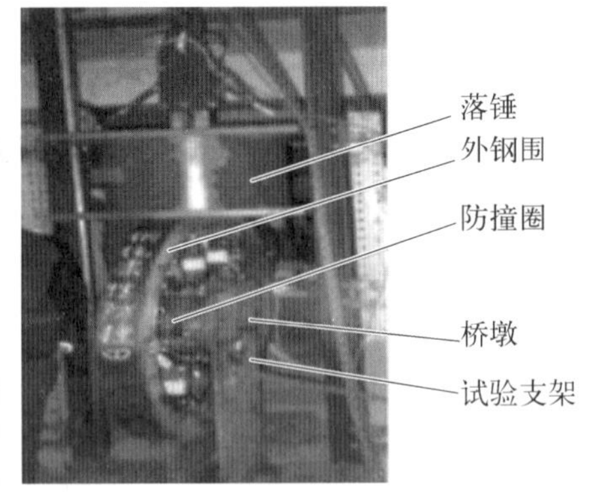

(b) 外钢围和防撞圈组装后置于落锤试验机内

(b) The mode of anti-collision equipment with rings and outer steel gate put in the drop hammer testing machin

图 7 利用外钢围测定防撞圈共同受载的试验装备

Fig. 7 The testing equipment with anti-collision rings and outer steel gate to determination the loading synchronism

将模拟桥墩和防撞装置的组合放倒,即按工作状态旋转 90°,支撑住桥墩,用自由落锤试验机的落锤作为来撞的船,对防撞装置的外钢围进行撞击。支撑装置具有两点支撑和圆弧支撑两种方式,以模拟船从正面和侧面撞击。分别测定两圈受压、两圈受压两圈受拉、两圈受压两圈受拉两圈受剪和一拉一压四圈受剪等各种情况的试验,测定"力-变形"图。

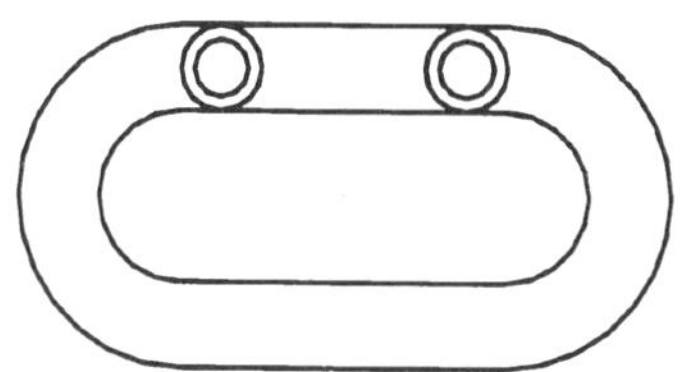

(a) 两圈受压
(a) Two rings behind the outer steel gate in the drop hammer test machine

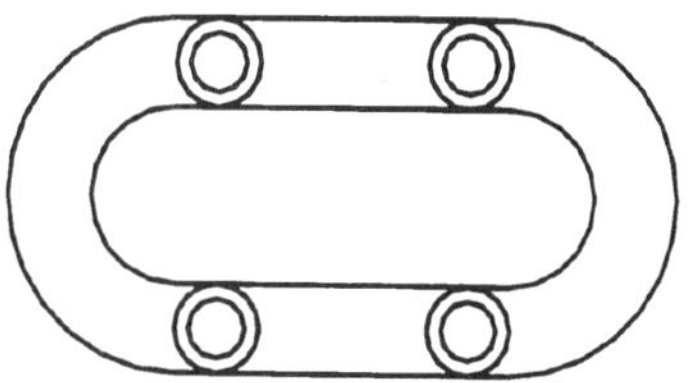

(b) 两圈受压两圈受拉
(b) Four rings behind the outer steel gate in the drop hammer to test the tensile and pressed

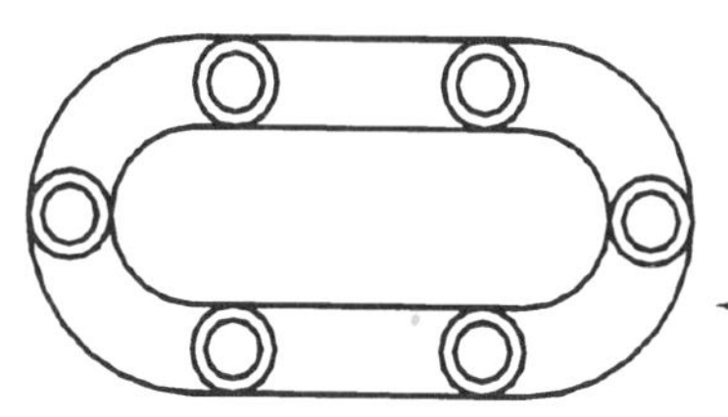

(c) 两圈受压两圈受拉两圈受剪
(c) Six rings behind the outer steel gate in the drop hammer to test the tensile, shear and pressed

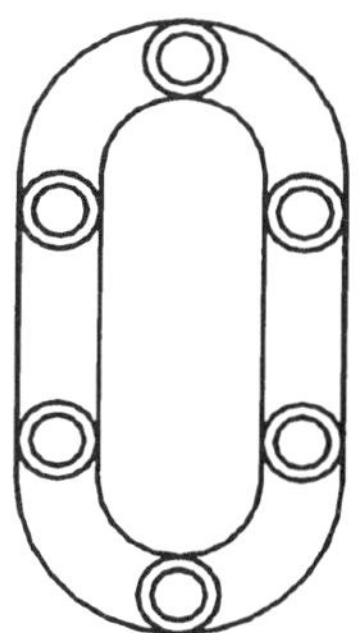

(d) 一拉一压四圈受剪
(d) Six rings behind the outer steel gate in the drop hammer4 to test the shear 1 tensile, and 1 pressed

图 8 利用外钢围测定防撞圈共同受载的各种工况试样布置图
Fig. 8 The samples with rings and outer steel gate used to determination the synchronism under difference situations

5 ϕ800 型防撞圈与外钢围单层并联组成 1∶1分段的试验

在做完了多个 ϕ300 mm 黏滞性耗能柔性防撞圈在外钢围包络下同期作用的试验之后,开始进行 1∶1分段的试验。这一阶段试验的目的是从试验室走向工程,尽量接近工程的情况。工程准备用 ϕ800 mm 的防撞圈,试验就做 ϕ800 mm 的防撞圈,工程有外钢围,试验就做外钢围,只是试验仅做一小段,1∶1的分段。

这一部分分为两个阶段。第一阶段仅用钢丝绳防撞圈(由钢丝绳紧密缠绕而成),尚未复合外层的橡胶主要是为节省工序和争取时间,但是外层橡胶的作用便试验不出来了。

先用外钢围与 4 个并联的裸钢丝绳防撞圈组成分段,测定“力-变形”(见图 9)。

第二阶段是用氯丁橡胶复合在钢丝绳防撞圈的外面,与钢丝绳紧密黏结在一起。黏结紧密程度是保证能够经受防撞圈的额定载荷,也就是说,每个防撞圈受到 50 ~ 60 kJ 的冲击功后,橡胶与钢丝绳均不裂不离。外层橡胶的作用,除了保护钢丝绳在海洋环境下不被腐蚀之外,还能帮助钢丝绳恢复,同时也增加一点防撞圈所能承受的冲击功。图 10 是外钢围与 4 个并联复合钢丝绳防撞圈的分段冲击装置和“冲击力-冲击位移”曲线。

(a) 外钢围与4个并联裸钢丝绳防撞圈组成的试样置于落锤试验机下

(a) The sample with 4 rings and outer steel gate under the drop hummer testing machine

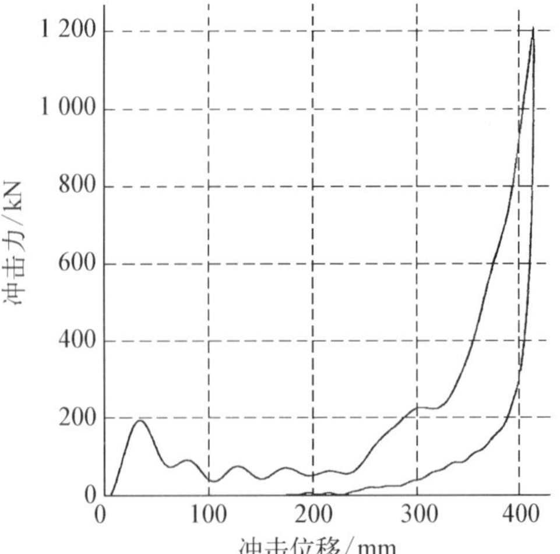

(b) 外钢围和4个钢丝绳防撞圈组成的分段作出的冲击"载荷-位移"图

(b) The loading and deformation curve of sample with 4 rings and outer steel gate

图9 用外钢围与4个并联的裸钢丝绳防撞圈组成分段测定载荷与位移

Fig. 9 The testing sample with 4 rings and outer steel gate used to determination the loading and deformation when they are paralleled

(a) 外钢围与4个并联复合钢丝绳防撞圈组成的单层防撞圈试样置于落锤试验机下

(a) The sample with 4 composite rings and outer steel gate under the drop hummer testing machine

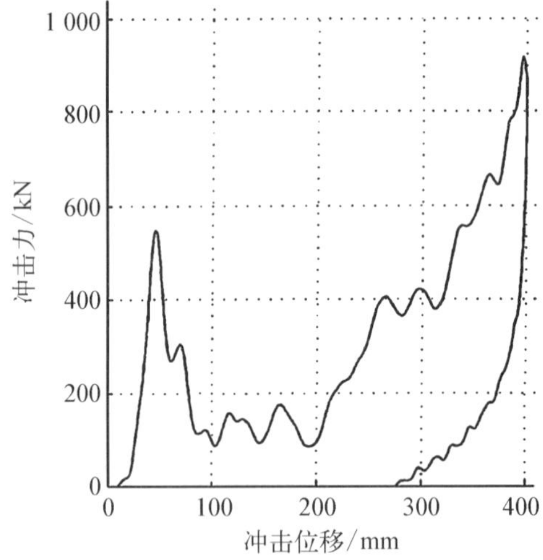

(b) 外钢围和4个钢丝绳防撞圈组成的单层防撞圈分段冲击试验的"冲击力-冲击位移"曲线

(b) The loading and deformation curve of sample with 4 composited rings and outer steel gate

图10 有外钢围的单层防撞圈并联试验

Fig. 10 Monolayer anti-collision ring test in parallel connection

6 ϕ800 mm 防撞圈与外钢围双层并联、串联组成 1:1 分段的试验

这一阶段试验的目的仍然是从试验室走向工程,更进一步地接近工程的情况。工程准备用双层 ϕ800 mm 的防撞圈,试验就做双层的 ϕ800 mm 的防撞圈;工程有外钢围,试验就做外钢围;工程准备用复合防撞圈,试验就用复合防撞圈。同样,试验只能做一小段,1:1的小分段。这一阶段试验,出现了新的问题——找不到足够大能量的试验机。这个试验分段需要在 4 m/s 的速度下能够给出 400 ~ 480 kJ 的落锤试验机。

同样,这一部分试验也分为两个阶段。第一阶段仅用钢丝绳防撞圈(2 层 8 个),尚未复合外层的橡胶主要是为节省工序和争取时间,但是外层橡胶的作用便试验不出来了。

先用外钢围与 2 层(串联)4 个(并联)的裸钢丝绳防撞圈组成分段,测定"力-变形"图(图略)。再用 2 层(串联)4 个(并联)的复合钢丝绳防撞圈组成分段。两种情况下均未能得到额定的功,达不到要求的变形量(见图 11)。

(a) 外钢围与 8 个串联、并联裸钢丝绳防撞圈组成的试样置于落锤试验机下

(a) The sample with 8 rings and outer steel gate in parallel and series under the drop hummer testing machine

(b) 外钢围与 8 个串联、并联复合钢丝绳防撞圈组成的试样置于落锤试验机下

(b) The sample with 8 composite rings and outer steel gate in parallel and series under the drop hummer testing machine

图 11　双层 8 个防撞圈串联、并联试验

Fig. 11　Double deck anti-collision rings test in parallel and series connection situation

7 陆上车辆撞击试验

陆上车辆撞击试验证明,柔性防撞装置是可以多次使用的。在陆上桩柱外装有 6 个 ϕ400 mm 复合高耗能防撞圈,防撞圈外面有外钢围,撞击车装有力传感器,如图 12 所示。

(a) 模拟桥墩、防撞圈和外钢围
(a) Simulate pier, anti-collision rings, and outer steel gate

(b) 模拟车撞向防撞装置
(b) Simulate car collision with the anti-collision equipment

图 12 陆上模拟装置试验(由宁波大学、宁波高等级公路建设指挥部等单位提供)

Fig. 12 Simulate anti-collision equipments for test on the ground

8 柔性防船撞装置实船试验简介[3]

2011 年 9 月 3 日,在浙江象山白墩港的一个混凝土试验桥墩进行了实船撞桥墩的试验。试验条件简述如下:

(1) 防撞装置有内、外两钢围(浮箱围子),安装在混凝土承台外,内、外两钢围(浮箱)之间装有 14 组共 28 个防撞圈;防撞圈与内、外钢围之间装有力传感器,如图 13 所示。

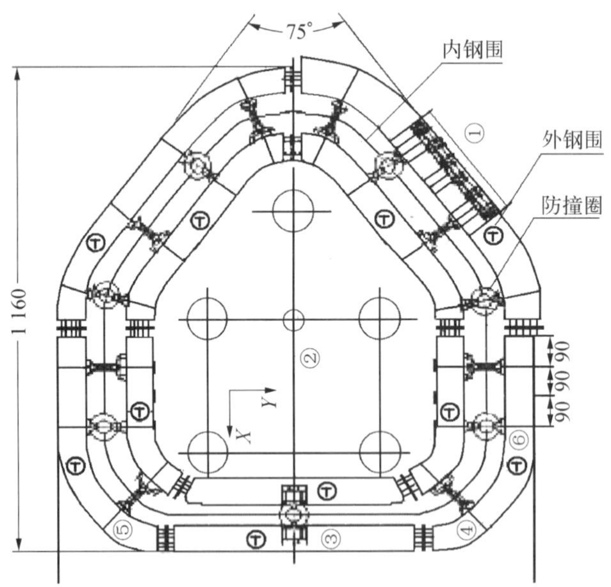

图 13 柔性防撞装置在桥墩的布置及安装图

Fig. 13 The installation drawing of flexible anti-collision equipments for test with solid vessel impact to a solid pier in water

(2) 选用载重量 400 t 的自航式沿海货船;空船撞击试验时排水量 250 t;满载排水量可达 625 t。做有载撞击试验时,载钢铁 150 t,当时排水量为 400 t。

(3) 撞击时航行速度选定为 5 节、6 节和 8 节,仪器记录的撞击速度与试验设计误差不超过 1 节。船的质心附近有三维加速度传感器和陀螺仪,记录船舶加速度和运动方向的变化。从低速到高速,从空载到有载,航线方向从 0°到 26°,共撞了 12 次。

(4) 撞后船头轻微损伤,防撞装置完好,人员站在离撞击点 1 m 的甲板上和离撞击点 2 m 的承台上,感觉轻微(类似船靠码头的震动)。按时间顺序截屏图如图 14 所示。

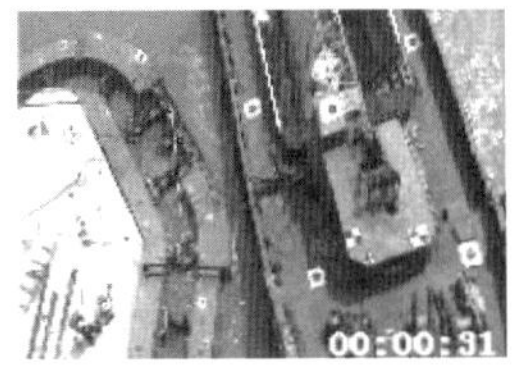

图 14　一次有载撞击过程(截屏)[7](按图中时序:撞前,撞上后滑动船头被拨转,离开防撞装置,继续前进)

Fig. 14　Once impact process with loading vessel (along the time with in the Fig.: before collision; just collision, glide, the bow had been dialed; departed from the anti-collision equipment; went on)

经过检索,防撞装置经过实船撞击成功地使船回到航线上的试验,是世界首次。不但形象地证明了"三不坏"防撞装置的实用性,更重要的是验证了所应用的程序软件。使工程设计人员有信心地进行设计和计算。

9　防撞元件从弹性、弹塑性发展到黏滞性

黏滞性高耗能防撞元件是在弹性和弹塑性防撞元件已应用之后发展研制的。弹性防撞元件不会消耗大量的能(很少发热),因此回弹时能量外放,可能造成撞击对象(例如船)的损坏;弹塑性防撞结构能够消耗能量,但不能恢复撞前形状,防撞装置被撞一次修一次,且因其刚性与船头相当,船头损坏与防撞装置相当;黏滞性高耗能复合钢丝绳防撞元件与弹性外钢围等组成的防撞装置,被撞后消耗掉部分撞击能量(发热),且不马上回弹,随后在外钢围和外复合层共同作用下慢慢恢复,并能够大部分恢复,多次使用。图 15 为三类防撞元件及其力学特征。

黏滞性高耗能防撞元件的表现有点像湿面团,力的上升和下降回线包围的面积就是消耗掉的能量,其比例较大。制造黏滞性高耗能防撞元件可以有气体、液体和固体的方法。用集束钢丝绳外包橡胶制成复合的固体黏滞性高耗能防撞元件,使用可靠,维修方便,体积小(其耗掉的能量,比例较大,通常超过外加功的 60%)。

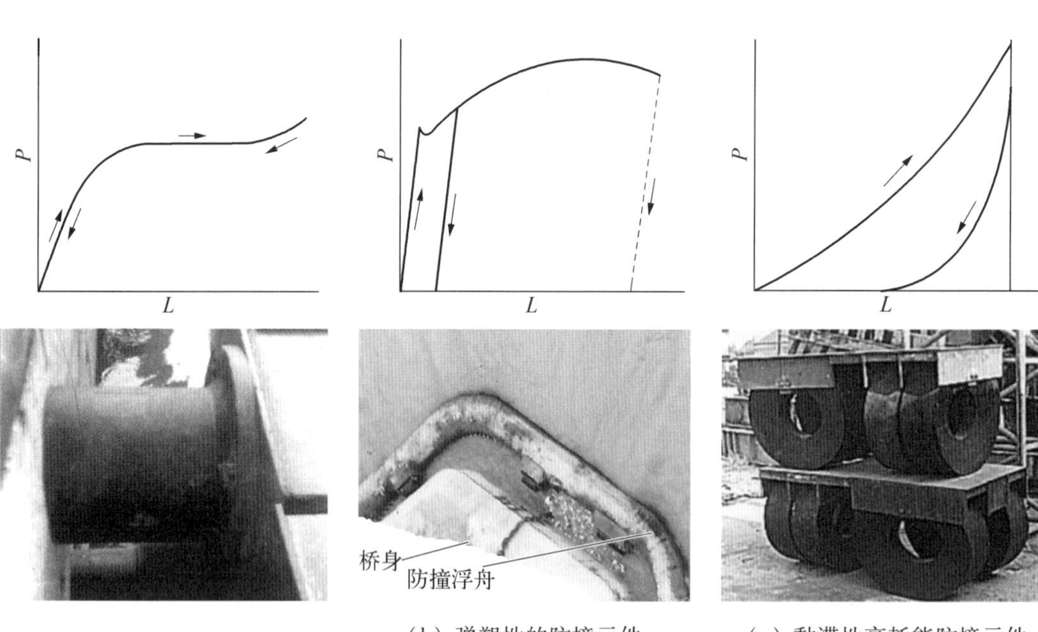

(a) 弹性的防撞元件
(a) Elastic anti-collision parts

(b) 弹塑性的防撞元件
(b) Elastic-plastic anti-collision parts

(c) 黏滞性高耗能防撞元件
(c) Viscidity high consumer energy anti-collision parts

图 15　三类防撞元件及其力学特征(典型化"力-变形"曲线)

Fig. 15　The three type anti-collision parts and its mechanics character

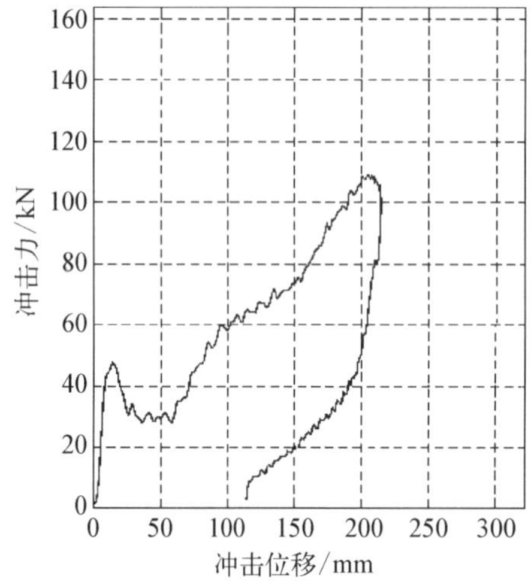

图 16　黏滞性高耗能防撞元件试验曲线

Fig. 16　The experiment curve of Viscidity high consumer energy anti-collision parts

黏滞性高耗能防撞元件的试验曲线如图 16 所示。

此试验曲线有如下特征：首先,其上升曲线基本上是一条凹曲线,前半段变形大而力较小(与凸曲线比较),实现后退和避让;其次,消耗的功很大,占的比率很高(占作用于圈的功的 60%以上);第三,回程不到 0,要想别的办法使其恢复形状;第四,冲击开始接触时,有一个消耗能量的小峰值。

对于第三点,在防撞圈的外面复合橡胶,因橡胶处于弹性状态,可帮助钢丝绳圈恢复形状;外钢围设计得比较强,在它处于弹性状态时也能帮助钢丝绳圈恢复形状。

黏滞性高耗能柔性防撞装置的动态冲击力-冲击位移曲线的前半段形状为凹曲线,变形大,力上升慢,充分体现黏性耗能缓冲了撞击过程,延长了撞击历时,降低了船撞力,使撞击的集中力为分布载荷,充分发挥了柔性防撞装置的整体作用,缩短了整个撞击过程,减少了能量交换,使船头尽早滑离,带走了尽量多的剩余动能。以钢丝绳防撞圈为主要元件

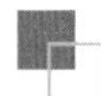

的柔性防撞装置是这一防撞理念的工程应用实例。

10 总结

从钢丝绳防撞圈元件到黏滞性高耗能湛江海湾大桥复合防撞装置,经过18年坚持不懈的研究、探索、创新,反复试验实践,多种方案论证,数值计算分析,各种模型试验直到1:1分段试验,陆上撞击试验,实船撞墩试验,汇集各方力量,“产、学、研”相结合,终于研制成功黏滞性高耗能柔性复合防撞装置,并成功应用到湛江海湾大桥和象山港大桥。成果鉴定会议认为,湛江海湾大桥防撞装置“达到国际领先水平”“是近年国内桥梁工程取得的罕见国际领先科技成果之一”[2]。

参考文献

[1] 曹映泓. 广东省交通厅首批科技示范工程. 湛江海湾大桥. 第二册. 技术创新[M]. 北京:人民交通出版社,2008.

[2] 湛江海湾大桥柔性吸能防撞设施世界首创[N]. 湛江晚报,2007-12-21.

[3] 董新龙,周风华,郑维钰,等. 桥墩柔性防撞装置实船撞击过程的试验研究——装置及撞击力的测量与分析[C]. 中国土木工程学会桥梁及结构工程分会. 第二十届全国桥梁学术会议论文集. 北京:人民交通出版社,2012:1188-1192.

[4] 湛江海湾大桥有限公司. 用户证明[R]. 2013-08-21.

发表于:国际船桥相撞及其防护学术研讨会论文集[M].
北京:中国铁道出版社,2014:42-51.

Published at: Proceedings of International Symposium on Ship-Bridge Collision and Its Protection. China Railway Press, 2014: 42-51.

桥梁抗船撞柔性防护方法及实船撞击实验

Flexible anti-collision method for ship with bridge and the impact experiments of an actual ship

杨黎明[1]　吕忠达[2]　王礼立[1]　陈国虞[3]　陆宗林[4]

（1. 宁波大学机械工程与力学学院;2. 浙江省宁波市高等级公路建设指挥部;
3. 上海海洋钢结构研究所;4. 同济大学）

YANG Liming[1], LU Zhongda[2], WANG Lili[1], CHEN Guoyu[3], LU Zonglin[4]

(1. The Mechanical engineering and Mechanics Institute of Ningbo University Zhejiang Ningbo 315211;2. Zhejiang Ningbo High-class Highway Construction Headquarter 315192;3. Shanghai Marine Steel and Structure Research Institute 201204; 4. Tongji University)

摘　要　自主创新研发的由防撞圈和内外钢围组成的桥梁抗船撞柔性防护装置的设计方法,基于冲击动力学理论分析和数值模拟,研究柔性防撞装置的冲击响应,以及各主要部件的关键设计参量。为了检验新型的桥梁抗船撞柔性防护技术的有效性和可靠性,在宁波象山白墩港组织实施了国内外首次采用实船撞击柔性防撞装置的实验。实验采用的船舶自重 250 t、载重量 400 t,以不同的航速、载重量和撞击角度对柔性防撞装置进行撞击实验。实验测得的船撞力与数值模拟结果基本一致。实验验证了新型的“桥梁抗船撞柔性防护装置”可以达到既保护桥梁,同时避免船舶损毁,也保护环境的目的。

关键词　桥梁柔性防船撞装置　实船撞击实验　船撞力

Abstract: This paper introduce the flexible anti-collision equipment constructed by the anti-collision rings, the outer steel gate and the inside steel gate. Which anti-collision equipment is self-dependent innovation at our country. This paper introduce the design method, theoretical analysis, numerical modeling. It also study the shock response, the design parameters of the main parts for examine the technical effectiveness and reliability of the new flexible anti-collision equipment. At Baidun port of Zhejiang Ningbo Xiangshan, we organized and carry out the first experiment of

actual ship collision with the bridge, which has the anti-collision equipment. This experiment used the ship with deadweight 400 t, and itself have lightweight 250 t, carry out the impact with difference route speed, difference loading and difference angle of impact to the flexible anti-collision equipment. The impact force, which we got from the experiment fit with the result of the numerical modeling. The experiment had been verification the new flexible anti-collision equipment may protect the bridge at the same time avoid the damage of the ship and also to protect the environment.

Keywords: flexible anti-collision equipment of bridge, impact test of actual ship with the bridge, force of ship collision with bridge

1 引言

随着河、海航运量加大与船舶吨位和航速的增加，以及河、海桥梁的大量兴建，船舶碰撞桥梁的概率越来越大。一旦船桥相撞，严重时不但将造成船毁人亡、桥梁倒塌等重大事故，经济损失巨大；还可能由于船体破损泄漏进一步引起灾难性环境污染。近年来，仅我国就发生了多次此类事故。

自20世纪80年代初，国际上对船撞桥以及桥墩防护问题的研究开始得到关注，关于船撞桥第一次国际研讨会于1983年在哥本哈根举行。20世纪80年代中后期国际上根据船桥碰撞的动能或动量原理，提出了桥梁设计的新标准，特别是1991年美国各州公路和运输官员协会（AASHTO）出版了《船舶碰撞公路桥梁设计指南》和1993年O. D. 拉森（O. D. Larsen）写的IABSE（*International Association for Bridge and Structural Engineering*）文件《船舶碰撞桥梁》。同时开展了一系列的实验研究、理论分析，提出了许多计算碰撞力的经验公式和半经验公式，作为桥梁的抗船撞设计基础[1-4]。发展了多种有效的桥梁抗船舶撞击的方法，例如，已被采用的桥梁抗船撞设计有“人工岛”、“防护桩”和加大承台等刚性防护装置，以及木栅、钢链和浮舟等柔性设施[4][5]。前者的刚性较强，虽保护了桥梁，但无法避免船舶的破坏；后者虽然可保护桥也能保护船体，但这些防护设施难以满足大吨位和高速度船的撞击的防护要求。为保证大型桥梁受船撞时的安全，国内外的桥梁设计师历来倾向于建造高刚度、高强度的防护设施。但桥墩防护设施愈坚固，船只则会受损愈严重。即使保护了桥墩，也可能导致船毁人亡、环境污染，并且为了吸收船舶的巨大动能，需要建造庞大的防护结构，并且对桩基的抗撞击的设计要求将提高，造价昂贵。

进一步的研究表明，船舶的尺寸、航速、船艏形状、撞击角和船体及桥墩的材料力学性能等都将对撞击力有明显的影响[6,7]。船撞桥本质上是一个复杂和困难的冲击动力学问题。很难要求用一个简化公式来描述这么复杂的冲击动力学问题。因此，人们开始转向采用动态有限元方法（例如LS－DYNA）针对各个具体问题作进一步的数值模拟分

析[7-9]。然而,数值模拟分析结果的可靠性和有效性往往容易受到工程技术部门的质疑。为此,研究人员进行了船撞桥的相关实验研究,如采用模型缩比实验等。美国佛罗里达大学于 2004 年在圣乔治岛上即将拆除的贝里安型(Bryant Pattern)桥上进行了实船撞击桥墩的实尺实验[10]。在两个桥墩上共进行了 15 次驳船与桥墩的碰撞实验。但是,实船撞击桥梁防船撞装置的实验至今未见报道。

本文介绍新型的"桥梁抗船撞柔性防护装置",当船舶偏航撞向桥墩时,承台外围的柔性防护装置可以起到隔阻强冲击波、减少撞击力的效果。尤其是柔性防撞部件延长低载荷下撞击时间,使得船舶有时间和空间转向,达到拨转船舶航向的效果。船舶能沿防撞装置外侧滑走,从而带走了船的大部分动能,大幅降低了船-桥撞击过程中的能量交换,降低了船舶的撞击力。本文采用冲击动力学理论分析和数值模拟,研究由防撞圈和内外钢围组成的柔性防撞装置的冲击响应,以及各主要部件的关键设计参量。为了检验我国自主创新研发的"桥梁抗船撞柔性防护技术"的有效性和可靠性,在宁波象山白墩港组织实施了国内外首次采用实船撞击柔性防撞装置的实验。

2 桥梁抗船撞柔性防护方法

2.1 基本结构和防护原理

"柔性防撞装置"主要由外钢围、防撞圈和内钢围构成(见图 1、图 2)。内、外钢围可以采用浮箱(全水密,箱梁结构)设计,其间通过众多的防撞圈相联系,使得柔性防撞装置作为一个整体围绕着桥墩承台、浮在水面,其高程随着水位的变化而上下浮动。内、外钢围可以采用非全水密的箱梁结构设计,其间同样可通过众多的防撞圈相联系,柔性防撞装置作为一个整体固定在桥墩承台周围。当船舶撞击桥墩时,将撞击在柔性防撞装置外钢围的外侧面。

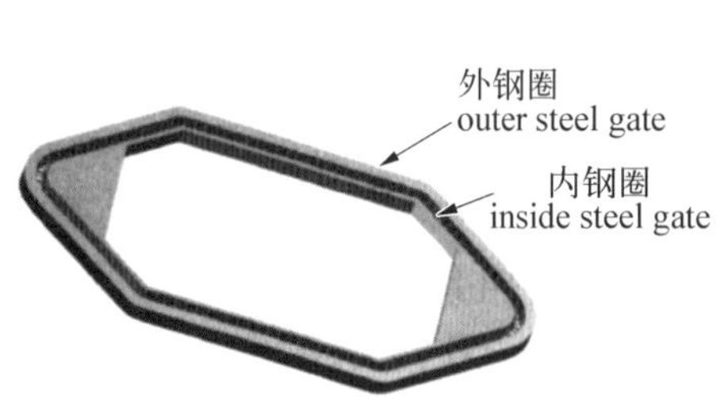

图 1　柔性防撞装置示意图

Fig. 1　The sketch map of flexible anti-collision equipment

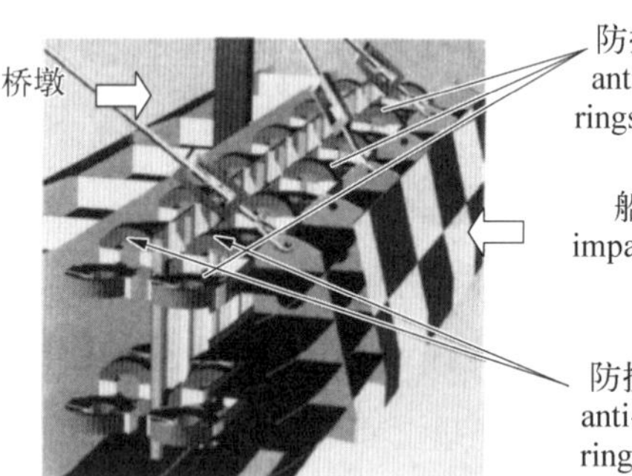

图 2　柔性防撞装置内部结构示意图

Fig. 2　The inside construction of the flexible anti-collision equipment

在发生船撞事故时,利用柔性防撞装置结构内各部件的共同作用,使得船撞桥产生的冲击波不直接传到桥墩,而是经过柔性耗能的防撞圈后传到桥墩,柔性防撞圈起到隔阻强冲击波、减少撞击力、缓冲(延长低载荷下撞击过程时间)、吸收撞击能的多种效果。尤其是延长较低载荷下撞击过程时间和防撞装置外钢围较大的移动,可使船舶有时间和空间转向,再利用水流的升力作用,将船舶推离桥墩,使船舶沿防撞装置外侧滑走,从而带走船的大部分动能,大大降低了船-桥撞击过程中的能量交换。达到“四两拨千斤”的功效。从而实现既保护桥梁,又能避免(或大大降低)船舶受到损伤的目的。

2.2 结构关键设计参量

(1) 防撞装置的刚度设计。当船舶撞到防撞设施的外钢围时,外钢围需要有足够的刚度,使得撞击过程中所有的防撞装置中的防撞圈共同受力,即撞击过程中,外钢围有很大的整体位移,但局部变形很小。同时,外钢围还需要一定的支撑,即外钢围抗整体位移的能力,使得在受到撞击过程中,对撞击体(船舶)施加一定的作用力,以期改变船舶的运动方向;由于这种施加在船舶上的作用力,也一定将传递到桥墩上,所以这一作用力不能太大(不能超过桥墩允许的最大横向撞击力)。为此,要研究使用多少数量的防撞圈并联支撑于外钢围的内侧(见图2),才能产生适当大小作用力作用于船舶上。外钢围刚度的设计取决于船舶的动能量级以及防撞圈的数量和强度,可以采用数值模拟方法确定,也可通过理论分析确定[11]。

(2) 防撞装置的柔性设计。当船舶撞到防撞设施时,防撞设施还需要有很好的柔性(即外钢围能够产生足够大的刚性位移),这种柔性由防撞圈提供。在受到撞击过程中,由于支撑外钢围的防撞圈表现出足够的柔性,船舶推压着外钢围运动。由防撞圈的力学行为所决定,在外钢围后退的初期,产生的力较小(防撞圈的力-位移曲线有一较大范围的力平台),后退一定距离后,作用力加大。船舶在这一平台作用力下,有时间和空间改变其运动方向,这样船舶的大部分动能可保留在船舶上,继续沿着外钢围外表侧向前运动,船舶的大部分动能在撞击过程中不参加交换。这样大幅降低了桥墩所受到的船舶撞击力、有效保护桥梁,同时,船舶受到的撞击力也大幅降低,也保护了船舶。对不同的桥梁,受到具有不同动能量级的船舶的撞击时,需要选用不同大小的防撞圈。例如对于受到具有高动能船舶的撞击的桥墩设防装置,需要使用大尺寸的防撞圈;大尺寸的防撞圈可以使得外钢围有相对大的运动距离和相对长的撞击过程时间以及承受较大的撞击力。根据需要,还可以将多个防撞圈串联起来使用,以延长外钢围的运动距离和撞击过程时间。总之,将根据数值计算结果或力学分析[11],研究如何选用和组构防撞圈和设计钢围结构,以使得防撞设施所具有的柔性适合用于不同的动能量级下的结构抗撞击防护。

(3) 外钢围迎撞角。外钢围在迎撞击方向上做成一定角度的尖形(例如90°、75°等,如图3所示),使得船舶碰撞到防撞设施的外钢围时,受到偏离原方向的向外分力,从而使船舶向离开桥墩的方向运动;经历一定时间之后,船舶将改变其运动方向,带着尽可能多的剩余动能沿外钢围的外侧滑走,起到太极推手“四两拨千斤的作用”。结合数值计算结果,分析在给定的船舶撞击条件下外钢围迎撞角的有效取值范围。研究表明,当外钢围的迎撞角设计为75°时,该柔性防船撞装置可以起到拨转船舶航向的功效。

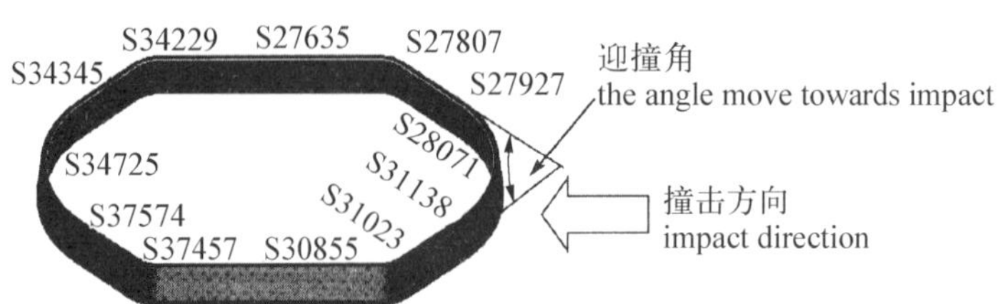

图 3 柔性防撞设施的外钢围迎撞角示意图

Fig. 3 The sketch map on the angle move towards impact of outer steel gate of the flexible anti-collision equipment

3 实船撞击实验

3.1 实验装置

实船撞击实验是利用宁波象山白墩港大桥主桥墩前方的一个防撞墩，将柔性防船撞装置安装在该防撞墩上（见图 4）。柔性防撞装置的内、外钢围采用浮箱（箱梁结构）设计，其间通过 28 个防撞圈（上下两排，如图 5a 所示）相联系，可以浮在水面。其迎撞角为 75°，外钢围的刚度与防撞圈强度的关系设计依据理论分析确定。为了测量船舶对桥墩的撞击力和船舶受到的撞击力，以及船舶的运动随时间的变化，在防撞装置和实验使用的船舶上布置、安放一系列的传感器。在防撞圈与内钢围之间装设力传感器（见图 5a），记录桥墩受到的撞击力，在外钢围上设计一个船舶撞击区，在撞击区内布置有 12 个压力传感器（见图 5b），记录船舶与外钢围之间的撞击力。在船舶的质心附近设置有三维加速度传感器和陀螺仪，记录船舶加速度以及船舶运动方向的变化，利用测量得到的船舶加速度时程曲线，也可以求得船舶受到的撞击力时程曲线。

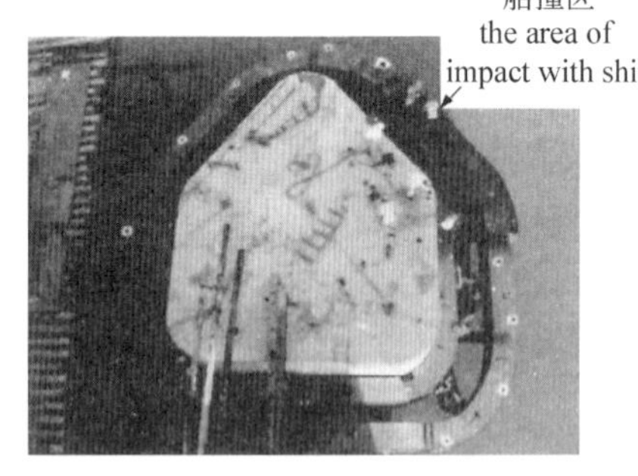

图 4 用于实船撞击实验的柔性防船撞装置

Fig. 4 The flexible anti-collision equipment for the experiment of actual ship impact to bridge

3.2 撞击实验

实验采用的船舶的空载重量为 250 t，载重量为 400 t，满载排水量约 650 t。实验中，船舶撞击速度 1 ~ 4 m/s，船舶的排水量范围：250 ~ 400 t。对不同的船舶航速、重量和撞击方向，共进行了 12 次实船撞击实验（见图 6）。实验测得船撞力时程曲线、船舶撞击后的运动轨迹，以及柔性防船撞装置的冲击响应等。船舶在撞击 12 次后仅受到轻微损伤；而防撞装置完好，可以继续工作；承台则没有发现任何损伤。实验结果表明：

（1）柔性防撞装置具有拨转船舶航向的功能，即使船舶偏航撞击角度达到 25°，该装置仍能够拨转船舶航向，使其沿着外钢围外侧滑走。

(5a)

(5b)

图 5　柔性防船撞装置局部结构

Fig. 5　The local structure of the flexible anti-collision equipment

(6a)

(6b)

图 6　实船撞击实验

Fig. 6　The experiment of actual ship impact to bridge

(2) 船舶航速在撞击后的变化很小，当船舶偏航撞击角度较小(5°)时，撞击后、前的船舶航速比达到 90% 以上，即使对于 25°的船舶偏航撞击角度，撞击后、前的船舶航速比仍达到 80% 以上。可见柔性防撞装置使得船舶在撞击后，其大部分动能没有参加能量交换，仍以动能的形式保留在船舶上。

(3) 柔性防撞装置不仅保护了桥梁(包括桥墩承台)，而且可以保护船舶，同时装置本身也可以不受损坏，可以达到“三不坏”。

(4) 设置于防撞圈与内钢围之间的力传感器测得的力时程曲线如图 7 所示，

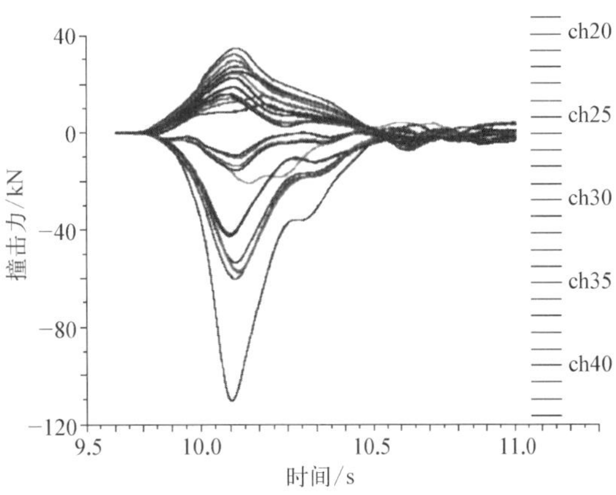

图 7　防撞圈的受力同期性

Fig. 7　The force synchronism of the anti-collision rings

虽然每个防撞圈到船舶撞击点的距离不同,但却有很好的受力同期性。图 7 表明:外钢围的刚度设计达到了要求,即外钢围在受撞过程中作刚性移动,变形很小。

(5)桥墩受到的最大撞击力略小于船舶受到的最大撞击力。

3.3 实验结果与数值模拟的比较

为了与实验结果进行比较,针对实验条件,采用有限元商用软件 LS - DYNA 进行了数值模拟。模拟三种工况下(如表 1 所示),船舶撞击未装设防撞装置的承台(裸撞,如图 8 所示)和装设柔性防撞装置的承台的撞击力时程曲线,其最大船撞力见表 1 所示。

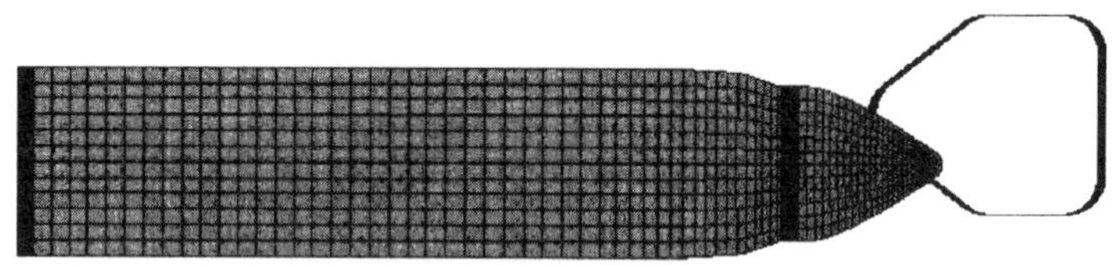

图 8 裸撞有限元模型

Fig. 8 The finite element model of naked collision

表 1 数值模拟工况及结果比较

Table 1 The compare of numerical modeling results of different working conditions

船舶重量 /t	船舶航速 /m·s⁻¹	船舶偏航撞击角 /(°)	数值模拟最大船撞力/kN		实测最大船撞力/kN
			裸撞	柔性防撞装置	柔性防撞装置
250	2.3	26	2 700	800	650
250	3.0	0	1 600	750	650
400	3.5	0	2 300	1 100	1 000

实验实测的船撞力时程曲线与数值模拟结果的比较见图 9 ~ 图 11。

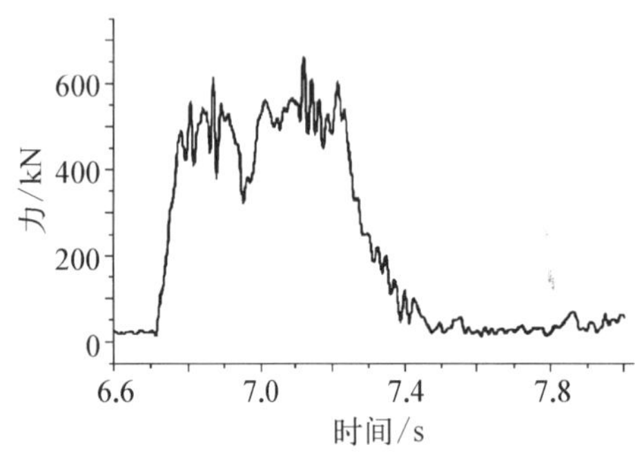

(a) 实验实测的船撞力时程曲线

The experimental impact curve of force-time histories of an actual ship

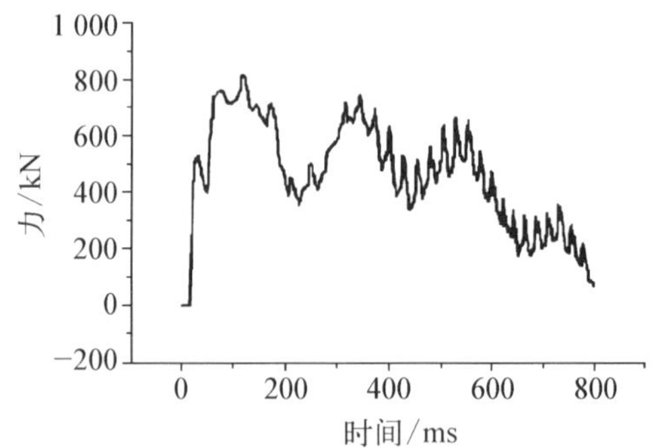

(b) 数值计算的船撞力时程曲线

The numerical calculation impact curve of force-time histories

图 9 船重 250 t,航速 2.3 m/s,船舶偏航撞击角 26°

Fig. 9 The ship have lightweight 250 t, with route speed 2.3 m/s, and impact with off-course angle 26°

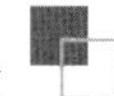

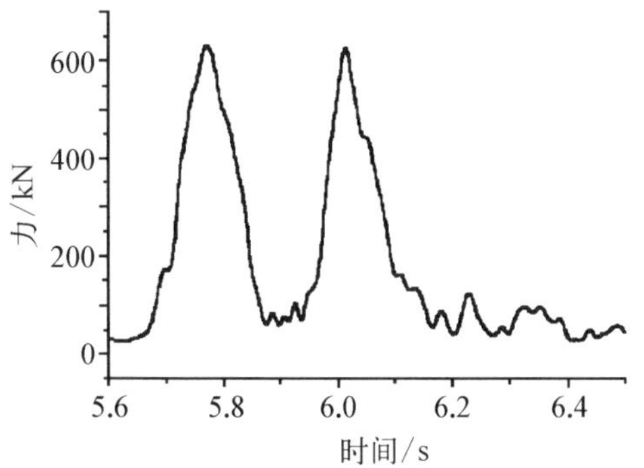

(a) 实验实测的船撞力时程曲线
The experimental impact curve of force-time histories of an actual ship

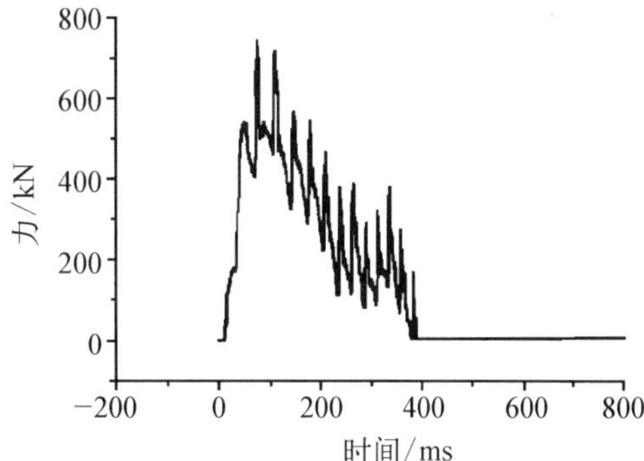

(b) 数值计算的船撞力时程曲线
The numerical calculation impact curve of force-time histories

图 10 船重 250 t,航速 3 m/s,船舶偏航撞击角 0°

Fig. 10 The ship have lightweight 250 t, with route speed 3 m/s, and impact with off-course angle 0°

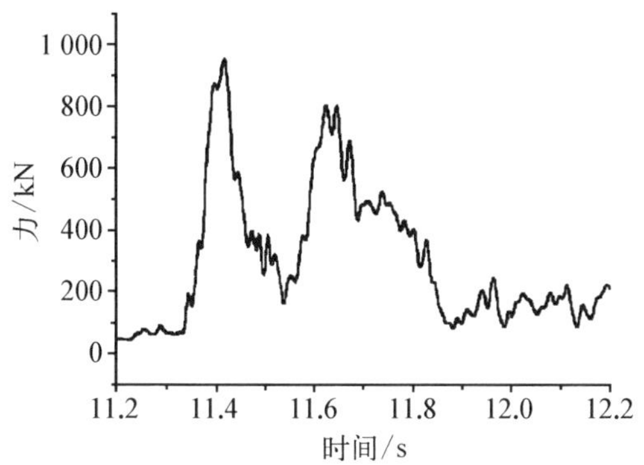

(a) 实验实测的船撞力时程曲线
The experimental impact curve of force-time histories of an actual ship

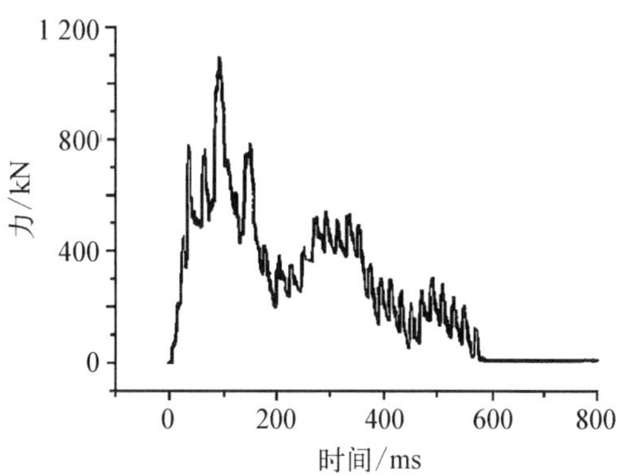

(b) 数值计算的船撞力时程曲线
The numerical calculation impact curve of force-time histories

图 11 船重 400 t,航速 3.5 m/s,船舶偏航撞击角 0°

Fig. 11 The ship have displacement 400 t, with route speed 3.5 m/s, and impact with off-course angle 0°

上述的比较可见,数值计算得到的最大船撞力与实验测量值基本一致,两者得到的碰撞历时也基本相同。因此,对最大船撞力的数值模拟结果是可靠的。表 1 表明,柔性防撞装置可以大幅降低船舶对桥墩的撞击力(降低 50% 以上)。

但两者的船撞力时程曲线的形貌有所偏差。如下因素可能造成这种偏差:

(1) 水流的影响:在有限元模型中,水流的影响是以附连水质量的形式体现,这可能在船舶具有角速度变化的运动时,产生一定的误差。

(2) 实际的船首钢板质量的影响:在有限元模型中,使用的船首钢板的材料参数是刚出产的钢板材料参数,然而实际的船首钢板已经受到海水相当严重的腐蚀,即实际的船首的刚度和强度要比有限元模型中的弱,这也是导致数值模拟的船撞力均略大于实验测量值(表1)的一个原因。

4 结论

经过有限元数值分析和实船撞击实验研究,得到如下结论:

(1) 新型柔性防撞装置能够起到缓冲、拨转船舶航向的作用,船舶具有的大部分动能在碰撞过程中没有参加能量交换,仍以动能的形式保留在船舶上,大幅降低了船舶对桥墩的撞击力(降低50%以上)。

(2) 柔性防撞装置不仅可以保护桥梁(包括桥墩承台),而且可以保护船舶,同时装置本身也可以不受损坏,可以达到"三不坏"。

(3) 柔性防撞装置的关键设计参量(外钢围刚度、迎撞角和防撞圈的组构设计)可以通过理论分析和数值模拟确定。

(4) 实验表明采用有限元数值计算方法模拟最大船撞力,得到的结果是可靠的。

参考文献

[1] Larry D, Olson P E. Dynamic Bridge Substructure Evaluation and Monitoring. Report No. FHWA-RD-03-089, U. S. Federal Highway Administration,2005.

[2] International Association for Bridge and Structural Engineering (IABSE). Ship Collision with Bridges and Offshore Structures, Preliminary Report, IABSE Colloquium. Copenhagen, Denmark, 1983.

[3] Jones N. Structural Aspects of Ship Collisions[M]. Structural Crashworthiness, Butterworths Publishers, London and Boston, 1983: 308 - 337.

[4] 陈国虞,王礼立.船撞桥及其防御[M].北京:铁道工业出版社,2006.

[5] 项海帆.桥梁设计概念[M].北京:人民交通出版社,2011.

[6] Terndrup Pedersen P, Valsg ~ rd S, Olsen D, et al. Ship impacts: bow collisions[J]. International Journal of Impact Engineering, 1993, 13: 163 - 187.

[7] Gary R Consolazio, David R Cowan Nonlinear analysis of barge crush behavior and its relationship to impact resistant bridge design[J]. Computers ~ Structures, 2003, 81: 547 - 557.

[8] 王礼立,张忠伟,黄德进,等.船撞桥的钢丝绳圈柔性防撞装置的冲击动力学分析[A].洪友士.应用力学进展[M]——祝贺郑哲敏先生八十华诞.北京:科学出版社,2004.

[9] Lili Wang, Liming Yang, D@ n Huang, et al. An impact dynamics analysis on a new crashworthy device against ship-bridge collision[J]. International Journal of Impact Engineering, 2008, 35: 895 - 904.

[10] Gary R. Consolazio Barge impact testing of the st. george island causeway bridge[R]. 2004.

[11] 杨峰,杨黎明.桥墩柔性防撞装置的静力学模型研究[J].固体力学学报,2011(32).

发表于:中国土木工程学会第20届全国桥梁学术会议论文集[M].
北京:人民交通出版社,2012:948 - 954.
Published at: CCES Proceeding of the 20th symposium of bridges.
Beijing: China Communications Press, 2012: 948 - 954.

船与墩的撞击力实验室研究和实船试验与数值模拟比较

Experimental study and actual test of impact force on bridge sustained collision by ship

陈国虞[1]　倪步友[1]　李玉节[2]　杨黎明[3]

(1. 上海海洋钢结构研究所,上海 201204;

2. 中国船舶科学研究中心,无锡 214082;3. 宁波大学,宁波 315211)

CHEN Guoyu[1], NI Buyou[1], LI Yujie[2], YANG Liming[3]

(1. Shanghai Marine Steel and Structure Research Institute, Shanghai 201204, China;

2. China Ship Scientific Research Center, Wuxi 214082, China;

3. Ningbo University, Ningbo 315211, China)

摘　要　运用理论推导、实验和数值计算这三种方法对铁路规范中船撞力公式的动能折减系数进行了研究。在我国铁路桥梁规范中列入的船撞力公式 $F=\gamma v\sin\alpha[W/(C_1+C_2)]^{0.5}$ 中,考虑了撞击系统中各物体的刚度,比较符合冲击动力学的原理。公式中的动能折减系数 γ,规范推荐选用 0.2 和 0.3。试验中,将钢对钢面接触、钢对钢线接触、钢对混凝土面接触以及钢对橡胶接触这 4 种情况进行了测定,得到钢对钢面接触时(背面有防撞元件——对应于高效的防撞装置)系数 γ 比较高的结论(最高可达 0.8 左右),建议在修订规范时,进行全面的设计试验,以测定之。还对专门建造的桥墩进行了实船撞击的试验,并将试验测得的力与数值模拟计算的结果进行比较。研究结果已用于指导 4 座大桥的 20 个桥墩的防撞装置的设计,其中 12 个桥墩的防撞装置已经建造。研究结果对船舶及海洋工程领域的结构物设计也有一定参考价值。

关键词　桥梁　铁路桥梁规范　船撞桥的力　动能折减系数　试验研究

Abstract: It is necessary to estimate ship-bridge collision force by using semi-empirical formulae during preliminary design of a bridge. There is a formula, that is $F = \gamma v\sin\alpha[W/(C_1+C_2)]^{0.5}$, which includes the stiffness of each body in impacting system and meets the principle of impact dynamics. Reduced coefficient of kinetic energy γ in the formula is proposed: $\gamma=0.2$ or $\gamma=0.3$ in the railway bridge

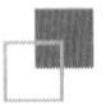

specification. In this paper, coefficient γ is determined experimentally under 4 different conditions: surface contact for steel-steel, line contact for steel-steel, steel-rubber contact, and steel-concrete contact. It is proposed that coefficient γ be determined with a comprehensive experiment at revision of the specification mentioned. Second, results of collision of an actual ship with an actual bridge pier are given in the paper. A comparison of the force from measurement with that of calculation is made. The results of this paper have provided guidance to the design of up to 20 piers for 4 bridges, within which 12 piers have been built.

Keywords: bridge, specification of railway bridge design, force of collision of ship with bridge, reduced coefficient of kinetic energy, experimental study

1 引言

20 世纪 60 年代后,由于行驶于跨桥梁的航道上的船愈来愈大、愈来愈多、愈来愈快,因而船撞桥的事故日渐被工程界重视。为防止船撞桥墩和船撞桥梁的下弦,人们曾经设置过多种主动和被动的防撞设施。因此,在设计桥梁的开始阶段,估算船撞桥的力,以便算出多大的桥墩能够不被撞塌,同时算出相撞时船的破坏情形、货物外泄数量、环境污染程度等。为了给跨航道桥梁的设计者在选定桥型、讨论航道中设置桥墩与否提供依据;早期利用半经验公式简单地估算船撞桥的力是必须的、有用的。

2 船与桥墩的撞击力的 5 个半经验公式

20 世纪 80 年代,人们估算船撞力时,废弃了单变量公式(例如[4]中的 $P = 0.5(DWT)^{0.5}$),采用双变量和多变量公式。国内外多在冲击能量原理或冲量原理的经典公式中加上经验系数,形成半经验公式;其中,中国铁路规范公式计及撞击系统中各物体的刚度,体现了冲击动力学的基本观点[1]。这些半经验公式中使用较多的有以下 5 个。

1) 我国铁路规范公式

该公式原来只有 C_1 和 C_2 两个系数,当在桥墩周围增加防撞装置情况下,可将防撞装置的弹性变形系数定义为 C_3;该式修订后[5],墩台承受船只或排筏的撞击力可表达为

$$F = \gamma v \sin\alpha [W/(C_1 + C_2 + C_3)]^{0.5} \tag{1}$$

式中,F 为撞击力,kN;γ 为动能折减系数,s/m(当船只或排筏斜向撞击墩台、船只或排筏驶向与撞击点处墩台面法线方向不一致时,可用 0.2;当正向撞击墩台、船只或排筏驶向

与撞击点处的墩台面法线方向一致时,可用 0.3);v 为船只或排筏撞击墩台时的速度,m/s(该速度对于船只采用航运部门提供的数据,对于排筏采用运送排筏的水流速度);α 为船只或排筏驶向与墩台面撞击点切向构成的夹角,应根据具体情况确定,如有困难,可采用 $\alpha=20°$;W 为船只重(或排筏重),kN;C_1、C_2、C_3 分别为船只(或排筏)的弹性变形系数、墩台的弹性变形系数和防撞装置的弹性变形系数,m/kN。

2)我国公路规范公式

漂流物撞击力可按下式估算:

$$P = Wv/(gT) \tag{2}$$

式中,P 为漂流物撞击力,kN;W 为漂流物重力,kN(应根据河流中漂流物情况,按实际调查确定);v 为水流速度,m/s;T 为撞击时间,s(应根据实际资料估计,在无实际资料时,一般用 1 s);g 为重力加速度,9.81 m/s^2。

3)敏诺斯基-捷勒-沃以信(Minorsky-Gerlach-Woisin)公式[4]

$$P = 0.024(vD_{max})^{2/3} \tag{3}$$

式中,P 为撞击力,MN;v 为船速 m/s;D_{max}为船的满载排水量,t。

4)诺特-索尔-格林那(Knott-Saul-Svelsson-Greiner)公式[4]

$$P_{max} = 0.88(DWT)^{1/2}(v/8)^{2/3}(D_{act}/D_{max})^{1/3} \tag{4}$$

式中,P_{max}为最大撞击力,t;DWT 为船的载重量,t;v 为撞击时的船速,m/s;D_{act}为撞击时的排水量,m^3;D_{max}为船只满载排水量,m^3。

5)美国各州公路和运输工作者协会(AASHTO)的公式[3]

$$P_s = 1.2\times10^2 v(DWT)^{0.5} \tag{5}$$

式中,P_s为船只的等效正面静撞击力,kN;DWT 为船只的载重吨数,t;v 为船只的撞击速度,m/s。

上述 5 个半经验公式中,只有铁路规范[2]公式中含有撞击系统各物体的刚度。

一般,在桥梁设计的“工程可行性研究”阶段,就要求根据桥位处的通航情况,对桥墩抵御航船撞击的水平力作出估算,称为该桥采用的“标准”船撞力,这个“标准”是一个准静态力。

在桥梁初步设计或防撞装置设计阶段,通常根据海洋工程结构物(例如:桥梁、船舶或海洋平台结构)的构造图纸,设计者用数值计算的方法,使用动态有限元程序,计及各种防撞元件在撞击力作用下的变形特征以及防撞结构中各种材料在动态加载下的特性,综合地考虑包括防撞装置和桥墩基础在内的整个桥墩系统的动态响应,详细地计算船撞力。

除了上述 5 个半经验公式计算和数值计算方法之外,在需要和有条件时,还利用实验手段用以验证结果、校核计算软件等。这就是现代工程力学处理问题常用的 3 种方法。半经验公式在桥梁设计的初始阶段是很有用的,而且还会在以后继续使用。

3 半经验公式发展现状

1991 年,O. D. 拉森[4]总结了各国使用的船撞力的半经验公式共 14 种,这些公式有的是双变量公式,但与我国铁路规范公式相比,都相形见绌。中国铁路规范公式把附连水系数计入 W 内(即:W 包括了 2 个变量),再计及防撞装置的刚度[5],共可计入 8 个变量,公式的理论基础是明确而直接的。

冲击动力学认为,冲击力与冲击系统中各元件的刚度有关。由于铁路桥梁规范公式体现了冲击动力学的原理,又可计入 8 个变量,比其他公式具有很大的优越性;且已经过论证:现有的半经验公式都是同源的[8]。现在的任务不是去创造新的公式,而是完善铁路桥梁规范公式,选择正确的参数。2006 年中国土木工程学会全国桥梁学术会议上有论文提出:将铁路桥梁规范中的船撞力公式作为铁路、公路和城建等各种桥梁共同使用的公式[7]。

本文的工作与参考文献[5]一致,也是为了完善铁路规范公式。

4 铁路规范船撞力公式中的动能折减系数的意义

两物体表面撞击时,会发声、发热,有时会发光(火花等);撞击消耗了能量,使撞击力下降。从冲击的动态“力-变形”曲线图(见图 1)来看,冲击开始时曲线出现一个峰值(峰值下有一块面积);而且,曲线与横坐标包围的功可分为三部分:Ⅰ是初打击时的表面消耗功;Ⅱ是防撞系统(包括防撞元件)消耗的功;Ⅲ是防撞系统返回给打击物(船头、船身、锤头等)的功,Ⅰ、Ⅱ、Ⅲ之和就是外加功(见图 1)。

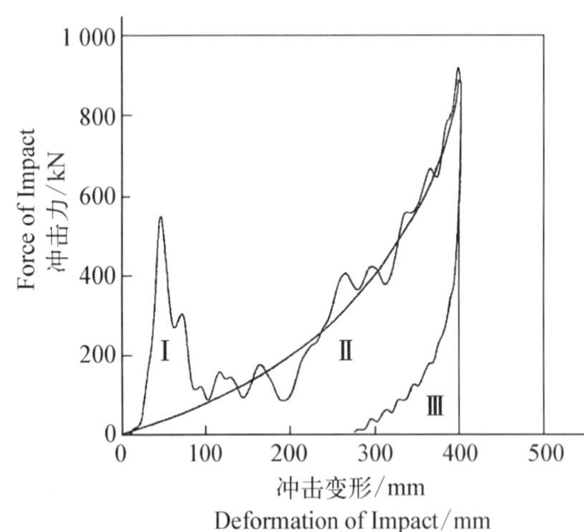

图 1 冲击的“力-变形”曲线下面三部分功

Fig. 1 Three parts of works under the“force-deformation” curve of impact

当然,有一部分发声、发光的功不包括在“力-变形”曲线之内。在船撞桥墩的速度范围,发光是比较少的;在钢结构背后有柔性低抗力、大变形、高耗能的防撞元件,试验时的声音是很小的。如果不计及这两种耗能,在撞击开始时,撞击力高峰部分的耗能(即:“力-变形”曲线中的第Ⅰ部分)代表的功,有特殊意义。

5　实验室试验设备及其原理

船头与桥墩之间增加弹性(弹塑性、黏性或低刚度的)防撞装置,使船头和防撞装置这个系统的撞击便有一个新的系统撞击时程。延长该撞击时程可引致撞击力下降,这是防撞装置的作用。因此,只要能测定相撞系统(包括:船头、防撞装置和桥墩)在船与桥墩相对速度下的撞击时程,并代入公路规范公式便可算出撞击力;表 1、表 2 所列的试验是在中国船舶研究中心进行的[8],其单自由度系统(见图 2)的运动方程为

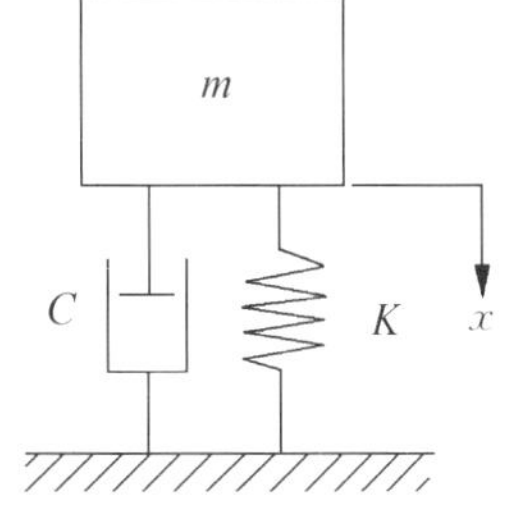

图 2　单自由度系统[8]

Fig. 2　Single-degree-of-freedom system

$$mx'' + Cx' + Kx = mg \tag{6}$$

式中,m 为落锤质量,kg;C 为试件阻尼,Ns/m;K 为试件刚度,N/m;g 为重力加速度,9.81 m/s^2。

只要用一个加速度传感器,测得“力-变形”图的纵轴数值,将测得结果积分 2 次,便可得出横轴数值。图 3 为落锤冲击试验机,图 4 为 8 个防撞圈所组成的试验分段。

图 3　落锤冲击试验机(单圈试验)[8]

Fig. 3　Drop-hammer-impact testing machine

图 4　八个防撞圈所组成的试验分段

Fig. 4　Test section with 8 protecting rings

6　四种接触情况的撞击表面耗能定量分析

6.1　实验室试验结果

在研制防撞装置的过程中,利用落锤试验方法[6]标定了一些防撞元件(ϕ300 ~

800 mm 的防撞圈)和一些防撞装置分段(4 ~8 个防撞圈与外钢围共同组成的防撞装置的模拟分段以及 1∶1实样分段)的“力-变形”曲线,共有 80 多幅,选取其中有代表性的曲线,其分别为: 钢平面直接打在橡胶面上(见表 1);钢对钢平面的接触(背后有防撞圈,模拟防撞装置斜面与船接触,见表 2);钢平面对钢线的接触(模拟尖船头崁入钢结构);钢对混凝土(平面);共 4 种情况,每种情况举 1 ~2 幅图为例,见图 5。

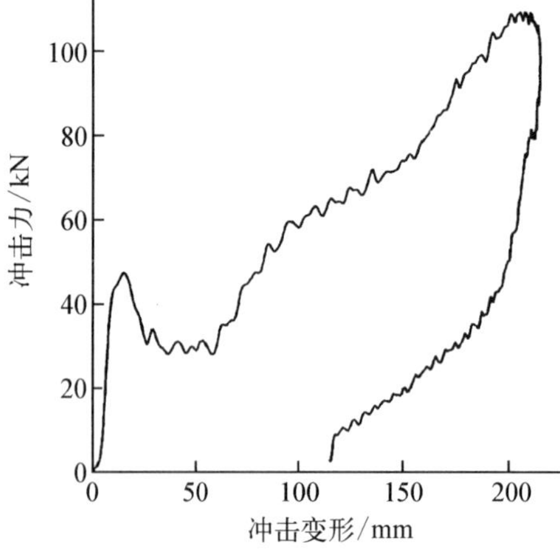

(a) 钢平面直接打在橡胶面上(表 1 之 1)
Steel plane impact to the rubber face of protection ring (1th of table 1)

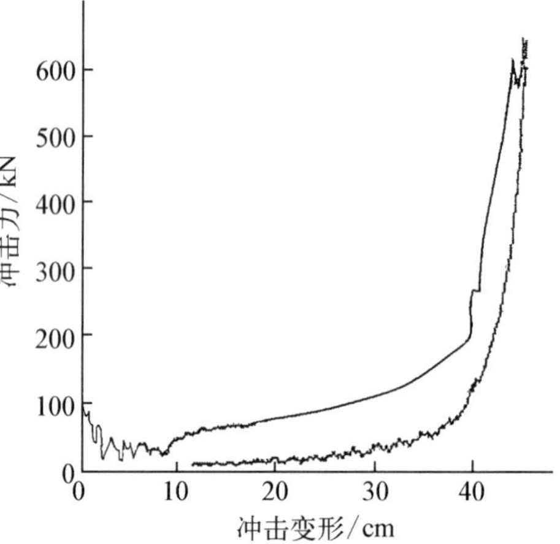

(b) 钢平面直接打在橡胶面上(表 1 之 11)
Steel plane impact to the rubber face of protection ring (11th of table 1)

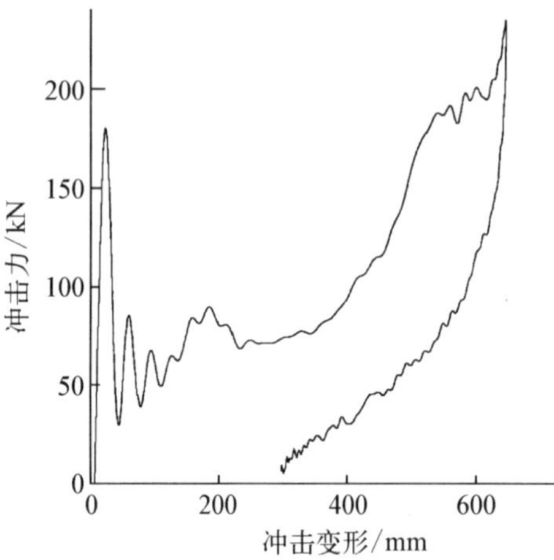

(c) 钢对钢平面接触(背后有防撞圈,表 2 之 6)
Steel plane impact to steel plane of outer gate (there are rings at the back) (6th of table 2)

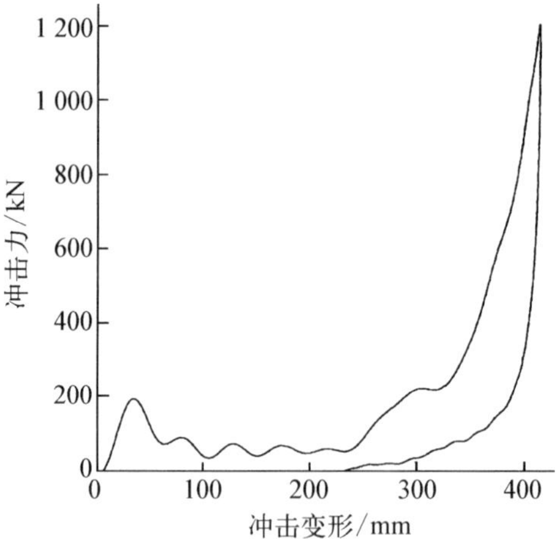

(d) 钢对钢平面接触(背后有防撞圈,表 2 之 8)
Steel plane impact to steel plane of outer gate (there are rings at the back) (8th of table 2)

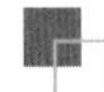

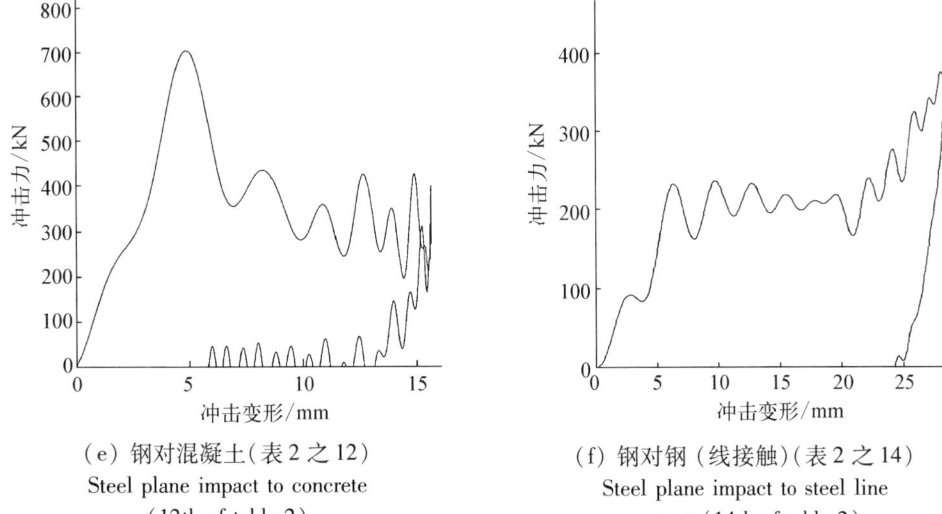

(e) 钢对混凝土(表2之12)
Steel plane impact to concrete
(12th of table 2)

(f) 钢对钢(线接触)(表2之14)
Steel plane impact to steel line contact (14th of table 2)

图5 冲击试验"力-变形"曲线举例

Fig. 5 Examples of the "force-deformation" curve of impact tests

表1 **钢对橡胶防撞圈撞击时表面耗能及系数(对应图5a、5b)**

Table 1 **The energy dissipation and its coefficient of steel plane impact to the rubber face of protection ring (reciprocal diagram 5a、5b)**

序号	撞击初速度/m·s^{-1}	接触形式和材质	外加功/J	总耗功/J	表面耗功/J	总耗功与外加功之比值/(%)	表面耗功与外加功之比值/(%)	试验日期
1	4.4	钢对橡胶	13 122	9 202	994	70	7.6	20020107
2	4.4		14 141	9 839	865	70	6.1	20020107
3	3.0		41 900	34 240	1 097	82	2.6	20021206
4	3.4		65 388	44 279	2 162	75	3.3	20030303
5	3.1		57 996	45 459	2 931	78	5.1	20030303
6	3.4		65 388	49 279	3 798	75	5.8	20030303
7	3.1		7 440	4 915	1 393	66	18.7	20040826
8	4.4		13 539	8 927	2 582	66	19.1	20040826
9	3.1		7 455	4 558	1 389	61	17.8	20040826
10	4.4		13 559	8 507	2 486	63	18.3	20040826
11	3.0		59 168	35 497	4 170	60	7.0	20060911
12	3.0		58 460	33 748	6 010	58	10.3	20060911
13	3.1		62 436	39 160	3 935	63	6.3	20060927
14	3.1		62 162	38 546	4 144	62	6.7	20060927
15	3.1		62 230	37 206	4 660	60	7.5	20060927
16	2.9		56 988	35 332	5 804	62	10.2	20060930
17	3.0		58 112	38 604	6 931	66	11.9	20060930
18	3.0		57 858	39 001	5 893	67	10.2	20060930
19	3.0		58 472	37 365	5 921	64	10.1	20060930

注:钢对橡胶外加功之表面消耗(%)范围:2.6%~19.1%;平均值:9.7%(粗略地取用10%)。

表 2　钢对钢的面接触、钢对钢的线接触和钢对混凝土撞击的表面耗能及系数(对应图 5c 至 5f)

Table 2　**The energy dissipation and its coefficient of steel plane impact to steel plane (there are protection rings at the back), to steel line and to the concrete (reciprocal diagram 5c to 5f)**

序号	撞击初速度 /m·s^{-1}	接触形式和材质	外加功 W_m/J	总耗功 W_a/J	总耗功与外加功之比值/(%)	表面耗功 W_f/J	表面耗功与外加功之比值/(%)	试验日期
1	4.0	钢对钢(面接触)	10 094	7 783	77	1 480	14.7	20011119
2	4.0		10 230	7 075	69	2 261	22.1	20011119
3	3.6		8 320	6 903	83	1 889	22.7	20011119
4	3.6		8 235	5 723	69	1 084	13.2	20011119
5	4.4		12 210	9 935	81	2 137	17.5	20011119
6	3.1		69 830	37 840	54	14 417	20.6	20020121
7	4.4		113 700	112 300	99	16 334	14.4	20020121
8	4.4		86 090	64 830	75	10 397	12.1	20020121
9	4.4		92 554	68 114	74	30 661	33.2	20030313
10	5.6		121 603	104 612	86	23 484	19.3	20030313
11	4.4		92 554	68 114	74	27 404	29.6	20030313
12	3.1	钢对混凝土	5 562	5 258	95	471	8.5	20040826
13	3.1		6 535	6 535	100	2 838	43.4	20040826
14	3.1	钢对钢(线接触)	5 702	5 185	90	0	0	20040826
15	4.4		11 068	10 748	97	0	0	20040826
16	4.4		11 281	11 018	98	0	0	20040826

注:(1) 对应表 1 表 2 的全部图见文献[10];(2) 钢对钢面接触的耗功与外加功之比率为(12.1~33.2)%,平均值为19.9%;(3) 表中1~11 项可见,总耗功与外加功之比值为54% ~99%,平均为76.5%;(4) 表中各次试验试样的防撞圈数和防撞圈内钢丝绳圈的构成略有不同。

6.2　讨论和建议

6.2.1　讨论

如果认为:动态"力-位移"曲线的上升段与横坐标之间的功是船的撞击功,初始峰下面的面积是表面消耗的功;那么,钢船首侧平面与这种防撞装置钢板面接触时,该表面耗能系数相应为0.8。

钢对钢的线接触的试验太少,仅发现一个现象:声响基本没有,曲线初始代表表面功的部分没有,初始的峰值也没有,一开始线状船头就压入钢板引起弹塑性变形,大部分能量都显示为变形功,表面耗能接近于零。

混凝土表面受撞击的试验太少,其现象是:撞击发出较大闷声时,其粉碎的试样表面耗能小;该撞击开始的能量峰的面积比例较大,但不能判断其为表面耗能,因为随后的曲

线下面积很小,在冲击开始阶段混凝土便粉碎了。

6.2.2 建议

根据实验结果,原有规范[1]中的:“当船只(或排筏)斜向撞击墩台(指船只或排筏驶向与撞击点处墩台面法线方向不一致)可采用0.2,正向撞击(指船只或排筏驶向与撞击处墩台面法线方向一致)时,可采用0.3;”这一段话就显得不正确了。在下次规范修订前,应设计比较全面的试验,得出结果后加以修订。

7 用测定实船撞桥墩的力验证模拟数值计算和铁路规范公式船撞力

得到交通部门和浙江省的基金支持,经过3年的准备,于2011-09-03在浙江象山白墩港,进行了钢船头对混凝土桥墩外面的柔性防撞装置撞击的实船试验,实验条件简述如下:

(1)选用船舶载重量400 t的自航式沿海货船“嘉工58号”(见图6),空船撞击试验时排水量250 t;有载撞击试验时,载钢铁150 t,排水量400 t。

图6 实船撞墩试验用船“嘉工58号”

Fig.6 Actual ship “JA-GONG 58th” for the ship impact to the actual pier test

(2)防撞装置有内、外两个钢围(浮箱围子),安装在混凝土承台外,内、外两个钢围(浮箱)之间装有15组共30个防撞圈;防撞圈与内、外钢围之间装有力传感器,如图7、图8、图9所示。

(3)撞击时航行速度选定为5 kn、6 kn和8 kn,仪器记录的撞击速度与试验设计误差不超过1 kn;船的质心附近有三维加速度传感器和陀螺仪,记录船舶加速度和运动方向的变化,从低速到高速、空载到有载、航线方向从0°到26°,共撞击12次。

(4)撞击后船头轻微损伤,防撞装置完好,人员站在离撞击点1 m的船的主甲板上和离撞击点2 m的承台面上,感觉轻微(类似于船靠码头的震动)。

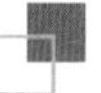

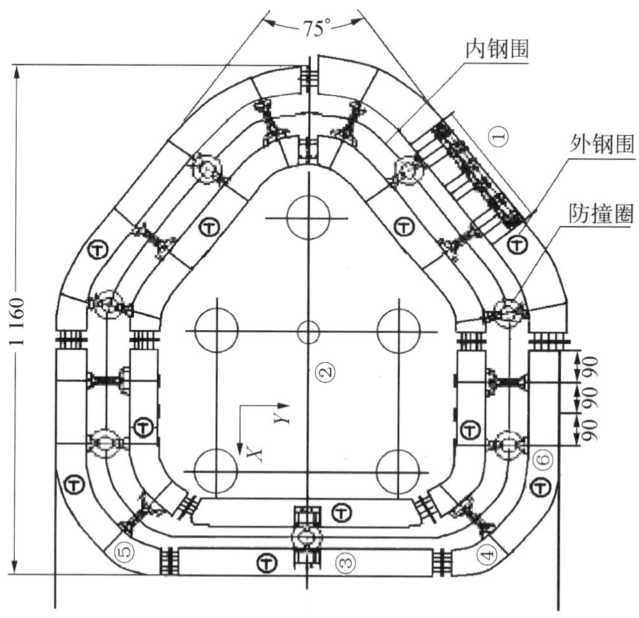

图 7　柔性防撞装置在桥墩的布置及安装图

Fig. 7　The location of flexibility anti-collision equipment around the actual pier

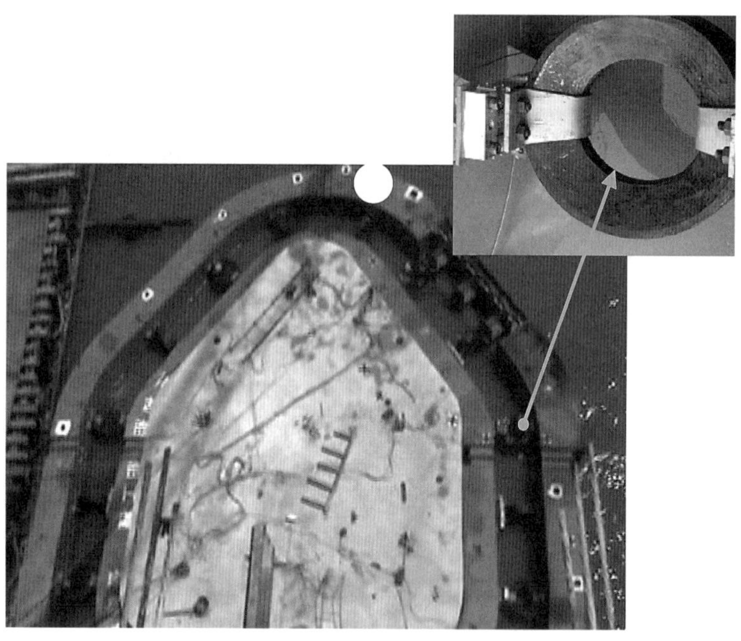

图 8　迎撞面点阵设置的压力传感器布置

Fig. 8　The pressure sensors location at the anti-collision equipment around the pier and face to the coming ship

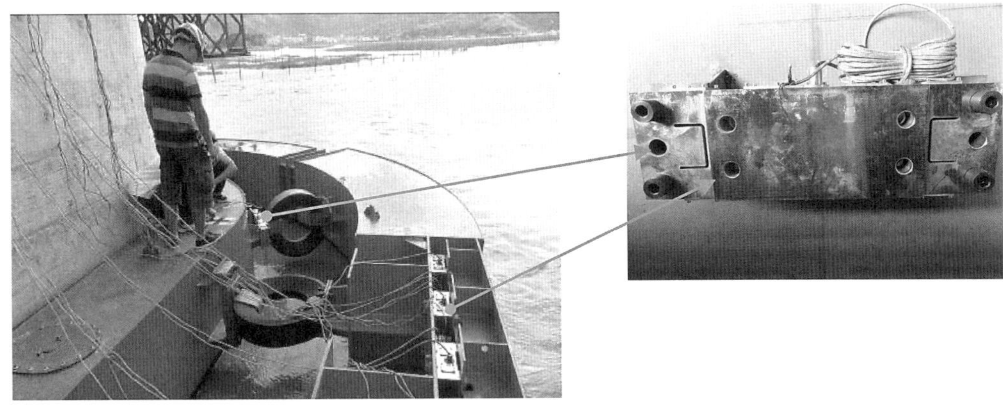

图9 迎撞面及防撞圈背面的压力传感器布置

Fig. 9 The pressure sensors location face to the coming ship and at the back of the ring

8 选取典型工况数值模拟、半经验公式与实船测力结果比较

表3为选取典型工况数值模拟、半经验公式与测力结果比较，图10为一次有载撞击过程（截屏）。

表3 选取典型工况数值模拟、半经验公式与测力结果比较

Table 3 The result comparing of numerical modeling, semi-empirical formula and force measurement on typical working condition

设计工况和顺序号	船舶排水量/t（计算）	船舶航速/$m \cdot s^{-1}$（计算/实测）	船舶偏航角/（°）（计算/实测）	数值模拟最大船撞力/kN		柔性防撞	
				裸撞	柔性防撞	实测最大船撞力/kN	铁道公式船撞力/kN
空载正撞 3002	250	3.0/2.27	0.0/3.8	1 600	750（616）*	568	650
空载大角度撞 3101	250	2.3/1.57	26.0/25.5	2 700	800	824	836
有载正撞 0201	400	3.5/3.27	0.0/−3.1	2 300	1 100	980	920

注（1）*括号内数值是经用实测的船速和角度数值的校正值；（2）C_1+C_3在图10的初始段取为0.004 m/kN，C_2取为0。γ在角度较小的两个工况取为0.5，大角度撞的工况取为0.75。

9 铁道规范动能折减系数γ的应用

自从“上海海洋钢结构研究所企业标准：桥墩的船撞力计算及柔性耗能防撞装置设计指南”[9]于2006年公开出版之后，每2年修订一次，到2010年已是第5版了。该企标规定：在设计跨航线桥梁时，桥梁开始设计阶段，应该根据通航船舶的情况，用半经验公

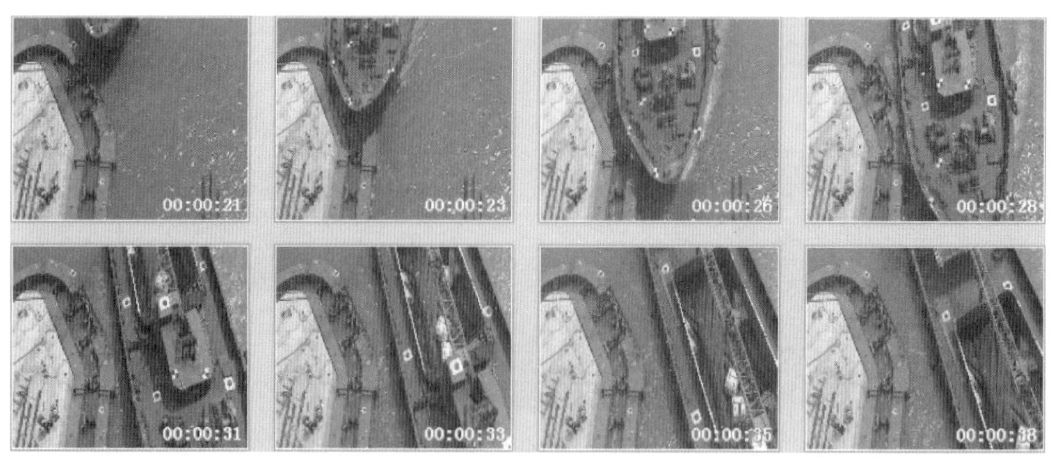

图 10 一次有载撞击过程(截屏)[7]
(按图中时序:撞前,撞上,滑动,船头被拨转,离开防撞装置,继续前进,远离防撞装置,继续前进)
Fig. 10 An impact process with loaded ship to the pier (cut-off frequency)
(By the time sequence in the fig.: before impact, just impact, glide, the ship bow pushed aside, leave from the anti-collision equipment, went on, leave away from the anti-collision equipment, and went on)

式估算船撞力。同时使用的 5 种半经验公式估算,其估算值相差不应超过 25%(应用铁道规范公式时,已将公式中的动能折减系数按试验研究结果进行了修正),现将应用的几个实例汇总于表 4。

10 总结

本研究的结果已用于指导 4 座大桥的 20 个桥墩的防撞装置的设计,其中 12 个桥墩的防撞装置已经建造。本研究结果对船舶及海洋工程领域的结构物设计也具有参考价值。

表 4 **五个半经验公式在桥梁设计前期对 3 座桥梁船撞力的估算**
Table 4 **The estimation of ship impact force with 5 semi-empirical formulas for 3 bridges at the preliminary design**

序	公 式	湛江海湾大桥主墩		重庆双碑公路桥		安庆铁路桥主墩	
		取 值	船撞力/MN	取 值	船撞力/MN	取 值	船撞力/MN
1	中国公路规范公式	v = 3 m/s W = 625 000 kN t = 2.5 s	84	v = 4.16 m/s W = 220 000 kN t = 1.9 s	48.2	v = 6.0 m/s W = 23 540 kN t = 0.6 s	24.0
2	中国铁路规范公式	W = 625 000 kN C_1 = 0.000 07 v = 3 m/s γ = 0.9	78	W = 22 000 t C_1 = 0.000 12 v = 4.16 m/s γ = 0.9	51.9	W = 23 540 kN C_1 = 0.000 13 v = 6.0 m/s γ = 0.9	24.8

续表

序	公　式	湛江海湾大桥主墩		重庆双碑公路桥		安庆铁路桥主墩	
		取　值	船撞力/MN	取　值	船撞力/MN	取　值	船撞力/MN
3	敏诺斯基-捷勒-沃易苏公式	v = 3 m/s DPT = 62 500 t	71	v = 4.16 m/s DPT = 20 000 t	45.7	v = 6.0 m/s DPT = 2 200 t	—
4	索尔-诺特-格林那公式	v = 3 m/s DWT = 50 000 t D/D_{dpt} = 0.8	86	v = 4.16 m/s DWT = 12 000 t D_{act}/D_{dpt} = 0.8	58.1	v = 6.0 m/s DWT = 1 650 t	26.2
5	美国公路规范公式	v = 3 m/s DWT = 50 000 t	80	v = 4.16 m/s DWT = 12 000 t	54.7	v = 6.0 m/s DWT = 1 650 t	29.2

参 考 文 献

[1] 陈国虞,王礼立. 船撞桥及其防御[M]. 北京：中国铁道出版社,2006：36 - 42.

[2] 中华人民共和国铁道部. TB10002. 1—2005 墩台承受船只或排筏的撞击力[S]//铁路桥涵设计基本规范,北京：中国铁道出版社,2005.

[3] 美国各州公路和运输工作者协会(AASHTO). 船只撞击[S]//美国公路桥梁设计规范. 辛济平,等,译. 北京：人民交通出版社,1998：97 - 112.

[4] O. D. 拉森. 交通船只与桥梁结构的相互影响[R]. 国际桥梁和结构工程协会(IABSE),1993. 广东虎门技术咨询公司,译. 1995.

[5] 陈国虞. 有防撞装置时计算船撞桥的力——铁路桥梁规范中船撞力公式的延伸修订[J]. 铁道标准设计,2004,47(1).

[6] 陈国虞,倪步友,等. 水中桩柱用钢绳柔性冲击吸能器试验研究[J]. 交通部上海船舶运输科学研究所学报,1995,31(2).

[7] 陆宗林,陈国虞,张澄. 统一我国两个桥涵设计规范中船撞力公式的探讨[C]//第 17 届全国桥梁学术会议论文集,北京：人民交通出版社,2006：1247.

[8] 王礼立,杨黎明,陈国虞,陆宗林. 船桥相撞的冲击力分析[C]//第二届国际自动化和工程控制会议论文集,2011,vol(7),呼和浩特 ISBN 078 - 1 - 4244 - 9438 - 5,5850 - 5853.

[9] 上海海洋钢结构研究所企业标准 QB/HY02—2010 桥墩的船撞力计算及柔性耗能防撞装置设计指南[S]. 上海海洋钢结构研究所,2010.

[10] 陈国虞. 铁路规范船撞力公式中动能折减系数的试验厘定[C]//城市桥梁养护管理、维修加固技术交流研讨会论文集,上海：城乡建设部,2008：88 - 95.

发表于：中国造船,2013,54(增刊 2)：507 - 515.

Published at：Ship Building of China, Vol. 54, Special 2, 2013：507 - 515.

第五部分

桥梁防船撞遇到的几个具体问题

Some detail problems of bridge anti-collision technology

跨海湾(河湾)桥非通航孔柔性拦船防撞装置

Anti-collision flexibility cable hold up net for the pier of un-navigation bore of long bridge in bay

陈国虞[1] 倪步友[1] 张澄[1] 刁金龙[2] 严景[2] 马海友[3]
(1. 上海海洋钢结构研究所 201204;2. 旗鱼绳网公司——原上海绳网厂 201400;
3. 农业部绳索网具质量监督检查测试中心 200090)
CHEN Guoyu[1], NI Buyou[1], ZHANG Cheng[1], DIAO Jinlong[2], YAN Jing[2], MA Haiyou[3]
(1. Shanghai Marine Steel and Structure Research Institute 201204;
2. Shanghai Sailfish Rope Net Co. Ltd. Formerly Shanghai Rope Net Factory 201400;
3. Rope and Net examination and supervise center of Ministry of Agriculture 200090)

摘 要 桥梁防撞装置中有主要防御船撞桥墩的、有防御船撞上部结构的;有在撞上时桥墩直接受力的和桥墩不受力的;有只保护桥的和既保护桥又保护船的……各种不同分类法。本题目着眼于主通航孔以外的辅助墩、过渡墩、水中引桥墩等的防撞,这部分桥墩通常占有较宽的水面,这水面原是小船的航道。提出一种方式是:既能拦住大船又不妨碍小船通行,而且能在几百米范围内,为水中各墩防撞的柔性缆索吸能方式。本文阐述其原理、措施和某些重要的细节。

关键词 拦船索 柔性防撞 海湾桥 非通航孔 水中引桥

Abstract: Within the equipment for anti-collision of bridge, there are equipments for protection the piers, and the others for protection the supper structure of the bridge. There are equipments when the ship collision with the bridge the collision force action to the piers, and the others the collision force is not action to the piers. There are equipments only protection the bridge and the others is also protection the ship and the circumstance when it protecting the bridge. This paper focus to protection the pier out of the main pier, include assistant pier, transition pier and the approach pier at the water area. Commonly these piers are having a lower strength then the main pier, and these piers occupancy a large water area and these areas just the route of the boats and yachts. So, this paper brings forward a new method. It can be hold up the big vessels and let the boats and yachts passes. It can be action in several hundred meters and protected every piers in this water area. This paper mentions the theory, measures and some coefficient for design.

Keywords: cable for hold up the vessels, flexibility collision protection, bridge in the bay, un-navigation bore, the bridge approach in water area

1 前言

桥梁防撞装置中,有主要防御船撞桥墩的、有主要防御船撞桥上部梁的;有当船撞上桥时桥墩直接受力的和桥墩不受力的;有只保护桥的和既保护桥又保护船的……

本文着眼于通航孔以外的辅助墩、过渡墩和水中引桥墩的防撞。这部分桥墩通常占有较宽的水面(见图1),这水面正是小船的航道(丰水期偏航的大船会撞上这些桥墩)。如果予以封航将影响数量比例甚高的小船。有时流速较急,小船本来航速低,若小船被迫绕道中间航道则根本无法前进。而且一定要小船挤到大船的航道,则大船避让频繁,本身的安全也会受到影响。为此本文提供一种方式,是既能柔性地拦住走歪了的大船,又不妨碍小船通行,而且能在港湾、河湾几百米的水面上为水中各墩防撞的柔性缆索吸能防撞方式。它成本低,拦住船舶保护桥的同时又不损伤船。这样桥、船和环境三方面都得到保护。

这种在主通航孔以外宽距离拦阻的方式,适用于类似杭州湾跨海大桥(海湾)、安庆铁路桥(河湾)以及广东九江大桥(河口宽阔水面)等场合。

图1　图左侧为水中引桥所占的广阔水面

Fig. 1　The vast expanse water area of approach span on the lefe side of the picture

2 拦船网构成及其能量计算

2.1 拦船网构成及布置

拦船网布置在航道的右侧(见图2),因为现在推行航船右驶规则[1],偏航船舶向右撞

向辅助墩、过渡墩(边墩)或水中引桥墩等,这些墩比较弱小(例如广东九江桥所撞的),因此须将船拦阻在它的前面。属于间接防撞方式,桥墩不受力。阻拦网两侧布置能固定拦网的设施(如锚泊的浮船、水中墩桩或岸边墩桩),举例如图3所示。

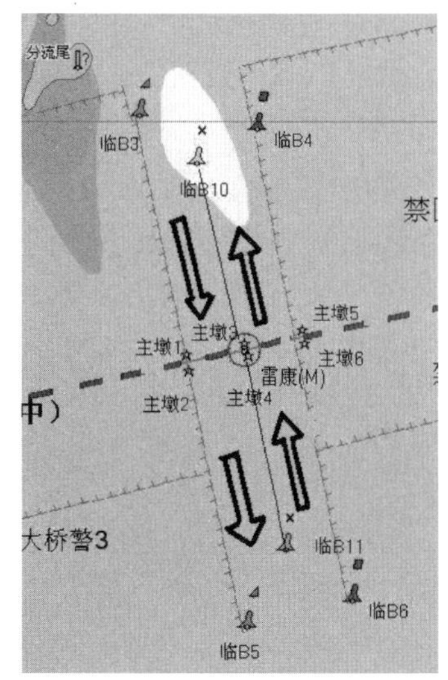

图2　一幅海事局公告的右行航道图

Fig. 2　A right channel picture of a maritime bureau announcement

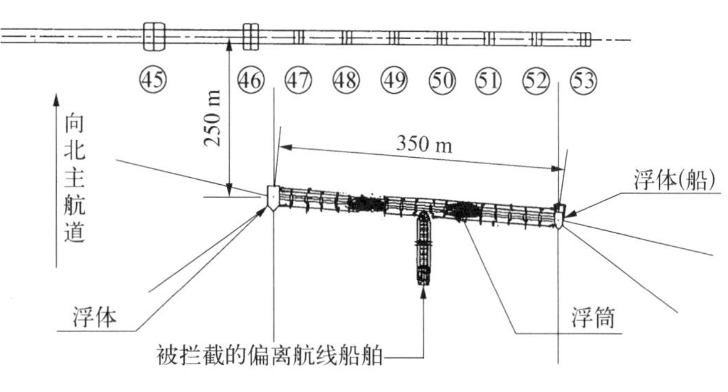

图3　拦船网设施布置举例

Fig. 3　Sketch of block vessel net

2.2　将船舶拦阻至停止所需吸收的能量

将船舶从运动状态拦阻至停止所需要吸收的能量由船舶大小和航速所决定。船速是海事部门对每一条航线具体规定的,水上航行安全监管规定中所规定通过该航线、航段所能使用的限速[1,2,3],即为最高限速,由于船舶航经有水工结构物附近均采取减速航行,所以大部分时间的实际航速是低于最高限速的一个速度,通常取最低最高航速之间的0.75作为该航速段最常出现的航速,作为防撞航速进行计算(例如水上航行安全监管规定中所规定通过该航线段的最低航速为4 kn,最高限速为8 kn,则取7 kn为防撞计算航速)。拦船网所需吸收的船舶动能:

$$E_{动能} = (1/2)mv^2$$

式中,m为船的排水量;v为防撞计算船速。

例如9 000 t排水量的船,以7 kn(≈3.5 m/s)航速代入,拦阻该船至停止所需吸收的能量为:

$$E_{动能} = (1/2)9\,000(3.5)^2 \approx 55\ \text{MJ}$$

3　拦船网原理和吸能计算

3.1　平时让小船通过

撞后抬起的拦船网由柔性绳索密封钢管(浮)和浮筒等组成(见图4),如设计其允

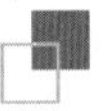

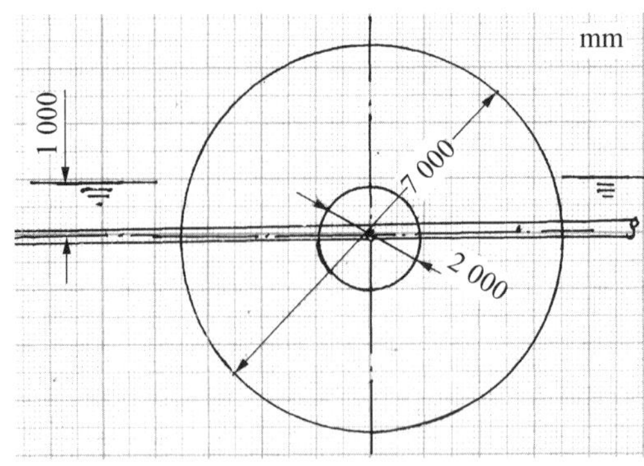

图 4　拦船索在水下 1 米处示意图(从浮筒尖部看过去)

Fig. 4　Sketch of block vessel net under 1 m water (look from the tine area of the float)

许通过吃水 1 m 的小船,则将网放在水面下 1 m 的水中,吃水小于 1 m 的小船便可以通过。

3.2　大船来时网抬起

大船撞第一根缆,网绕浮筒中心转动,对面的缆便会撬起来。浮筒做得比主航道通航船舶的宽度更宽一些,两端呈橄榄形(见图 5)。不管船从正面或斜面撞来,均不会将浮筒压倒船底(斜向力将浮筒推向船的一侧),拦网撬起的功能得以发挥。

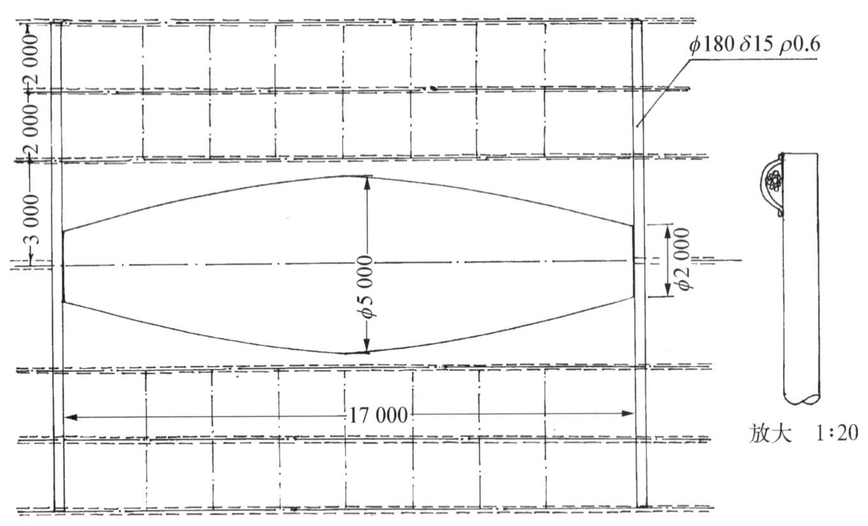

图 5　拦船网及其浮筒(顶视图)右面放大图为顶部侧投影

Fig. 5　Top view of block vessel net and float

3.3　拦船柔性索的计算

拦网布置在桥前约 250 m 处,留下两个 50 m 供拉紧锚链和储备之用,则可得到供拉船的耗能航程为 150 m,在航程 150 m 时拦船索约伸长为 31.0% ~31.5%(见图 6)。

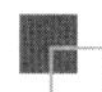

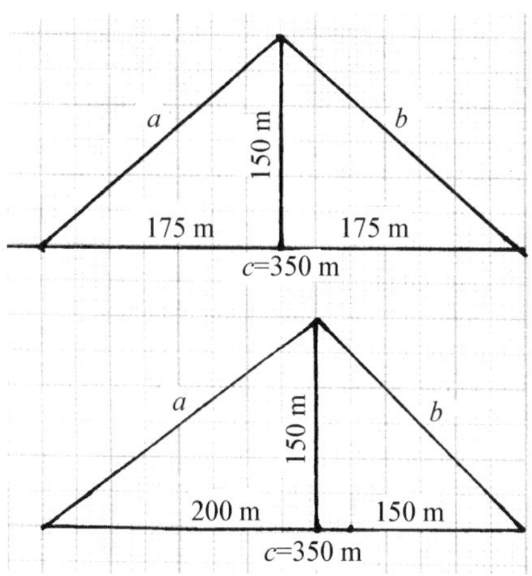

图6　航程内可将拦船索伸长30%

Fig. 6　Displacement of the block net under crashing

一根3 m长的缆索试样,工作段约长1 m,延伸至40%时吸能0.328 MJ;延伸至30%时吸能0.1 MJ左右。本设计布置6根拦船索,每根350 m,可以有较大的吸能富裕。

4　柔性拦船索的选择与设计系数

4.1　柔性拦船索的选择

本系统缆索的主要功能是吸收动能(拉断载荷×延伸率)锦纶复丝绳吸收能量比其他绳大,不易脆断,先比较其优缺点(见表1)。

表1　各种纤维绳索的特点和用途[4]

Table 1　Features and use of various kinds of fiber rope[4]

品　种	锦纶(复丝)	涤　纶	丙　纶	维　伦	高分子量聚乙烯	白棕绳(基准绳)
强度/%(干)*	292	242	182	148	1 200***	100
强度/%(湿)*	251	242	182	124	1 200***	100
延伸率/%	40~50***	25~40	40~45	25~33	4.5**~8***	13~18
吸能	最高	中	中	中	低	中
在海水中	不腐蚀	耐腐蚀	耐腐蚀	耐腐蚀	耐腐蚀	耐腐蚀
使用工艺性	柔软	柔软、不滑脱	不滑脱	不滑脱	不滑脱	耐磨、抗寒摩擦系数大
密度/g·cm^{-3}	1.14	1.38	0.91	1.26	0.97**	1.45

* 干强度和湿强度均以白棕绳为100,其余各种绳表示为对白棕绳的百分比。

** 大成新材料科技股份有限公司[7]

*** 国家绳网监督检验测试中心[6]

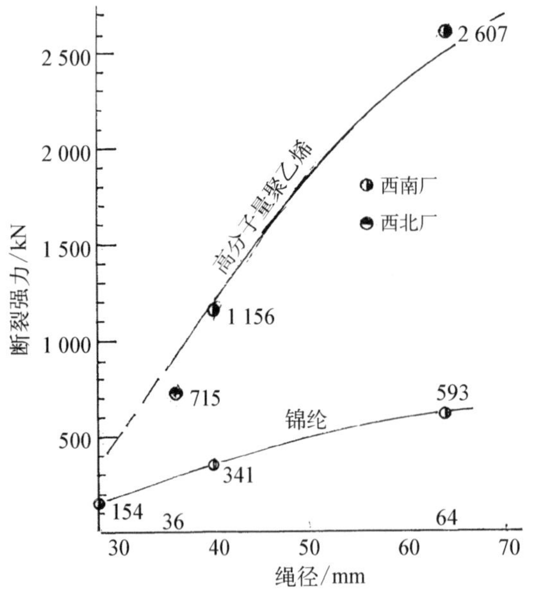

图 7　高分子量聚乙烯与锦纶复丝绳强度比较

Fig. 7　Strength comparison of HMWPE and nylon multifilament string

图 8　高分子量聚乙烯绳变形特征（DSM）

Fig. 8　Deformation characteristics of HMWPE（DSM）

图 7 和表 1 中高分子量聚乙烯编成的绳子，强度较锦纶复丝编成的绳子高 3 ~ 4 倍，用树脂复合高分子量聚乙烯的丝编成的绳子延伸率可达 8%（见图 8），价格约为锦纶复丝绳 6 ~ 8 倍（已计及比重因素）。

如若选用高分子量聚乙烯编成的绳子，应采用防御紫外线措施延缓其老化。可采用高分子量聚乙烯作心层，编成复合绳子；也可以采用黑色橡胶（人造橡胶）水龙带做缆绳的外套。

此外，还应在设计时选用折扣系数，大幅度地降低许用抗拉强力，以备锦纶绳子吸潮后仍然保留足够的强度。

锦纶绳生产历史长久，质量稳定，并有多种直径的绳子做过吸收能量数据的测定，可供设计选用。

4.2　柔性拦阻索的吸能测定

为了表明绳索系统拦阻的可重复性、耐久性，体现使用中多次拦阻的能力，对拦阻索进行多次加载和卸载，加载的大小（与强度极限的百分比）与实际设计的使用载荷相匹配。

选取 ϕ28 mm 和 ϕ40 mm 两种直径的锦纶索进行多次加载和卸载的试样，每种进行两次试验。试验结果说明所选材料重复性很好。能够进行多次拦阻。

两种直径锦纶绳的试验结果，如图 9b 和图 9c 所示。

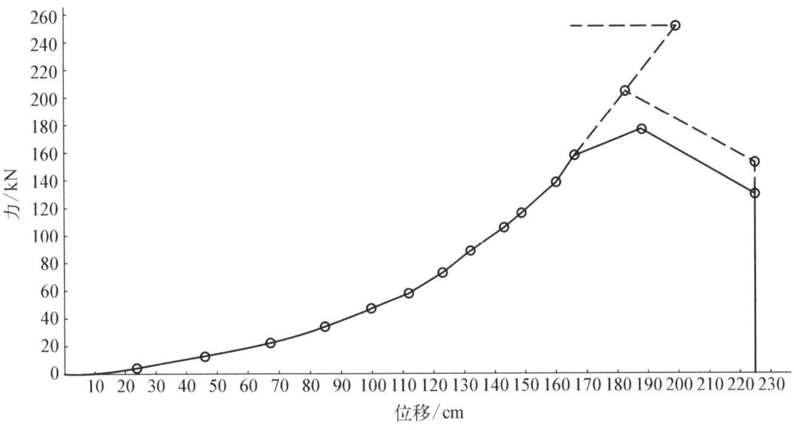

(a) 校核试验绘出的“力-位移”曲线

(a) force-displacement curve of control test draw

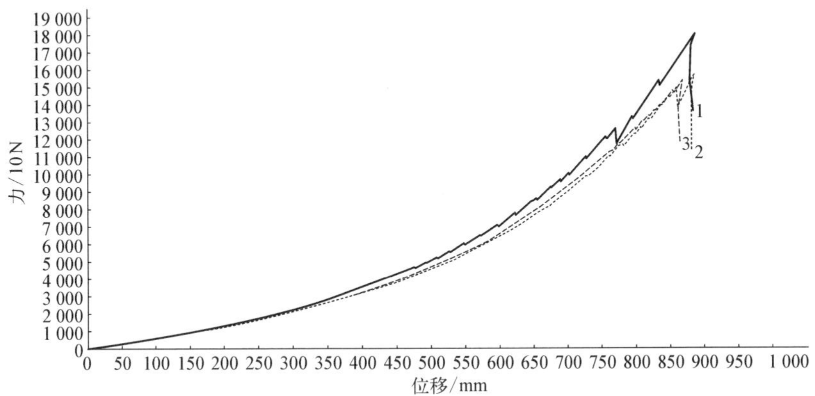

(b)“力-位移”曲线的均衡性试验(ϕ28 mm)

(b) Balance test of force-displacement curve (ϕ28 mm)

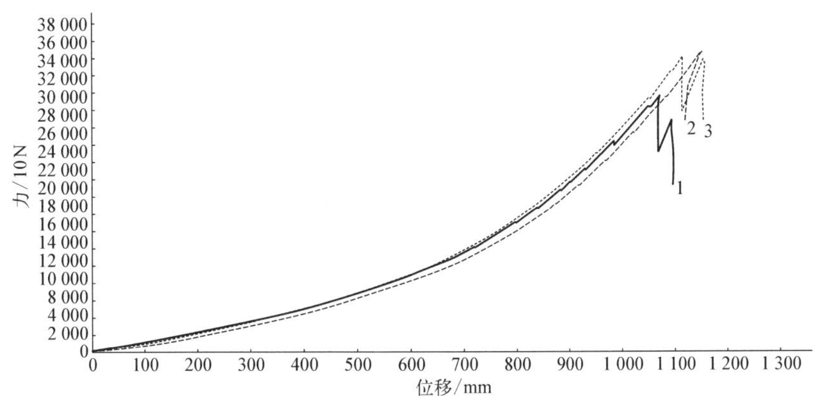

(c)“力-位移”曲线的均衡性试验(ϕ40 mm)

(c) Balance test of force-displacement curve (ϕ40 mm)

图 9　柔性拦阻索的吸能测定

Fig. 9　Energe absorption determination of block vessel net

4.3 计算吸能时选用的折扣系数

(1) 锦纶绳吸水后抗拉力呈指数曲线下降,图 10 中曲线 4 所示为充分吸水后的强度下降,从 70 MPa 下降至 35 MPa 左右,故取湿强度为 50%。

即

$$k_1 = 0.5$$

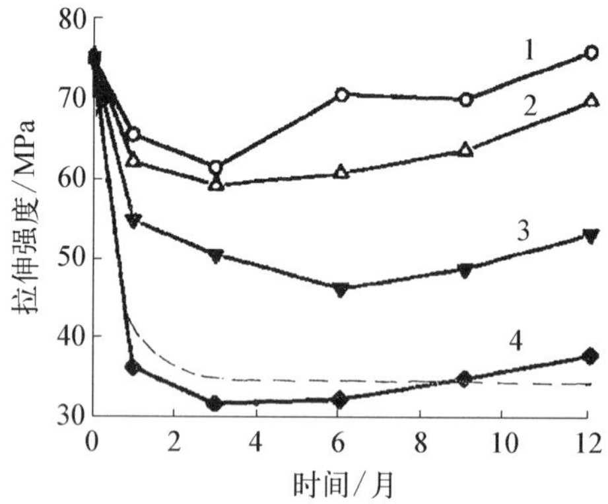

图 10 锦纶吸水后的抗拉力下降[8]

Fig. 10 Tensile strength decrease of polyamide fiber after absorbing water[8]

(2) 锦纶复丝绳在 40% 的延伸时测得的吸收能为 0.328 MJ,在 30% 延伸时只有其 33%(见图 11),故其吸能发挥系数为 $k_2 = 0.33$

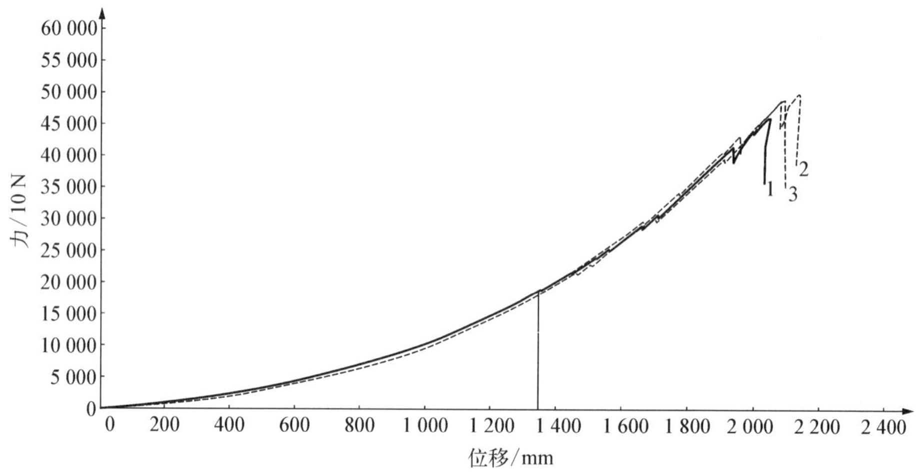

图 11 锦纶绳(缆)在延伸 30% 时的吸能(ϕ64 mm)

Fig. 11 Energy absorption of Polyamide fibre rope after expanding 30% (ϕ64 mm)

(3) 锦纶复丝做成的拦船网在拦船时绳索发挥吸能有先后,设 6 根绳子有 4 根正常发挥,所以 $k_3 = 0.67$

用这 3 个系数进行吸能计算,在船被拦阻的 150 m,6 根主绳吸收的功 $E_{绳}$ 如下:

$$E_{绳} = 6\text{根} \times 350\ \text{m/根} \times (\phi 64\ \text{mm 工作段长 1 m 的锦纶绳断裂功}) \times k_1 \times k_2 \times k_3$$

$$= 6\text{根} \times 350\ \text{m/根} \times 0.328\ \text{MJ/m} \times 0.33 \times 0.5 \times 0.67 = 76.1\ \text{MJ}$$

对前述的船的动能给予10%的富裕,即55 MJ×1.1=60.5 MJ,设计校核结果通过。

4.4 耐久性措施

用黑色内层的(防紫外线)复合消防龙带作为外套(见图12),350 m内无接头(用穿电线管的方法在工作广场上拉入)。两端用热收缩型塑料管套扎紧,并置于两端浮体上高出水面的联结点(见图13),防止水进入龙带内部。

图12 双层复合黑色(防紫外线)消防龙带包裹示意图(尚未用热缩性塑料管套)

Fig. 12 schematic diagram of rope package

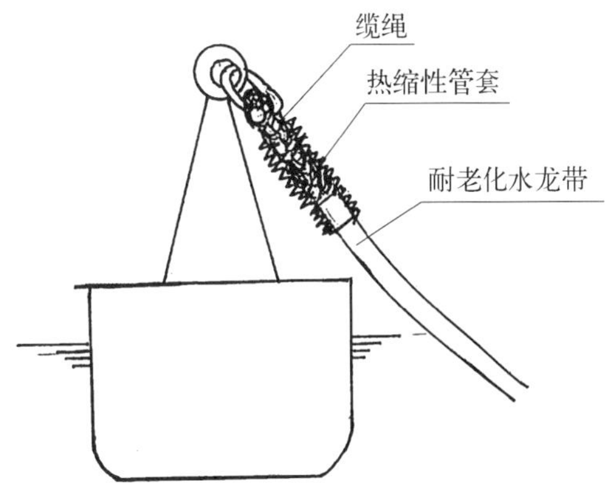

图13 拦船索两端在水面上

Fig. 13 schematic diagram of block vessel net ends

4.5 浮体设计

两端的浮体按船舶设计,建造有不沉性要求,设计有多个密封舱,以便在风浪中自保的同时不失去工作能力。

4.6 锚泊设计

本系统的锚泊,集中在两端浮体,因为全长是作为一根绳子发挥变形作用的,所以中间不系锚。

柔性防撞的特点是初受力时变形很大,力是渐增的,而且初受力时力比较小,锚泊的力要按最后将拦船网主索拉至耗能末端(指延伸率40%及以上)时的力计算,举例说,每根ϕ64锦纶绳拉直40%时载荷为700 kN左右。设计6根横网,每根的连接部分都设计成离开水面,并且钢构能受700 kN水平力。

锚链直接用大抓力锚(或混凝土锚块)固定在海床底上,拉入海床底土中,单向受力,愈拉愈深。船撞受力后快速拉紧,不希望有大的位移,锚链受力在(3~6)×700 kN之间(可选用工作载荷≥2 100 kN,破断载荷≥4 200 kN,用二锚分力设计)。

5 总结

(1)在一条运输线上的桥梁各跨各墩中,只要断了一处,全线中断,所以保护薄弱易

断的桥墩是必须的,用柔性缆绳拦船装置在保护桥的同时,也保护了船,因此也保护了环境。

(2)航船偏向,撞向辅助墩、过渡墩和水中引桥墩等桥墩,这些桥墩本身承受水平力的能力较差,极易撞坏,所以设计使用此种将船拦于墩外而桥墩不受力的间接防撞方式。

(3)以某航线为例经过装置设计和能量计算,此拦阻装置可以拦住载重量为5 000 t的从主航道偏航的船舶。

参考文献

[1] 福州海事局. 平潭海峡大桥施工期间通航安全管理规定(试行)[R],2007.

[2] 中华人民共和国上海港务监督. 上海水上安全监督规则[R],1995-03-01.

[3] 中华人民共和国湛江海事局. 湛江海上安全监督管理规定[R],2000-02-15.

[4] 中华人民共和国交通部. 公路桥涵设计通用规范[S]JTG D60—2004. 北京:人民交通出版社,2004.

[5] 张承源等. 船舶材料手册[M]. 北京:国防工业出版社,1989.

[6] GB/T 18674—2002(2004修订). 中华人民共和国. 国家标准. 渔用绳索通用技术条件[S].

[7] Q/VAQG 2—2008. 上海市企业标准. 船用缆绳产品技术条件[S].

[8] 朱本玮等. 环境湿度对尼龙66性能的影响及其时间效应[J]. 现代塑料加工,2008(5).

[9] 德. G. Klust著. 钟若英译. 渔用网材料[M]. 上海水产大学,1990.

[10] 上海旗鱼绳网有限公司. 产品目录"旗鱼绳网"[R]. 上海:奉贤,2009.

[11] 宁波大成新材料股份有限公司. 产品目录. 高科技超强纤维高性能系列产品[R]. 浙江:慈溪,2009.

[12] 浙江四兄绳业有限公司. 产品目录[R]. 浙江:台州市,杜桥镇,2009.

发表于:广东造船,2011(1):38-41,31.

Published at: Guangdong Shipbuilding, 2011(1): 38-41,31.

对双壁钢围堰兼做防撞设施功能的探讨

The discuss on the function of double steel wall cofferdam concurrently as anti-collision equipment

陆宗林[1]　陈国虞[2]

（1. 同济大学，上海 200092；2. 上海海洋钢结构研究所，上海 201204）

LU Zonglin[1], CHEN Guoyu[2]

（1. Tongji University, Shanghai, 200092, China;
2. Shanghai Marine Steel and Structure Research Institute, Shanghai 201204, China）

摘　要　随着航运的发展，人们日益重视桥墩要防止因船只撞击而受损的问题。目前有不少桥梁将施工用的双壁钢围堰作为防撞的主结构。探讨此双壁钢围堰在船只撞击时的防撞功能及其合适的应用场合。同时指出船撞力应按冲击动力学的原理进行计算更为合理。

关键词　桥梁桥墩防撞　双壁钢围堰　船撞力

Abstract: Along with the development of the shipping, people increasingly recognition to the problem of damage from the ship collision with the bridge pier. Now, there are a few bridges use the construct double steel wall cofferdam as the main structure of the anti-collision equipment. This paper discuss the anti-collision function and its suitable applied situation of the double steel wall cofferdam, when the ship collision with the pier. And points out when we calculate the force of ship collision with the pier may be use the impact dynamics is reasonable.

Keywords: anti-collision of bridge pier, double steel wall cofferdam, force of ship collision with the pier

江河是船只航行的通道，它对陆上交通是个障碍，通过它最常用的方法是在水面上建造桥梁。但受建桥技术和经济等因素的制约，通常要在较宽江河的水中设置桥墩，以支撑桥梁的上部结构。这些桥墩就成为船只航行的障碍物。船只的航行会受到气候（风、雾）、水文（流速、水位）及船只的工况（机械故障，失锚）等的影响，更多的是人为的失误，如驾驶员的

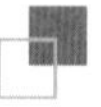

判断错误、误操作、注意力分散甚至是醉酒、瞌睡，致使船只在航行时偏离正常的航线而导致与水中桥墩碰撞。因此，即使留有“足够”通航净空的桥梁也要考虑船只在非正常航行时与桥墩碰撞的可能性。必要时要设置防止桥墩被船只撞损（毁）的有效防撞设施。

近年来，我国对此也日益重视，更多的桥梁在设计、建造时同时考虑了桥墩的防撞措施。1995 年建设的湖北黄石长江公路大桥主桥墩采用浮式钢套箱作为防撞设施。它能适应高达 17 m 的水位变化，防止船只直接撞击较为柔弱的双肢薄壁桥墩。21 世纪初建设的苏通长江大桥原来也拟采用类似的浮式钢套箱防撞设施，以防载重 50 000 t 级散货轮以 4 m/s 航速横桥向撞击主塔墩（最大撞击力可达 132 MN 左右）。在桥墩承台周围安装防撞设施后，利用船舶碰撞动力模拟程序进行计算，52 300*DWT* 散货船满载工况和空船压载工况的计算成果见表 1，碰撞力的时程曲线见图 1。

表 1　**不同工况下计算结果**

Table 1　**Calculation results on difference conditions**

船舶载重工况	t	载重 52 300（*DWT*）	空船压载
船舶总排水量（含连附水）	t	68 750	25 342
船舶吃水	m	12.50	5.34
碰撞速度	m/s	4.0	4.0
正撞最大碰撞力	MN	90.7 - 100	58.5
船首破坏长度（深度）	m	4.89	
设施破坏长度（深度）	m	10.1	
碰撞持续时间	s	4.9	2.98

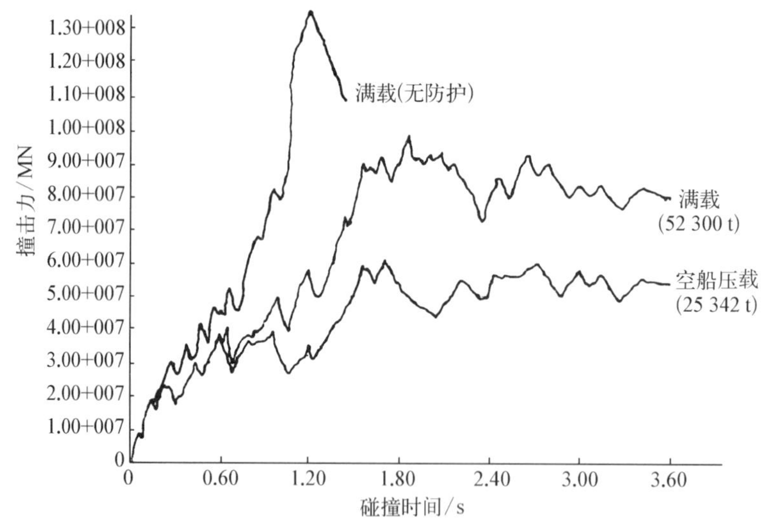

图 1　碰撞力-时间历程

Fig. 1　force of collision-time course

根据这些数据，浮式钢围箱防撞设施的钢箱截面在船只的冲撞力和桥墩承台的抵承力共同作用下变形，把船只的动能转换为船头和钢套箱的变形能。承台受到的最大水平力降为 100 MN 左右。同时钢套箱也隔离了船只和承台，避免了承台表面混凝土因船只直接撞击发生的碎裂脱落（见图 2）。

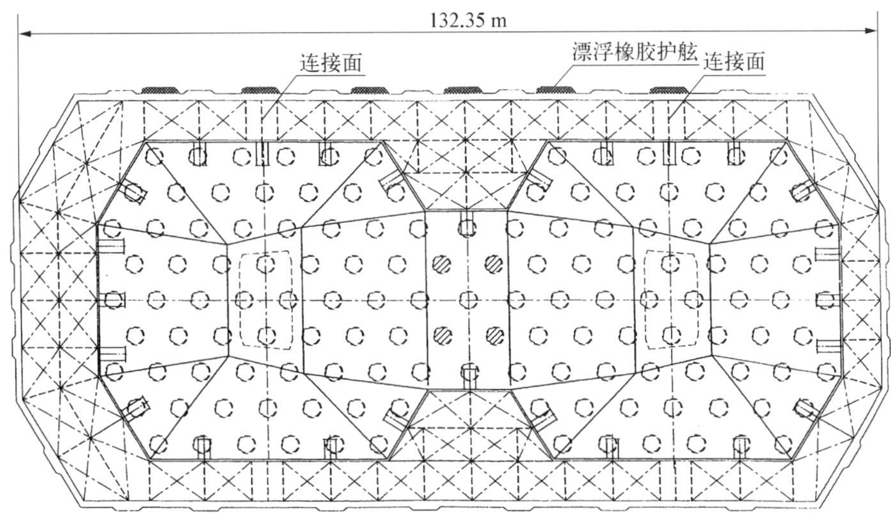

图 2　苏通大桥基础和钢套箱平面图

Fig. 2　Plane drawing of steel wall cofferdam on pier of Sutong Bridge

随着设计工作的深入，苏通大桥采用 A 型索塔，基础承台的体型特别巨大，承台平面尺寸达 48 m×114 m，下有 135 根 ϕ2.5 m～2.8 m 钻孔灌注桩，本身的水平抗力已能承受船只的最大撞击力，初期如果仅考虑桥墩可以不必建造防撞设施；以后如需建一些保护船的柔性装置则可以另议。

为了防止承台表面混凝土被撞裂，就将用于承台施工的双壁钢围堰（厚 2 m）不予拆除，并部分填混凝土，作适当加强。用以保护承台的侧壁，并增加船头球鼻首与基桩的距离，减小它碰撞桩基的概率。

船只与桥墩的碰撞力，目前大多用准静态的公式（程序）来计算，实质上它是一个冲击动力学的课题。冲击应力波的传递与碰撞两物体的物理力学性能和碰撞速度有关。应变率的提高会使碰撞材料的屈服强度和强度极限值提高，延伸率降低、屈服滞后等。根据冲击动力学的原理，运用计算机通用程序，用混凝土、钢两种材料的弹性模量，分别对钢－钢，钢－混凝土两种工况进行计算。以某桥为例，按相同速度和重量的钢质船只与钢质套箱碰撞的撞击力要比钢质船只与混凝土承台相撞的撞击力增大约 10%。这个结果与霍布金森装置上的冲击试验结果的趋向是一致的（见图 3），要引起注意。

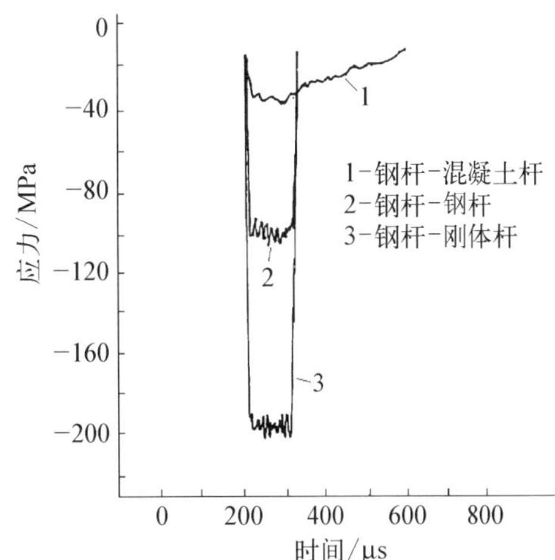

图 3　霍布金森装置冲击试验

Fig. 3　Impact test on Hopkinson equipment

近年来正在设计或施工,有防船撞要求的大桥不少都把厚度为 2 m 左右的双壁钢围堰作为代替浮式钢套箱作为桥墩防撞主体结构。表面上看它是“一物两用”,节省了很多,实际上它箱体单薄,消不了多少动能!特别是套箱原是为桥墩承台施工设置的,且是固定的。它的位置是由承台的高程确定的,常不能与通航水位相适应,有可能发生船艏撞击墩(塔)身或船只的球鼻艏在水下撞击基桩。引发桥墩的墩(塔)身或基桩损毁的严重事故,危及桥梁的安全。

浙江金塘大桥的通航孔的防撞标准与苏通大桥一样是 50 000 t,4 m/s,该桥是菱形索塔的斜拉桥。主塔承台平面尺寸为 34 m×63.3 m,下设 42 根 ϕ2.5 m~2.85 m 钻孔灌注桩。采用 2 m 宽的双壁钢围堰作防撞设施(见图 4)。它消不了多少船只的动能,船撞力主要仍由承台承受。该承台及桩数要比苏通大桥小(少)甚多。承受不了高达 >100 MN 的撞击力,似为此而把通航标准降为 50 000 t 船只空载压舱,甚为费解。此航道有空船航行,必会有满载的船通过。当满载的船通过时,万一不慎碰到桥墩,其后果就不堪设想了。满载的 50 000 t 海轮的吃水深度为 12.5 m,在低通航水位时,船只的球鼻首更有可能会直接撞到基桩(见图 5)。

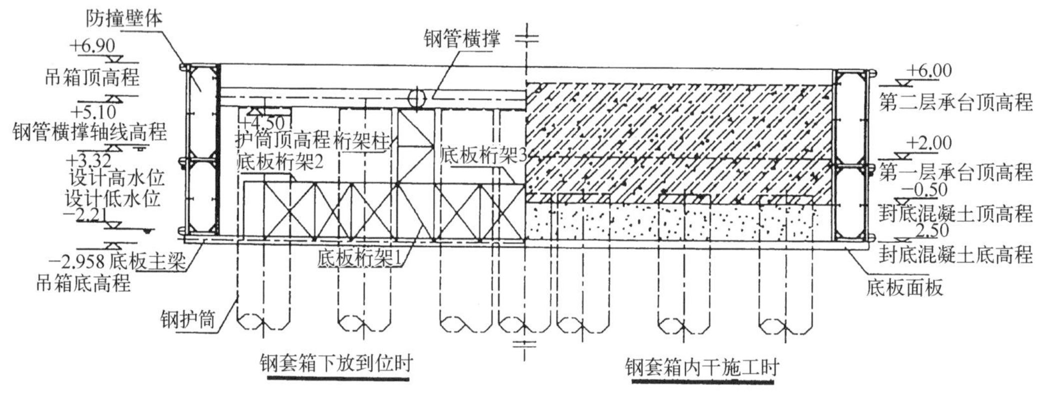

图 4　钢套箱总体布置

Fig. 4　General arrangement of steel wall cofferdam

浙江象山港大桥的主桥桥型与金塘大桥相似,它的通航孔防船撞标准也为 50 000 t 级的海轮,过桥航速为 3.7 m/s。最初也拟采用 2 m 厚的双壁围堰作为防撞措施。它的承台高程较高,最低通航水位几乎与封底混凝土的底面齐平。在此水位若要挡到船只的球鼻首,需要将围堰向下延长 9 m。可是这段背后没有承台实体挡住,处于悬臂状态下的钢箱,抗弯刚度是很差的。稍受船头碰撞,它不会变形消能,而会整体向内弯曲,将使桩基更早受到围堰钢箱的挤压甚至损坏(见图 6)。最终放弃了这个防撞方案。

我们认为,双壁钢围堰如要“兼”作防船撞的消能设施,需要考虑下列因素。

1. 作为承台施工的临时围护结构,一般比较单薄,面板薄、支撑少,如要兼作永久的防撞设施,它必须要做得很厚实。不仅要经得起船只的碰撞,还要考虑(海)水的锈蚀影响。

2. 钢围堰的厚度一般根据承台施工操作要求设计,不会做得很厚,它的消能能力有限。应只适用于防止小型、低速船只碰撞的场合。

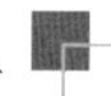

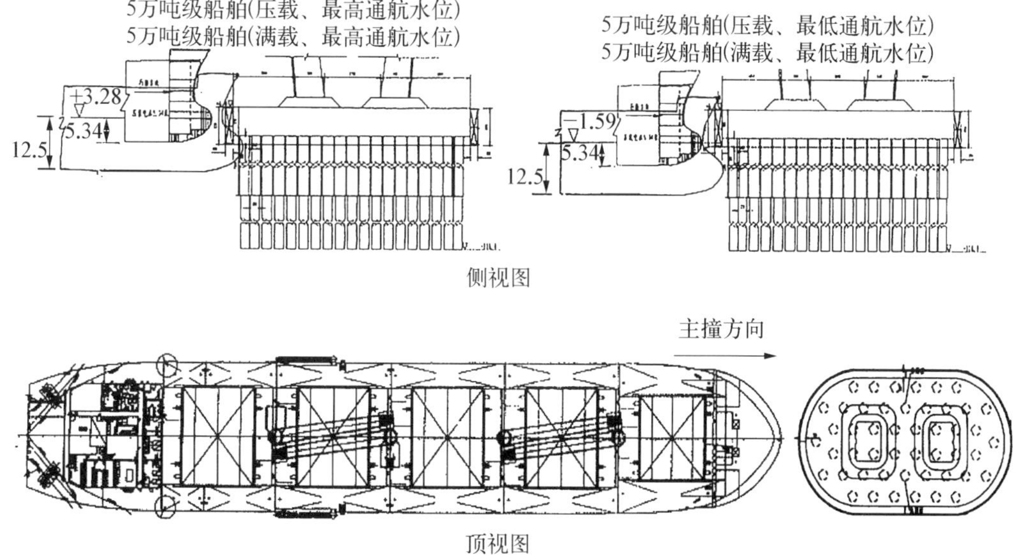

图5　金塘大桥撞击工况(5万吨级船舶)

Fig. 5　Impact condition of Jintang Bridge

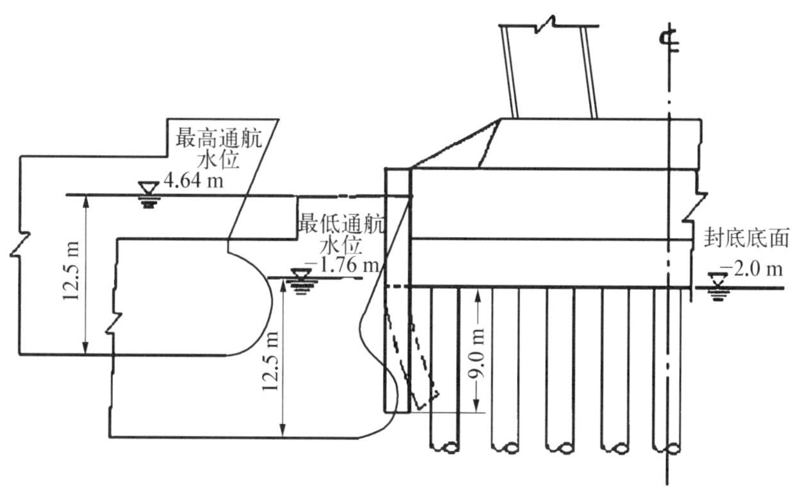

图6　象山港大桥撞击工况(钢套箱方案)

Fig. 6　Impact condition of Xiangshan Port Bridge (project of steel wall cofferdam)

3. 钢围堰的位置高程,通常与承台的高程一致,当它与通航水位不一致,因此在此两者不能协调的桥上不宜采用。

参考文献

[1] 王礼立. 应力波基础(第二版)[M]. 北京:国防工业出版社,2005.

[2] 史元熹,金允龙,徐骏. 黄石长江大桥主墩防撞设施设计[R]. 船撞桥论文选. 上海:上海海洋钢结构研究所(内部). 2000-05,P75-81.

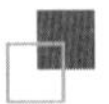

[3] 上海船舶运输科学研究所.苏通长江公路大桥基础防撞结构研究[R].上海,2003.

[4] 陈国虞,张澄,杨黎明,周凤华.紧靠混凝土承台的直接式防撞装置的选择[C].中国公路学会2009年全国桥梁学术会议论文集.北京:人民交通出版社,2009.10,pp.156-163.

[5] 白雨东,王晓阳.金塘大桥主通航孔桥下部结构设计[C].中国公路学会2008年全国桥梁学术会议论文集.北京:人民交通出版社,2008.10,pp.52-57.

[6] 许宏亮,宋华清,曾平喜,周玉娟,彭强.金塘大桥主墩防撞钢套箱设计[C].中国公路学会2008年全国桥梁学术会议论文集.北京:人民交通出版社,2008.10,pp.62-71.

[7] 上海船舶运输科学研究所.宁波象山港大桥船舶防撞研究补充报告[R].2008.

发表于:中国土木工程学会桥梁及结构工程分会第十九届全国桥梁学术会议论文集[M].北京:人民交通出版社,2010:1338-1343.

Published at: CCES Proceeding of the 19th symposium of bridges. Beijing: China Communication Press, 2010: 1338-1343.

桥墩防撞设计中对驳船队撞墩的分析和处理

Analysis and transact on barge fleet collision with the pier in the design of bridge anti-collision with ship

陈国虞

（上海海洋钢结构研究所 201204）

CHEN Guoyu

（Shanghai Marine Steel and Structure Research Institute 201204）

摘　要　驳船队比较宽、比较长，再加上操纵不灵便，在桥梁设计开始阶段，对桥型、通航宽度和撞上概率等三方面对它及早考虑是应该的。但是，由于驳船的使用日渐减少，驳船队一撞就散，撞击力比较小，因此驳船队的撞击力不成为撞塌桥墩的控制因素。从驳船队连接特点出发，求出两边驳船对被撞驳船的附加力；并从冲击动力学的理论出发，计算出后面驳船对被撞驳船压力峰值与第一撞击力峰值的时间差，说明叠加之后远小于该航道上相当载重量的单船的撞击力。所以，计算航行船舶对桥墩的撞击力时，主要应该考虑单体船。也对我国公路桥梁设计规范源出于驳船队的规定和美国各州公路和运输工作者协会（AASHTO）的指南中关于驳船队的研究进行了讨论。

关键词　驳船队　驳船撞墩　通航宽度　峰值的时间差　边驳的附加力

Abstract: The barge fleet have its long and breadth are big then the mono-hull ship. And also due to its manipulate ineffective, so, in the beginning stage of bridge design, the designer would consider about these three factor influence the bridge type, the navigation width and the probability of the ship collision with the pier. But, the usage of the barge fleet has decrement. And when the collision happened, the barge fleet may disperse at once. Also due to its collision force is small, so, the collision force would not be the control factor in the ship collision with the bridge pier.

This paper discussed the peculiarity of the link between the barges in the fleet. And got the append force from the two close barge. From the theory of dynamics and got the interval time between two peak value of force. And when the two peak values of forces are pile up the result is far small from the peak value of the mono-hull ship. So, when calculate the force of the collision we should consider the mono-hull ship.

In this paper also discussed the guide idea about the barge collision with the bridge in the guide of AASHTO.

Keyword: barge fleet, barge collision with the bridge, navigation width, interval time between two peak values, Appends force from two close barges

1 驳船队的现状

大型驳船队,我国主要在武汉以下的长江中下游从事载货运输,曾每年为马鞍山钢铁公司、武汉钢铁公司运输矿石 1 000 万 t 以上(上水),为沿江各电厂运输煤炭 2 000 万 t(上、下水)。另外,驳船队为下游的建筑工地运送砂石也是非常经济的。

1 ×4 413 kW(6 000 hp) +20 ×2 000 t 的驳船队为载重最大的驳船队之一,如图 1 所示,其载重量达到 4 万 t。

图 1　1993 年 4 月 16 日,4 413 kW(6 000 hp)的长江 26004 号,4 排 5 列顶推 20 艘 2 000 t 分节驳(载重量 40 000 t)上水通过九江长江大桥

Fig. 1　1993 - 04 - 16, the towboat Changjiang 26004(4 413 kW, 6 000 hp) push 20 ×2 000 t fleet (4 tiers 5 lines, dead weight 40 000 t) up-bound through the Jiujiang Changjiang bridge

在河流下游的水网地区,流速比长江低些,往往几百马力的拖船就可以拉几千吨的货,运输成本比较低。可以看见一字长蛇形的拖驳船队,如图 2 所示。

驳船队这种运输方式大约风行了几十年。“进入 21 世纪,船运公司增多,货源分散;北煤南运,港口建成,水运煤由江转到海上。大批载重量为 5 000 ~30 000 t 的江海联运浅吃水肥大型散货船投入运输。它们自航,调度方便,靠离码头不需港作拖船帮助,不花港

图 2　水网地区的小运河中 1 + 11 拖船队

Fig. 2　1 + 11 fleet at a small cannel in the area crisscrossed by waterways

作规使费。船上防浪防潮设备好，可载多种货品，适应港口大型化和港口装卸高速化。因此港口和货主倾向自航货船，大多数货主不再接受 2 000 t 以下驳船。”[1]

驳船公司为了维持本身的竞争力，采用建造大载重量驳船的补救办法：批量建造 5 000 t 舱口驳，以缩短码头掉靠驳船的时间，减少使用港作拖船的费用；建造 8 000 ~ 10 000 t甲板驳，以承运大件货物。

“但由于补救办法仍未能彻底改变驳船队运输‘不适港，不适货’的总趋势，所以驳船队退出江湖是必然趋势。2009 年 11 月 4 日，国内最大的内河水运企业凤凰公司将 106 艘 2 000 t 中分节驳退出市场。长江航运进入自航船舶时代。”[1]

2　驳船队撞墩的实例描述

“1998 年夏，长江中上游发生特大洪水，全线封航，9 月 2 日洪水消退恢复通航，就在这天晚上，长 22033 轮第 23 航次顶推 1 000 ~ 1 500 t 空驳 7 艘顺水而下，航速 18 km/h。8 时刚过，与黄石长江公路桥 3#主墩防撞设施相撞。船队编结如图 3 所示。

碰撞发生后，多根系结缆绳断裂，船队分解，分别从防撞设施两侧漂下，各个驳船损伤程度不一……”[2] 因为是 21237 号驳船撞 3#墩，所以“21237 驳左舷发生长 6 m高 2 m 凹陷 0.25 m 的破裂穿孔；甲板拱凸 8 m^2。21169 驳首尖舱水线(2.4 m)以下全部破损，5 根钢丝绳(2 英寸 4 根。3 英寸 1 根)断裂。81058 驳首尖舱左舷近第一空舱处破损凹进 2 处，各为 1 000 mm × 50 mm，第一舱左舷侧板破裂 12 000 mm × 600 mm，系结

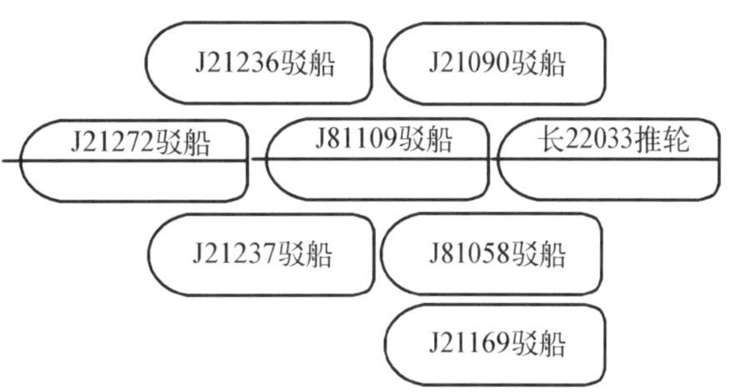

图 3　被撞散前的船队编结图

Fig. 3　Ties diagram of fleet to collision disperse

钢丝绳断损 3 根。”[2]

从上面描述可以看出,驳船队是用钢丝绳系结起来的,撞墩之后钢丝绳断裂,驳船散队。而且空驳船的惯性力就足以拉断连接钢丝绳,致驳船队散队。

这个概念要从船舶流体阻力出发去理解,驳船之间的连接钢丝绳是为了推船(从前俗称拖头、推轮)推带驳船前进、转弯和靠泊之用的,而船舶在低速度时,基本没有兴波阻力,要使驳船前进只需比克服摩擦阻力大一点的力便可以了,驳船队选择的运行速度比较低,使用的连接钢丝绳比较细就够了。

3 驳船队系缚驳船的方式——驳船之间力的传递

驳船队对撞击桥墩的影响大致有两个方面:一是驳船队的宽度影响到通航净宽的选定[7];二是驳船队对桥墩撞击力的大小,而要决定撞击力的大小就必须弄清楚旁边的驳船是怎样对撞上的驳船传递作用力的。

研究发生撞击时驳船之间力的传递,必须了解驳船之间是如何连接的。驳船有拖带和顶推两种方式。因为顶推的效率比较高,多艘驳船的大编队多用顶推。窄小河流用前拖,一字形编队。单只驳船用前拖和侧面绑拖都可以。两只驳船可以用左右绑拖或前拖。顶推驳船编队常用的有:梭形、燕形和梅花型。如图 4 所示。

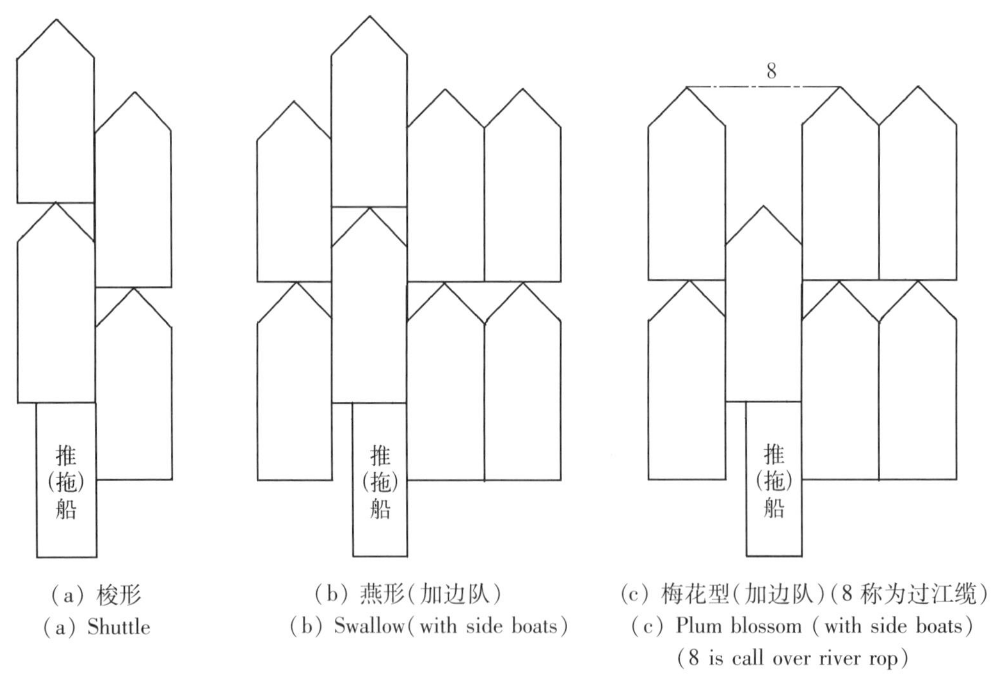

(a) 梭形
(a) Shuttle

(b) 燕形(加边队)
(b) Swallow(with side boats)

(c) 梅花型(加边队)(8 称为过江缆)
(c) Plum blossom (with side boats)
(8 is call over river rop)

图 4 三种常用的顶推驳船编队方式
Fig. 4 3 types common tie diagrams of pushed fleet

驳船队中推船与驳船和驳船与驳船之间大多数是用钢丝绳连接的[3]，个别曾用过钢搭扣，现已不多见了。驳船队连接的钢丝绳，按其作用和位置，常用的有 8 种称呼：1 包头缆，2 横缆，3 拖缆，4 倒缆，5 连接缆，6 尾缆，7 操纵缆和 8 过江缆。其中“8 过江缆”示于图 4(c)，其余 7 种如图 5 所示：

钢丝绳是不能传递推力的，凡是受推力的地方钢丝绳是松的，它能够传递拉力；每根系结钢丝绳所能传递的最大拉力，是该钢丝绳的破断拉力。前后驳船之间是能够传递推力的，当前面的驳船速度低于后面的驳船时，后面的驳船便通过缓冲垫（通常是橡胶材料制成）给予推力。下面将讨论这两种力的传递。

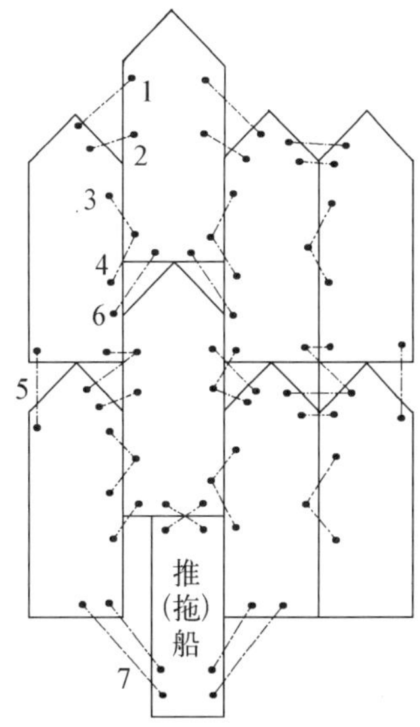

1 包头缆，2 横缆，3 拖缆，4 倒缆，5 连接缆，6 尾缆，7 操纵缆
1 over head rope, 2 across rope, 3 towing rope, 4 converse rope, 5 linking rope, 6 tell rope, 7 control rope

图 5 用钢丝绳连接驳船队的典型例子

Fig. 5 The typical diagram of people to tie the fleet by rope

4 应力波在钢质驳船内的传递——峰值判断

4.1 从冲击动力学理论分析

冲击载荷使构件受载后产生的变形有局域性，即变形和损坏集中在受力区附近。当第一艘驳船受桥墩撞击时（例如桥墩撞击船头）撞击点附近即受载、变形，形成损坏，这时有两个后果：

(1) 被撞的一艘驳船减慢，其他驳船继续前进，在这一瞬间动作中，其他驳船通过受拉力的钢缆给第一艘驳船加载直至钢缆拉断为止——撞散。这是大多驳船被撞后发生的情况。

(2) 后面的一艘驳船将两船间的空隙压缩，在惯性力的作用下后一艘船将撞击前一艘船的尾部，这种载荷需要时间，这样与第一艘船撞力产生的峰值便会不同时产生，可能出现第二个撞击峰值。第二艘船压向第一艘船尾部的时候，会引致两船接触部分的损伤（局域性），这儿也会消耗能量。因在第二艘船的头部和第一艘船的尾部存在橡胶垫块，橡胶垫块延长了撞击过程的时间也减低了撞击力，同时也延缓了在接触处的第二次撞击力的时间。

对第一艘驳船与桥之间的撞击力，应考虑两项直接的作用：其一是第一艘驳船的速度、自重和船头刚度等；其二是通过钢索在撞击瞬间能够加上去的载荷。

4.2 通过钢索在撞击瞬间能够加上去的载荷

由于第一艘船被撞受阻，和其他各船之间产生速度差，使受拉的钢丝绳载荷增加，导致这些钢丝绳拉断，驳船队散开。按照图示的几种绑扎方式，例如实例燕式加边，当撞到 21237 驳时，有 4 处钢丝绳受拉，每处两根钢丝绳，共 8 根。通常用 2 英寸（老叫法，即圆周 50.4 mm，相当于国标中直径 16 mm)：3 英寸钢丝绳(即圆周 75 mm，直径 24 mm)，若按 GB/T 8918—1996，6×37+FC 结构，1 670 MPa 强度级的钢丝绳其主参数如表 1。

表 1　**驳间连接用 GB/T 8918—1996，6×37+FC 结构，1 670 MPa 强度级的钢丝绳主参数**
Table 1　**The common broken force of a linking point, when the ropes manufactured from 1 670 MPa wires**

直径/mm	1 670 MPa 强度级时的拉断力/kN	
	4 根	8 根
ϕ16 mm	4×126	8×126
ϕ24 mm	4×283	8×283

这个数量级相当于满载驳船撞击力的 20% 左右(在上述实例中，连接钢丝绳被空载驳船拉断，也说明是这个数量级)，如果考虑到钢丝绳拉断有先后，这个系数还要折减。粗略地说，首驳撞墩导致侧驳通过钢丝绳加上去的力，相当于首驳"船撞力"的 20%，因此建议在以后的计算中，用驳船质量乘上一个系数(1.2)的办法处理。

4.3　二次撞击的撞击力叠加的时间差

后一艘驳船撞击前一艘驳船的尾部的二次撞击力为橡胶垫所传递的力。根据试验，橡胶传力一般在 0.1～0.14 s(100～140 ms)左右才能达到峰值；再加上应力波传递的时间：在惯性力的作用下，从第二艘船的中部质心传到第二艘船的船头有半个船长，第一艘船的船尾传到第一艘船的船头，有一个船长，因此与第一次撞击相比，延后了 $1.5L/C$(L=一艘驳船的长度，C=船中的应力波传递速度)。设驳船长 $L=100$ m，应力波传递速度应算为 $C=5\ 000$ m/s，所以应力波传递时间为：$1.5L/C=30$ ms(延后总共 130～170 ms)。在船撞力的时程曲线中，过了峰值一百多毫秒(下面讨论用平均值 150 ms)后叠加的二次力对峰值影响已经不大了，下面用曲线讨论两个因素对峰值的共同影响。

4.4　峰值判断

以燕式绑结方式(图 5(b)不加边)为例，6 艘载重量为 3 000 t 的驳船(在长江现在还有使用)连接成驳船队(见图 6)。总载重量约 20 000 t，航速为每秒 4 m，最前面的一艘驳船撞墩，该桥墩已装有柔性耗能防撞装置。

在驳船队各次撞击力的叠加的示意图中，撞墩首驳船撞击力时程曲线为曲线 0，两边都有钢丝绳附加值(1.2×1.2)，故乘以 1.4，得到曲线 1；约 150 ms 后叠加后面驳船的力得到曲线 2，得到峰值 5；再过 150 ms 后叠加推船的力曲线 3，由于拖船的质量不大，约 1 000 t 得到峰值 6。

曲线 4 是载重约 25 000 t 的自航单体货船以每秒 4 m 的速度撞墩力的时程曲线。可以看出，曲线 4 的峰值(约 52 MN)大于驳船撞击力叠加后的峰值。

船队峰值示意图如图 7 所示。

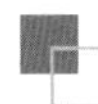

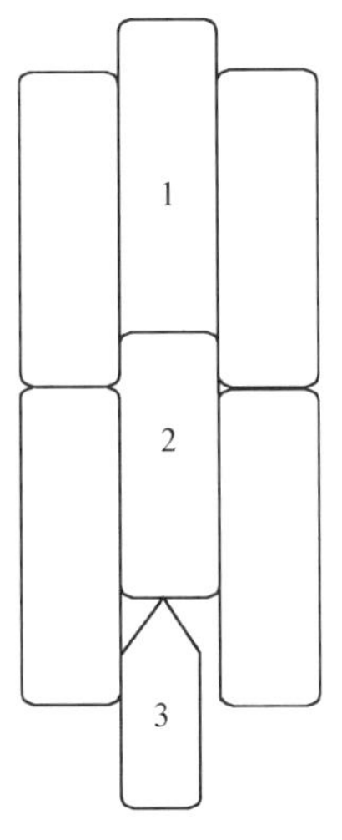

图6　峰值判断驳船队示例

Fig. 6　The sketch of example for jadgement the peak valae

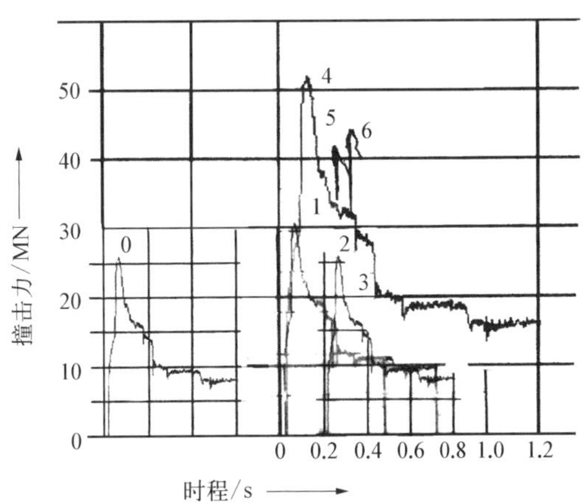

图7　驳船队各次撞击力的叠加示意图

Fig. 7　The sketch map of over laying every time of impact force in the fleet

5　桥跨净宽、净高的趋势

我国两个桥梁设计规范中对桥跨的净高有一些规定，对净宽则要求符合 JTJ 311—97 通航海轮桥梁通航标准[10]和 GB 50139—2004 内河通航标准[9]的规定。

后者对桥跨的宽度主要是考虑驳船队，而且仅考虑了矩形的驳船队。根据现在的发展，驳船队少了，宽度小了，“撞上”的概率就小了。但，单只自航的船大了、快了，船撞力变大；船的上层建筑大了高了，风流压偏角变大；这些都要求桥跨加宽。船撞因素对桥梁开始阶段的选型，越来越重要。

6　总结

经过研究认为：由于驳船队撞击桥墩的力叠加后的峰值远小于同样载重量的自航货船（或集装箱船）的撞击力的峰值。而且发展的方向是自航的货船取代驳船队。单体货船载重量较大，速度较快，撞击力较大，对船撞墩起决定性的影响。应选择自航货船作为设计防御船撞桥时船撞力的代表船型。

在桥梁设计的开始阶段，考虑桥型、通航宽度和船撞上桥墩的概率时，可对现在仍有的驳船队的宽度加以考虑（虽然船撞力已经不起控制作用）。

附录：对美国船撞桥设计指南中关于驳船两则条文的讨论

美国船撞桥设计指南[4]中关于考虑驳船的意见见于 3.12 节和 3.13 节：

“3.12　驳船对桥墩的撞击力

驳船正面撞击桥墩时，撞击力可以按以下方法计算：

$$a_B < 0.34 \text{ 时}, P_B = 4\,112(a_B) \quad (3.12-1a)$$

$$a_B \geqslant 0.34 \text{ 时}, P_B = [1\,349 + 110(a_B)] \quad (3.12-1b)$$

这里：P_B = 驳船撞击等效静力（千磅），B_B = 驳船宽度（英尺），a_B = 驳船船头损坏深度（英尺）”。

指南中，对于4艘以内的运泥驳船队有计算好的线图。一般的驳船如欲根据船头损坏深度计算驳船对墩的撞击力，则有：

“3.13　驳船船头损坏深度

驳船船头的损坏深度应当按如下公式进行计算：

$$a_B = \left[\left(1 + \frac{KE}{5\,672}\right)^{1/2} - 1\right]\left(\frac{10.2}{R_B}\right) \quad (3.13-1)$$

这里：a_B = 驳船船头损坏深度（英尺），KE = 驳船撞击能量（千磅－英尺）。

$$R_B = \frac{B_B}{35}\text{”}$$

对此，讨论几点：

（1）有了驳船宽度并计算出驳船撞击能量之后，代入公式（3.13－1）计算出驳船船头损坏深度，看计算出驳船船头损坏深度是大于还是小于0.34，然后再用公式（3.12－1a）或（3.12－1b）计算出驳船对墩的撞击力。——这种用冲击能去计算冲击力的理念，由于不符合牛顿力学的基本原理（冲击力与物体质量、速度和刚度有关，不是冲击能的单变量函数），在26年前我国铁路规范[8]的冲击力公式中已经表明，并提出了不同的处理分法。因为撞击力不是冲击能的单变量函数，它还受撞击过程时间（牛顿力学的冲量公式）、撞击系统刚度等因素的影响[5]，怎能用冲击能加一个驳船头的宽度就决定了呢？该协会指南也许对特定种类的驳船有用（不是普适的）。

（2）在该协会船撞桥设计的补充指南中，对驳船头被撞深度给予足够重视，我认为可以预防驳船头破损而致的环境受污染，这是很好的。但是，在桥梁设计的开始阶段，桥梁设计人首先关心的是选择桥位和桥型。他们首先想知道在航道中航行的船舶万一撞上时会有多大的力，他选择的桥墩会不会被撞倒，因此必须更直接地求出船撞力（不同型号的驳船有不同的船头刚度，应有不同的船头撞深计算方法）的方法。

（3）美国船撞桥设计指南中的实例，选择路易斯安那州新奥尔良附近的一座桥，该地区属于水网地区，宽的窄的河道都有。美国专业人员在这个地区也进行过驳船撞击闸门和驳船撞击水中桩柱（模拟桥墩）的实船试验[5]。有的试验用的是一只驳船，并没有看到关于驳船队的驳船之间力传递的处理办法（处理对象从单只驳船到驳船队必须解决的方法）。

参考文献

[1] 王孙. 长航驳船队“退位”新船型等待加冕[N]. 北京：中国船舶报. 2009-11-20.

[2] 史元熹,金允龙等. 黄石长江大桥主墩防撞设施设计. 上海：船撞桥论文集. 上海海洋钢结构研究所,2000：75-81.

[3] 上海河运学校,船舶操纵[R]. 教材.

[4] 美国各州公路和运输工作者协会(AASHTO)：公路桥梁船撞设计指南[R]2009 第二版 中译 2010 上海海洋钢结构研究所.

[5] 倪步友,陈国虞,郑丹,陈明栋. 中、外船撞桥实验评述[J]. 桥梁工程与技术(直投媒体),2009(6)：29-38.

[6] 中华人民共和国铁道部. 墩台承受船只或排筏的撞击力 TB10002. 1—2005 铁路桥涵设计基本规范[S]4. 4. 6 条. 北京：中国铁道出版社,2005.

[7] 中华人民共和国交通部. 公路桥涵设计通用规范[S]JTG D60—2004. 北京：人民交通出版社,2004.

[8] 中华人民共和国铁道部. 墩台承受船只或排筏的撞击力 TBJ2—85. 铁路工程技术规范[S]第二篇 3. 4. 6 条. 北京：中国铁道出版社,1985.

[9] 中华人民共和国国家标准,GB50139—2004,内河通航标准[S].

[10] 中华人民共和国行业标准 JTJ311—97,通航海轮桥梁通航标准[S].

发表于：广东造船,2012(1).

Published at：Guangdong Shipbuilding, 2012(1).

杭州内河92座桥梁防撞评估与增设防撞装置建议

Evaluation of ship collision with pier and suggestion of set up anti-collision equipment for 92 bridges of Hangzhou inland river

廖 娟[1] 陈国虞[2]

（1. 浙江大学城市学院310015，2. 上海海洋钢结构研究所201204）

LIAO Juan[1], CHEN Guoyu[2]

（1. Institute of Architecture and Civil Engineering, Zhejiang University 310015
2. Shanghai Marine Steel and Structure Research Institute 201204）

摘　要　2007年，从6月15日（广东九江大桥被撞塌）到年底，全国海事部门开展了防船撞防泄漏的整治工作。杭州城市管理部门认为对现有桥梁的防撞能力评估，整治危桥，是一项很重要的工作。对杭州市钱塘江北岸6条内河河道上92座桥做了初步评估，并对建设柔性防撞装置做出建议。计调查了：京杭大运河桥27座，余杭塘河桥11座，杭钢河桥8座，电厂河桥6座，上塘河桥16座，西塘河桥24座。评估后给出建议：一跨过江、已有防撞装置和无需装设防撞装置的桥梁26座；对已通航的4条河流的桥梁除按交通部要求完善航行标志外，应增设柔性防撞装置的桥梁20座；其余的桥梁或需改建、或属于危桥待拆、或需在其余2条河流进行通航整治时统一考虑。此20座桥梁装设柔性防撞装置之后，万一船撞上桥墩时，可做到桥梁不倒塌，船舶少泄漏，水体得到保护。从而提高该4流域通航的安全性。文中有对92座桥的建议总表和20幅建议桥梁图。

关键词　桥梁　防撞　评估　增设

Abstract: In 2007, from June 15th, Guangdong Jiujiang Bridge was fall, till the end of this year; the department of maritime of China expensed a work of anti-ship collision with the bridge and anti-leakiness of ships.

The city management in Hangzhou thinks the evaluation on ability of anti-collision with ship for the existing bridge, cure shaky bridge, is a very important work.

This thesis give out the first step valuation for 92 bridges over 6 inland rivers in Hangzhou City on the north of Qiantang River, and also give out the suggestions on set up the soft-anti-collision equipment.

The following river has been investigated: The Grand Canal (Beijing-hangzhou) in hangzhou city is 27 s, Yuhangtang river is 11 s, the Hang-Steel river is 8 s, the Electric-Plant river is 6 s, the Super-Pond river 16 s, and the West-Pond river is 24 s.

Give the suggestion after evaluate: One span over the river, had been constructed the anti-collision equipment and do not need to equip the anti-collision equipment are 26 bridges;

For the 4 navigated rivers, except in addition to requesting the symbol according to the Ministry of Communications, 20 bridges should set up the soft-anti-collision equipment.

The other bridges may be rebuild, may belongs to shaky bridge to treat to dismantle, or need at the rest 2 rivers to carry on navigation whole cure unify consideration.

After this 20 bridges set up the equipment, when the ship collision with the bridge, it does not full down, the ship and the water body gets a protection.

The navigations safety of thus 4 river valleys' has been raised.

Keywords: bridge, anti-collision, valuation, to set up the equipment

1 前言

2007 年 6 月 15 日,广东九江大桥被撞塌,引起公路交通和海事部门的重视,交通部向全国海事局发出船舶碰撞防泄漏的通知[1],佛山市、杭州市等交通部门开展对现有桥梁的防撞能力评估,整治危桥。交通部要求各地在 2007 年底作出总结。比较认真的城市道桥管理部门组织桥梁和航道多个专业进行评估,也有委托科技部门进行评估的,由于工作较繁重,故延续至 2008 年,甚至更长的时间。

杭州市城管部门委托浙江大学城市学院成立专题,进行调研,对钱塘江以北 6 条杭州市的内河(京杭大运河、余杭塘河、杭钢河、电厂河、上塘河和西塘河)上的桥梁进行防撞能力评估[2],此 6 条河中前 4 条通航,后两条河待整治后通航,现在已有小船在河中航行(由桥墩边上的撞擦痕迹可以证明)。6 条河上的桥名和数量见图 1 和表 1。

本文在评估报告的基础上,除建议补齐通航标志、增加非结构性的主动防撞设施之外,首批选出 20 座桥梁建议增设结构性柔性防撞设施。

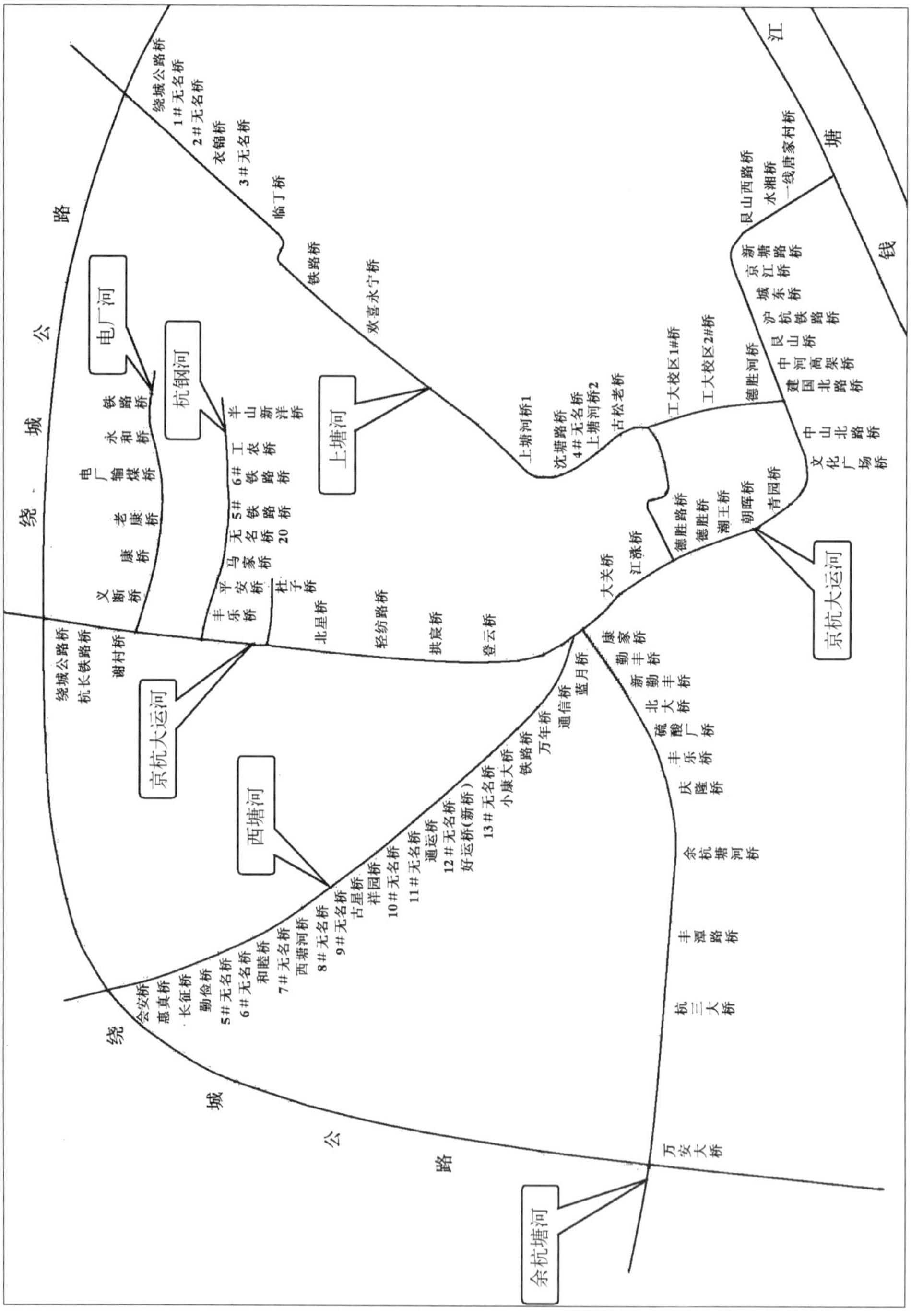

图 1　杭州 6 条内河桥梁分布图

Fig. 1　The distributing map of bridges on 6 inland rivers of Hangzhou City

表 1 杭州市 6 条内河的通航等级和桥梁数
Table 1 The navigation grades and the number of bridge on the 6 inland rivers of Hangzhou City

序	名　称	通 航 等 级	通行最大船	净高×净宽/m	桥 梁 数
1	京杭大运河	4 级	500 吨级船	8×55	27
		5 级	300 吨级船	5×45	
2	余塘河	6 级	100 吨级船		11
3	杭钢河	6 级(货运)	100 吨级船		8
4	电厂河	6 级(货运)	100 吨级船		6
5	上塘河	客运一类(旅游)		3.5×18	16
6	西塘河	客运二类(旅游)		2×12	24

2　建议增设柔性防撞设施的原则

(1) 对已有防撞装置的桥墩不增设柔性防撞装置。

(2) 对通航船舶较多,现在撞擦痕迹较重的桥墩;对双柱墩或多柱墩的桥墩,建议增设柔性防撞装置。

一般来说双柱墩在增设防撞装置时,首先将其两墩之间进行结构连接,使受撞时船撞力由多柱共同承担。一般认为新桥在材料使用相当的情况下,设计成扁墩,抗撞力可以提高到 4~5 倍。

(3) 对近期有可能拆除的桥梁,暂缓增设柔性防撞装置。

(4) 对将来整治后才能正式通航的两条河流,现不增设柔性防撞装置。

3　对杭州内河 92 座桥梁增设柔性防撞装置的建议

根据上述原则,分别对 92 座桥梁梳理后,建议分为:不建、应建和缓建 3 类,列在表 2 最右项。所建议增设柔性防撞设施的桥梁见图 2~21。

表 2 杭州市 6 条内河 92 座桥梁建设防船撞装置的建议
Table 2 The suggestion on construction equipment for anti-ship collision with bridge on the 6 inland rivers of Hangzhou City

序号	桥　名	结 构 形 式	通航净宽/m	通航净高/m	情　　况	防撞装置建议
京　杭　大　运　河						
1	绕城公路桥	混凝土三跨连续梁	70.0	7.0	中孔通航、撞击可能性小,墩大	缓建
2	杭长铁路桥	钢桁架	60.0	7.1	船停靠时容易刮擦;桥墩椭圆	缓建
3	谢村桥	钢筋砼箱型连续梁	70.0	7.0	在河道的交叉口,有防撞设施	不建

续表

序号	桥　名	结构形式	通航净宽/m	通航净高/m	情　况	防撞装置建议
4	杜子桥	4跨梁桥	缺	缺	船速慢，被撞概率低，桥墩弱	缓建
5	北星桥	钢筋砼箱型连续梁	45.0	5.5	中孔通航	应建
6	轻纺路桥	钢筋砼箱型连续梁	45.0	4.5	桥墩有刮擦的痕迹	应建
7	拱宸桥	石拱桥	15.7	7.0	撞致吉祥物雕塑与防撞墩错位	不建
8	登云桥	V型刚构	63.0	5.5	净高牌被树枝遮挡	缓建
9	大关桥	钢筋砼双悬臂梁	42.8	4.5	刮擦严重桥墩端部有钢筋外露	应建
10	江涨桥	钢筋砼悬臂梁	46.0	4.5	盖梁上有刮擦，桥墩遭受过撞击	应建
11	德胜路桥	钢筋砼箱型连续梁	57.5	4.5	承台较高，防撞击的能力好	缓建
12	德胜桥	钢筋砼双曲拱	22.8	3.9	主拱已被加固，桥台腐蚀严重	缓建
13	潮王桥	钢筋砼双悬臂	45.5	4.5	交角大，撞击多，钢筋外露	应建
14	朝晖桥	钢筋混凝土系杆拱	46.5	4.5	一跨过江	不建
15	青园桥	钢筋砼桁架梁	48.0	4.5	桥墩薄、刮擦明显	应建
16	文化广场桥	钢结构连续梁	45.0	4.5	有防撞装置东边净高牌、缺桥标	不建
17	中山北路桥	钢筋砼箱型连续梁	44.5	4.5	承台高、桥墩薄，有刮擦	应建
18	建国北路桥	钢筋砼箱型连续梁	44.0	4.5	实体墩台有刮擦	应建
19	中河高架桥	钢筋砼箱型连续梁	45.0	4.5	四座桥梁在一起，视线较差	应建
20	艮山桥	钢筋砼T型简支梁	46.0	4.5	斜交桥，桥墩有撞击的痕迹	应建
21	沪杭铁路桥	钢筋砼箱型梁桥	16.0	4.1	河道中间桥墩容易被撞	缓建
22	城东桥	钢筋砼T型简支梁	46.0	4.5	有撞擦痕迹	应建
23	京江桥	钢筋砼箱型连续梁	44.0	4.5	主梁在四分点处有对称斜裂缝	应建
24	新塘路桥	钢筋砼系杆拱桥	51.0	4.5	河道中无桥墩	不建
25	艮山西路桥	钢筋砼双悬臂	45.5	4.5	桥宽，扁墩，路面曾塌陷待改造	缓建
26	水湘桥	钢筋砼桁架桥	51.0	4.7	河道中无桥墩	不建
27	一线唐家村桥	钢筋砼桁架桥	51.0	4.7	船速小，撞击可能性小	不建
余　杭　塘　河						
1	康家桥	钢筋砼梁板	17.2	4.37	多柱墩，桥墩部位有加固	应建
2	勤丰桥	钢筋砼双曲拱	15.0	4.23	易撞、有撞击的痕迹，危险	缓建
3	新勤丰桥	刚架桥	未得	未得	在建，桥墩不占航道	不建
4	北大桥	钢筋砼简支梁	26.0	4.48	有简易防撞柱，高2 m，共4个	不建
5	硫酸厂桥	钢筋砼桁架拱	17.2	4.40	危险，建议拆除	缓建
6	丰乐桥	钢筋砼拱桥	27.6	4.00	危险，建议拆除	缓建
7	庆隆桥	钢筋砼拱桥	15.5	3.75	有桥标；桥梁结构很薄弱	缓建
8	余杭塘河桥	钢筋混凝土板梁桥	23.0	4.62	撞击概率较高，3柱墩有刮痕	应建
9	丰潭路桥	混凝土梁桥	22.0	4.5	河道中无桥墩，墩墩实体，边墩悬壁	缓建

续表

序号	桥　名	结构形式	通航净宽/m	通航净高/m	情　况	防撞装置建议
10	杭三大桥	钢筋砼简支梁	18.7	4.21	3跨预制梁桥中跨在河中有刮擦	应建
11	万安大桥	钢筋砼桁架拱	21.5	3.67	桥老	缓建
			杭　钢　河			
1	丰乐桥	钢筋砼梁板	15.8	4.05	位于炼油厂处,江中独墩为圆形	应建
2	平安桥	钢筋砼梁板	16.0	3.89	新旧桥并排老桥墩弱,刮擦严重	应建
3	马家桥	钢筋砼梁板	20.0	3.95	单跨独墩,墩靠桥台外,刮擦严重	应建
4	无名桥20	下承钢筋砼桁拱	24.5	4.45	桥墩在岸上结构防撞安全;要拆	缓建
5	5#铁路桥	钢筋砼梁板	7.1	3.25	江中无墩,净宽不足,刮擦严重	缓建
6	6#铁路桥	钢筋砼梁板	10.0	3.65	独墩航道中刮擦严重,净宽不足	缓建
7	工农桥	钢筋砼双曲拱	16.3	2.85	河道中无桥墩;桥侧外边有刮擦	缓建
8	半山新洋桥	钢筋砼桁架拱桥	11.3	4.58	河道中无桥墩;主拱有加固	缓建
			电　厂　河			
1	义断桥	钢筋砼双曲拱桥	19.5	4.05	桥墩不占河道,桥老	缓建
2	康桥	钢筋砼梁板桥	22.0	3.90	桥墩在河道中间,有多处刮擦	应建
3	老康桥	钢筋砼梁板桥	22.3	4.05	桥墩在河道中间,有多处刮擦	应建
4	电厂输煤桥	钢筋砼梁板桥	40.5	8.10	4跨独柱墩有简易防撞措施被撞	不建
5	永和桥	钢筋砼梁板桥	17.5	3.60	独柱墩,刮擦严重,桥老	缓建
6	铁路桥	钢桁架桥	30.4	5.20	河道中无桥墩	不建
			上　塘　河			
1	绕城公路桥	梁式桥	24.9	4.34	未通航,净宽9.71 m,河道深约1 m	缓建
2	1#无名桥	T形梁桥	9.7	3.35	未通航,板梁桥,无桥墩	不建
3	2#无名桥	旧桥T形梁新桥板梁	10.8	2.85	净高2.85 m,江中无桥墩,钢筋外露	缓建
4	衣锦桥	拱桥	12.8	6.30	未通航,古桥需要保护	不建
5	3#无名桥	拱桥	12.8	3.60	未通航,拱肋有被撞击的痕迹	缓建
6	临丁桥	两座连续箱梁桥	≈70	5.20	未通航,桥轴与河斜交角较大	不建
7	铁路桥	简支梁桥	8.7	3.40	未通航,河中无桥墩,净宽不足	缓建
8	欢喜永宁桥	拱桥	11.2	5.50	古桥,拱桥侧壁有刮擦的痕迹	不建
9	上塘河桥1	梁桥	20.0	4.28	未通航3跨梁桥江中两排多柱墩	应建
10	沈塘路桥	梁桥	23.4	4.70	未通航,3跨,航道中	应建
11	4#无名桥	梁桥	18.3	3.43	未通航,航道中两排多柱墩	应建
12	上塘河桥2	梁桥	26.0	4.90	双柱墩,有刮擦痕,未通航	应建
13	古松老桥	石拱桥	12.2	5.60	古桥,未通航	不建
14	工大校区1#桥	中承钢管拱桥	32.8	1.96	未通航,通航净高1.96 m	缓建
15	工大校区2#桥	梁桥	13.7	2.20	钢桥3跨,均为3柱墩,净高2.2 m	缓建
16	德胜河桥	梁桥	8.9	1.85	净高1.85 m无法通航,2柱和3柱墩	缓建

续表

序号	桥　名	结构形式	通航净宽/m	通航净高/m	情　　况	防撞装置建议
西　塘　河						
1	会安桥	拱桥	6.7	3.7	3 条航道,河道淤塞较厉害	不建
2	惠真桥	刚架桥	10.0	3.2	净宽不够,河道淤塞较厉害	缓建
3	长征桥	双曲拱桥	18.3	3.3	通航净空够了,河道淤塞较厉害	不建
4	勤俭桥	混凝土板梁桥	~	6.5	桥墩在岸上,无撞击可能	不建
5	5#无名桥	梁桥	5.9	3.9	2 个桥墩在航道中,条石墩	应建
6	6#无名桥	梁桥	7.4	4.8	有两座桥并排,一座高架桥	不建
7	和睦桥	拱桥	9.8	5.0	通航净宽不够,河道淤塞	缓建
8	7#无名桥	梁桥	19.7	8.3	两排多柱墩	应建
9	西塘河桥	梁桥	32.0	6.0	通航净空够了	不建
10	8#无名桥	梁桥	48.0	4.0	通航净空够了	不建
11	9#无名桥	梁桥	10.0	2.0	通航净宽不够	缓建
12	古星桥	拱桥	~	~	是一条旱桥	不建
13	祥园桥	梁式桥	12.5	3.0	三跨连续梁桥,多柱墩	应建
14	10#无名桥	刚架桥	14.5	2.9	通航净高不够	缓建
15	11#无名桥	梁式桥	8.1	3.0	通航净宽不够	缓建
16	通运桥	3 跨梁桥	12.8	3.9	航道中两排多柱墩,疏浚后通航	应建
17	12#无名桥	拱式桥	17.9	3.6	拱桥,清理后通航	不建
18	好运桥(新桥)	梁式桥	14.4	2.8	三跨梁桥,通航净高不够	缓建
19	13#无名桥	拱桥	~	3.5	拱桥,老,净高 3.5 m,桥面砼破裂	缓建
20	小康大桥	梁式桥	9.0	2.4	通航净空不够	缓建
21	铁路桥	梁式桥	17.4	7.0	河道无法通行	不建
22	万年桥	拱式桥	13.6	~	混凝土刚构桥,老,属危桥	缓建
23	通信桥	梁式桥	13.8	4.4	一跨过河,无桥墩	不建
24	蓝月桥	梁式桥	11.5	2.6	桥较新,通航净高不够	缓建

图 2　北星桥承台损伤情况

Fig. 2　The scar on the cushion cap of Beixing bridge

图 3　轻纺路桥河道中间承台有刮擦痕迹

Fig. 3　Some scrapes on the pier (in the middle of route) of Qingfanglu bridge

图4 大关桥桥墩位于河道中间

Fig. 4 The pier of Daguan bridge put in the middle of route

图5 江涨桥桥墩有刮擦痕迹

Fig. 5 Some scrapes on the pier of Jiangzhang bridge

图6 潮王桥桥墩情况

Fig. 6 The pier fig of Chaowang bridge

图7 青园桥立面

Fig. 7 The stand fig of Qingyuan bridge

图8 中山北路桥立面图

Fig. 8 The stand fig of Zhongshangbeilu bridge

图9 建国北路桥立面图

Fig. 9 The stand fig of Jianguobeilu bridge

图10 中河高架桥承台混凝土被撞碎

Fig. 10 The concrete cushion cap of Zhonghe high way bridge had been crack-up by collision

图11 艮山桥立面图

Fig. 11 The stand fig of Yinshan bridge

图 12　城东桥全景

Fig. 12　The panorama of Chengdong bridge

图 13　京江桥全景

Fig. 13　The panorama of Jingjiang bridge

图 14　康家桥桥墩情况

Fig. 14　The panorama of pier on Kangjia bridge

图 15　余杭塘河桥桥墩刮擦严重

Fig. 15　The severity scrapes on the pier of Yuhangtanghe bridge

图 16　杭三大桥立面图

Fig. 16　The stand fig of Hangsan bridge

图 17　丰乐桥立面图

Fig. 17　The stand fig of Fengle bridge

图 18　平安桥桥墩布置情况

Fig. 18　The piers disposal fig of Ping-an bridge

图 19　马家桥被撞击和摩擦的情况

Fig. 19　The collision and frictional fig of Majia bridge

图 20　康桥桥墩，刮擦严重

Fig. 20　The severity scrapes on the pier of Kang bridge

图 21　老康桥立面图

Fig. 21　The stand fig of old Kang bridge

4　结论

杭州市钱塘江以北 6 条内河有 92 座桥梁，对其中已通航的 4 条（京杭大运河、余杭塘河、杭钢河和电厂河）河流中的 52 座桥梁，在防撞能力评估报告的基础上，建议其中 20 座桥梁增设柔性防撞设施。经过精心设计和详细计算，要求达到：通航船舶万一撞上桥墩时也要做到桥墩不垮、船舶损失不大。

参 考 文 献

[1] 中华人民共和国交通部. 关于开展防船舶碰撞防泄漏专项整治活动的通知[D]. 北京：交海发[2007]304 号，2007-06-17.

[2] 杭州市城市管理办公室. 杭州市内河桥梁防撞能力评估与对策[D]. 杭州：浙江大学城市学院，2008-03.

[3] 中华人民共和国交通部. 内河通航标准(GB50039—2004)[S]. 北京：中国计划出版社，2004.

[4] 国家技术监督局. 内河助航标志(GB5863—93)[S]，1993.

[5] 陈国虞等. 长江中游桥墩防撞——钢绳柔性吸能防撞器试验研究[J]. 航海科技动态，1995.

[6] 陈国虞. 防御船撞桥装置的历史和新发展——“三不坏”桥墩防撞装置. 力学 2000. 北京：气象出版社，2000：657-658.

[7] 陈国虞，杨黎明，周风华，张澄. 紧靠混凝土承台的直接式防撞装置选择. 桥梁养护管理与维修加固技术交流研讨会(西安)论文集[C]. 北京：住房和城乡建设部，2009.

[8] 方辉. 杭州拱宸桥防撞墩设置[J]. 市政设施管理，2006.

[9] 新华网浙江频道. 杭州桥梁排查情况. 三大症状缠绕百座问题桥梁[W]，2007.

第六部分

对国内外一些桥梁防船撞规范的评析

Analysis on some guides for defends collision of ship with bridge

有防撞装置时计算船撞桥的力

——铁路桥梁规范中船撞力公式的延伸修订建议

The front force of ship collision to a protected pier

陈国虞

（上海海洋钢结构研究所，上海 201204）

CHEN Guoyu

（Shanghai Marine Steel and Structure Research Institute, Shanghai 201204, China）

摘　要　我国铁路工程技术规范的桥涵篇中有船撞桥墩力的计算公式，该公式用："撞后镶住不动，动能全部耗尽"的状态，考虑了船的质量、速度，以及船和桥墩两者的刚性，计算出最大正撞力，再考虑相撞时的角度和能量耗散得出船撞桥墩的力。但若相撞时两者之间有防撞装置呢？将防撞装置的刚性与船和桥墩两者的刚性同样对待，以防撞装置弹塑性曲线的割线斜率作为平均弹塑性系数 C_3，推导出有防撞装置时的船撞力。建议在修订规范时在公式中增加 C_3。文中还反对对本公式作过分的简化。

关键词　铁路规范　船撞力　防撞装置

Abstract: In the Rules of the design for railway of China, there are a formula on the force of ship collision with the bridge pier. According to the state of: when collision is happened, the ship inlaid with the pier, $v \to 0$, all the energy of motion had been waste, we got the maximum collision front force. There are consider with the mass and velocity of ship, the angle function and energy waste on collision and the rigidity of ship and pier. But, we how to consider the protection equipment of the pier? In this paper, the protection equipment treat as the ship and pier, join C_3 behind C_1 and C_2 to calculation the force of ship collision to pier with the protection equipment. In this paper, we oppose excessive simplify this formula.

Keywords: Force of Ship Collision with pier, Collision force of ship to protection pier

1　前言

我国铁路工程技术规范反映了制定它时的技术水平,在下次修订前的使用期内,科技发展会不断提出修改意见,作为每次再版前的意见都反映了这一个使用周期内科技的发展。

第 15 届全国桥梁学术会议的分组会讨论了船撞桥的研究进展。陈兴冲、周世忠、顾永宁和本文作者等桥梁和造船专业工作者出席讨论,认为:没有防撞装置时,当船头比桥墩软得多,船头决定了船撞力的大小。防撞装置与船头的刚柔程度差不多,他们共同起作用,共同决定船撞力的大小。铁路规范计算船撞力公式已考虑了船头和桥墩的刚性,现将防撞装置的刚性也考虑进去,便可在计算船撞力的公式中反映出防撞装置的作用。

铁路规范第 3.4.6 条“墩台承受船只或排筏撞击力可按下式计算[1]:

$$F = \gamma v \sin\alpha [W/(C_1 + C_2)]^{0.5}$$

式中:F——撞击力,kN;

γ——动能折减系数(s/m$^{0.5}$),当船只或排筏斜向撞击墩台(指船只或排筏驶近方向与撞击点处墩台面法线方向不一致)时可采用 0.2,正向撞击(指船只或排筏驶近方向与撞击点墩台面处法线方向一致)时可采用 0.3;

v——船只或排筏撞击墩台时的速度(m/s)。此项速度对于船只采用航运部门提供的数据,对于排筏可采用筏运期的水流速度;

α——船只或排筏驶近方向与墩台撞击点处切线所成的夹角,应根据具体情况确定,如有困难可采用 $\alpha=20°$;

W——船只重或排筏重,kN;

C_1、C_2——船只或排筏的弹性变形系数和墩台圬工的弹性变形系数,缺乏资料时可设 $C_1 + C_2 = 0.0005$ m/kN。”

2　铁路规范船撞力公式的物理意义——公式的推导

当有一艘质量为 M 速度为 v 的船,船头正撞桥墩时。设撞后船头被镶住不动,船的速度由 $v\to0$,船的动能由 $(1/2)Mv^2\to0$,这个动能(ΔE)引致船头、桥墩和防撞装置三者的变形,简单地认为通过三者的力是一样大的,它引致桥墩、船头和防撞装置三者的变形(位移),依次称为 L_1, L_2, L_3。

在力与变形的“$F-L$”图上,设其为线性做功,即:$\Delta E = 1/2(FL)$,得到:

$$1/2(Mv^2) = 1/2[F(L_1 + L_2 + L_3)]$$

现将斜率的倒数(1/斜率)称为 C,即 $C = L/F$, $L = FC$, 对桥墩、船头和防撞装置三者的 C 分别称为 C_1, C_2, C_3 则上式可写为:

$$1/2(Mv^2) = 1/2(FL_1 + FL_2 + FL_3) = 1/2(FFC_1 + FFC_2 + FFC_3)$$
$$= 1/2[F^2(C_1 + C_2 + C_3)]$$

移项得到:

$$F = v[M/(C_1 + C_2 + C_3)]^{0.5} \tag{1}$$

将式中 M 用船的重量 W(满载排水量 · 附连水系数)表示,考虑撞击能量耗散系数写作 γ,即得到铁路规范中角度折减前有防撞装置的最大正撞力公式(1):

$$F = \gamma v[W/(C_1 + C_2 + C_3)]^{0.5} \tag{2}$$

C 的物理意义:当桥墩的刚性大于船头的刚性几十倍,变形也小几十倍,这样桥墩吸收的能量很小,经过计算认为将其忽略不计时($C_2 = 0$)误差可接受。如果这时也没有采用防撞装置,则式中只有 C_1, C_1 的割线意义表示如图 1,这是将一艘 40 000 t 载重量的油船[2]撞桥时的变形时程曲线与力的时程曲线整合而得的“力-撞深”曲线。图中的直线斜率的倒数就是 C_1。

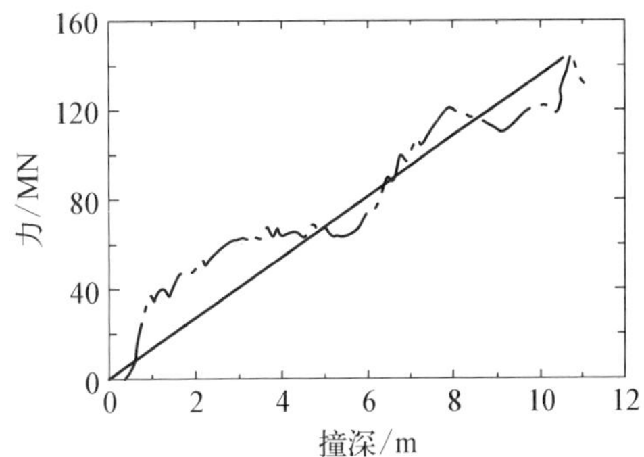

图 1　40 000 t 油船“力-撞深”曲线的割线(斜率 = $1/C_1$)

Fig. 1　Secant of 40 000 t oil tanker “force-impact depth” curve (slope = $1/C_1$)

从物理意义比较明确、公式参变量比较多和采集公式数据的可能性几方面来说,这是现有各公式中比较好的一个。但仍有一些缺陷如:第一,此式以最高点以下的面积与全部变形能($0.5Mv^2$)相对应,实际上到达最高点后能量还在交换;第二,此式认为相撞力是一个通过船、桥都不变的力,实际上船头在变形,船头各处受力并不相同;如考虑到应力波的传递则还会有波长与元件的关系、界面影响等。故“比较好”只是在一定程度上而言的。

船若直接撞到碰垫上,碰垫受力和变形,适用厂商提供的“力-变形”图,若多个防撞圈(或碰垫)一齐用,则多了一个联系各防撞圈的钢围,它也参加变形。如果钢围刚性足够大,钢围和防撞圈组成的防撞装置的变形规律便可用防撞圈的规律来代表。

图 2 是两种碰垫和复合防撞圈的“$F - L$”曲线,鼓形碰垫用于防撞时由于曲线太硬——凸曲线,反力大变形小。管形碰垫解决了这个问题,得到了凹曲线,即初撞便后退。此两种碰垫均为弹性的橡胶,变形过程吸能很小。钢丝绳复合防撞圈是凹曲线且吸能很多,“吸能比”很大,做到了又软又吸能。此三曲线图上可以看出割线斜率 $1/C$ 代表刚柔程度的意义,至于能量吸收和放出,及其对船体破坏的影响等均非此图讨论范围。

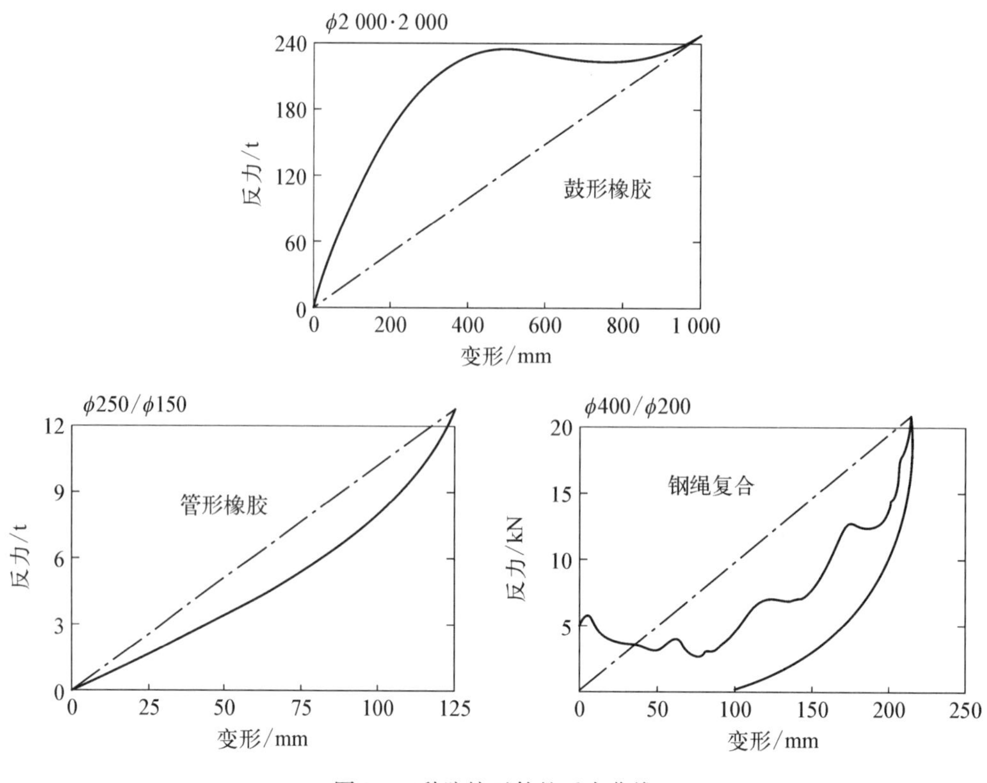

图 2　三种防撞元件的反力曲线

Fig. 2　Reaction force curves of the three typies anti-collision element

3　撞击过程中各个瞬时的力

从上面公式推导看出与原有铁路规范船撞力公式相比较，仅将 C_1+C_2 变成了 $C_1+C_2+C_3$，因此称为延伸修订，使用起来也很方便，式中的 C_3 不论是鼓形橡胶、管形橡胶还是钢丝绳复合型，都是由制造厂提供“$F-L$”曲线中可得出。

原公式公布于 1985 年，近 20 年来防撞理论、防撞元件和防撞计算都有了较大的发展，新制成的钢绳复合型防撞圈也可作为防撞元件以其参数进入计算。图 2 是当有外钢圈和 700 个防撞圈时有限元计算结果，图中横线为铁路公式计算结果，公式使用的数据为：船的载重量为 50 000 t，满载排水量乘以附连水系数 1.1 后为 687 500 kN，$C_1=0.000\,07$，$C_2=0$，$C_3=0.000\,068$，$C_1+C_3=0.000\,138$ m/kN，$\gamma=0.2$，$\sin 20°=0.34$，代入公式后得到 $F=14.4$ MN。

在有限元方法得出的力的时程曲线中，应该用哪一个时间的力与公式算出的力相比较呢？用哪一个力去计算桥墩？所以尽管有这两种方法，仍应继续设法用实验或实际测量力的方法加以验证。

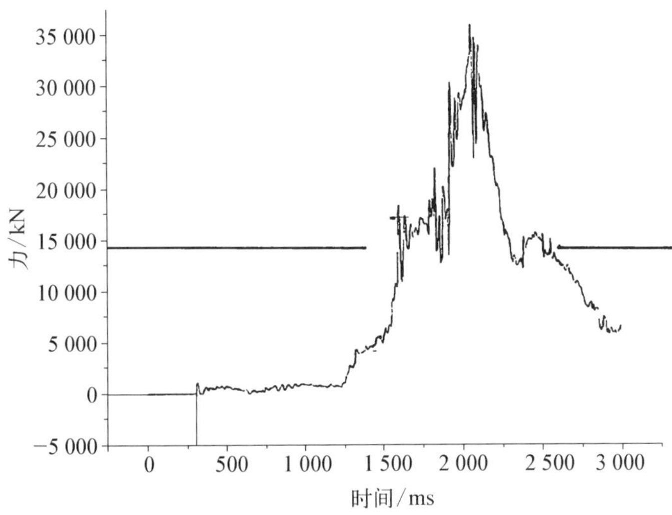

图 3　船与防撞装置以 20°夹角相遇时的桥墩受力

Fig. 3　Reaction force between ship and anti-collision device by impact angle 20°

4　建议不要用过分简化的公式

美国各州公路和运输工作者协会(AASHTTO)的公路桥梁设计规范[5]中,使用的船撞力公式是我国铁路规范公式的一种简化形式,现证明如下:将(2)式中的 W 写成:

$$W = \eta\Delta = \eta(1/K)DWT$$

式中 η 为附连水系数,从 1.04 ~ 1.1 左右;Δ 为排水量,DWT 是载重量,K 是载重量与排水量之比(DWT/Δ)。

在国际桥梁和结构工程师协会(IABSE)的指南[6]中对 K 值给出如下:

油船:$DWT = 0.9\Delta$;　货船:$DWT = 0.8\Delta$;　集装箱船:$DWT = 0.6\Delta$。

这个简表从具体船归纳而来,每艘船都有一个 DWT 和 Δ,遇到表内不能概括的船,可以查船的资料。这样,将式(2)写成美国规范的形式是:

$$F = \gamma[\eta(1/K)/(C_1 + C_2 + C_3)]^{0.5} \cdot V \cdot (DWT)^{0.5} \tag{3}$$

比较式(3)和式(4)可看出美国公路规范的船撞力公式将有 6 个变量的系数:

$\gamma[\eta(1/K)/(C_1 + C_2 + C_3)]^{0.5}$ 简约成常量 1.2:

$$F = 1.2V \cdot (DWT)^{0.5} \tag{4}$$

也就是说:不同情况下的能量耗散系数,不同船种时的载重量与排水量之比例,船头、桥墩和防撞装置的刚柔程度以及附连水系数等统统不能逐个考虑,而一齐简约为一个常量 1.2,这种做法当然是不可取的,作者建议设计者不要采用这个过于简化的公式。

5　应用铁路规范船撞力公式时厘定式中系数的方法[3]

此公式共有 8 个变量,分为三类: 船的排水量,从船的资料上可以得到;船的速度也是可知的;此外还有 6 个变量,在运动状态下船的附连水系数一般取 1.1,至于桥墩的 C_2 由于桥墩变形量很小,与船头和防撞装置相比若把它看作 0,其误差可以接受。余下 4 个变量: γ 在规范中分为两挡,已有规定,仍旧沿用。系数 $K = DWT/\Delta$, 在各型船的资料中有,船长保管的资料中也有一份。最后剩下 C_1 和 C_3。C_1 的厘定现有两种方法: 一种是用实验法,即将船拉上船排,用刚性重锤正向打击船头,测定其变形和力,在拆船厂打击各类型的待拆船舶便可得到一系列的 C_1;另一种方法是模拟计算法,我国很多学者计算过不少船头弹性变形系数[2]。C_3 是防撞装置的弹塑性变形系数,也可用实验法或计算法去厘定。

所以防撞设计研究工作者如能把 C_1 和 C_3 这两个系数厘定得准确一些,船撞力自然就计算得准确一些了。

6　总结

(1) 只要承认原来的公式用割线代表曲线的简化(即仅为了计算最高点的力,忽略达到最高点的过程),则可用同样原理将防撞装置的刚柔程度导入公式内,作为一个参变量,公式反映船撞桥的情况更贴切了,建议规范修订将采用此新公式(2)。

(2) 知道公式中各参数的意义,便知道美国规范船撞力公式用常数 1.2 代表的是 6 个变量,因此建议不要用过于简化的公式。

参 考 文 献

[1] 中华人民共和国铁道部: TBJ2—85 铁路技术工程规范[S]第二篇 桥涵 1985.

[2] 刘建成,顾永宁. 船桥碰撞数值仿真[C]. 第 15 届全国桥梁学术会议论文集. 上海: 同济大学出版社,2002.

[3] 陈国虞. 船对桥墩的正撞力[C]. 第 15 届全国桥梁学术会议论文集. 上海: 同济大学出版社,2002.

[4] 陈国虞,沈文玮. 船对桥墩的侧撞力[C]. 第 15 届全国桥梁学术会议论文集. 上海: 同济大学出版社,2002.

[5] 美国各州公路和运输工作者协会(AASHTO): 美国公路桥梁设计规范[S]中译. 人民交通出版社,1994.

[6] 国际桥梁和结构工程师协会(IABSE): 航行船舶与桥的相互影响[R]. 同济大学译,1991.

发表于: 铁道标准设计,2004(1).

Published at: Railway Standard Design, 2004(1).

统一我国两个桥涵设计规范中船撞力公式的探讨

Discuss on the unification of the impact force formula in two design criterion on ship collision with bridge

陆宗林[1]　陈国虞[2]　张澄[2]

（1. 同济大学，上海 200092；2. 上海海洋钢结构研究所，上海 201204）

LU Zonglin[1], CHEN Guoyu[2], ZHANG Cheng[2]

(1. Department of Bridge Engineering, Tongji University, Shanghai, 200092, CHINA;
2. Shanghai Marine Steel and Structure Research Institute, Shanghai 201204, CHINA)

摘　要　目前我国在桥梁设计中，计算船撞桥的力时，有的不使用规范的公式而使用外国的公式；有的只用数值计算，其结果与规范相距甚远，也不作处理。新的公路桥涵设计通用规范（JTGD60—2004）有了一些改进，载入一些切合实际的观点和规定。但所列船撞力表格不符合航运和力学的基本原理，所列公式需要的条件和数据也不够，公式运用起来有困难。建议公路和铁路两个桥涵设计规范计算船撞桥的力时，使用统一的公式，提出一个经过延伸修正的公式，试算了若干使用这公式时所需的数据，供主管部门在修订规范时采用。

关键词　公路桥涵　铁路桥涵　设计规范　船撞力

Abstract: Now, in China, some bridge designer does not use the formula in the criterion to calculation the force of ship collision with bridge. Some one used the formula abroad, another only use the numerical calculation method. When the result far from the criterion, some one does not take order with them. There are some progress in the general criterion of high way bridge (JTGD60—2004), some view points and regulates are effective. But, its table of impact force of ship collision with bridge does not accord with the shipping practical and foundation theory of mechanics. Its impact force formula is with out necessary data. So this formula is difficult to use. This paper discussed and suggests when we design the high way and railway bridge use the same formula to calculation the impact force of ship. This paper has give out a revised formula. It is extend from the railway criterion formula.

And also give out many data for used this formula to calculation. Devote to the member in charge as refer for recession the criterion.

Keywords: high way bridge, railway bridge, design criterion, impact force of ship collision with bridge

1 前言

1.1 船撞力近似公式的使用

目前,求船撞桥的力通常有3种方法:基于刚体或弹性体理论的近似(半经验)公式法、数值计算法和模型试验法。

在一座桥梁的设计初期,通常采用近似公式法对船撞力进行估算,我们认为是可取的,对于重要桥梁在设计的后期,我们推荐使用冲击动力学的数值法进行仔细的计算。如果计算所需的数据不充分或需要验证计算结果时,还需进行试验[6]。因此,在规范中选择一种优良的近似(半经验)公式,就显得非常必要了。

1.2 公路桥涵设计通用规范的使用现状

目前,我国在桥梁设计中,计算船撞桥的力时,有的不使用规范的公式而使用外国的公式;有的只用数值计算,其结果与规范相距甚远,也不作处理。这一方面是由于规范还有较大的缺陷,满足不了设计人的要求;另一方面是设计人对规范的严肃性认识不够,遵守规范的意识薄弱,这两种情况都须尽快加以改变。

自从2002年有学者[1]指出,我国公路桥涵设计规范对船撞桥的条款"设计思想和设计策略不明确"之后,我国研究防御船撞桥的科技工作者对我国两个桥涵设计规范中关于船撞力的计算方法提出了不少改进的建议,如:[2]、[3]、[4]、[5]。2004年公布施行新的公路桥涵设计通用规范虽然有了一些改进,载入一些符合实际的观点和规定,但船撞力表格和漂浮物撞击力公式运用起来仍有困难,表列数值也不符合航运和力学的基本原理,公式所需的条件也不够,数据不易确定。

2 公路桥涵设计通用规范(JTGD60—2004)关于船撞力的条文

该规范中载明的、符合实际的、进行船撞力估算时应该遵循的条文及其说明有以下几点:

(1)"在通航河流上,当基础采用桩基础时,承台底面应置于低水位以下,以免船舶或漂流物直接作用于桩上。"

(2)"位于流水中的桥墩……宜做成圆形、圆端形或尖端形,以减少流水压力。"这也是减少船撞力的有效结构措施。

(3)“跨越江、河、海湾的桥梁,必须考虑船舶或漂流物对桥梁墩台的偶然作用。船舶或漂流物与桥梁结构的碰撞过程十分复杂,其与碰撞时的环境因素(风浪、气候、水流等)、船舶特性(船舶类型、船舶尺寸、行进速度、装载情况以及船首、船壳和甲板室的强度和刚度等)、桥梁结构因素(桥梁构件的尺寸、形状、材料、质量和抗力特性等)及驾驶员的反应时间等因素有关,因此,精确确定船舶或漂流物与桥梁的相互作用力十分困难。”

(4)“从实际情况看,在航道顺直、桥位较正的情况下,船舶或漂流物与桥梁发生正面撞击的机会很小,斜向撞击桥梁墩台的较多。一般斜向撞击的角度 α 小于 45°。当桥位与航道斜交时,正向与斜向撞击墩台的可能性均存在。由于撞击角度不容易预先确定,故在计算撞击作用时,应根据具体情况加以研究确定。”

(5)“总体而言,对于船舶与桥梁撞击力的计算,各国学者通过实验模型分析或结构计算分析,总结而得的计算方法不尽相同,这些试验或计算公式的结果出入也很大。在实际桥梁设计中,应综合考虑船桥相撞的各种因素,通过多方面比较之后再作确定。”

3 公路桥涵设计通用规范 4.4.2 节运用时的问题

3.1 用表格中固定的船撞力作为计算依据是不妥的

规范中列上这些表格的原因,似是受了 20 多年前的沃以信(Woisin)公式的影响:沃以信公式中只有一个变量,表达为:“船撞力仅与船的大小有关。”因其考虑因素太少,目前国外已经不采用了——1983 年诺特(Knott)提出必须对索尔(Saul)和沃以信(Woisin)的公式加以修正[2],在公式中加上速度变量 v,即将:

$$P_{\max} = 0.88(DWT)^{1/2} \pm 50\% \quad [\text{沃以信公式}]$$

改为:

$$P_{\max} = 0.88(DWT)^{1/2} \cdot (v/8)^{2/3} \quad [\text{诺特-索尔-格林那公式}]$$

20 年来人们使用的有船重(DWT)和船速(v)两个主要参数的公式有 5 个[2]。仅有船重(DWT)一个变量的公式基本上已不用了。

由于两物体相撞时的碰撞力不仅与物体大小有关,且与两物体相撞的速度有直接关系。公路桥涵设计通用规范中 4.4.2 节中,两个船舶撞击作用力的表(4.4.2.1;4.4.2.2)仅与船舶大小有关,不反映速度是不妥的。

该节中所列计算排筏撞击力的公式,已经考虑到船重(DWT)和船速(v)两个因素,所以说:表格相对公式是一种倒退。

3.2 船撞桥墩的力不因船只在海上或河上航行而变化

2004 年的公路桥涵设计通用规范规定,同一艘船(航速相同)出海口前撞上桥墩力就小;出了海口后,撞上桥墩力就大。

对船撞桥墩的力进行近似估算时,规范的公式表明,该力随船的质量和速度而变,不因在海或河中而变。例如,同一艘 3 000 t 在海河联运航线的船只,出海口前撞上桥墩,其作用力为 1 400 kN(表 4.4.2.1);出了海口后撞上桥墩,其作用力为 19 600 kN(表 4.4.2.2);

竟然相差 14 倍！是解释不通的。

3.3 船撞桥墩的力不能因桥墩的结构形式是“钢筋混凝土桩墩”而减半

大家都知道船撞桥墩的力是受桥墩刚度影响的。当其他条件不变且刚度相同时，船撞力也相同，所以不能一遇到钢筋混凝土桩墩就减半。

3.4 公式中的时间很难确定

公路桥涵设计通用规范 4.4.2 的公式 $FT = mv$ 是从牛顿力学的冲量公式来的。撞击过程时间 T 直接影响 F 的大小，此 T 值在小船或大船相差很远，且与碰撞的两种材料有关，不宜用一个数值。从国内有关试验的一组数据（见表 1）也说明了这一情况。

表 1　模拟船头撞上桥墩及防撞装置的撞击过程时间试验数据[2]

Table 1　Impact time list by crash test used to simulate ship-pier or ship-device crash[2]

序	相撞的一方（模拟船头）	相撞的另一方（模拟桥墩及防撞装置）	撞击过程时间/s
1	钢	刚性（钢筋混凝土）	0.051 ~ 0.084
2	钢	弹性（鼓形橡胶碰垫）	0.13 ~ 0.14
3	钢	黏性（柔性耗能防撞圈）	0.29 ~ 0.65

由上表可以看出，公路桥涵设计通用规范 4.4.2 所载：“在无实际资料时可用 1 s，”对不设防撞装置的桥墩（大多为圬工结构）而言，此值显然偏大，将导致碰撞力算小了。

既然确定撞击过程时间 T 如此困难，而同样根据牛顿力学导出来的还有一个没有 T 的公式用起来可能更方便一些。这个公式就是铁路桥涵设计基本规范（TB 10002.1—99）4.4.6 节的船撞力公式。它又隐性地反映了碰撞时间这个因子。我们对这个公式再做些延伸补充，建议可作为公路和铁路两个桥涵设计规范计算船撞桥的力使用的统一公式。

4 各国桥涵设计规范中船撞力公式的比较

由于两物体撞击的力与两物体相撞时的速度有直接关系，欧洲和美洲公路设计规范或指南的公式中，能将速度作为变量与质量平行地代入进行计算的有 3 个公式[2]，加上我国公路和铁路规范中的公式（式中均有质量和速度作为变量），这样便有 5 个公式。

对这 5 个公式的原理进行验证，对公式中可代入的各变量的具体数值进行分析、搜集、统计，对各公式间的差异进行协调，便可利用我国及世界上已有的研究成就，发展出解决问题的方法，求出船对桥的正撞力（即规范中的横桥向力）。

船撞墩后镶住不动的正撞力是一个理论上的最大值，如果不让船镶住不动，动能便会保留在船上，而不是全部参与交换，关键是怎样让船撞上之后不镶住，拨开船头让船继续前进。例如桥墩两头作成 60°，正撞变成 30°斜撞，船撞力减半了，船头也不易镶住。

这 5 个公式中，能以具体数值代入的变量有多有少？列于表 2。

表 2　　5 个常用公式的变量表

Table 2　　**Variables of five commonly used formulas**

序号	公 式 名 称	变量数	变 量
1	公路桥涵设计通用规范[8]	2 *	M, v
2	铁路桥涵设计基本规范[7]	5 **	M, v, γ, C_1, C_2
3	敏诺斯基-捷勒-沃以信(Minorsky, Gerlach, Woisin)	2	M, v
4	索尔-诺特-格林那(Saul-Svelsson, Knott, Greiner)	2	M, v
5	美国各州公路和运输工作者协会(AASHTO)	2	M, v

*：规范说明此公式使用于漂流物和排筏。

**：此式还有考虑斜撞的角度变量 $\sin\alpha$,本文仅讨论正撞力故未列入。

5 推荐我国公路-铁路桥涵设计规范共同采用的撞击力公式[4]

墩台承受船只或排筏的撞击力可按下式计算[4]：

$$F = \gamma v \sin\alpha [W/(C_1 + C_2 + C_3)]^{0.5}$$

式中：F——撞击力,kN；

γ——动能折减系数($s/m^{0.5}$)；当船只或排筏斜向撞击墩台(指船只或排筏驶近方向与撞击点处墩台面法线方向不一致)时可采用 0.2,正向撞击(指船只或排筏驶近方向与撞击点墩台面处法线方向一致)时可用 0.3；

v——船只或排筏撞击墩台时的速度(m/s)。此项速度对于船只采用航运部门提供的数据,对于排筏可采用筏运期的水流速度；

α——船只或排筏驶近方向与墩台撞击点处切线所成的夹角,应根据具体情况确定,如有困难,可采用 $\alpha = 20°$；

W——船只重*或排筏重,kN；

C_1——船只或排筏的弹性变形系数(m/kN)；

C_2——墩台圬工的弹件变形系数(m/kN)；

C_3——防撞装置的弹件变形系数(m/kN)；

*：船只重系船只排水量和附连水之和。

此公式也是从牛顿力学来的,在[6]中已讨论了它的推导过程,各参数每一项的物理意义和 γ 的冲击动力学意义。在[4]中已阐明将此公式延伸加入 C_3的过程。

对 C_1, C_2, C_3等参数进行系列计算后即可列成附表,以供广大桥梁工作者查用。表 3 和表 4 提供 C_1, C_2的算例,设计人可按照实桥工况计算、选用。而 C_3可由防撞装置设计人计算提供。

表 3　　模拟计算的船头平均弹性系数 C_1

Table 3　　Average elastic coefficient C_1 of the bow for simulation calculation

序号	船　　型	排水量 /t	撞击初速度 /m·s^{-1}	最大力 /MN	变形 /m	船头平均弹性系数* C_1/m·kN^{-1}
1	79.54 m 客船	2 510	5.35	9.23	2.29	0.000 25
2	5 000 吨级多用途船	9 839	5.0	46.8	5.40	0.000 12
3	万吨级散货船	18 917	5.0	56.5	6.85	0.000 12
4	万吨级集装箱船	17 670	3.0	16.5	0.77	0.000 047
5	3.5 万吨级散货船	45 807	5.0	97.5	9.11	0.000 093
6	6.5 万吨级油轮	76 189	5.0	290.0	6.44	0.000 022

* 由于船撞桥动态力的局域性，所以船头刚度也与动态参数（例如速度）有关。

表 4　　桥墩吸能刚度系数 C_2 算例

Table 4　　Example list of energy absorbtion and stiffness coefficient C_2 for piers

序　号	桥　名	桥墩型式	桥墩水平抗力 /MN	桥墩位移 /cm	桥墩吸能 /kJ	C_2 /m·kN^{-1}
算例 1	武汉长江一桥	连续梁桥的混凝土墩	10.1	0.8	40	0.000 000 8
算例 2	湛江海湾大桥	斜拉桥的高桩承台	30.0	3.0	450	0.000 001 0

注：算例 1 的衡准是桥墩的危险截面的最大应力值小于第一级应力（第一级应力指该截面不出现拉应力）。

6　总结

（1）在一座桥梁设计的初期，采用近似公式法对船撞力进行估算是必要的，且要便于使用。因此，在规范中选择优良的船撞力近似（半经验）公式，就显得非常必要了。

（2）以现行的公路桥涵设计通用规范 4.4.2 的方法来选用或计算墩台承受船只或排筏的撞击力是不合理的。建议放弃这些表和公式。另以一个也是从牛顿力学导出的公式替代之。

（3）作者认为采用本文推荐的公式较为合理可行。它与原来的公式也同出于牛顿力学。推荐的公式考虑了船撞力的 7 个因素：船的质量、船的速度、船与墩相撞的角度、船与墩相撞时的能量耗散、船的刚度、桥墩的刚度和防撞装置的刚度。应是现有的船撞力近似（半经验）公式中能够考虑相撞过程参数最多的一个公式。其计算结果更接近实际工况。

（4）采用本文推荐的公式则可把我国公路和铁路两个桥梁规范中的船撞力公式统一起来，也为建设公-铁两用桥梁创造了有利的条件。

（5）为使从业人员能便捷正确的使用此公式，需编制公式中 C_1，C_2，C_3 各参数数值的表格附于规范公式之后，便于在计算时查用。

（6）当桥梁所处的航道或港口设有指导船只航行的“船舶航行服务系统”（VTS）：并

且通过桥梁的巨型船只装有完善通讯导航设施,它们将大大减少船舶的偏航角度,进而在设计防撞装置时,研究取消正撞、减小侧撞角的可能性,调整相应的参数,最终降低船舶与桥墩碰撞的概率。

(7) 船对桥墩的侧撞力不在本文讨论之内。铁路桥涵设计规范中的船撞力计算公式内也有斜撞角度因子 α。也可参考文献[3]的讨论进行厘定、计算或修正。

参 考 文 献

[1] 项海帆,范立础,王君杰. 船撞桥设计理论的现状与需进一步研究的问题[J]. 同济大学学报,2002(4).

[2] 陈国虞. 船对桥墩的正撞力[C]. 第十五届全国桥梁学术会议论文集. 上海: 同济大学出版社,2002: 222-227.

[3] 陈国虞,沈文玮. 船对桥墩的侧撞力[C]. 第十五届全国桥梁学术会议论文集. 上海: 同济大学出版社,2002: 228-232.

[4] 陈国虞. 有防撞装置时计算船撞桥的力——铁路桥梁规范中船撞力公式的延伸修订[C]. 铁道标准设计,2004(1).

[5] 汪克来,宋玉祥. 关于桥梁船舶撞击力的设计与计算初探[R].(铜陵长江大桥管理局)

[6] 王礼立. 船撞桥的钢丝绳圈柔性防撞装置的冲击动力学分析[M]. 应用力学进展. 北京: 科学出版社,2004.

[7] 中华人民共和国铁道部. 墩台承受船只或排筏的撞击力 TB10002.1—99. 铁路桥涵设计基本规范[S]4.4.6 节. 北京: 中国铁道出版社,2000.

[8] 中华人民共和国交通部. 船舶或漂流物的撞击作用. 公路桥涵设计通用规范[S]4.4.2 节. 北京: 人民交通出版社,2004.

[9] 国际桥梁和结构工程协会(IABSE). 交通船只与桥梁结构的相互影响[R](1993). 广东虎门技术咨询公司译,1995.

[10] 陆宗林. 一种新型的柔性吸能防撞装置[C]. 中国公路学会 2004 年全国桥梁学术会议论文集. 北京: 人民交通出版社,2004.

发表于: 中国土木工程学会第十七届全国桥梁学术会议论文集[M]. 北京: 人民交通出版社,2006.

Published at: CCES Proceeding of the 17th symposium of bridges. Beijing: China Communications Press, 2006.

6个桥梁防船撞指南比较研究

The comparative study between six guides of defends collision of ship with bridge

陈国虞
（上海海洋钢结构研究所，上海 201204）
CHEN Guoyu
（Shanghai Marine Steel and Structure Research Institute, Shanghai 201204, China）

摘　要　为了更好地丰富和发展中国的桥梁防船撞设计指南，学习了"欧洲规范"EN1991－1－7(2006)，它是一个对结构受到各种冲击外载产生响应的全面规定，其中有一部分谈到船撞桥；也学习了美国各州公路和运输工作者协会(AASHTO)的"公路桥船撞设计指南"(2009)，它是一个基于载荷与抗力系数设计法，对桥梁防船撞进行设计的指南，它的概率估算方法已载入美国公路桥梁设计规范中。其他三个是北京、上海和重庆三家研究单位的研究报告或征求意见稿。在船撞上桥的速度、船撞桥概率、全桥防撞问题和防船撞对桥梁设计的要求等几个问题上，将我国最早出版的指南(企业标准)与上述几个桥梁防船撞指南作比较。

关键词　桥梁防船撞　桥梁防船撞设计指南　欧洲规范　美国指南　比较研究

Abstract: For the development of our design guide, we study the *European norm* EN1991－1－7(2006), it is an overall provision that the structure is subjected to various impact to carry a creation to respond, within this standard have a part to speak of the ship collision with bridge. The *Vessel Collision Design of Highway Bridge* (2009) is a guide of AASHTO. It based on the loading and resistance coefficient method, and its probability calculation method had been write in the design code of American high way. And the other three guides are the study report or the exposure draft of the institute on Beijing, Shanghai and Chongqing. This paper discussion the different and similar between these five guides to a standardize document published by

a home institute on the four field: the collision speed of ship with bridge pier; probability of collision and collapse; whole bridge (all the piers in the water) to defend the ship collision and the demands from defend the ship collision to the bridge design.

Keywords: bridges defend ship collision, design guide of defend collision vessel with bridge, European norm, American guide, comparative studies

1 前言

中国的桥梁设计规范,包括铁路桥和公路桥的规范,都对桥梁防船撞有一定的要求:铁路桥梁规范要求设计桥墩具有足够的水平抗力,规范中给出了计算船撞力的公式,我们曾在多种场合推荐这个公式。代入这个公式的参数需要认真选择,我们曾为使用这个公式的人提供了多个供选参数表[1]。公路桥梁规范中有 6 处提出桥梁防船撞的要求[2],首先是墩台轴线应与主流方向一致,通航净空和桥孔布置应满足"通航标准",还规定船撞力作为偶然作用 100% 地加入永久作用和可变作用进行计算,考虑流水压力和流冰压力和船舶及漂流物的撞击力,给出了撞击力的计算公式,我们为这个公式需要的时间参数也提供了一个数据表,最后明确规定可能遭受大型船舶撞击的桥墩应设置防撞设施。除了这 2 个必须遵守的规范之外,中国另有 4 个指南,还从国外引入 2 个指南。

欧洲规范 EN1991 - 1 - 7(2006)是一个关于结构受到各种冲击外载产生响应的全面规定,其中有一部分谈到船撞桥[3]。

美国各州公路和运输工作者协会(AASHTO)的"公路桥船撞设计指南"(2009 年第二版,其第一版发布于 1991 年)是一个基于载荷与抗力系数设计法对桥梁防船撞进行设计的指南,它的概率估算方法已载入美国公路桥梁设计规范中,它比较全面,且可操作性强[4]。

中国最早的桥梁防船撞设计指南是一个企业标准(标准化文件的最低一级)。始于 2002 的《桥墩的船撞力计算及柔性防撞装置设计指南(征求意见稿)》,当时是作为一个设计乙方向甲方说明一种黏滞性高耗能柔性防船撞装置设计所遵循的方法。到 2005 年成为上海海洋钢结构研究所的企业标准《桥墩的船撞力计算及柔性耗能防撞装置设计指南(2005)》,于 2006 年由中国铁道出版社出版[7]。后经过广东湛江海湾大桥 5 年的使用和修改,成为《桥梁的柔性防船撞装置设计指南(2008)》。近两年经过铁路安庆长江大桥的使用和修改,最新版本为《桥墩的船撞力计算及柔性防撞装置设计指南(QB/HY02—2012)》,于 2013 年发表在《桥梁防撞理论和防撞装置设计》中[9]。

2010 年,招商局重庆交通科研设计有限公司提出了《重庆市三峡库区跨江桥梁船撞设计指南(征求意见稿)》;2011 年,同济大学提出了《桥梁船撞性能设计样板指南》;2013 年,中交公路规划设计院有限公司提出了《公路桥梁抗撞防撞设计指南(送审稿)》。

本文对这 6 个标准和指南作对比研究,先谈 5 个问题,最后提出建议。

2 关于船撞墩的速度

美国(AASHTO)指南中指出,航道上船舶的航行速度应能反映诸如风、水流、能见度、迎面来船以及航道的几何尺度等典型条件。对于选择船只的“典型”航速,该指南规定,船撞速度在航道范围内为正常速度;航道范围以外,船撞速度随桥墩距航道中线的距离而正比下降,即撞速呈线性降低(见图1)。将该方法用于天然航道上的桥梁,难以反映“美国指南”所述(如风、水流、能见度、迎面来船以及航道的几何尺度等)诸因素。

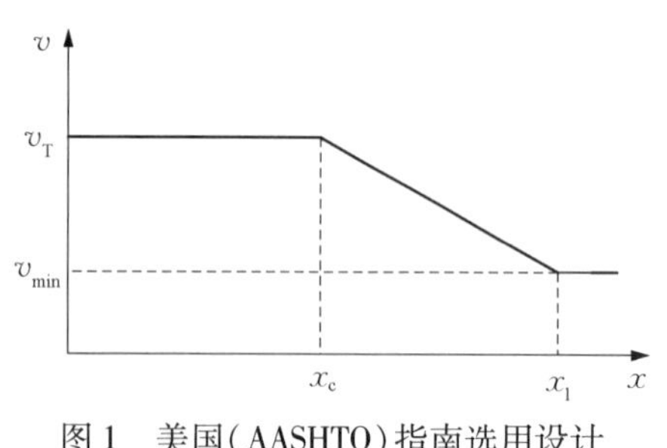

图1 美国(AASHTO)指南选用设计撞击速度分布图

Fig. 1 Design impact speed (from AASHTO 2009)

实际上,船速由静水航速与流速合成(流速有方向:内河有流向、港湾有潮汐、大海有洋流),流速有水工部门实测数值,静水速度应取在该航段操船者(大副等)经常采用的速度。船撞桥墩的速度,应采用船的静水速度与墩位处流速叠加,方向与船对桥墩的相对位置有关。

图1中,美国指南 x_1 为距离航道中线3倍船长,如果航道的宽度与 x_1 差不多,则与实测的误差可能不大(比较窄的内河航道,或者河渠化的港湾航道)。若是天然的大江大河,差别就比较大了。

桥位处水工部门实测流速数值举例如下:2006年10月28日,长江委员会长江下游水文水资源勘测局对某桥区河段进行了水文测验工作,将墩位标在图上便得到各墩位处的流速。水文测验结果如下:测时水位为5.32 m,测时流量为16 700 m^3/s。所测得桥位流速分布如图2所示。

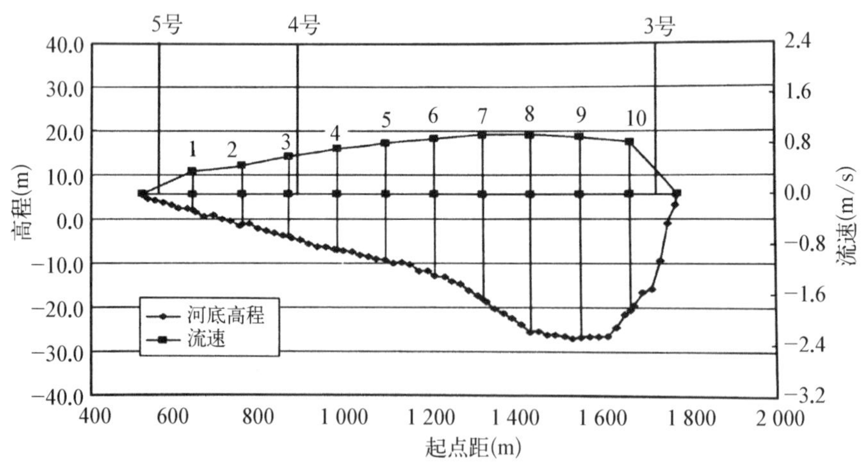

图2 某铁路长江大桥桥位实测流速和水深

Fig. 2 The actual measurements of the flow velocity and water depth at a railway bridge on Yangtze River

分别按照美国(ASSHTO)指南推荐的船速折减方法和中国考虑流速折减的方法得出船舶撞击速度沿桥向分布比较如图 3 所示。图中坐标原点表示桥梁主跨的中心。

进行桥墩防撞设计时,船舶撞击速度是计算船撞力的重要参数之一,它直接影响到船撞力的大小和桥梁的设防标准。在分析各国船舶撞击桥墩的速度选取方法的基础上,我们曾研究了实际发生船撞时的速度和船舶偏航时船撞速度沿横向的变化趋势,指出了目前世界各国所使用的五种方法存在的不足,提出了考虑船撞速度沿桥轴线方向的分布及船舶意外失速等因素综合影响下的撞击速度的计算方法[10]。

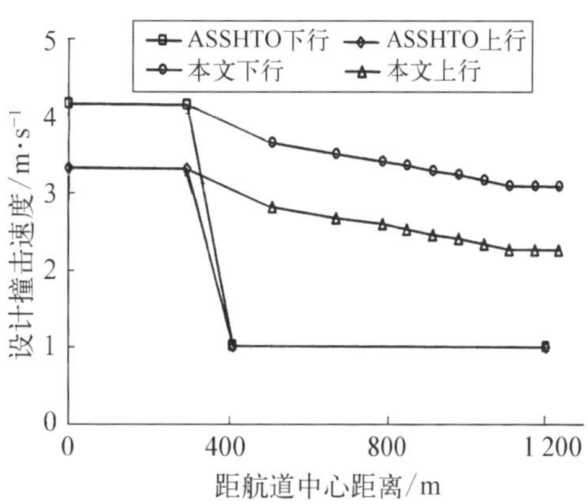

图 3　某长江大桥船舶撞击速度沿桥向分布图

Fig. 3　The distribution diagram of design impact speed along the bridge direction at a railway bridge on Yangtze River

3　关于撞上和撞塌

船在桥下和桥墩边上走了几百几千次,撞上桥墩(或桥上的梁)一两次,这是一个概率问题。但撞上之后倒塌不倒塌,则取决于船撞力大小和桥梁抵抗水平力的结构强度,例如武汉长江大桥(图 4)有记录的被撞 70 余次,没有撞塌;有的桥(例如图 5)结构强度不足,一撞就塌。这不是一个概率问题。

图 4　武汉长江大桥被撞第 70 次(钢笔画)

Fig. 4　The 70th times impacted of Wuhan Yangtze Bridge (pen drawing)

图 5　美国第 40 号州际公路阿肯色河桥

Fig. 5　The 40# interstate highway bridge at Arkansas River

在讨论船舶和漂流物撞击时,先讨论受各种因素的影响而撞上的可能性,即撞上概率。撞上之后倒塌与不倒塌视其撞击力大小及结构强度而定。后者是一个现代工程计算能够解决的问题,撞击力大于该方向上的强度,桥便塌了,反之则不塌。这是必然事件,不是概率问题。

既不需要专门的数学术语,也不需要繁深的公式推导,便可以讲清楚这个道理。

用来表示随机事件 A 发生的可能性大小的量,称为此事件的概率(见《辞海》)。概率用 $P(A)$ 表示,必然事件的概率为 1,即 $P(A)=1$;不可能事件的概率为 0,即 $P(A)=0$。

随机事件是指在一定条件下可能发生也可能不发生的事情。它需要满足 3 个条件:

(1) 重复性——试验可以在相同的情形下重复进行;

(2) 可知性——试验的所有结果都是明确的,并且不止一个;

(3) 随机性——每次试验总是恰好出现这些结果中的一个,但在一次试验之前却不能肯定这次试验会出现哪一个结果。

当小船撞大桥墩,例如美国旧金山跨海湾大桥的大桥墩(包括悬索桥的锚墩),承台边上装有钢木结构的格栅护舷,将船撞坏了而桥墩无损;杭州市内的京杭运河多座桥梁,桥墩被撞出几十道痕迹,却仍一直在使用;武汉长江大桥建桥后 53 年间被撞了 70 多次,伤痕最深的一次,混凝土墩被刮出 2.0 m 长、0.15 m 深的伤,也没有影响火车通行,这些都是 $P(A)=0$。

撞上了塌不塌是必然事件　船在桥下和桥墩边上走几百几千次,撞上桥(是受各种因素影响才发生的)是一种随机事件、偶然事件,所以讨论其概率,可以称为撞上概率。

一旦撞上之后桥倒塌不倒塌,这是可以通过现代工程力学计算的,结构能抵御的水平力和船撞力都是可以计算出来的。

当结构能抵御的水平力 > 船撞力,即美国指南用的(结构能抵御的水平力/船撞力) >1,这时虽撞上而不倒。

当结构能抵御的水平力 < 船撞力,即美国指南用的(结构能抵御的水平力/船撞力) <1,这时撞上就垮塌了。

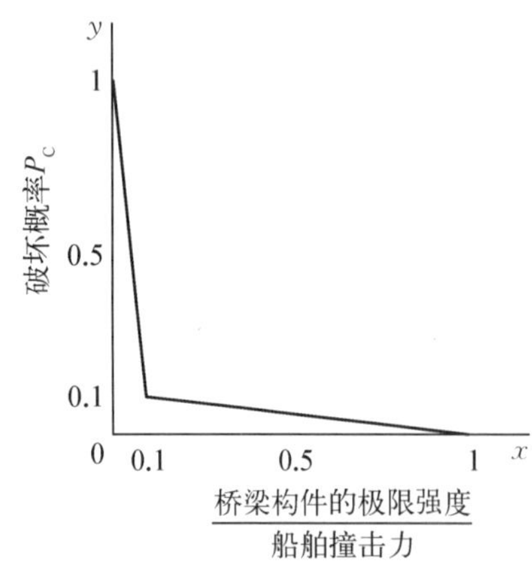

图 6　美国公路规范 3.14 节中构件破坏概率 P_C 分布

Fig. 6　Probability of collapse distribution in the section 3.14 of specification of American highway

由于材料力学、结构力学和其他工程力学学科发展的结果,可以算得比较准确,工程材料生产和施工质量的现有水平,使桥梁强度性能比较均衡,这样上述式中的力,能够算出确定的量,所发生的是必然事件,不具有随机性,因而不是概率问题。

1998 年,我国出版了美国《公路桥梁设计规范(1991)》的中译本。该规范第 3.14 节认为,桥梁船撞力大于桥墩抗撞能力时,还会有桥墩被撞塌的概率。它采用图 6 所示分布的倒塌概率,用 P_C 表示,即当桥梁构件强度大于船舶撞击力时,$P_C=0$;当桥梁构件强度介于船舶撞击力的 10% 和 100% 之间时,P_C 在 0 到 0.1 之间线性变化;当桥梁构件强度小于船撞力的 10% 时,P_C 在 0.1 到 1 之间线性变化。

可以看出,上述美国公路规范的处理中:x 坐标上的交点(1, 0)是说桥梁构件的强度能经受撞击力,因此船撞时桥不坏($P_C=0$),这是大家能接受的;y 坐标上交点(0, 1)是说桥梁构件强度为零,一撞就塌($P_C=1$),这也是大家所能接受的。

中间一个交点(0.1, 0.1)是说当桥梁构件只能承受船撞力的0.1时撞塌概率为0.1,即一座强度只有船撞力1/10的桥梁撞塌概率为0.1(撞十次塌一次),此处有一点违背常识。质疑者认为此交点没有依据,当桥梁构件强度小于船撞力非常多时,一撞就塌(这是必然的),这样撞塌概率就不是0.1,而应该是1.0。

船撞力虽然受多种因素的影响,包括船舶尺度和形式、船首形状及船首舱压载、船舶行驶速度、撞击方向及撞击质量等,并且与防撞装置的种类、防撞装置降低船撞力的程度等有关;桥墩的抗撞强度与设计的抗撞能力(包括:形式、大小和选材等)及其建造质量有关。在现今工程力学和工程设计计算中,两者都是可以得到确定数值的。

在计算得出桥梁的船撞力以及桥墩的设计抗撞能力两者的确定数值后,便可以评价发生单次撞击时桥墩的破坏。

当桥墩强度不足,例如只能够抵受的水平力为船撞力的0.9时,一撞就倒,等不到出现第二次撞击,因此不是一个多次出现的事件,不是一个概率问题。

4 桥梁防撞设计研究应该在桥梁设计的方案阶段进行

当桥梁设计单位接受用户提出的桥梁设计要求时,就开始考虑桥位和桥型,如果桥下有航线就应该考虑包括《铁路桥涵设计基本规范》和《公路桥涵设计通用规范》中各章节所包含的防船撞要求。应及时研究该航线、航段的水流和船舶运输情况,并应对船型发展规划、河道整治规划和港口建设规划尽可能地掌握或推算。发现桥位、桥型、桥跨选择对防船撞不合理时,应及早向用户提出修改建议(包括重新考虑桥位、桥型和桥跨等)。

为了符合桥梁防撞的要求,桥梁设计人必须在考虑永久作用的同时也考虑可变作用和偶然作用,必须在计算桥墩垂向力的同时也考虑足够的水平抗力。船舶受各种因素影响会偏航,在丰水期会驶到距离岸边较近的水域,特殊情况下还会撞上航道两侧离航道中心较远的桥墩,因而要求设计人增大桥梁跨距,减少桥墩数量,将水域尽量多地留给原来的航道。减少桥墩数量,必然会加强桥墩,从而提高每个桥墩的水平抗力。在方案设计阶段,估算出船撞力,让该船撞力传到桥墩时小于桥墩能够抵受的水平力,否则就应该加大桥墩或更改桥型,让桥墩能够抵受的水平力大于该船撞力传到桥墩时的值。

很明显,要增大桥梁跨距,减少桥墩数量,要尽量多地将原来的水面留给航道,就必须从桥型选择开始考虑。因此,桥梁防船撞问题应该在桥梁设计的方案阶段开始加以论证和设计。向用户提出的桥梁防船撞意义和建议,还应该从船桥互利相安、社会持续发展的观点,提出合理而充分的建议。

例如,1995 年建成的长江黄石公路桥,桥位选择在河流转弯处,对桥梁防船撞很不利。2010 年在其上游 926 m 处重新选择桥位,建成新桥,新桥位离开弯道,处于河流相对平直段。该桥1994年选择的桥型是混凝土连续刚构桥，主跨通航净宽为220 m，此桥型也不适应"船撞桥"形势严峻的桥位，所以发生了将驳船队撞散的事故。后重新选择桥型，建成一跨过江的斜拉桥——鄂东长江大桥。建一座长江大桥仅用15年就被取代，充分说明桥梁防船撞必须在其方案论证阶段加以充分考虑。

我国的桥梁防撞设计指南[7,8]都指出了这一点。

《公路桥梁抗撞防撞设计指南（送审稿）》中有桥梁防船撞总体设计一章，其中包括基本原则、桥位选择、桥轴线布置、桥梁类型、通航跨净空、非通航孔防撞和保护系统等内容。该指南指出"保护桥……还要适当减缓船舶损伤"（实际上我国已经做到不仅能减缓船舶损伤而且能够在万一船舶撞上之后仍然能够拨开船头，船舶完好无损），值得称赞。

关于桥梁防船撞总体设计一章，应该由起草单位提出，（学习美国的做法）写入桥梁设计规范中，由桥梁的总体设计师加以贯彻。

5 全桥防撞问题

路、桥和涵洞等组成一条公路运输线，只要其中一个环节出现问题，该公路运输线即中断。要想公路运输线有效，则主桥墩、辅助墩、水中引桥墩和上部结构的每一处都不能垮塌。因此各部分对防船撞的能力应该相当，不能一处大一处小。都有被船撞的可能性的环节，就不能一处设防而另一处不设防。

5.1 设计研究防船撞的机构应该适时提出全桥防撞的建议

用户提出防撞设计要求后，设计研究机构应及时研究该航线、航段的水流和船舶运输的情况，并对船型发展规划、河道整治规划和港口建设规划尽可能掌握或推算（很多情况是并没有百年规划），发现桥型、桥跨选择对防船撞不合理时，应及早向用户提出修改建议。

向用户提出的桥梁防船撞建议，应该包括《铁路桥涵设计基本规范》或《公路桥涵设计通用规范》中各章节所包含的防船撞要求，还应该从船桥互利相安、社会持续发展的观点，提出合理而充分的建议（即必要和充分两方面）。

5.2 柔性耗能防撞装置和绳索耗能柔性拦船装置

跨海湾（河湾、海峡等）的长桥，通常由主通航孔、辅通航孔、水中引桥和滩地引桥等组成。

主通航孔水比较深，高墩高塔投资较大，而且通航净宽比较宝贵，因此对柔性防撞装置降低船撞力的要求较迫切；辅通航孔、水中引桥孔等水比较浅，通航的船较小，一般要求的水平抗力相对较小。

主通航孔一般可采用有柔性防撞圈的防撞装置。水中引桥很长时，可以设置拦船装置，较早采用的如浙江朱家尖桥和杭州湾跨海大桥的钢链拦船装置；也可以设置绳索耗能柔性拦船装置[11]，如福建平潭海峡大桥采用的芳纶混合纤维拦船装置等。

6 桥梁防撞指南的使用对象

既然要求桥梁的总设计师在桥梁开始酝酿建设时，只要是跨过航线的桥就考虑防船撞问题，那么桥梁防船撞设计的原则性意见就应该是提供给桥梁的总设计师用的，因此桥梁防船撞的设计指南应该写入桥梁的设计规范。例如美国就将其列入桥梁设计规范，成为桥梁设计规范中的一节："3.14 节　船只撞击 CV"。

在整个桥梁的设计规范中，桥梁防船撞的设计仅是整个设计的一小部分，因此桥梁防船撞的指南应该写得简洁而易于操作。

7 总结

粗浅地进行对比研究后，有以下几点认识。

(1) 欧洲规范是一个关于结构受到各种冲击外载产生响应的全面规定，其中有一部分谈到船撞桥。涉及这一部分的规定是以冲击动力学作为理论支持的，相信其所给出的数据的后面应该有足够的计算作为依据。

(2) 美国指南比较全面，且"可操作性"强，更为可贵的是指南的核心部分已被列入美国公路桥梁设计规范中，非常值得我们学习。

但是美国指南的规定在某些方面与中国国情不符，应继续探讨：关于桥梁分为重要和一般，并分别给出"设"和"不设"防撞装置的标准；船撞墩速度简化选取；过分简化的船撞力公式；年撞塌概率的概念；关于驳船的参数等。

建议在现行的《铁路桥涵设计基本规范》和《公路桥涵设计通用规范》已有的 6 点关于防御船撞桥的规定的基础上，吸收《公路桥梁抗撞防撞设计指南》的优点，参考美国指南的做法写成一节，以便于贯彻。该节可称为"跨航线桥梁防船撞设计"。包含如下内容。

(1) 桥位选择。桥位宜避免处于弯道、汊道、险滩、分流口、汇流口、港口作业区、锚地等区域。

(2) 把尽量多的水面留给航道。桥梁设计跨越航线时，应该不碍航，主槽不设墩，把尽量多的水面留给航道。桥梁的通航净空应经过充分论证后设计，净空应该尽量大，地情和水情适合时，应选择一跨过江。

(3) 桥梁轴线与水流流向应垂直。跨越主槽的桥梁，其轴线与水流流向夹角不宜超过 5°。

(4) 通航河流桥梁墩台应设计成尖形或流线型。位于通航河流或有漂流物的河流中的桥梁墩台，设计时应考虑船舶或漂流物的撞击作用，其平面形状应设计成尖形或流线型。

(5) 可能遭受大型船舶撞击的桥墩应设置保护桥和船的防撞设施。可能遭受大型船

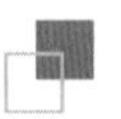

舶撞击作用的桥墩,应根据桥墩自身抗撞击能力、桥墩的位置和外形、水流流速、水位变化、通航船舶类型和碰撞速度等因素,作桥墩防撞设施的设计。防撞设施应考虑能够同时保护桥和船,从而也保护环境。

(6) 撞击力作为一种偶然载荷100%地计入水平力。船的撞击力作为一种偶然载荷,与永久作用和可变作用相结合时,规范规定是以其标准值计入的。规范原文是:“与其他作用相结合时采用:永久作用标准值效应与可变作用某种代表值效应、一种偶然作用标准值效应相结合。”

(7) 设计船撞力的选定。在桥梁规划开始时,可用经验公式或线图估算,初步设计有图纸后可用数值法计算,有条件时可用试验验证。各种方法得出的船撞力数值应当足够接近。

参考文献

[1] TB10002.1—2005. 铁路桥涵设计基本规范[S]. 北京:中国铁道出版社,2005.

[2] JTG D60—2004. 公路桥涵设计通用规范[S]. 北京:人民交通出版社,2004.

[3] 英标 BS EN1991-1-7 欧洲规范 Eurocode 1 结构作用 总体作用 偶然作用,2006.

[4] AASHTO. 公路桥梁船撞设计指南(第二版)[S]. 华盛顿:美国各州公路和运输工作者协会,2009.

[5] 王福敏,等. 重庆市三峡库区跨江桥梁船撞设计指南(征求意见稿)[S]. 重庆:招商局重庆交通科研设计有限公司,2010.

[6] 王君杰,等. 桥梁船撞性能设计样板指南[S]. 上海:同济大学,2011.

[7] 上海海洋钢结构研究所. 桥墩的船撞力计算及柔性耗能防撞装置设计指南(QB/HY02—2012)[S]//桥梁防撞理论和防撞装置设计[M]. 北京:人民交通出版社,2013.

[8] 赵君黎,等. 公路桥梁抗撞防撞设计指南(送审稿)[S]. 北京:中交公路规划设计院有限公司,2013.

[9] 陈国始. 浅谈用概率论研究船撞桥的几个方法问题[C]//中国土木工程学会桥梁及结构工程分会. 第十七届全国桥梁学术会议论文集. 北京:人民交通出版社,2006:1253.

[10] 陈国虞,陈明栋,郑丹. 计算船撞力选择撞击速度时考虑墩位流速的方法[J]. 广东造船,2010,(3):33-37.

[11] 陈国虞,倪步友,张澄,等. 跨海湾(河湾)桥非通航孔柔性拦船防撞装置[J]. 广东造船,2011,30(1):38-41.

发表于:国际船桥相撞及其防护学术研讨会论文集[M].
北京:中国铁道出版社,2014:17-23.
Published at: Proceedings of International Symposium on Ship-Bridge Collision and its Protection. China Railway Press, 2014: 17-23.

“防御船撞桥事故”研究中的概率问题

Probability analysis in “anti-collision accident between ship and bridge” research

陈国虞[1]　陈国始[2]

（1. 上海海洋钢结构研究所，上海 201204；2. 原长沙理工大学，长沙 410000）

CHEN Guoyu[1], CHEN Guoshi[2]

(1. Shanghai Marine Steel and Structure Research Institute, Shanghai 201204, China;
2. Changsha University of Science & Technology, Changsha 410000, China)

摘　要　船撞桥有概率问题，肯定了文献中对“撞上概率”的分析，但对文献中的“撞塌概率”经过分析后认为，其概念值得质疑。船撞桥的撞上概率问题可以用概率方法去分析，但船撞桥研究中的“撞上概率”分析与其他学科的概率分析比较，是既缺乏实际数据的积累也欠缺概率分布的理论。因此，目前还不能仅以概率分析就说此桥应作防撞装置或可不作防撞装置。其次，撞塌不是概率问题。船在桥下和桥墩边上走了几百甚至几千次，撞上桥墩或船顶上的桥梁一两次，这是一个概率问题。但撞上之后倒塌不倒塌，取决于船撞力的大小和桥梁抵御水平力的结构强度。有的桥被撞70余次没有撞塌，有的桥却因结构强度不足一撞便塌，这本来就不是一个概率问题。从正面说明以否定1998年从国外传入的一个协会指南，认为撞塌是一个概率问题，并给出示意线图，归纳借鉴而来的“应保尽保”方法取代仅“以概率分析决定建与不建防撞装置”。

关键词　桥梁毁塌　撞塌　概率　必然事件　“应保尽保”原则

Abstract: Ship-bridge collision is a problem with probability. This paper approves the analysis of “collision probability” in the literatures and questions the concept of “rammed probability”. The ship-bridge collision probability can be analyzed by probabilistic method, but this “collision probability” analysis is lack of actual data accumulation and the theory of probability distribution. Therefore, it cannot be concluded that the anti-collision device should be setup or not only depending on the probability analysis. This paper indicates that being rammed is not a problem of probability. It is not dependent on the navigable discharge, but dependent on the magnitude of impact force and the structural strength of the bridge to defend the horizontal force. Some bridges are all right under more than 70 times impact, and some collapse weakly. In 1998 an incoming association guide from abroad considered the being rammed is a problem of probability and provided schematic diagram. So it needs to be negated by positive explanation in this article. This article summarized the references as a principle that protection is given where it is required instead of the way only depending on probability analysis.

Keywords: bridge collapse, rammed, probability, certain event, "protection is given where it is required" principle

1 撞上和撞塌

船在桥下和桥墩边上走了几百几千几万次,撞上桥墩或桥顶上的桥梁一两次,这是一个概率问题。但撞上之后倒塌不倒塌,取决于船撞力大小和桥梁抵抗水平力的结构强度,例如:武汉长江大桥有记录的被撞77次,没有撞塌;有的桥水中引桥桥墩结构强度不足,一撞就塌。

桥梁受有多种载荷,有恒定的静载,变化的动载;有偶然一次的大载荷,还有反复多次的小载荷。如果按照桥梁设计规范,可分为永久作用、可变作用和偶然作用。

在讨论船舶和漂流物撞击时,必须先讨论受各种因素的影响而撞上的可能性,即撞上的概率。撞上之后倒塌与不倒塌,视其撞击力的大小与桥墩的结构强度而定,这是一个现代工程力学能够计算的问题,撞击力大于该方向上的结构强度,桥便塌了;反之不塌。这是必然事件,不是概率问题。

下面既不需要专门的数学术语,也不需要繁深的公式推导,便可以讲清楚这个道理,从而破除不合适的线图,建立正确的系数。

1.1 概率定义

概率又称或然率、概率或机会率。概率用来表示随机事件 A 发生的可能性大小的量,称为此事件的概率(见《辞海》)。概率用 $P(A)$ 表示必然事件的概率为 1,即 $P(A) = 1$;不可能事件的概率为 0,即 $P(A) = 0$。

当小船撞击大桥墩,例如:美国旧金山跨海湾大桥的大桥墩(包括:悬索桥的锚墩),承台边上装有钢木结构的格栅护舷,将船撞坏了,桥墩无损(见图 1);杭州市内的京杭运河多座桥梁,桥墩被撞留下的痕迹几十道,却一直在使用(见图 2);武汉长江大桥建桥后的 55 年间,被撞击了 70 多次,其中伤痕最深的一次,水泥墩被刮出 2.0 m 长 0.15 m 深的伤痕,也没有影响火车和汽车通行(见图 3);2012 年 5 月 12 日,万吨船撞上南京长江大桥 6 号墩,虽有伤痕但不影响通车(见图 4)。这就是撞上多少次,一次也没有撞塌,称为撞塌概率为零,表述为 $P(A) = 0$。

（a）桥墩外壁钢木结构护舷
（a）Wood and steel structure wall pier fender

（b）撞坏的船舶
（b）Wrecked ship

图 1　旧金山湾悬索桥船撞实例
Fig. 1　Example of the ship collision the San Francisco Bay Suspension Bridge

（a）杭州江涨桥桥墩刮擦痕迹
（a）Scraping marks found on the Hangzhou Jiangzhang Bridge piers

（b）杭州轻纺路桥桥墩承台刮擦痕迹
（b）Scraping marks found on the Hangzhou Qingfang Bridge piers

图 2　京大运河桥梁船撞痕迹
Fig. 2　Traces of ship collision of Beijing-Hangzhou Grand Canal bridges

图 3　1999－12－18，1 570 t 铁驳撞武汉长江大桥 7 号墩，墩身凹痕 0.15 m（钢笔画）
Fig. 3　1999－12－18, 1 570 t iron barge hit 7# pier, dent of 0.15 m in pier (pen drawing)

图 4　万吨船撞南京长江大桥 6 号墩
Fig. 4　Ten thousand tons of ship collision with the 6# pier of Nanjing Yangtze River Bridge

当弱墩被大船撞击，例如美国的佛罗里达的阳光大桥，船大墩弱，桥被撞塌了（见图5）；美国的阿肯色河桥，顶推驳船撞上双柱墩的一个柱，桥便塌了（见图6）；广东九江公路桥，一艘不很大的运砂船撞到引桥第一墩，桥塌了，表述为 $P(A) = 1$。

图5　船大墩弱，美国的佛罗里达的阳光大桥

Fig. 5　Large ship and weak piers, the Florida Sunshine Bridge in the United States

图6　美国阿肯色河桥，撞坏双柱墩的一柱

Fig. 6　The Arkansas River Bridge in the United States, one column of the double column pier crashed

图7　广东九江公路桥，运砂船撞到引桥第一墩，双柱墩的一柱

Fig. 7　Guangdong Jiujiang Road Bridge, the sand carrier hit of the first pier of approach span, one column of the double column pier

1.2　撞上了塌与不塌是必然事件

在船撞桥的例子中有两种情况。船在桥下和桥墩边上走几百几千几万次，撞上桥墩是受各种因素影响才发生的，这是一种随机事件、偶然事件，所以讨论其概率，可以称为撞上概率。

一旦撞上之后，桥倒塌与不倒塌，这是现代工程力学可以计算的问题，结构能抵御的水平力和船撞力都是可以计算出来的。

当结构能抵御的水平力 > 船撞力，即美国[1]所用的（结构能抵御的水平力/船撞力）>1，这时虽撞上而不倒。

当结构能抵御的水平力小于船撞力，即美国的（结构能抵御的水平力/船撞力）<1，

这时撞上就垮塌了。

由于材料力学、结构力学和其他工程力学学科发展的结果,可以算得比较准,工程材料生产和施工的高质量使桥梁结构和材料的性能都比较均衡,这样上述式中的力,能够算出确定的量[7-11],所发生的是必然事件,不是概率问题。

2　1998 年传入我国的一个桥墩被撞塌的估计方法

船撞力受多种因素的影响,包括船舶尺度和形式,船首形状,船舶行驶速度、撞击方向及撞击体的质量等,并且与桥墩被撞部位的刚度、防撞装置的种类、防撞装置降低船撞力的程度等有关。在计算得出桥梁的船撞力以及桥墩设计的抗撞能力后,可以评价发生单次撞击时桥墩的破坏。

2.1　美国公路桥梁设计规范中的撞塌线图

1998 年,中国翻译出版了美国 1991 版《公路桥梁设计规范》。在规范第 3.14 节中,讨论了偏航概率与几何概率,这对于讨论航船撞上桥墩是有意义的。但同一节中认为,当桥梁船撞力大于桥梁构件的极限强度(横坐标比值小于 1)时,还会有桥墩被撞塌的概率(即可能破坏或不破坏)。它采用图 8 所示分布的倒塌概率,用 P_c 表示,即:当桥梁构件强度大于船舶撞击力时,$P_c = 0$;当桥梁构件强度介于船舶撞击力的 1.0 到 0.1 之间时,P_c 在 0 到 0.1 之间呈线性变化;当桥梁构件强度小于船撞力的 0.1 时,P_c 在 0.1 到 1 之间呈线性变化。

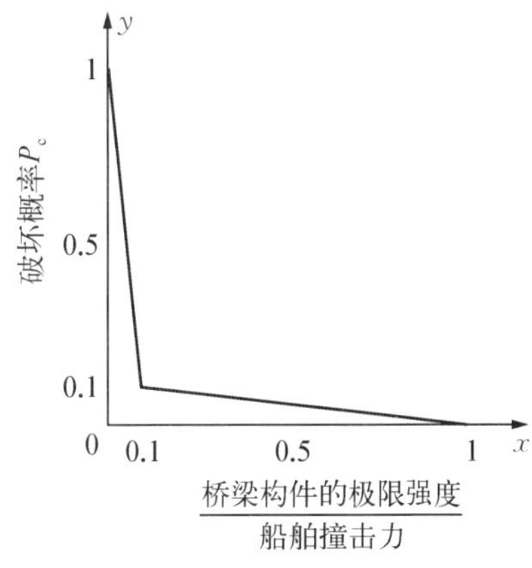

图 8　美国公路规范构件破坏概率 P_c 分布

Fig. 8　The highway standard component failure probability P_c distribution

可以看出,上述美国公路规范的处理中:x 坐标上的交点(1, 0)是说桥梁构件的强度能经受撞击力,因此船撞时桥不坏,这是大家能接受的;y 坐标上交点(0, 1)是说桥梁构件强度小于船撞力,一撞就塌,这也是大家所能接受的。图中间两条斜线的交点(0.1, 0.1)是当桥梁构件只能承受船撞力的 0.1 时撞塌概率为 0.1,即撞 10 次垮一次。质疑者认为此交点没有依据,当桥梁构件强度小于船撞力,一撞就塌,这样撞塌概率就不是 0.1,而是 1.0,即(0.1, 0.1)这个点不存在。

2.2　桥墩被撞塌是工程计算的确定事件而不是概率问题

船撞力虽然受多种因素的影响,包括船舶尺度和形式,船首形状,船舶行驶速度、撞击方向及撞击质量等,并且与防撞装置的种类、防撞装置降低船撞力的程度等有关;桥墩的抗撞强度与设计的抗撞能力(包括形式、大小和选材等)及其建造质量有关。在现今工程力学和工程设计计算中,两者都是可以得到确定数值的。

在计算得出桥梁的船撞力以及桥墩的设计的抗撞能力两者的确定数值后，便可以评价发生单次撞击时桥墩的破坏。

当桥墩强度不足，例如只能够抵受的水平力为船撞力的0.9时，一撞就倒。等不到出现第二次撞击，因此不是一个多次出现的事件，不是一个概率问题。如果一定要在美国规范的图上表示，应该如下图两段分开的实线所示。

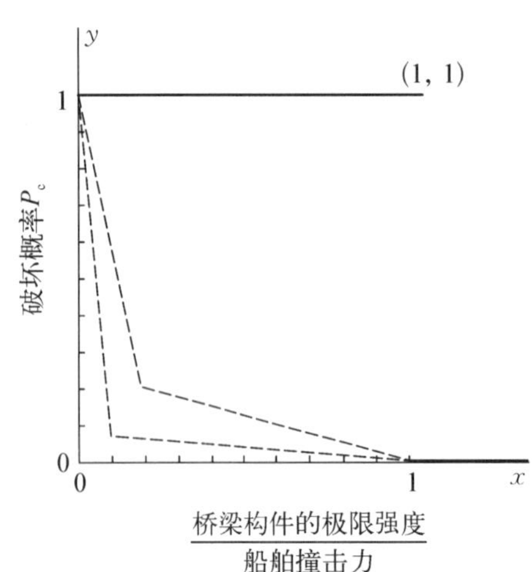

图9　实线为桥墩撞塌系数的概念（P_c只有1和0）

Fig. 9　The solid line is the concept of coefficient of rammed piers (P_c is only 1 and 0)

桥墩撞塌系数的选取办法。根据上述分析，应采用的桥墩撞塌分析方法是：桥墩经受水平力的能力大于船撞力（或经过加强桥墩和设置柔性防撞装置之后，桥墩经受水平力的能力大于船撞力的），此桥墩就撞不塌，处于x轴(1,0)点以右，如硬要套入美国规范的线图，则选取$P_c = 0$，如横坐标上的粗实线所代表；对桥梁构件经受水平力的能力小于船撞力的、没有装设柔性防撞装置或者防撞装置后仍达不到防撞效果，此桥墩一撞就塌，处于y轴(0, 1)点或以上，如要套入美国规范，选取$P_c = 1$，如图上方$y = 1$的一条粗实线所代表。在利用AF（桥墩受船舶碰坏的年频率）法计算时[2]，P_c只在0或1两个数值中取一个。

这样，桥梁计算撞塌概率，必须在计算出船撞力（或是装有防撞装置降低了的船撞力）并与桥墩（或加强了的桥墩）的抵抗力比较后，才能计算出结果。

2.3　撞塌公式内变量的讨论

美国《公路桥梁船撞设计指南》[2]中的撞塌公式为

$$AF = (N)(PA)(PG)(PC)(PE)$$

其中N为按船舶类型、大小、荷载状态分类后的年撞击桥梁构件的次数。

上面已经讨论过，撞上和撞塌是两个概念，小船撞很多次桥梁仍无动于衷，大到足够的船一次便把桥撞塌，所以年撞塌概率与撞上次数成正比的概念就不存在。众所周知，构件经受疲劳荷载时，当荷载小于某一数值时不管多少次撞击都不会损坏构件，所以将撞击次数正比地计入年撞塌概率值得讨论。

3　研究船撞桥的概率既缺乏实际数据积累也欠缺概率分布的理论

概率论是研究“船撞桥”问题可以应用的一种方法，但是，研究船撞桥问题的历史比

较短,所以借鉴一种相邻的、古老的学科——水文学,借鉴它运用概率论研究的方法。

船驶过桥下时撞到桥墩,历史上早已有之,那时桥小船的质量也小,危害不大;现在桥大船也大,若撞上了后果严重(船沉、桥塌、人亡),于是船撞桥成了值得大家研究的问题。最近30年,很多学者从不同的方面和角度、利用不同的学科基础(运动学、刚体碰撞理论、冲击动力学、黏性耗能理论、水力学、概率论等)去研究船撞桥。

众所周知,船撞桥这事隐含着一定的概率,于是想把概率论的概念用到船撞桥上去,这是研究的一个方面。概率论在工程上有不少的应用,在水文学上的应用比较成熟,且较为人知,而搞桥梁总体设计的人,大多对水文学有一定造诣。因此,可以借鉴水文学上的研究成果。

3.1 对于随机事件中"频率"概念的理解及应用

事件 A 在 n 次试验中出现了 m 次,则称: $W(A)$ 为事件 A 在 n 次事件中出现的频率,写成等式: $W(A) = m/n$。

概率是表示某一随机事件在客观上可能出现的程度,是一个稳定的常量。频率是个经验值或试验值,随着试验次数的增多频率趋近于概率值。

n 不大时,频率不稳定,当 n 在客观事物中可以收集到足够多的数据,即 n 值足够大,频率与概率之差便可任意小,即频率趋于概率(此点可由大数定理证明)[1]。

3.2 碰撞的风险

现在来讨论碰撞的风险[2]:根据碰撞的随机性,如设计碰撞定为 T 年一遇,大于或等于这种碰撞发生的概率为 $1/T$。如工程有效服务年数为 N 年,则在 N 年内至少发生一次(T 年一遇)的碰撞的概率 U 为

$$U = 1 - \left(1 - \frac{1}{T}\right)^{N} \tag{1}$$

这个 U 在水文学上称为"失事概率"或"破坏率"。这才是真正的工程所承担的碰撞风险。用(1)式可以制成表1。

表1 **在有效服务段内的碰撞概率 U(按%计)**

Table 1 **Collision probability within the effective service period U(%)**

		有效服务时段 N/年				
		1	25	50	100	200
设计碰撞平均重现期 T/年	25	4	64	87	98	100
	50	2	40	64	87	98
	100	1	22	39	63	87
	200	0.5	12	22	39	63
	1 000	0.1	2.47	5	9.5	18
	10 000	0.01	0.25	0.5	1	2
	100 000	0.001	0.025	0.05	0.1	0.2
	1 000 000	0.000 1	0.002 5	0.005	0.01	0.02

例如你设计某种船只的碰撞重现期为“百年一遇”(年被撞概率0.01),那么从表1可以查出,在桥梁的有效期(若按公路规范设计为100年)内,其碰撞概率为63%。

这63%是什么意思呢?假若有一千座同样的这种桥,在100年服务期内大概有630座会被撞一次以上(也就是一半以上挨撞),这个风险是很高的。

假如重现期为“千年一遇”(年被撞概率0.001),那么从表上可以查出,在桥梁的有效期(若按公路规范设为一百年)内,其碰撞概率为9.5%。

这9.5%是什么意思呢?假若有一千座同样的这种桥,在100年服务期内大概有95座会被撞一次以上(也就是接近十分之一被撞),这个风险还是很高的。

现引用水文学家提供的一句话作为参考:“因此很不安全。”“对于特别重要的工程,采用千年设计洪水标准,破坏率仍达10% ~20%,即使用万年洪水,其破坏率仍有1% ~2%。这就是水工《规范》对重要水库定出千年、万年一遇洪水或可能最大洪水作标准的原因。”[4]

由于服务期内的被撞概率并不是年碰撞概率,可见在讨论碰撞概率时,不应简单地认为碰撞概率就是$1/T$。

3.3 实际数据积累

资料越不足,其误差就越大。在水文学研究中,就有搜集洪水资料增多,洪水重现期改变的例子。例如长江三峡(宜昌站)历史上最大的1870年洪水[4,5],19世纪50年代考证期只能追溯到1530年,当时订1870年洪水的重现期为439年;到了20世纪70年代查到1154年资料,重现期改为830年;今年根据三峡大洪水研究取得的洪水资料,说明1870年洪水是2 500年中的首大项,其重现期应定为2 500年。表2为长江干流宜宾至宜昌段洪水痕迹及洪峰水位和流量的统计资料。

还有根据800多年来对洪水刻痕记录,得出洪峰水位和流量的例子。

表2 长江干流宜宾至宜昌段洪水痕迹及洪峰水位和流量的统计

Table 2 Statistics of flood mark, water level and flow rate of the Yangtze River Yibin-Yichang section

序号	洪水年份	洪痕和题刻总数/个	水位/m	流量/$m^3 \cdot s^{-1}$	发生日期(月-日)
1	1870	344	59.50	105 000	07-20
2	1227	4	58.47	96 300	08-01
3	1560	3	58.45	93 600	08-25
4	1860	19	58.32	92 500	07-18
5	1153	2	58.06	92 800	07-31
6	1788	21	57.50	86 000	07-23
7	1796	2	56.81	82 200	07-18

现在看船撞桥的记录。下面根据铁路系统公布的资料列出公铁两用桥和铁路桥被撞击的记录表(见表3),这一表格是我国近50年来积累的、公铁两用桥和铁路桥被撞击的历史记录。

表 3　　公铁两用桥和铁路桥开始记录被撞的年代
Table 3　　Record starting years of combined bridge and railway bridge collision

序号	开始记录船撞桥的年代	桥　　名
1	20 世纪 50 年代	武汉长江一桥，宜宾岷江大桥，白沙沱长江桥，沙溪口闽江桥，佳木斯松花江大桥，南平闽江桥，三棵树松花江大桥
2	20 世纪 60 年代	南京长江一桥，京广线建河桥，京广线涝刀河桥，三道坎黄河桥，浙赣线樟树桥，资许线鲤鱼江桥，湘桂线湘江桥，京广线汨河桥，湘黔线 K21 桥，鹰厦线永安闽江桥，牡圆线 K28、K83、K89 桥
3	20 世纪 70 年代	广深线石龙北桥，广三线珠江西桥，牙林线牛耳河桥，汉阳汉水桥
4	20 世纪 80 年代	九江长江大桥，枝城长江大桥，湘潭市湘江桥，京广线汨河桥，平齐线嫩江桥，宁芜线当涂桥，京广线新地河桥，汉丹线唐白河桥，京广线二道河桥，广旺线嘉陵江桥

由于公路桥管理比较分散，希望各公路管理局的安全处等单位对其积累的桥梁被撞击的记录进行研究，加入学术讨论，其结果亦将会对船撞桥的概率研究提供有益的帮助。

可以看出，我国船撞桥的记录，无论在时间跨距上还是次数上，都明显不足，这在统计学上称为“样本容量太小”。

同样地，船撞桥的概率机理分析还未见系统的讨论，概率密度曲线的理论分析工作还未见端倪，如果现在就用概率论来指导设计，将“船撞塌桥概率”作为指导性规定，作为“必须设置或不需设置”的指标，步伐就显得仓促了一些。

4　“应保尽保”方法

美国某协会的“以概率分析决定建与不建防撞装置”方法可以表述为：先将桥梁分为“关键性桥梁”和“一般性桥梁”，当“年撞塌频率”分别小于 0.000 1 和 0.001 时可不设防撞装置。由上述讨论得知，应用这种方法尚嫌“样本容量太小”，需要寻求更全面更有说服力的方法，取代仅“以概率分析决定建与不建防撞装置”的方法。

“应保尽保”方法是本文归纳借鉴而来的，在积累样本时期采用的可靠方法。这个方法的目标如下。

（1）凡是可能被船舶碰撞的桥墩应作桥墩防撞设施。这是参照我国《公路桥涵设计通用规范》[12] 中第 4.4.2 条之 3“可能遭受大型船舶撞击作用的桥墩，应根据桥墩自身抗撞击能力、桥墩的位置和外形、水流流速、水位变化、通航船舶类型和碰撞速度等因素作桥墩防撞设施的设计”而来。

（2）水面宽阔的桥位应作船舶偏航论证，因为桥梁及其连接线中，只要撞断一处全线便不通了。尽量考虑多变的自然条件，考虑多大的船可能偏航到哪一个桥墩，相应地做出防撞装置。利用浅滩、水工构筑物、航标、水面养殖设施等作为防止船舶偏航撞上航道边上桥墩的措施。

（3）可能被船舶碰撞的桥墩，如水平抗力过低，经过加强或装设减低船撞力的防撞装置仍然不足以抵御来撞船舶的,可作拦船装置。

"应保尽保"方法在我国科研中已是屡见不鲜。例如周总理在发展两弹一星时提出了"严肃认真、周到细致、稳妥可靠、万无一失"的十六字方针。起初有人认为万无一失的提法不符合科研规律,经过实践,大家知道它是贯穿科研过程的一种态度和要求。以2011年俄、中、美三国运载火箭发射数量与成功率为例,中国运载火箭的发射成功率位居世界前茅(见表4)。"应保尽保"除"万无一失"的态度和精神之外,还多了一种对桥梁及连接线"一塌全断"的认识。

表4 **贯彻"万无一失"精神的成果**

Table 4 **Adhering to the principle of "nothing goes wrong"**

国　别	发射次数	失败次数	成功率/%
中　国	19	1	94.7
俄罗斯	18	1	94.4
美　国	33	4	87.8

5　总结

"应保尽保"方法,就是对凡可能被船舶碰撞的桥墩均作桥墩防撞设施;考虑多大的船可能偏航到哪一个桥墩,相应地设置防撞装置;直接式防撞装置(缓冲装置)不足以保护的时候,可采用拦船装置。

"应保尽保"就是对美国指导文件中的"关键性桥梁"和"一般性桥梁",当"年撞塌频率"分别小于0.000 1和0.001不做防撞装置,放弃的这一部分也加以防护,也可叫做"全桥防护(或全桥防撞)"。

参 考 文 献

[1] 美国各州公路和运输工作者协会(AASHTO).美国公路桥梁设计规范[S].北京:人民交通出版社,1998.

[2] 美国各州公路和运输工作者协会(AASHTO).公路桥梁船撞设计指南[S].上海:上海海洋钢结构研究所,2010.

[3] 雒文生.水文学[M].北京:中国建筑工业出版社,2001:44.

[4] 詹道江,谢悦波.古洪水研究[M].北京:中国水利水电出版社,2001:2-4.

[5] 刘俊民,余新晓.水文与水资源学[M].北京:中国林业出版社,1992:66.

[6] V. Klemes. Dilettantism in Hydrology [J]. Transition of Destiny Water Resources, 1986, Vol.22, No.9:1775-1885.

[7] 陈国虞.有防撞装置时计算船撞桥的力[J].铁道标准设计,2004(1).

[8] J JTJ311—97.通航海轮桥梁通航标准[S].北京:人民交通出版社,1998.

[9] 陈国虞,王礼立.船撞桥及其防御[M].北京:中国铁道出版社,2006.

［10］陈国虞. 桥墩防撞设施的历史及其功能——“三不坏”桥墩防撞装置的诞生［C］//科学中国人十年优秀论文选. 北京：科学中国人杂志社，2002.

［11］Wang Lili, Yang Liming, Tang Changgang, et al. On the impact force and energy transformation during ship-bridge collisions.

［12］JTG D60—2004. 公路桥涵设计通用规范［S］. 北京：人民交通出版社，2004.

发表于：国际船桥相撞及其防护学术研讨会论文集［M］.
北京：中国铁道出版社，2014：205－212.

Published at: Proceedings of International Symposium on Ship-Bridge Collision and its Protection. China Railway Press, 2014: 205－212.

附录 1　Appendix 1

桥墩的船撞力计算及柔性防撞装置设计指南 QB/HY02—2014

Ship Collision Force Calculation for Pier and Design Guide of Flexible Anti-collision Device QB/HY02—2014

2014 - 09 - 01 发布　　2014 - 10 - 01 实施

上海海洋钢结构研究所发布

目　　录

1　前言

1.1　指南编写说明

1.1.1　本指南作为企业标准，指导设计桥梁柔性防船撞装置之用。

1.1.2　当本所被邀请对桥梁柔性防船撞装置设计进行评议或复核时，本指南作为主要评议依据之一。

1.1.3　自本企业标准生效之日起，本所原有的：《桥墩的船撞力计算及柔性防撞装置设计指南——征求意见稿》2002，《桥墩的船撞力计算及柔性耗能防撞装置设计指南2005》(2006出版[4])，《桥梁的柔性防船撞装置设计指南》2008和《桥梁的柔性防船撞装置设计指南》2012等4个文件被取代。

1.1.4　本企业标准拟定2年修订一次，请各参考、使用人员将发现的问题和意见及时反映，以便吸收改进。

1.1.5　本版指南主要修订人：陈国虞，张 澄，倪步友。

1.2　符号和单位(表1.2)

表1.2　**符号和单位**

序号	符号名称	符号	单位	备注
1	角度	α、β、γ、θ、ϕ	度、(°)或弧度	当用于特定条文时按该条文定义或定语
2	统计数群在横轴上的平均值	X_{CP}	与横轴单位相同	
3	统计数群在横轴上的均方差	σ_{n-1}	与横轴单位相同	
4	船(或排筏)撞桥的总体力	F P P_{max} P_S	kN, MN	F用于我国铁路规范；P用于我国公路规范和敏诺斯基公式；P_{max}用于索尔公式；P_S用于美国公路规范
5	船撞桥的相对速度	v	m/s	对漂流的排筏用水流速度
6	动能折减系数	γ	$s/m^{0.5}$	
7	船或排筏的重量(重力)	W	kN, MN	
8	船和桥墩的弹性系数	C_1, C_2	m/kg	
9	撞击时间	T	s	
10	重力加速度	g	m/s^2	
11	桥墩设防力	$[P]$	kN, MN	
12	船的载重量	DWT	t	标记在船的证书上
13	船的满载排水量	DPT, D_{max}	t	标记在船的证书上
14	撞桥时船的实际排水量	D_{act}	t	由船长提交或算出
15	桥墩吸能、能量增量	ΔE	J, kJ, MJ	

1.3 术语定义和释义

1.3.1 撞击船。指船对桥墩撞击发生时的实船,也可指进行设计和研究时假定的一艘典型船舶。根据不同的防撞设施设计方法,典型船舶可以是上级文件中规定的,也可以是用统计方法得出,还可以是用其他方法论证出的。

1.3.2 正撞力。船舶正面撞击桥墩的理论最大撞击力(一般设定为钢船撞上水泥墩)。在进行数值计算时为正撞工况撞击时程曲线的峰值。

1.3.3 侧撞力。船舶侧面撞击桥墩或船头撞击桥墩的侧面的理论最大撞击力。侧面撞击有不同角度等多种情况,乃有各种情况下的侧撞力。在进行数值计算时为侧撞工况时程曲线的峰值。

1.3.4 两类桥梁防船撞装置, 间接结构防撞装置和直接结构防撞装置。利用天然岛礁或沙滩以及围堰、护桩等称为间接结构,使船舶及早搁浅或不能与墩接触,在船桥碰撞过程中桥是不受力的。对保护桥是很有效的,但通常不能保护船。有些场合(例如桥墩处水很深)不便于采用间接结构,就要使用直接结构。即碰撞过程中该防撞装置与桥接触,船撞力通过防撞装置传到桥上。

1.4 桥梁柔性防船撞装置的适用性

1.4.1 柔性防船撞装置可以设于桥墩或间接式防撞结构的外面。设于桥墩外面的直接式柔性防撞结构,能大幅度地降低船撞力,使作用于桥墩的水平力小于桥墩能够承受的水平力。达到既保护桥又保护船,船的破损和泄漏减少,也就保护了环境。又因为它的结构体积较小,占用航道较少,不易引起堆积、冲刷、淤填、回流等现象,因而对环境影响较少。设于天然岛礁或围堰、护桩等间接式防撞结构外面的柔性防船撞装置由于大幅度地降低了船撞力, 因而达到保护船也保护环境的防护目标。

1.4.2 本指南供新建桥梁和原有桥梁增设柔性耗能防撞装置时之用。本指南中关于船撞力的部分章节可供设计柔性耗能防撞装置以外的防船撞装置时参考。

1.4.3 本指南适用于桥下有(或可能有)航船通过的桥梁。既适用于主桥桥墩的防船撞,也适用于引桥桥墩的防船撞。仅有竹木流筏、流冰或兼有竹木流筏、流冰的桥梁可参考使用。

1.4.4 桥梁柔性防船撞装置从安装方式来说有 2 种形式: 浮动式和固定式。一般说来潮差比较大或汛期水位变化比较大的多选用浮式。

1.4.5 设计协调。不论浮式或固定式,桥梁柔性防船撞装置作为港口中的水工结构,或是航道两侧浮动设施,均应与船检、港口、航道和航政等海事部门进行协调。

1.4.6 车辆通道防撞。本指南可供设计公路弯道和其他车辆通道防车辆撞击装置参考使用。

1.5 引用文件

下列文件中的条款通过本指南的引用而成为本指南的条款。由于柔性耗能防撞装置的发展超出下列文件原适用范围,本标准对下列文件亦应有补充和发展,这时与本指南不符合的部分,均不适用于本标准。鼓励运用本指南的各方,研究是否可使用这些文件的最

新版本或修改后的版本。

1）中华人民共和国交通部 JTG，D60—2004 公路桥涵设计通用规范。

2）中华人民共和国铁道部，TB10002.1—2005 铁道桥涵设计基本规范。

2　船舶撞击桥墩的作用力

2.1　船撞桥墩的力

桥梁装设防船撞装置的主要目的之一就是降低桥墩所受的船撞力，所以正确估算船撞力是十分必要的。本指南推荐对船舶撞击桥墩的作用力大小可用规范、经验公式法和动态有限元数值法两种方法进行计算。

我国有两个规范公式：公路规范（漂浮物公式）源于动量公式；铁路规范源于能量公式。在这两个规范中，选定代入公式的数据需要进行很多工作。设计公路铁路两用桥梁时，必须同时符合这两个规范，所以本指南推荐的撞击力应取这两个规范分别计算得到的撞击力的较大者。在规范公式法得到初步估算值之后，建议采用动态有限元数值计算对撞击力进行详细校核。

2.2　船舶撞击桥墩的方向和角度

如果桥墩正面（迎撞面）作成尖的（尖角形），船舶撞击桥墩正面尖部时，桥墩反力可拨开船头，该反力的大小随该尖角的减小而降低。

船舶撞击桥墩侧面或船的侧面撞击桥墩时的力称为侧撞力，其大小视船与墩侧面的夹角而定，它随该夹角的减小而减小，而该夹角受航道的风和流等条件对失控船舶的影响而不同。

2.3　计算船撞力时的速度选择

船撞墩的速度应仔细厘定，通常计算船撞力所选择的速度应是桥被撞时最可能出现的速度。选择方法是：先调查航行法规允许的最大速度，再访问通过桥位诸航线的船长和驾驶员，了解该航线在各种水情时的实船航速，然后选取最可能出现的速度。

应分别计算水中各墩的撞击速度。利用桥位处航道横截面上流速分布图，给出该桥各墩位处的流速[6]，综合考虑船速、流速和偏航情况后给出撞击速度的向量值。

故意违规的船舶的速度及其方向，另行考虑或不予考虑。

不采用过分简单的速度分布假设[3]。

2.4　源出动量公式的船撞力计算公式（公路规范公式）[2]

船舶或漂浮物的冲击作用力按（1）式计算

$$P = Wv/(gT) \tag{1}$$

式中：P——漂流物撞击力（kN）；

W——漂流物重力（kN）。应根据河流中漂流物情况，按实际调查确定；（参看表2.6）

v——对漂流物是水流速度（m/s）；对船来说是船舶相对桥墩的撞击速度；

T——撞击时间(s)(应根据实际资料估计,在无实际资料时可用1 s);

g——重力加速度,可取9.81 m/s^2。

T 值的实际资料:

钢—钢筋混凝土　0.05～0.08 s

钢—单个鼓形橡胶隔震垫　0.13～0.14 s

钢—单个钢丝绳吸能防撞圈　0.25～0.75 s

设计者应根据实际情况对 T 值进行计算或实验厘定。使用钢丝绳吸能防撞圈串联和并联时应综合计算。

表2.4是国内各单位对船撞桥墩时间的计算结果,可供有关船撞桥三方单位参考。

表2.4　**钢船头撞击桥墩(全部能量交换)过程的时间举例**

序号	船　型	总长/m	船宽/m	型深/m	载重/t	排水量/t	速度/m·s⁻1	时间/s
1	1 000 t级多用途货船	68	12	4.9	1 120	1 600	5.0	1.40
2	3 000 t级多用途货船	93	16	7.8	3 220	4 600	3.0	2.10
3	5 000 t级油船	107	15.0	7.5	5 263	7 235	4.0	1.86
4	5 000 t级散货船	107	17.6	9.0	6 900	9 400	4.0	1.90
5	万吨级多用途船	137	22.4	11.0	10 475	17 000	4.0	1.90
6	万吨级散货船	140	22.0	12.2	13 189	19 000	4.0	2.46
7	4万吨级油船	150	30.0	17.0	40 000	50 500	5.1	3.28
8	5万吨级油船	197	32.3	19.2	50 000	62 500	4.0	3.00
9	5万吨级散货船	182	32.3	17.2	52 300	62 500	3.0	4.50

注:表中数值从各家计算收集而来,冲击力下降至峰值的1/4左右即认为过程结束。如用柔性防撞装置或有斜面滑动船头,时间会增加,交换能量会减少。

2.5　源出能量公式的船撞力计算公式(延伸修订的铁路规范公式)[1]

墩台承受船舶或排筏的撞击力可按下式计算:

$$F = v\gamma\sin\alpha[W/(C_1 + C_2 + C_3)]^{0.5} \tag{2}$$

式中:F——撞击力,kN;

γ——动能折减系数($s/m^{0.5}$):当船只或排筏斜向撞击墩台(指船舶或排筏驶近方向与撞击点处墩台面法线方向不一致)时可采用0.2,正向撞击(指船舶或排筏驶近方向与撞击点处墩台面处法线方向一致)时可用0.3;

v——船只或排筏撞击墩台时的速度(m/s)。此项速度对于船舶采用航运部门提供的数据,对于排筏可采用筏运期水流的速度:

α——船舶或排筏驶近方向与墩台撞击点处切线所成的夹角,应根据具体情况确定(如有困难可采用 α=20°);

W——船舶重或排筏重,kN;

C_1, C_2, C_3——船舶或排筏、墩台圬工和防撞装置的平均弹性变形系数(原注:缺乏

资料时可假定 $C_1 + C_2 = 0.0005\ m/kN$）。

此式可用于计算正撞力和侧撞力。

此式有一个动能折减系数,按撞击方向不同而有两种取值。与撞击时的动能耗散有关。

α 角在计算正撞力时仅与墩尖角度有关。在计算侧撞力时应根据具体情况作一分析。

C_1, C_2和 C_3由各设计者用不同的方法进行计算: 对国内多位学者的模拟计算结果中包含有 C_1。

桥墩刚性较大(如武汉一桥、南京一桥)C_2比 C_1小 2 ~3 个数量级,可以不计入(即设为 0),引起的误差不大;高桩立于沉积层软土地基等桥墩,应进行计算。

C_3根据防撞装置而定。

表 2.5　**计算出的船头平均弹性系数 C_1**

序号	船　型	排水量 /t	撞击速度 $/m \cdot s^{-1}$	最大力 /MN	变形 /m	船头平均弹性系数 $C_1/m \cdot kN^{-1}$
1	79.54 m 客船	5 102	5.35	9.23	2.29	0.000 250
2	5 000 t 级多用途船	9 839	5.0	46.8	5.40	0.000 120
3	万吨级散货船	18 917	5.0	56.5	6.85	0.000 120
4	万吨级集装箱船	17 670	3.0	16.5	0.77	0.000 047
5	3.5 万吨级散货船	45 807	5.0	97.5	9.11	0.000 093
6	4 万吨级油船	50 500	6.7	148.0	10.50	0.000 071
7	5 万吨级散货船	62 500	3.0	99.0	6.97	0.000 070
8	6.5 万吨级油船	76 189	5.0	290.0	6.44	0.000 022

表注: 除船头结构外,由于动态力的局域性,船头刚度亦与动态参数(例如速度)有关。

2.6　与国际上常用的半经验估算公式相比较

将上述计算与国际上常用的半经验公式相比较时,至少选择下述两个公式:

1) 敏诺斯基,捷勒,沃易荪(Minosky, Gerlach, Woisin)公式;

2) 索尔,诺特,格林那(Saul-Svensson, Kaott, Greiner)公式(使用本公式时,可参考表 2.6 求出满载排水量)。

当此两公式与(2)式的结果相差小于 25% ,可认为代入(2)式时所选参数算出的结果与国际常用半经验式相一致。

表 2.6　**货运船舶的载重量与满载排水量表**

序号	船　型	载重量/t	满载排水量 t/	载重系数
1	5 000 t 级油船	5 263.0	7 235.0	0.73
2	5 000 t 级沿海散货船	6 399.0	8 670.0	0.74
3	7 000 t 远洋干货船	7 228.0	10 940.0	0.66

续表

序号	船　型	载重量/t	满载排水量 t/	载重系数
4	10 000 t 级油船	9 927.0	12 548.0	0.79
5	12 000 t 级江海直达货船	12 000.0	20 997.7	0.57
6	700TEU 集装箱船	12 300.0	18 466.1	0.67
7	13 000 t 级油船	13 144.0	16 964.0	0.77
8	15 000 t 经济干货船	15 572.0	20 881.0	0.75
9	15 000 t 级油船	15 786.0	21 020.0	0.75
10	G2 型 20 000 t 散货船	20 400.0	26 485.0	0.77
11	1 700 TEU 集装箱船	20 700.0	30 166.0	0.69
12	25 000 t 级油船	24 774.0	32 319.0	0.77
13	27 000 t 运木散货船	27 635.0	33 852.0	0.82
14	28 000 t 多用途货船	28 450.0	38 242.3	0.74
15	30 000 t 级油船	32 397.0	39 830.0	0.81
16	35 000 t 浅吃水散货船	35 603.0	45 807.4	0.78
17	35 000 t 级油船	36 665.0	45 141.0	0.81
18	40 000 t 运木散货船	42 196.0	53 144.0	0.79
19	3 108 TEU 集装箱船	42 210.0	57 251.0	0.74
20	3 800 TEU 集装箱船	42 876.0	71 263.0	0.60
21	52 300 t 散货船	52 104.0	62 078.0	0.84
22	70 800 t 自卸船	59 654.0	77 201.0	0.77
23	63 000 t 级油船	62 200.0	76 250.0	0.82
24	5 600 TEU 集装箱船	69 285.0	93 885.0	0.74
25	90 000 t 级油船	90 261.0	105 160.0	0.86
26	110 000 t 级油船	110 296.0	126 622.0	0.87
27	175 000 t 散货船	170 800.0	193 227.0	0.88

2.7　桥墩抗船撞能力的校核

2.7.1　当桥墩设计者给出桥墩设计抗船撞强度，即能承受的水平力（X 向和 Y 向），这时只要将船撞墩的力沿 X，Y 方向分解，这两个船撞力分量必须均不超过相对应的允许撞击力。

2.7.2　对不同标高的撞击点应分别校核桥墩危险截面的强度，包括抗剪强度和抗弯强度或其组合，因为桥墩受到的船撞力矩与船舶的撞击位置相关，所以应考虑桥墩的危险截面到船撞部位的距离（应与航道水位有关）。

2.8　侧撞力的估算

船舶撞击桥墩墩侧面或船舶侧面撞击桥墩时的撞击力即为侧撞力。侧撞力 $P_{侧可}$ 用下式估算：

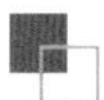

$$P_{侧} = P \cdot \sin \alpha_{侧撞角}$$

式中：P 为正撞力。$\alpha_{侧撞角}$的确定：

$$\alpha_{侧撞角} = |\theta_{风流压偏角}| + |\phi_{桥法线偏角}|$$

$\theta_{风流压偏角}$随该时间的自然条件和船舶条件而定，在自然条件正常、桥位设置正常、符合港航规定时，风流压偏角不大于15°，所以，普通货船、驳船均可取 $\alpha = 20°$。

2.9 有限元数值计算船撞力

由于影响船撞力的因素很多，如船舶和桥墩的材料和结构特性、船舶和桥墩的几何尺寸、撞击加载速度等都将影响船舶对桥墩的撞击力及其强度，可采用有限元数值计算校核。

采用有限元数值计算的正撞力时程曲线峰值，通常大于上述各公式计算得到的船撞力。若进行桥墩动态响应计算时，注意了防撞元件应使用典型实验曲线进行正确的拟合；桥墩对水平力的响应计及了桥梁元件和材料的动态性能等因素，有限元数值模拟计算校核通过即可。

3 全桥防船撞设计

3.1 对桥型、桥垮的及时建议

用户向防船撞的专门单位（本所、乙方）提出防撞设计要求后，乙方应及时研究该航线、航段的水流和船舶运输的情况，并应对船型发展规划、河道整治规划和港口建设规划尽可能的掌握或推算，如发现桥型、桥跨选择对防船撞不合理时，应及早向用户提出修改建议。

向用户提出的桥梁防船撞建议，应该包括铁道桥涵设计基本规范和公路桥涵设计通用规范两个规范中各章节所包含的防船撞要求，还应该从船桥互利相安、社会持续发展的观点，提出合理而充分的建议[8]。

3.2 有柔性耗能防撞圈的装置和绳索耗能柔性拦船装置

跨海湾（河湾、海峡等）的长桥，通常由主通航孔、辅通航孔、水中引桥和滩地引桥等组成。分别有不同的情况：

主通航孔水比较深，高墩高塔投资较大，而且通航净宽比较宝贵，因此对柔性防撞装置降低船撞力的要求较迫切；辅通航孔、水中引桥孔等水比较浅，通航的船较小，一般要求的水平抗力相对较小。

主通航孔一般可作有柔性防撞圈的防撞装置[6]，水中引桥很长时，可设计绳索耗能柔性拦船装置[9]。

3.3 关于船撞桥的概率研究设计[7]

（1）由于船撞桥的统计样本较少，一般不仅以统计结果作为设计或不设计防撞装置

的依据。

(2) 应用户要求,可提交概率分析研究报告,作概率分析研究时,船撞速度应计及各墩所处位置的实际流速[5];偏航概率在具体航线和航段的水流情况,应予以具体考虑;几何概率应根据桥梁初步设计的桥墩形状予以考虑,如桥墩形状不符合规范或不符合水流和船舶运输的具体情况,应及时向用户提出;经过柔性防撞设计降低了船撞力后,桥墩水平抗力仍不能满足要求时,应及时向用户提出加强桥墩。

(3) 经过上述反复设计和修改之后,船撞上桥墩的概率可以得出,但撞塌概率已经为0(即船撞上后的撞力 < 桥墩水平抗力)。

4　桥梁柔性防船撞装置的原理和基本结构

4.1　桥梁柔性防船撞装置的原理[6]

“桥梁柔性防船撞装置”是利用其结构内各部件的共同作用,使得船撞桥产生的冲击不直接作用在桥墩上,而是经过柔性的防撞部件缓冲后传到桥墩。柔性缓冲部件起到隔阻强冲击波、减少撞击力、延长低载荷下撞击过程时间的多种效果。尤其是延长撞击过程中,低载荷下的时间,并由于防撞装置具有较大的缓冲移动,使船舶有时间和空间转向,将船舶推离桥墩,使船舶沿防撞装置外侧滑走,从而带走船的大部分动能,降低了船-桥撞击过程中的能量交换,达到“四两拨千斤”的功效。从而实现既保护桥梁,又能避免(或大幅度降低)船舶受到伤害的目的。

4.2　桥梁柔性防船撞装置的基本结构

桥梁柔性防船撞装置的基本结构:主要由防撞圈、外钢围和内钢围三部分构成,防撞圈位于外钢围和内钢围之间,而内钢围的内壁与桥墩相接触,即桥墩位于内钢围之内侧。当发生船撞事件时,船舶撞在外钢围的外壁上,船撞力通过支撑在外钢围内壁上的防撞圈的缓冲作用后,经内钢围传递到桥墩上。

4.2.1　外钢围。外钢围是环状钢箱形结构,箱梁的局部结构刚度不小于来撞典型船舶的船首刚度,并需要适当的动态结构刚度。使得在受到撞击过程中,外钢围不会因变形的局域化而镶住船头。但由于支撑在外钢围内壁上的防撞圈的刚度相对较小,在船撞作用下,具有较强结构刚度的外钢围迫使这些防撞圈同期受力、变形和运动,同时造成外钢围整体产生足够大的位移。

4.2.2　外钢围迎撞角。外钢围的正面(迎撞面)作成锥角形(尖角形,该角度不应大于90度),船舶撞击柔性防撞装置的外钢围外壁尖部时,外钢围的反力可拨开船头,该反力的强度随该尖角的减小而降低。考虑到工程的造价和施工方便,该尖角的角度不宜小于45度。

4.2.3　防撞圈。在柔性防撞装置的外钢围和内钢围之间串联并联地布置着几十个至几百个防撞圈,防撞圈提供了柔性防撞装置的非线性柔性,使得外钢围整体可以产生大的位移。在外钢围后退的初期,防撞圈产生的阻挡力较小,后退一定距离后,作用力逐渐

加大。并联组构的防撞圈越多,对外钢围(相当于对船舶)产生的作用力越大;串联组构的防撞圈越多,外钢围(相当于对船舶)整体位移量越大。防撞圈的组构形式取决于来撞之船舶的大小。还可根据需要,设计防撞圈的刚度和尺寸。

4.2.4 内钢围。主要为了支撑防撞圈、传递作用力以及隔离船头而设计。

4.2.5 浮式或固定式。根据桥区的水位变化情况,桥梁柔性防船撞装置可设计成浮式的或固定式的。若是浮式的,外钢围和内钢围应设计成水密性的,并分别具有 4 ~ 6 个或更多独立的水密舱。采用 2 舱不沉设计,即当有两个水密舱被船舶撞坏漏水时,该防船撞装置仍不至于沉没。

5 桥梁柔性防船撞装置的设计步骤

5.1 计算船舶撞击力

5.1.1 确定典型船。通过对桥下通航船舶密度、船型、吨位等的调查(可以作一个时期的通航船舶直方图,应取平均值加 3σ 选择船舶的大小)以及该航道的发展规划(通常应该为 50 ~ 100 年,规划不详细时,由设计人给予补充)的调查,基于防撞保证率研究、选择,回过来确定计算船撞力用的典型船,包括船型、吨位和航速。

5.1.2 根据航道的流速及风向,分析船舶的风流压偏角。采用半经验公式初估、再用有限元程序计算船舶撞击力,并分析计算得到的船撞力的可靠性。

5.1.3 计算船撞力降低。根据强度校核,确定所装设的柔性防撞装置能够使得桥墩受到的船撞力降低多少。

5.2 桥梁柔性防船撞装置的初步设计

5.2.1 选定采用浮式或是固定式。根据桥墩的结构设计、桥位、桥形,以及水位和通航条件的资料,确定柔性防船撞装置是采用浮式或是固定式,以及柔性防船撞装置主体框架结构,包括柔性防船撞装置与桥墩的位置关系和联系形式。

5.2.2 设计迎撞角。根据对柔性防船撞装置降低船撞力的百分数的要求,设计柔性防船撞装置外钢围的迎撞角角度。

5.2.3 防撞圈设计。根据船撞力和撞击船能量的大小,设计柔性防船撞装置中的防撞圈的组构形式,以及防撞圈的大小和数量。

5.2.4 外钢围刚度。设计柔性防船撞装置外钢围的局部刚度不小于典型船的船首刚度。

5.2.5 防船撞装置整体的强度。设计柔性防船撞装置整体的强度不小于桥墩的设计抗船撞强度。

5.2.6 绘制船与防撞设施和桥墩的相遇图。

船与防撞设施和桥墩的相遇图用以确定:所设计的防撞装置,其所具有的尺度和功能,当船接触到防撞装置系统且受力变形后,船头(含设计水线上、下部分)在最低、最高通航水位时,均触及不到桥梁任意一点。

绘制船桥相遇图应使用结构动力学或冲击动力学方法进行分析或有限元数值计算。如果应用其他方法求冲击力与变形,则应分成足够多的时段并辅以试验修正和证明。

5.3 桥梁柔性防船撞装置设计的完善

完成桥梁柔性防船撞装置的初步设计后,对其进行有限元数值仿真分析,为改善设计提供依据。动态数值仿真分析内容包括:在船撞过程中,桥墩所受到的动态撞击力,船舶受到的动态撞击力,船舶在撞击过程中的动态能量转换,该装置关键技术设计参量:外钢围刚度设计、迎撞角的角度设计、该装置的整体强度设计以及防撞圈的组构设计等。基于数值仿真分析结果,改进柔性防撞装置设计。其步骤如下:

桥梁柔性防船撞装置总图设计⇒数值仿真计算⇒优化设计(修改,再计算……)⇒数值仿真计算验证⇒设计防撞装置施工图

即:对修改后的设计方案重新进行数值仿真分析研究,验证防撞装置是否达到设防要求。若未能达到要求,继续改进设计,重复:优化设计⇒仿真验证之过程,直到防撞装置达到设防要求。

5.4 桥梁柔性防船撞装置设计的细部结构设计

应参照船舶的钢结构设计方法进行。

5.5 桥梁柔性防船撞装置设计的施工方案和零件设计

应参照船舶的钢结构设计方法进行。

6 船舶撞击桥墩数值计算

通过数值计算可得到撞击系统(船、防撞装置和桥墩)的力、能量和变形随时间的变化过程以及防撞圈的受力同期性、外钢围弹塑性变形直至局部毁坏的图像,和船舶的运动轨迹。

6.1 计算软件

推荐使用商用有限元软件,如 LS-DYNA、ABQUES 等作为动态有限元分析用软件。

6.2 划分单元

对于撞击系统:船、防护装置和桥墩分别划分单元,视其结构的繁简进行划分,构建有限元模型。船头每个构件各自成为单元,到防撞舱壁以后可以进行简化,但保持其重心,作用力和变形等的特征不受因简化而产生的影响,应避免简化不当而影响计算结果。当发现简化会影响计算结果时,应改变简化方法。

6.3 材料模型

在材料模型中,应考虑材料参量的应变率敏感性,采用应变率相关的材料模型,包括:钢、混凝土、防撞圈,特别是防撞圈应采用应变率相关的材料模型。

6.4 计算

计算时,可利用多台微机分别平行计算或大型计算机的多个 CPU 同时运算,后者需

要有供多个 CPU 同时运算的软件,以加速数值计算进程,缩短防撞装置的设计周期。

6.5　从计算结果中取出报告所需数据

这部分工作极需注意表达方式,应合乎桥梁工程师们的想法,符合工程习惯,易于接受。

6.6　将计算结果与材料和结构的动态性能对比

材料和结构在动态载荷作用下,其强度、变形和断裂等性能均有不同的表现。因此,应以动态性能与动态计算结果相比较,才能得出正确的衡量。

7　钢丝绳(柔性耗能)防撞圈参数及组合形式

7.1　钢丝绳(柔性耗能)防撞圈

它的内层由钢丝绳压接而成,外面复合橡胶,变形时钢丝之间摩擦,并有弹塑性变形,表现出黏滞性,所以有很大的耗能率,消耗掉大部分撞击能;同时可产生较大的变形,起缓冲作用、降低撞击力。

实验表明,在同样外载条件下:柔性耗能防撞圈较同样体积的橡胶减震垫,耗能率约增大3倍,撞击时间延长至2倍,撞击力大幅下降。

柔性耗能防撞圈的"力-变形"曲线为凹曲线,在初始加载阶段,防撞圈在较低的作用力下产生较大的变形。

7.2　钢丝绳(柔性耗能)防撞圈的应用

应用在桥梁柔性防船撞装置中,为该装置提供了恰当的柔性,达到大幅降低船撞力,既保护桥也保护船的目的。由于单个柔性耗能防撞圈的承载力、吸能值不大,在桥梁柔性防船撞装置中通常使用几十个、几百个防撞圈,这些防撞圈串联和并联组合,固结于内外钢围之间,所采用的紧固元件必须设计可靠。

由于柔性防撞装置高功效,因此,需要一定的建设成本,在桥梁建设初期应予估计。

7.3　钢丝绳(柔性耗能)防撞圈参数

在桥梁柔性防船撞装置设计中应根据来撞船舶的动能大小,选用不同规格的防撞圈。防撞圈的参数如表7.3-1、表7.3-2和图7.3。

表7.3-1　　**高耗能柔性复合防撞圈的尺寸、重量和允许偏差**

型　式	型　号	外形尺寸/mm									重量/kg
		D_1	D_2	B_1	B_2	B_3	c	d	e	f	
按图1	A400	400	190	120	42	42	15	145	100	177	25
	A600	600	300	170	44	44	25	160	120	280	76
	A800-3	800	400	228	80	80	30	200	150	370	180
	B800-4	800	450	195	70	70	30	200	150	425	140
允许偏差		±2%	±2%	±2%	±2%	—	—	—	—	—	±2%

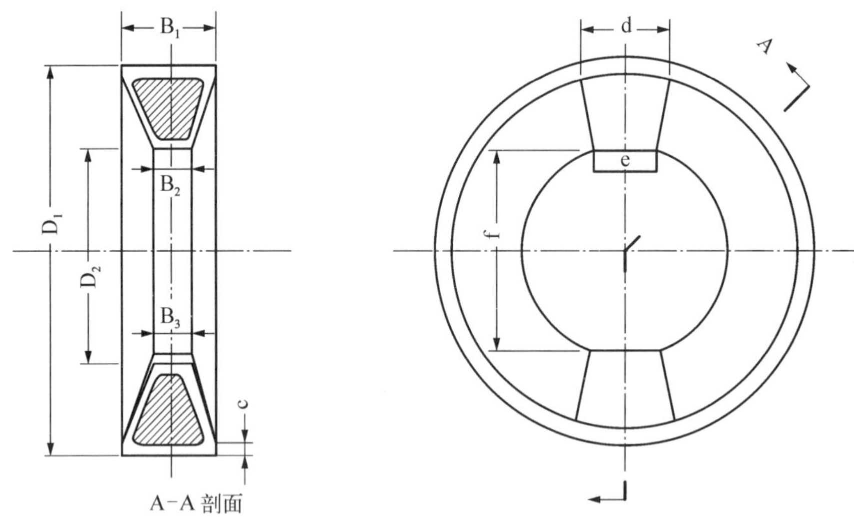

图 7.3　高耗能柔性复合防撞圈的形状和尺寸符号

表 7.3-2　防撞圈的能量消耗指标

	额定外加之功/J	能量消耗值(功)/J
A800-3	≥50 000	≥30 000
B800-4	≥30 000	≥22 500

7.4　钢丝绳(柔性耗能)防撞圈的组构

在桥梁柔性防船撞装置中,防撞圈按其布置可分为并联和串联两种组构。为使并联和串联各组之间正常传力,可适当设计紧固的结构。

8　浮体设计

8.1　浮体审图检验

船舶检验单位属交通部海事局领导,在上海和武汉分别设有海洋和内河船舶(包括海洋工程浮动结构)的审图中心。本防撞装置的浮体就是一艘具有大月亮井的趸船,其月亮井形状与桥墩外形相配。故应按其所处水域,向相应单位申请船舶检验(有的船舶检验单位不予受理,理由是她不航行,故亦可报告港务部门)。

8.2　浮体要求

8.2.1　按水位(包括最大水位、通航水位.最低水位等)要求设计浮体。浮体在各水位时,均应使防撞设施实现其功能。

8.2.2　浮体,如果不是按照外钢围或内钢围设计的,应在防撞装置受撞时自身不直接受到撞击,以免损坏。

8.2.3　浮体可分块制造、组装,或分块使用。

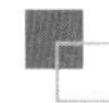

8.2.4 外钢围和内钢围应分别具有4～6个或更多独立的水密舱,当有两个水密舱被船舶撞坏漏水时,该防船撞装置仍不至于沉没。

8.3 位移空间

防撞圈需有很大的位移空间,浮体要承受防撞圈的重力,并要给予变形时的滑动位移空间,滑动处需有润滑措施。

8.4 防腐设施

钢结构应采用表面保护的最新长效措施进行防腐。可在钢结构上先用喷涂锌铝伪合金长效防腐蚀涂层系统外加牺牲阳极阴极保护。

此外,由于经常有水的环境(干舷较小),可以用海洋工程水舱保护涂层进行防护。

8.5 适应水位变化的滑动设计

浮体为适应水位变化,设计成沿桥墩外表面滑动的,要求浮体沿着桥墩上下能够滑动,必须在间隙处精心设计,使其不致卡住。应采取合适的间隙、分布合理的支点以及选用最佳的减摩材料触点。

如果是设计成固定式,优点是没有浮体,结构就简单了;缺点是当水位变化较大时需用防撞装置的尺寸太大,不利于降低设计物的成本。

9 桥梁柔性防船撞装置的其他附属设备

9.1 撞击记录仪

桥梁柔性防船撞装置外层的钢围子上,可设置冲击传感器,以记录船舶撞击桥墩的力度和防撞效果,纪录仪设置在桥塔或桥墩上的路面附近,用隔热房子保护,便于随时或定期检查、取阅记录。记录仪采用有信号即启动的方式,设定门槛值,冲击达不到此门槛值记录仪不启动。

9.2 非结构性防撞装置

9.2.1 标志及灯标导航系统,桥墩有规定的标志灯及标志,也可以自行设计标志灯及其系统,但须与港航部门协调。

9.2.2 加强雷达与导航系统,设置专门的导航站进行导航,当船偏离最佳航线时对其发出警告。

10 桥梁柔性防船撞装置的防腐设计及维修保养

10.1 防腐设施

桥梁柔性防船撞装置主要由钢结构组成,长期处于水中,甚至处于腐蚀性极高的海水中,并且还长期受到波浪的冲刷,必须设计用于钢结构表面保护的长效措施进行防腐。推荐使用多重防护,以达到长期使用而维修较少的目的。应该使用计算方法求得各种保护措施实现保护的年限。在桥梁柔性防船撞装置安装完毕后,应检查连接部位的防腐层,发现问题及时修补。

10.2　装置撞坏后的维修

10.2.1　小面积损伤。当防撞装置受到船舶擦碰时,可能发生局部损伤,当受损程度不大时,可按类似于船舶修理方法进行局部结构拆换处理,然后对结构的防腐涂层进行必要的修补。

10.2.2　大面积损伤。当防撞装置受到船舶的强烈撞击时,可能发生大面积损伤,应对损伤部件、甚至单体(如受损的水密浮箱)进行更换等必要的修复工程。

10.2.3　定期维护。定期维护是保证桥梁柔性防船撞装置长使用寿命的一个关键点,可每半年进行一次例行检查。检查内容包括:防撞装置外表面是否损伤、防腐体系是否受到损害、钢结构有无出现局部锈蚀、连接部位有否松动等。发现问题,及时修复。

10.3　整体维护

桥梁柔性防船撞装置每使用5年可进行一次整体维护,内容包括:

10.3.1　用高压水清洗,清除表面的寄生生物。

10.3.2　在锈蚀部位进行打砂除锈。

10.3.3　检查钢结构的受损(腐蚀)程度,当钢板厚度因受损减少10%时,应更换该部件。

10.3.4　更换出现破损或失效的防撞圈、紧固件等。

10.3.5　全面检查防腐设施,发现问题,进行修复,甚至按设计配套进行重涂。

参 考 文 献

[1] 陈国虞. 有防撞装置时计算船撞桥的力——铁路桥梁规范中船撞力公式的延伸修订[J]. 铁道标准设计,2004(1).

[2] 陆宗林,陈国虞,张澄. 统一我国两个桥涵设计规范中船撞力公式的探讨[C]. 第十七届全国桥梁学术会议论文集. 北京:人民交通出版社,2006.

[3] 王礼立,杨黎明,陈国虞,陆宗林. 船桥相撞时撞击力和动态能量转换的冲击动力学分析[C]. 英文版发表于:第七届国际冲击工程研究会议论文集. 2010年7月,华沙.

[4] 陈国虞,王礼立. 船撞桥及其防御[M]. 北京:中国铁道出版社,2006.

[5] 陈国虞,陈明栋,郑丹. 计算船撞力选择撞击速度时考虑墩位流速的方法[J]. 广东造船,2010(3).

[6] 陈国虞,张澄,王礼立,黄德进. 柔性消能防撞装置的技术特点[C]. 桥梁,2007(4):58-62.

[7] 陈国始. 浅谈用概率论研究船撞桥的几个方法问题[C]. 第十七届全国桥梁学术会议论文集. 北京:人民交通出版社,2006.

[8] 陈国虞. 评议桥梁防撞设计的依据[C]. 城市道桥与防洪,2011(6).

[9] 陈国虞,倪步友,张澄,刁金龙,严景,马海友. 跨海湾(河湾)桥非通航孔拦船防撞装置[C]. 广东造船,2011(1).

附录 2　Appendix 2
主要作者"船撞桥及其防御"方面论文一览表
The list of main writer's other papers on "ship collision with bridge and its defense"

(文章以发表先后为顺序)

(sequence by the time of published)

1. 三不坏桥墩防撞装置的设计　陈国虞
发表于：船撞桥论文选(非正式).上海海洋钢结构研究所,2000－8－17
On "Three-uninjured" Equipment for Protect the Collision Ship to Bridge　Chen Guoyu
Published at *The proceedings of ship collision against bridge*. Shanghai Marine Steel and Structure Research Institute, 2000－8－17
2. 黄峙江连续钢构桥,船对墩的冲撞力分析　陈国虞　陆宗林
发表于：船撞桥论文选(非正式).上海海洋钢结构研究所,2000
Analysis on Force of Ship Collision to Pier of Huangshi River Continuous Solid Structure Bridge　Chen Guoyu　Lu Zonglin
Published at *The proceedings of ship collision against bridge*, Shanghai Marine Steel and Structure Research Institute, 2000
3. 防御船撞桥的桥墩防撞装置　陈国虞
发表于：航海技术,2001(1)
The anti-collision equipment of pier for recovery collision ship with bridge　Chen Guoyu
Published at *Marine Technology*, 2001(1)
4. 从美国阿肯色河桥被撞塌谈起　陈国虞　张　澄
发表于：中国水运,2002(12)
Talk from the Bridge Collapse at Arkansas River due to Ship Collision with the Bridge — Happening Every Year and Half in America (Abstract)　Chen Guoyu　Zhang Cheng
Published at *China Water Transport*, 2002(12)
5. 船对桥的正撞力　陈国虞

发表于：中国土木工程学会第15届全国桥梁学术会议论文集. 同济大学出版社,2002

The front force of ship collision with bridge Chen Guoyu

Published at *The Proceedings of 15th countrywide bridge technical Conference of The Associationon bridge and structure of China Civil Engineering Society.* Tongji University Press, 2002

6. 船对桥的侧撞力 陈国虞 沈文玮

发表于：中国土木工程学会第15届全国桥梁学术会议论文集. 同济大学出版社,2002

The side force of ship collision with bridge pier Chen Guoyu Shen Wenwei

Published at *The Proceedings of 15th countrywide bridge technical Conference of The Association on bridge and structure of China Civil Engineering Society.* Tongji University Press, 2002

7. 有防撞装置时计算船撞桥的力——铁路桥梁规范中船撞力公式的延伸修订 陈国虞

发表于：铁道标准设计,2004(1)

The Front Force of Ship Collision to a Protected Pier Chen Guoyu

Published at *Railway Standard Design*, 2004 (1)

8. 怎样实现桥墩柔性防撞 陈国虞 张澄 倪步友 王礼立 黄德进 张忠伟

发表于：中国土木工程学会第16届全国桥梁学术会议论文集. 人民交通出版社,2004

The Practice on flexible Protection for Ship Collision with Pier

Chen Guoyu Zhang Cheng Ni Buyou Wang Lili Huang Dejin Zhang Zhongwei

Published at *The Proceedings of 16th countrywide bridge technical Conference of The Associationon bridge and structure of China Civil Engineering Society.* People Communication Press, 2004

9. 船撞桥的钢丝绳圈柔性防撞装置的冲击动力学分析 王礼立 陈国虞等

发表于：应用力学进展. 科学出版社,2004

Dynamic analysis of a new flexible, energy-dissipating crashworthy device with steel wire bight used for anti-collision on ship with bridge Wang Lili Chen Guoyu etc.

Published at *Advances in Applied Mechanics.* Science Press, 2004

10. 一种新型的柔性吸能防撞装置 陆宗林 陈国虞等

发表于：中国公路学会2004年全国桥梁学术会议论文集. 人民交通出版社,2004

A new flexible, energy-dissipating crashworthy device for ship collision with bridge

Lu Zonglin Chen Guoyu etc.

Published at *Proceedings of 2004 Conference of CHINA Society of Highway Engineering Sub-society of Bridge and Construction.* People communications Press, 2004

11. 统一我国两个桥涵设计规范中船撞力公式的探讨 陆宗林 陈国虞 张澄

发表于：中国土木工程学会第十七届全国桥梁学术会议论文集. 人民交通出版社,2006

Discuss on the unification of the impact force formula in two design criterion on ship collision with bridge Lu Zonglin Chen Guoyu Zhang Cheng

Published at *The Proceedings of 17th countrywide bridge technical Conference of The Associationon bridge and structure of China Civil Engineering Society*. People Communication Press, 2006

12. 桥墩防撞问题研究的进展 陈国虞

发表于：中国公路学会 2005 年全国桥梁学术会议论文集. 人民交通出版社,2005

The Progressing on Research of Ship Collision with Bridge pier Chen Guoyu

Published at *Proceedings of 2005 Conference of CHINA Society of Highway Engineering Sub-society of Bridge and Construction*. People communications Press, 2005

13. 防御船撞桥的新装置及其机理 陈国虞

发表于：船舶工程 2007 年 29 卷(4)

New equipment for defence the ship collision with the pier and its mechanism research Chen Guoyu

Published at *SHIP ENGINEERING*, 2007 Vol. 29 (4)

14. 防御船撞桥的两类设施 3 种任务 陈国虞

发表于：城市道桥与防洪,2008(6)

The 3 tasks on anti-collision of ship and bridge Chen Guoyu

Published at *Urban Roads Bridges & Flood Control*, 2008(6)

15. 柔性耗能防撞装置中采用的新技术 陈国虞

发表于：城市道桥与防洪,2008(7)

The new technique in the flexible equipment for anti-collision with ship and bridge Chen Guoyu

Published at *Urban Roads Bridges & Flood Control*, 2008(7)

16. 水中桩柱防撞新技术 陈国虞

发表于：中国海洋产业：海洋工程,2008(4),北京：国联直投媒体,13－18

New technique of anti-collision for pile and pole in water Chen Guoyu

Published at *China's Marine industry*: *Marine Engineering*, 2008(4)

17. 三个“桥墩防撞设计指南、规范”的对比研究 陈国虞

发表于：城市道桥与防洪,2009(2)

The contrast study of three “guide or specification” of the design on anti-collision for ship with bridge Chen Guoyu

Published at *Urban Roads Bridges & Flood Control*, 2009(2)

18. 安庆长江铁路大桥防船撞研究 陈明栋 陈明 陈国虞 郑丹

发表于：重庆交通大学学报(自然科学版),2009(2)总第 28 期

Study On Anti-collision of Ship for Anqing Yangtze River Railway Bridge

Chen Ming dong　Chen Ming　Chen Guoyu　Zheng dan

Published at *Journal of Chongqing Jiaotong University*(*Natural Science*), 2009(2)

19. 中外船撞桥实验评述　　倪步友　陈国虞　郑丹　陈明栋

发表于：中国桥梁行业专业直投媒体 桥梁工程与技术,2009(6)

Experimentation on Ship Collision with Bridge of China and Other country

Ni Buyou　Chen Guoyu　Zheng Dan　Chen Mingdong

Published at *Bridge engineering and technology*, 2009(6)

20. 紧靠混凝土承台的直接式防撞装置选择　　陈国虞　张澄　杨黎明　周风华

发表于：中国公路学会桥梁和结构工程分会2009年全国桥梁学术会议论文集. 人民交通出版社,2009

The choose of the directness type anti-collision equipments closed the concrete cushion cap

Chen Guoyu　Yang Liming　Zhou Fenghua

Published at *Proceedings of 2009 Conference of CHINA Society of Highway Engineering Sub-society of Bridge and Construction*. People communications Press, 2009

21. 船桥相撞时撞击力和动态能量转换的冲击动力学分析

王礼立　杨黎明　唐长刚　张忠伟　陈国虞　陆宗林

On the Impact Force and Energy Transformation During Ship-Bridge Collisions

Lili Wang, Limuing Yang, Changgang Tang, Zhongwei Zhang, Guoyu Chen, Zonglin Lu.

Published at *ISIE Book of Proceedings*, 2010

22. 桥梁防撞设施及其最新发展　　陈国虞

发表于：桥梁船撞研究与工程应用(论文集). 人民交通出版社,2011

Anti-collision Establishments of Bridge and its New Developments　　Chen Guoyu

Published at *Research and Engineering Application of Bridges Against Vessel Impact* (*Proceedings*). People communications Press, 2011

23. 学习外国公路桥防船撞设计指南的四点思考　　陈国虞

发表于：桥梁船撞研究与工程应用(论文集)发表时用"桥梁防撞设计规定的研究"作为标题. 人民交通出版社,2011

Fore studies points between the foreign highway guide and a home guide about how to anti-collision of ship with bridge　　Chen Guoyu

Published at *Research and Engineering Application of Bridges Against Vessel Impact* (*Proceedings*). People communications Press, 2011

24. 关于老桥防船撞问题　　陈国虞

发表于：广东造船,2011(6)

Anti-collision with ship for the old bridge　　Chen Guoyu

Published at *Guangdong Shipbuilding*, 2011(6)

25. 因地制宜选用桥梁防撞设施 陈国虞
发表于：中国桥梁行业专业直投媒体，桥梁工程与技术，2011(6)中国桥梁行业专业直投媒体
Choose the anti-collision equipment suit the local condition Chen Guoyu
Published at *Bridge engineering and technology*, 2011(6)

26. 船桥相撞时撞击力和能量转换的冲击动力学分析 王礼立 杨黎明 陈国虞 陆宗林
发表于：第二届国际自动化和工程控制会议论文集，2011(7)
Impact dynamics analysis on impact force and energy transformation during ship-bridge collisions Wang Lili Yang Liming Chen Guoyu Lu Zonglin
Published at *Proceedings of the second international automation and engineering control*, 2011(7)

27. 钢丝绳圈防撞装置力学建模与船撞桥数值模拟研究 张忠伟
发表于：道客巴巴-www. doc88. com/p-78247318946...-2011－10－25；
豆丁网-www. docin. com/p-124217005. html&endPro = true-2011－2－13；
Modeling of Steel-Wire-Loops Crashworthy Equipment and Its Application to Numerical Simulation of Ship-Bridege Collision Zhang Zhongwei
Published at *www. doc88. com/p-78247318946...-2011－10－25* & *www. Docin. com/p-124217005. html&endPro = ture-2001－2－13*

28. 试论几座大桥在防御船舶撞击方面值得提高的地方 陈国虞
发表于：中国土木工程学会桥梁及结构工程分会 第二十届全国桥梁学术会议论文集. 人民交通出版社，2012
Some Discussions on Improve of Anti-collision of a few big bridges Chen Guoyu
Published at *The Proceedings of 20th countrywide bridge technical Conference of The Association on bridge and structure of China Civil Engineering Society*. People Communication Press, 2012

29. 对武汉长江大桥被船撞76次事故的反思 朱海涛 陈国虞
发表于：中国土木工程学会桥梁及结构工程分会 第二十届全国桥梁学术会议论文集. 人民交通出版社，2012
Some introspection on 76 times of accidents of collision with ship and bridge at Wuhan Changjiang Bridge Zhu Haitao Chen Guoyu
Published at *The Proceedings of 20th countrywide bridge technical Conference of The Association on bridge and structure of China Civil Engineering Society*. People Communication Press, 2012

30. 加速度法测量实船与柔性防护装置碰撞的撞击力
唐长刚 吕忠达 徐爱敏 王永刚 杨黎明
发表于：中国土木工程学会桥梁及结构工程分会 第二十届全国桥梁学术会议论文

集. 人民交通出版社,2012

Used acceleration method to measure the force of actual ship collision with flexible Anti-collision equipments

Tang Changgang　Lv Zhongda　Xu Aiming　Wang Yonggang　Yang Liming

Published at *The Proceedings of 20th countrywide bridge technical Conference of The Association on bridge and structure of China Civil Engineering Society*. People Communication Press, 2012

31. 桥梁柔性防撞装置设计的关键技术研究 刘　军　吕忠达　徐爱敏　周刚毅　杨黎明

发表于: 中国土木工程学会桥梁及结构工程分会 第二十届全国桥梁学术会议论文集. 人民交通出版社,2012

The study on key technique of design on flexible anti-collision equipment of bridges

Liu Jun　Lv Zhongda　Xu'Aiming　Z Gangyi　YANG Liming

Published at *The Proceedings of 20th countrywide bridge technical Conference of The Association on bridge and structure of China Civil Engineering Society*. People Communication Press, 2012

32. 桥墩柔性防撞装置实船撞击过程的实验研究——装置及撞击力的测量与分析

董新龙　周风华　郑维钰　李来则　段　忠　周刚毅　杨黎明

发表于: 中国土木工程学会桥梁及结构工程分会 第二十届全国桥梁学术会议论文集. 人民交通出版社,2012

Experimental study on the process of actual ship to the flexible anti-collision equipment — the Equipment and the measure, analysis of the collision force

DONG Xinlong　ZHOU Fenghua　Zhen Weiyu　LI Laize　DUAN Zhong　GHOU Gangyi　YANG Liming

Published at *The Proceedings of 20th countrywide bridge technical Conference of The Association on bridge and structure of China Civil Engineering Society*. People Communication Press, 2012

33. 实船与有防护装置桥墩碰撞实验的数值模拟　　秦　焜　杨黎明　王永刚

发表于: 中国土木工程学会桥梁及结构工程分会 第二十届全国桥梁学术会议论文集. 人民交通出版社,2012

The numerical simulation of experimental on the actual ship collision with the pier protected by the flexible anti-collision equipment　QIN Kun　YANG Liming　WANG Yonggang

Published at The Proceedings of 20th countrywide bridge technical Conference of The Association on bridge and structure of China Civil Engineering Society. People Communication Press, 2012

34. 船撞力估算公式中动力折减系数的一种试验评议　　陈国虞　倪步友

发表于: 2012 年中国公路学会桥梁和结构分会全国桥梁学术会议(马鞍山)论文集.

人民交通出版社,2012

A discussion by experiment on the dynamic factor in the estimation formula of collision force with ship and bridge Chen Guoyu NI Buyou

Published at *Proceedings of 2012 Conference of CHINA Society of Highway Engineering Sub-society of Bridge and Construction*. People communications Press, 2012

35. 答读者问——论桥梁柔性防撞 陈国虞 倪步友

发表于：中国桥梁行业专业直投媒体 桥梁工程与技术,2013(1)

Answer to the Readers — Flexible Anti-collision When the Ship collision with Pier

Chen Guoyu NI Buyou

Published at *Bridge engineering and technology*, 2013(1)

36. 我国桥梁防船撞的回顾和展望 朱海涛 陈国虞 倪步友

发表于：2013 年中国公路学会桥梁和结构分会全国桥梁学术会议(沈阳)论文集. 人民交通出版社,2013

Retrospect and prospect of bridges against ship in China

ZHU Haitao Chen Guoyu NI Buyou

Published at *Proceedings of 2013 Conference of CHINA Society of Highway Engineering Sub-society of Bridge and Construction*. People communications Press, 2013

37. 我国已经可以防止船沉桥塌的严重事故 朱海涛 陈国虞

发表于：国际船桥相撞及其防护学术研讨会论文集. 中国铁道出版社,2014

Severe accidents of shipwreck and bridge collapse can be prevented in our country

Zhu Haitao Chen Guoyu

Published at *Proceedings of International Symposium on Ship-Bridge Collision and Its Protection*. China Railway Press, 2014

38. 有外钢围的桥梁柔性防船撞装置与复合材料消能防撞装置对比研究 倪步友 倪士强

发表于：国际船桥相撞及其防护学术研讨会论文集. 中国铁道出版社,2014

The comparison study on flexible defend devices with outer gate for ship-bridge collision to the defend devices made by fiber reinforced composite Ni Bu-you Ni Shi-qiang

Published at *Proceedings of International Symposium on Ship-Bridge Collision and Its Protection*. China Railway Press, 2014

39. 柔性防船撞装置数值分析技术与结构优化

赵彦龙 赵振宇 王 伟 杨祥磊 陈国虞

发表于：国际船桥相撞及其防护学术研讨会论文集. 中国铁道出版社,2014

Numerical analysis and structure optimization of flexible anti-ship-collision device

Zhao Yanlong Zhao Zhenyu Wang Wei Yang Xianglei Chen Guoyu

Published at *Proceedings of International Symposium on Ship-Bridge Collision and Its Protection*. China Railway Press, 2014

40. 从耗能出发谈几座钢构压溃式桥梁防船撞装置　陈国虞
发表于：中国桥梁行业专业直投媒体 桥梁工程与技术,2014(3)
Base on the energy dissipation to compression study some steel structure anti-collision equipment for ship collision with bridge　Chen Guoyu
Published at Bridge engineering and technology, 2014(3)

附录3 Appendix 3
主要作者简介 Brief introduction of the main authors

陈国虞 CHEN Guoyu	研究员,上海海洋钢结构研究所总工程师,宁波大学、重庆交通大学教授,原中国公路学会桥梁和结构分会理事,原中国钢结构协会海洋钢结构分会理事 Researcher. Chief engineer of Shanghai Marine Steel & Structure Research Institute. Professor of Ningbo University and Chongqing Jiaotong University. Former council member of Committee of Bridge and Structural Engineering, China Highway and Transportation Society. Former council member of Association for Marine Steel structures, China Steel Construction Society.
王礼立 WANG Lili	研究员,宁波大学教授,东京理科、法国梅兹、英国伊利诺斯和英国圣母院等大学客座教授,原中国力学学会爆炸力学专业委员会召集人 Researcher. Professor of Ningbo University. Visiting professor of Tokyo University of Science, Université de Metz, University of Illinois, University of Notre Dame, etc. Convener of Committee of Explosion Mechanics, Chinese Society of Theoretical and Applied Mechanics.
杨黎明 YANG Liming	宁波大学教授,钱江学者特聘教授、博导,曾在香港城市、美国北卡罗莱那州立、南卡罗莱那、新加坡国立等大学任教,中国公路学会桥梁和结构分会理事 Professor of Ningbo University. "Qianjiang" Special-Term Scholar, Ph. D. supervisor. Taught in City University of Hong Kong, NC State University, University of South Carolina, National University of Singapore, etc. Director of Committee of Bridge and Structural Engineering, China Highway and Transportation Society.
陈明栋 CHEN Mingdong	重庆交通大学研究员,硕士生导师,注册咨询工程师(投资)、重庆市建设工程评标专家、重庆市交委建设工程评标专家、兼任上海海洋钢结构研究所桥梁防撞研究顾问

Researcher of Chongqing Jiaotong University. Master's supervisor. Registered Consulting Engineer (Investment). Construction project bid evaluation expert of Chongqing Transport Commission. Bridge collision avoidance research consultant of Shanghai Marine Steel & Structure Research Institute.

倪步友 NI Buyou
上海士强起重索具有限公司总工程师,上海海洋钢结构研究所产学研负责人
Chief engineer of Shanghai Shiqiang rigging Co. Ltd. The head of Industry - Academia - Research in Shanghai Marine Steel & Structure Research Institute.

朱海涛 ZHU Haitao
高级工程师,原中铁大桥局集团有限公司、上海海洋钢结构研究所桥梁科学技术顾问
Senior Engineer. Former in China Major Bridge Engineering Co. , Ltd. and Technical consultant of bridge science of Shanghai Marine Steel & Structure Research Institute.

陆宗林 LU Zonglin
同济大学教授级高级工程师,上海海洋钢结构研究所桥梁科学技术顾问
Professor of engineering in Tongji University. Technical consultant of bridge science in Shanghai Marine Steel & Structure Research Institute.

吕忠达 LU Zhongda
博士,教授级高级工程师,宁波市高等级公路建设指挥部总指挥
Doctor. Professor of Engineering. General command of Ningbo high grade highway construction headquarters.

周风华 ZHOU Fenghua
研究员,钱江学者特聘教授、博导,宁波大学力学与材料研究中心负责人
Researcher. "Qianjiang" Special - Term Scholar, Ph. D. supervisor. The head of mechanics and materials research center of Ningbo University.

张　澄 ZHANG Cheng
原上海船舶设计研究院高级工程师,上海海洋钢结构研究所钢结构设计顾问
Former senior engineer of Shanghai Merchant Ship Design and Research Institute. Steel structure design consultant of Shanghai Marine Steel & Structure Research Institute.

郑　丹 ZHANG Dan
博士,重庆交通大学河海学院副教授,上海海洋钢结构研究所水文水工研究顾问
Doctor. Associate professor of Hehai College, Chongqing Jiaotong University. Hydrological engineering research consultant of Shanghai Marine Steel & Structure Research Institute.

廖　娟 LIAO Juan
博士,浙江大学城市学院副教授,上海海洋钢结构研究所桥梁顾问
Doctor. Associate professor of Zhejiang University City College. Bridge

	consultant of Shanghai Marine Steel & Structure Research Institute.
赵振宇	西安交通大学在读博士
ZHAO ZhenYu	Doctoral student in Xi'an Jiaotong University.
王建强	中交第一公路勘察设计研究院有限公司产业化中心产品研发主管
WANG Jianqiang	Chief of product research and development , Industrialization department of CCCC Highway Consultants Co. , Ltd.